THE ORIGIN
OF NEGATIVE DIALECTICS

The Origin
of Negative Dialectics

Theodor W. Adorno,
Walter Benjamin,
and the Frankfurt Institute

Susan Buck-Morss

THE FREE PRESS
A Division of Macmillan Publishing Co., Inc.
NEW YORK

The Free Press
A Division of Macmillan Publishing Co., Inc.
866 Third Avenue, New York, N.Y. 10022

Collier Macmillan Canada, Ltd.

First Free Press Paperback Edition 1979

Library of Congress Catalog Card Number: 76-55103

Printed in the United States of America

printing number
HC 1 2 3 4 5 6 7 8 9 10
SC 1 2 3 4 5 6 7 8 9 10

Library of Congress Cataloging in Publication Data

Buck-Morss, Susan.
    The origin of negative dialectics.

    Bibliography: p.
    Includes index.
    1. Adorno, Theodor W., 1903-1969. 2. Benjamin,
Walter, 1892-1940. 3. Frankfurt am Main. Institut für
sozialforschung. I. Title.
B3199.A34B8   193   76-55103
ISBN 0-02-904910-5
ISBN 0-02-905150-9 pbk.

To my parents

Contents

Preface

In the 1960s, Theodor W. Adorno became the most controversial theoretician of the German New Left. He and Max Horkheimer had reestablished the exiled *Institut für Sozialforschung* (Institute for Social Research) in Frankfurt after the war, and since Horkheimer's retirement in 1959, Adorno had been acting director. The Institute, which spent the Nazi years in the United States, was identified with Critical Theory, an original method of Freudo-Marxist analysis that developed there when Horkheimer first became director in 1931 and Herbert Marcuse was one of its more illustrious members.

Critical Theory looked to Marxism as a method rather than a cosmology, and it considered dialectical thinking to be the core of that method — dialectics as the tool for a critical analysis of society, not for building metaphysical systems. Instead of trying to fit present historical conditions dogmatically into Marxist theory, it applied Marx's method to the present, and its critique of the most contemporary, psychological phenomena of late bourgeois society — the "culture industry," mass media, conformism — spoke to students of the fifties and sixties with an urgency which a classical analysis of wage labor would not have achieved. Its criticism of the patterns of authoritarian domination within bourgeois society applied to the purportedly "revolutionary" societies of Soviet Russia and Eastern Europe as well.

The intellectual influence of Adorno and Horkheimer was even greater than that of Marcuse, who chose to stay in the United States, as they had a decisive impact on not one, but successive generations of postwar students. They attracted some of the best to the Institute, the first place in postwar Germany where one could study Marxist sociology and Freudian psychology in order to comprehend analytically the fascism which had outlawed them both. The preeminence of the Institute had its source in the paradox of its historical situation: its members were totally immersed in the German intellectual tradition which they criticized. Exiled by Hitler because they were Leftist and Jewish, these "outsiders" provided by their personal survival and return a link to the best of the German past, its Enlightenment and humanist tradition, which the Nazi experience had all but obliterated. Critical Theory gave students the opportunity to reject the Germany of their fathers and yet find a home in its intellectual traditions. Its analysis was thus both the negative critique and the positive redemption of that German *Geist* which had proven such an ambivalent legacy, and it played an important role in Germany's intellectual reconstruction. Almost singlehandedly Adorno and Hork-heimer reestablished a kind of radical social analysis which relegitimized Marxist thinking, so that it once again became part of the national political debate. As a result, although they shunned affirmative, political participation, their work contributed indirectly to the end of the Christian Democrats' monolithic rule and the victory in 1971 of Willie Brandt's Social Democratic Party.

But at the height of the student movement the goal was revolution rather than reform. The demonstrations of workers and students in Paris in May, 1968 seemed to indicate that socialist revolution was not only desirable but possible. Students in Germany entered an antiauthoritarian phase of counterculture and anarchist praxis. Whereas Marcuse in the United States gave some degree of theoretical support to such activism, Adorno at the Frankfurt Institute did not. As a result, young radicals who had shortly before crowded the aisles to hear the erudite, eloquent Adorno speak on Hegel's *Logic* or Goethe's *Iphigenea*, dis-rupted his lectures. They attacked him because his revolutionary theory seemed to leave no space for revolutionary praxis. In May 1969, students occupied the Institute, and when Adorno did nothing to stop the police from evicting them, their sense of betrayal was complete. Adorno met with SDS leaders, who had learned from him their radical criticism of society but now charged him with not being radical enough. He told them that precisely because of his revolutionary goals he was critical of anarchist tactics as ineffective, and he was clearly worried by the students' impatience with theory. Their glorification of action, their counterculture, and even their hashish echoed the abortive protest of the intel-lectual *avant-garde* of his own generation, which had proven no match for fascism.

By then the student confrontation had spread well beyond Frankfurt. One after another, student assemblies voted to strike. During that year, I was study-ing in Tübingen, and the disruption of the university in the summer of 1969 was my introduction to Marxist theory in general and to Adorno in particular. The universities were turned over to continuous debate in plenary sessions and "work groups," where the writings of Adorno, Horkheimer and Marcuse, but also Marx, Lenin and Mao were attacked or defended with passion.

The student strikes were an intellectual explosion, and they had some lasting success in transforming the power structure, the syllabus, and the method of instruction in German universities. But in achieving their major goal — the forma-tion of a revolutionary political movement — students here were not more suc-cessful than in other Western countries, and Adorno's skepticism was perhaps justified. The possibility of further dialogue, however, was cut short when Adorno died suddenly from a heart attack in August of that year. The euphoria of anti-authoritarianism dissipated, and the sense of solidarity that underlay this rebellion against the Establishment began to reveal its superficiality. Some students, stung by remorse, became ardent apologists for Adorno, attempting to prove his legit-imacy as the heir of the tradition of Marx. Others abandoned him as a pretender, and turned to Lenin or Mao on questions of theory and organizational discipline. A few (including Angela Davis who studied with Adorno from 1966–1967) joined the Communist Party. The sectarian struggles that followed splintered the New Left, and one of the casualties was the Institute itself.

When I returned to Germany the following summer to begin research for this study, the Frankfurt Institute was museumlike and ghostly silent. Horkheimer was in retirement in Montagnola, Switzerland, where he died in 1973. The younger generation of Critical Theorists had moved elsewhere, joined research institutes or university faculties, and had begun their own theoretical writing. Jürgen Habermas, the senior member of this second generation, soon moved to the *Institut für Friedensforschung* in Starnberg, where he began a long-term socio-psychological project. The critics of Critical Theory congregated largely in Berlin, where journals like *Alternative* still made sporadic attacks against the revisionism of the Frankfurt School.

As the aura and immediate presence of the Institute began to evaporate, the question of historical origins became significant. How was it that Adorno and Horkheimer, born at the turn of the century and reared in Weimar Culture, be-came the articulators of a theory which half a century later captured a movement renown for its youth, its rejection of tradition and suspicion of age? What histor-ical network linked the American with the German New Left and led not only Angela Davis, but a whole group of students from the United States to study at the Institute in Frankfurt? It was an American, Martin Jay, who wrote the first scholarly history of the Institute, tracing its development from 1923–1950.* In a pioneering effort of intellectual road-mapping, Jay unearthed a web of con-nections which embraces a surprisingly large segment of Weimar culture. His book discusses the involvement of Theodor Adorno, Walter Benjamin, Erich Fromm, Leo Lowenthal, Herbert Marcuse – all at one time members of the Institute's "inner circle" – and others who as members, journal contributors, friends, or enemies played a role in the Institute's history. The list reads like a roster of this century's intellectuals. Included were Hannah Arendt, Raymond Aron, Bruno Bettelheim, Bertolt Brecht, Ernst Bloch, Otto Kirchheimer, Siegfried Kracauer, Paul Lazarsfeld, Georg Lukács, Karl Mannheim, Paul Massing, Thomas Mann, Franz Neumann, Friedrich Pollock, Wilhelm Reich, Gershom Scholem, Paul Tillich, and Karl August Wittfogel.

Jay quite rightly chose to focus his study on Max Horkheimer and the decades of the thirties and forties which were Horkheimer's most productive years. For it was Horkheimer who held the Institute together as it wandered from Germany to New York, from New York to California, and back again to Frankfurt sixteen years later. And it was Horkheimer who, by inspiring personal loyalty, managed to maintain a degree of theoretical cohesiveness among the strong-willed, bril-liantly individualistic thinkers to whom he gave intellectual and economic shelter.

*Martin Jay, *The Dialectical Imagination: A History of the Frankfurt School and the Institute of Social Research, 1923–1950* (Boston: Little, Brown, 1973).

But there are problems with Jay's approach when it tends to equate the intellectual development of Max Horkheimer with that of the Institute, and to speak of a Frankfurt "School" even though the *non*identities of its members' positions were sometimes as significant as their common assumptions.

In particular, Adorno remains a somewhat shadowy figure in Jay's account, all the more remarkable as Adorno became Horkheimer's close collaborator after 1938 and was the leading "Critical Theorist" at the Institute during the 1960s. The problem has been largely attributed to Adorno's esoteric language, to which, in fact, the Critical Theory of the Frankfurt "School" fails to provide a sufficient key. The search for such a key has prompted the present study. My research into the historical origins of Adorno's philosophy was done in Frankfurt from 1970 to 1973, during which time the documents from Adorno's Estate were being assembled in preparation for the publication of his complete works. I had access to hitherto unpublished writings, and they contained some surprises. Particularly revealing was Adorno's inaugural lecture to the philosophy faculty at the University of Frankfurt in 1931. It outlined a program and a task for philosophy which was to guide his intellectual efforts for the rest of his life. As he himself recalled in 1962:

> Very much of what I wrote in my youth had the character of a dreamlike anticipation, and only from a certain shock-moment on, which may have coincided with the outbreak of Hitler's Reich, did I actually believe that I was right in what I had done.*

As the first articulation of his philosophy, which Adorno much later named "negative dialectics," the inaugural lecture demonstrates the remarkable consistency of his thinking over time. It also gives evidence that a shift which occurred in the Frankfurt Institute's position after 1938 reflected not only the external reality of Hitler and World War II but the internal one of Adorno's arrival in the United States as a full-fledged Institute member, the closest to Horkheimer in a personal sense, and increasingly in an intellectual sense as well. Ironically, the shift, which has been interpreted as a move by the Institute away from Marx, on the part of Adorno marked a move toward Marx, along with a greater recognition of the limits of intellectual praxis — hence the increased pessimism in the tone of his cultural criticism.

The really formative influence on Adorno occurred before 1931, and it came from Walter Benjamin. Adorno's inaugural lecture clearly documents this fact, which only increases the mystery surrounding the origin of his philosophy. The lecture lays out guidelines for a "dialectical," "materialist" theory which is

*Letter, Adorno to Ernst Bloch, cited in the editorial afterword of Theodor W. Adorno, *Gesammelte Schriften*, vol. 1: *Frühe philosophische Schriften*, ed. Rolf Tiedemann (Frankfurt am Main: Suhrkamp Verlag, 1973), p. 384. Translation from the German here, and those that follow, are mine. In cases where published English translations exist, I have used them or made my own at my discretion.

intentionally Marxist, yet it does so in language and conceptual categories borrowed from the non-Marxist, nonmaterialist early philosophy of Benjamin. The latter incorporated structural elements from such seemingly remote sources as Jewish mysticism, Kantianism, Platonism, and German Romanticism.

The question raised by Adorno's inaugural lecture is the puzzle which this study has tried to resolve: How does Benjamin's early, non-Marxist philosophy provide the key to Adorno's own dialectical, materialist method? The answer involves following Adorno in a double procedure, translating Benjamin's original conceptions into a Marxist theoretical frame, and grounding Marxist theory philosophically with the aid of those conceptions in order to prove immanently that dialectical materialism was the only valid structure of cognitive experience. This task distinguished Adorno's work from *Ideologiekritik,* the criticism of the ideological, social function of ideas, which was characteristic of essays written by other members of the Frankfurt Institute. Adorno not only wanted to demonstrate the untruth of bourgeois thinking; he wanted to show that precisely when the bourgeois project — the idealist project of establishing the identity of mind and material reality — failed, it expressed, unintentionally, social truth, thus proving the preeminence of reality over mind and the necessity of a critical, dialectical attitude of *non*identity toward it — proving, in short, the validity of dialectical, materialist cognition.

Adorno's project does not fit neatly into the Hegelian-Marxist philosophical tradition. In rejecting the concept of history as progress and in insisting on the nonidentity of reason and reality, it broke decisively from Hegel; in separating philosophy from all concern with the proletariat, it broke radically from Marx. Adorno was influenced by Husserl's phenomenology as much as by Hegel's. Indeed, it could be said that if Kierkegaard's existentialism and Marx's materialism represented the two branches of protest against Hegel, then there was a parallel in Heidegger's and Adorno's responses to Husserl. But if Adorno was on Marx's side in rejecting existentialism, endorsed by Kierkegaard and Heidegger, his understanding of dialectics was modeled more on aesthetic experience than, as with Marx, on the experience of economic production.

This last point is particularly significant. Adorno thought of himself as an artist, and the time he spent in the 1920s in Vienna studying Schönberg's compositional method with Alban Berg, although brief, left an indelible imprint. He and Benjamin both viewed art as a form of scientific knowledge. Perhaps their most important contribution was to redeem aesthetics as a central cognitive discipline, a form of secular revelation, and to insist on the structural convergence of scientific and aesthetic experience. They thereby challenged a fundamental dualism of bourgeois thought, the binary opposition between scientific "truth" and art as "illusion," which had characterized bourgeois thinking since the seventeenth century. Their intellectual careers demonstrate the promise and also the dangers of trying to reconcile these two cultures.

Despite, or perhaps because of, the closeness of Adorno's and Benjamin's philosophical thinking, they became involved in an extended debate, documented by their correspondence, in which Adorno found himself in the anomalous position of defending Benjamin's philosophy against the latter's own revisionism. But after Benjamin's suicide in 1940 his influence on Adorno's thinking remained, and his brilliantly eccentric mind haunts even the most empirical, social-scientific writings of Adorno's later years.

The story of their intellectual friendship forms the major theme of this study. The first part, introduced by a biographical chapter describing Adorno's early intellectual development, analyses his philosophical conceptions as they were first articulated in the early 1930s and demonstrates their debt to Benjamin. This section grew out of a dissertation completed in 1974. The second part returns to the chronological structure of the introductory chapter, tracing the theoretical debate between Adorno and Benjamin, and concludes with Benjamin's suicide and Adorno's reaction to it, in particular, his sublation of even the most daring Benjaminian techniques in the empirical research methodology of *The Authoritarian Personality* (1950), the pathbreaking social-psychological study for which he is best known in this country. The account ends in 1953 when, at the age of fifty, Adorno left the United States to return to Frankfurt and join Horkheimer at the newly reestablished *Institut für Sozialforschung*.

This book will have achieved its aim if it introduces "negative dialectics" to an English-reading audience, demonstrates the originality of Adorno's philosophical project when compared to other strands of Western Marxism, and, by showing the project's historical connection to the theory of Walter Benjamin, sets the discussion of Adorno's contribution within an accurate understanding of what it was that he hoped to accomplish.

Acknowledgments

I am deeply indebted to Rolf Tiedemann, without whose generosity and precious friendship this book could not have been written. I want to thank the *Deutsche Akademische Austauschdienst* for the stipend which supported my research in 1971-1972. Thanks are also due to Martin Jay, Hisham Sharabi, David Goldfrank, Norman Levine, and Marcus Raskin for their penetrating comments and criticisms, to my Frankfurt family, Wolfgang Bock, Gisela Engel, Fritz Hermanin, Claudia Honegger, Klaus Schröter, and Gunter Wegeleben, for their help and hospitality, to István Csicsery-Ronáy, Regina Schmidt, Neal Wadler, and Irving Wohlfahrt for their enthusiasm in long discussions, and to Maria Tokić for her help in preparing the manuscript. I am grateful to Elliott for his patient and good-humored support.

Finally, I want to thank four women whose teaching was inspiring: Dorothy M. Brown, Evalyn A. Clark, Gladys M. Kingsley, and Theresa L. Wilson.

Chapter 1. Intellectual Beginnings: A Biographical Essay

FRANKFURT AM MAIN

He was born Theodor Adorno Wiesengrund[1] in Frankfurt am Main September 11, 1903. His father, a successful wine merchant, provided him with the economic and emotional security of a comfortable bourgeois home, but seems otherwise to have been uninvolved with the training and development of this, his only child. Adorno was raised by the two women of the household, his mother, née Maria Calvelli-Adorno (who was thirty-seven years old when he was born),[2] and her unmarried sister Agathe.[3] They were Catholic, Corsican, daughters of a German singer and a French army officer of Genoese ancestry,[4] but most importantly they were musicians: Maria sang professionally; Agathe played the piano as accompanist for the famous singer Adelina Patti.[5] They furnished Adorno's earliest world with music. Even before Adorno could read the notes, he would follow the scores, reconstructing their sound from memory.[6] As he grew older, Agathe taught him piano, and together they played four-handed transcriptions of the classics of musical history. He recalled: "Four-handed playing laid the geniuses of the bourgeois nineteenth century as a gift at the cradle at the beginning of the twentieth."[7] Adorno was at home in this bourgeois, mostly German, cultural tradition. The large, green-bound volumes brought symphonic and chamber-music literature "into household life"; it was produced on the piano as a piece of family furniture, played "without fear of false notes and stops"; it "belonged to the family."[8]

But if domestic familiarity robbed music of one kind of aura, if for Adorno "serious" music was never untouchable and its "greatness" elicited no authoritarian reverence, it maintained an aura of another sort, the kind Walter Benjamin would claim was threatened with extinction in the modern age of art's mechanical reproducibility.[9] Unlike radio and phonograph recordings, this music was recreated with each reproduction. It was brought to life, actively produced rather than passively consumed:

Four-handed playing was better than the [reproduction of Arnold Böcklin's painting] "Island of the Dead" over the buffet; one had truly to acquire the symphony every time anew in order to possess it.[10]

His mother and aunt linked Adorno to a cultural heritage, giving him an intellectual orientation which proved far more influential than any social or religious identification. French-born, his mother's family had no social roots in Germany, nor were these provided by his Jewish, assimilated father. Adorno was baptized a Catholic, confirmed a Protestant — no doubt as a matter of expediency — and (except for a brief interest in Catholicism during the twenties)[11] he was, throughout his life, an atheist.[12] Because his father made no attempt to force his own religion or business occupation on him, Adorno, unlike many of his generation,[13] had no impulse to rebel against the world of his father. Yet because his social roots were shallow, this lack of rebellion did not bring with it intellectual conservatism. Frankfurt am Main was a secular, socially mobile city, retaining into the twentieth century some of the salutary characteristics of bourgeois liberalism, and an openness and lack of dogma were characteristic of its large Jewish population.[14] Anti-Semitism was of course not absent in the years before Hitler, but, as Adorno recalled, overt expression of it was "quite unusual in the trade city of Frankfurt."[15] Compared with Berlin, it was provincial; yet it had an active cultural life, a liberal press, and a new, relatively liberal university which attracted to its faculty some of the more original and critical thinkers in Weimar Germany.

There existed in Frankfurt that curious social phenomenon whereby a class enthusiastically feeds the intellectuals and artists that bite it. Yet despite the liaison, the two worlds remained distinct. Hence it was possible for the precocious and gifted Adorno, clearly destined from childhood for the world of intellectuals and artists, to grow up quite ignorant of the realm of business and practical politics. In 1914 he was too young to go to war, and was thus also protected from this brutal experience which traumatically affected so many slightly older intellectuals of his generation. In 1918-1919, while Germany was reeling from military defeat and political upheaval, the fifteen-year-old Adorno studied music and spent his weekend hours reading Kant. His Kant tutor was Siegfried Kracauer, fourteen years his senior and a friend of the family: "For more than a year, regularly on Saturday afternoon, he read with me the *Critique of Pure Reason.*[16] But it should not too quickly be assumed that here was the training of a German mandarin.[17] Adorno had no blind reverence for past culture and made no attempt to disdain the present by cloaking himself in its authority. He approached culture with a passion that was as intimately personal as it was authentic. As with his first exposure to music, what excited Adorno about this introduction to philosophy was that it demanded his active engagement. Kracauer did not teach Kant as a reified, closed system of thought that needed to be assimilated, but as thought which, for all its historical remoteness, was vitally relevant to the present:

Exceptionally gifted pedagogically, he [Kracauer] brought Kant to speech for me. From the start, under his guidance, I experienced the work not as a mere theory of cognition, as an analysis of the conditions of scientifically valid judgments, but as a kind of coded text, out of which the historical condition of the mind [*Geist*] could be read, with the vague expectation that thereby something of truth itself was to be won.[18]

In 1921 Adorno passed the *Abitur* exam, and left the Kaiser Wilhelm Gymnasium to enter Frankfurt's new university.[19] He was eighteen and already the author of two published articles: a short essay on expressionism[20] and a review of a new opera by his music teacher Bernhard Sekles.[21] Yet for all his accomplishments, he still had the excited intensity, the "brutish earnestness"[22] of the protégé. He was impressionable, seeking out intellectual companionship from men many years his senior. He went quickly through coursework, studying philosophy, sociology, psychology, and music, and received his doctorate in philosophy three years later in 1924. It was for him a time of mastering material rather than real intellectual originality. It was his initiation into the philosophical controversies which, largely the legacy of prewar thinkers, had come to dominate in academic circles.

European bourgeois culture, in self-proclaimed crisis since before the war, was flushed with the symptoms of what looked like a terminal fever — as was the political and economic structure in which it had developed. Significantly, the two cultural phenomena most threatened were precisely Adorno's passions: art and philosophy. While art was threatened from without by a technology which mechanized its production and altered aesthetic experience,[23] the prewar expressionist movement had liquidated bourgeois forms of music, painting, and literature from within. As Adorno wrote in his first published article, the very possibility of art was in doubt: "The art of the age stands before the question of its continued existence."[24] As for philosophy, it no longer presumed to provide an overarching system for all knowledge, and was in danger of receding into problems of formal logic while its traditional concerns became the property of the new social sciences. Relativism, both historical and scientific, eroded the foundation of bourgeois philosophy when Einstein overturned Newtonian physics and Dilthey questioned whether even the forms of cognition were timeless, challenging the universality of rational subjectivity.

If the bourgeois *Weltanschauung* was disintegrating, words had no power to make it whole. In the era of photography and the first silent films, the linear logic of the written word lost its monopoly. Moreover, poets and philosophers — Trakl, Hofmannsthal, the young Wittgenstein — had begun to wonder whether language was at all capable of communicating truth.

In short, there was universal agreement that bourgeois culture was in ruins. The debate was whether to applaud or lament the situation. To be young (with a full stomach) in this age of crisis was to have a golden opportunity for original contribution. In the twenties, still, it seemed "everything was allowed."[25] Given his Jewish and foreign background, Adorno had no political or social influence to lose, no vested interest in perpetuating the old order. It could be anticipated that he would join the intellectual *avant-garde*.

The year he entered the university Adorno read Ernst Bloch's *Geist der Utopie*,[26] and it impressed him greatly. Bloch, he wrote later in exile, was "the philosopher of expressionism, in which the word knowledge and expression are one and the same. Already that was not gladly seen [in Germany]."[27] Like Schön-berg with music, like Kandinsky with painting, Bloch developed the creative possibilities set loose by disintegrating forms. In the name of a utopian future, he broke radically with both the form and content of traditional academic philosophy. Politically engaged, he made his living as a writer outside the uni-versity. Adorno had not yet met him (they became friends after 1928), but Bloch's name conjured up a distinctive atmosphere:

> Dark as a passageway, roaring, dampened as a trumpet blast, he awakened an expectation of the extraordinary, which soon enough made me suspicious of the philosophy with which my studying had acquainted me, as stale and not living up to its own concept.[28]

Geist der Utopie took philosophical concepts and controversies out of the attic of academic scholasticism and made them current, expressing by the very tempo of its language the altered form of contemporary philosophical experience. Bloch

> . . . took the [Hegelian] dialectic, which taught overcoming the alienation of subject and object, so seriously that he despised the impartial, composed tone of academicians who perpetuate a cold disconnectedness with the object.[29]

Animated by a mystical, almost occult concept of art and a religious messi-anism,[30] yet committed to a secular, Marxist vision of sociopolitical utopia, Bloch dared philosophers to leave the safety of formal logic with its easily resolvable questions and confront, as religion and art confronted, the "unformulatable question" (*unkonstruierbare Frage*) of utopian realization.

But if Bloch brought philosophy back into the political arena, if he placed it in the service of Marxist goals, the transcendent, religious element of his thought was strongly opposed to the economic determinism and positivist, mechanistic view of history which had come to characterize orthodox Marxism. In his study of the Protestant radical Thomas Münzer (1921) he had argued that subjective as well as objective forces were the motors of historical development, and revolutions were moved by religious thinking; utopia could not be defined merely in socioeconomic terms.[31]

Bloch's heady combination of elements from religion, aesthetics, idealism, and political utopianism was not without problems. One of the tragic flaws of Weimar culture generally (which recurred in the New Left movement of the 1960s) was that to bring philosophy to bear on questions of social justice was to correct an *academic* failing, while it left social reality untouched. The fact that intellectuals adopted an advocacy position in no way guaranteed they would have the desired (or any) social effect. In 1918 left-wing expressionists and other intellectuals attempted to integrate cultural protest with political praxis; their failure became characteristic of the subsequent history of Weimar culture.[32] The problematic relationship between cultural revolt and sociopolitical revolution was, as will be demonstrated, a difficulty in Adorno's own theory, and in this sense his story is typical.

Among the books by writers who, like Bloch, reintroduced religious elements into philosophy in its present crisis, Franz Rosenzweig's *Der Stern der Erlösung* (The Star of Redemption), published in 1920, was significant, not because it influenced Adorno directly (although he was surely acquainted with both the book and the man), but because it returned to specifically Jewish religious thought in an attempt to redeem philosophy from its current atrophy. In a review of the 1930 edition of the book, Gershom Scholem testified to its impact in the 1920s among Jews and among radicals, including himself,[33] and in it there were elements which via the circuitous route of Scholem and Walter Benjamin found their place in Adorno's thinking. Rosenzweig was influenced by Hegel, but rejected Hegel's closed system, his metaphysical identity of the totality of reality with truth: "The monumental error of idealism consisted in thinking that the All was really wholly contained in its 'generation' of the All";[34] "the whole is simply not All, it is in fact only a whole";[35] "Reason is entitled to a home in the world, but the world is just that: a home; it is not totality."[36] The notion of the whole was a utopian hope for the future (better expressed by art than by philosophy):[37]

> Only in redemption, God becomes the One and All which, from the first, human reason in its rashness has everywhere sought and everywhere asserted, and yet nowhere found because it simply was nowhere to be found yet, for it did not exist yet.[38]

In place of Hegel's totalistic view, Rosenzweig insisted that reality was fragmentary, composed of a "plenitude" of individual, distinct phenomena:

> Whence they are coming or whither going has not been inscribed in their foreheads: They simply exist. But in existing they are individual, each one against all others, "particular," "not-otherwise."[39]

Knowledge of the object (this was a mystical motif) was bound to the "name," singular and particular, "incapable of utter absorption into the category, for there can be no category for it to belong to; it is its own category."[40] Knowledge was "revelation" which "looks back into the past. . . . But the past only becomes visible to revelation when and as revelation shines into it with the light of the present."[41] All of these conceptions were characteristic as well of Adorno's theory. Yet it was not Judaism which led him to them. Instead, it was his friendship with Walter Benjamin.

Adorno met Benjamin in Frankfurt in 1923.[42] The meeting was arranged by their mutual friend Siegfried Kracauer at the Cafe Westend am Opernplatz.[43] Adorno, eleven years younger than Benjamin, remembered being tremendously impressed:

> It is scarcely an illusion of memory when I say that from the first moment on, I had the impression of Benjamin as one of the most significant human beings that ever confronted me. I was 20 years old at the time. . . .[44]

If reading Bloch had opened Adorno's eyes to the inadequacies of current academic philosophy, it was Benjamin who pointed out the way to overcome them:

> It was as if through this [Benjamin's] philosophy it first dawned on me what philosophy must be if it was to fulfill what it promised, and yet has never contained since there crept into it the Kantian division between that which remains within experience and that which transgresses the boundaries of the possibility of experience.[45]

Specifically, it was Benjamin's ability to scrutinize the concrete and conceptless details of which, as Rosenzweig had argued, reality was composed, in a way which released a transcendent meaning, without ever leaving the empirical realm. Benjamin thus achieved insights which paralleled mystical revelation, while adhering to the Kantian antimetaphysical rule of staying within the data of experience. His goal, first formulated in 1918, was to establish, on a Kantian basis, "the virtual unity of religion and philosophy."[46]

In Benjamin's student years he had been part of a radical, Jewish, intellectual wing of the *Jugendbewegung.*[47] Here he met Gershom Scholem, his closest intellectual companion from 1916 to 1923.[48] Scholem was beginning what would become a lifelong task of scholarship in the Kabbalah, the then largely forgotten tradition of Jewish mysticism.[49] They studied Kant together, as Adorno had with Kracauer, fantasizing, "half earnestly, half in fun," about founding their own academy, as "there was so little to learn at the university."[52] They discussed Scholem's religious scholarship continuously. Benjamin (who despite several attempts never became proficient in Hebrew) acquired through this relationship a theological, mystical mode of expression which was preserved in a sublated form in even his most intentionally "Marxist" writings of the thirties. But unlike Scholem (or Rosenzweig or Bloch, whom he befriended in 1918), Benjamin sought and discovered the origins of mystical concepts in aesthetic rather than theological literature, in the theories of Novalis, Schlegel, and Goethe, and in the German tragic dramas of the Baroque era.[50] Benjamin's religiosity was secular and mundane, at the same time that he approached profane objects with a religious reverence. His was thus an "inverse" or "negative" theology[51] in which mysticism and materialism converged, and as a model for philosophical thinking it made no little impression on Adorno. But the really crucial period of Benjamin's influence on him would come later, after 1927, in connection with their common adaptation of Marxism.

As for Judaism and theology *per se,* they cannot be said to have influenced

Adorno in an affirmative sense. Unlike Benjamin, he joined no Jewish youth groups as a student; unlike Scholem, he was not attracted to Zionism;[53] nor did he participate with Siegfried Kracauer, Franz Rosenzweig, and Martin Buber in Rabbi Nehemiah A. Nobel's intellectual circle in Frankfurt.[54] Turning to theology to provide the sense of wholeness and security which the shattered bourgeois *Weltanschauung* could no longer provide was an option which Adorno felt compelled to reject.[55]

There was a tendency in the twenties for the revolt against academic sterility (as well as against modern society with its bureaucratically organized, "rationalized" structure) to take the form of an affirmation of the irrational. The theological revival was one manifestation of this, but there were many others: Sorelian voluntarism in politics, a renewed interest in Kierkegaard, Jungian psychiatry, the novels of Hermann Hesse, the advocacy of "culture" over civilization and "community" over society, and even an intellectual vogue for horoscopes and magic. A shift was occurring in intellectual alliances: the advocates of reason, since the Enlightenment identified with progressive social and political forces, had abandoned the impulses of revolution and passively accepted the "given" state of things. Rationality had become synonymous with compromise and resignation, manifested in political life by the *Vernunftrepublikaner* who, with a claim to being "reasonable," accepted without enthusiasm the given reality of the Weimar Republic, which was in many respects very unrepublican and undemocratic. On the other hand, revolt which grounded itself in irrationalism slipped easily into a formula for fascism. To their credit, Adorno and those individuals who were intellectually closest to him did not accept the new dichotomy that was developing. Rather than align themselves with one side of this polarity, they insisted that truth lay in the tension between the two, in the rationale of what appeared as irrational and in the irrationality of what was accepted as reason.

It was Benjamin's insistence that religion and Kantianism, that mysticism and materialism *converged* insofar as they were true that prevented him from fitting into either intellectual current. Adorno was fortunate to have as a mentor at the university a man also eccentric, also outside the intellectual mainstream: the philosophy professor Hans Cornelius,[56] in whose seminars Adorno came to know his lifelong friend, Max Horkheimer. Against irrationalists, Cornelius firmly defended the Enlightenment tradition, but not in its present, quasi-scholastic form. Cornelius was an *Aufklärer* of the old sort, a radical, philosophically speaking, more of a Kantian than Kant himself in his commitment to the "destruction of dogmatic theories and the establishment of those in their place which are grounded in experience and are assured for experience beyond doubt."[57] His rejection of the Kantian doctrine of the thing-in-itself, which he claimed was a metaphysical residue, was in effect slipping behind Kant to earlier British and French empiricism. It was also in accord with the neo-Kantianism of his Viennese contemporaries Avenarius and Mach. Yet if there was a positivist bent to Cornelius's interpretation of Kant, he lacked the positivists' uncritical acceptance of the "given" world and their passive notion of the subject. Cornelius was an artist and a bohemian.[58] To him the philosophical "subject" was not a uniform, transcendental universal, but a unique living individual, and philosophical experience was personal and lived rather than abstract and academic. All knowledge was based on prior experience, hence it was never complete; philosophy was no closed system, and there were no ontological absolutes. Despite the universality of the cognitive forms, the cumulative nature of experience guaranteed that reality was "unlimited possibility" and that "the objects always remain partially alien,"[59] not because they belonged to some noumenal realm, but because they appeared each time in a new configuration. In Cornelius's notion of experience, there was no being independent of consciousness, and no consciousness independent of being. This amounted to the abrogation of a philosophical first principle (*prima philosophia*), and it was one of the earliest and most constant tenets of Adorno and Horkheimer as well.

There was something refreshing in Cornelius's bohemian individualism, and the very un-German empiricism which he espoused. His idea of philosophy was "striving for the ultimate clarity," and it was "violently inimicable to any kind of dogmatism."[60] He encouraged Adorno and Horkheimer to respect the individuality of concrete phenomena, providing a down-to-earth counterweight to the far more esoteric Kantianism of Walter Benjamin. Yet like Benjamin, and because of his artistic sensitivities, he respected aesthetic and religious experiences as well as those of "scientific" reason. Critical of society (yet not politically active), he wrote in 1923:

> Men have unlearned the ability to recognize the Godly in themselves and in things; nature and art, family and state only have interest for them as sensations. Therefore their lives flow meaninglessly by, and their shared culture is inwardly empty and will collapse because it is worthy of collapse. The new religion, however, which mankind needs, will first emerge from the ruins of this culture.[61]

Cornelius's philosophy was well enough known to have been singled out for attack by Lenin in his critique of contemporary philosophy, *Materialismus und Empiriokritizismus* (1909).[62] Lenin claimed it remained subjectivist and idealist despite its opposition to Kant's idealism, and cited as evidence Cornelius's keeping the way open for the possibility of life after death, and his statement that "above all" the goal of learning was "training to respect — not the transient values of an arbitrary tradition, but the immortal values of duty and beauty — of the [Godly elements] within us and without us."[63] As for Cornelius, he accused materialism in general of the same "dogmatism" which he criticized in idealism, and claimed it treated men as "automatons."[64] He urged his students not to conform to any -ism, but to think for themselves: "Not Kant and not Marx, not Luther and not Fichte, and not anyone else should be your master, but only your own reason. . . ."[65]

Max Horkheimer had been Cornelius's student since 1918, and Pollock has written that the latter's "influence on Horkheimer can hardly be overestimated."[66] Born near Stuttgart in 1895, the son of a conservative Jewish, very successful textile manufacturer, Horkheimer had trained for seven years in the commercial aspects of his father's business (developing a financial acumen that later kept the Frankfurt *Institut* afloat) and traveled to Brussels, Paris, and London until the outbreak of World War I forced his return to Stuttgart. The war became an intense personal crisis for Horkheimer. His early diaries document his passionate condemnation of the war (in which he was forced to serve after 1917), as well as his hatred of the business occupation into which he was being channeled.[67] The twenty-year-old Horkheimer longed for a different existence:

> By my craving for truth will I live, and search into what I desire to know; the afflicted will I aid, satisfy my hatred against injustice, and vanquish the Pharisees, but above all search for love, love and understanding. . . .[68]

At that time he wrote a spate of novellas; all expressed the inhumanity of war and the anguish of being trapped against his will, chained, as he wrote, by a tyranny no less oppressive for its invisibility.[69]

Surely his was an adolescent rebellion, turning against his family the moral fervor which it had nurtured in him.[70] Yet it was not only filial duty which held him back from following his own desires. Horkheimer had a deep, nagging sense that the desire for social justice was "insanity," that all people, even the most self-righteous, were guilty, however indirectly, of perpetrating the world's evils.[71] Perhaps it was the essence of being human, this "striving for power, for domination, for acquisition": "Wherever human beings are, there will be war."[72] Horkheimer had been exposed to Schopenhauer's writings in 1913,[73] and the Schopenhauerian pessimism which began to permeate his writings in the 1940s (again, with the outbreak of world war) was a resurfacing of this, his earliest orientation, not a radical break in his intellectual development, as has been assumed.[74] From the start, Horkheimer's thinking resided in the tension between a commitment to foster social justice (more, "the happiness of each individual")[75] and his suspicion of the futility of the endeavor. The way to peace, he wrote in 1915, was "forgiveness, suffering, spirit, love. The world's history eternally roars past these things: blind, hopeless, irredeemable, insatiable — an eternally restless power."[76]

Released from fighting due to illness, Horkheimer left the business world and entered the university, studying first at Munich, then moving with Friedrich Pollock, his friend since childhood, to Frankfurt in 1918. Later, with a letter of introduction from Cornelius, he spent a semester in Freiburg to hear the lectures of Edmund Husserl, who impressed him greatly.[77] In 1921 he was back in Frankfurt, studying psychology with the Gestaltist Adhemar Gelb (as did Adorno), and he received his doctorate in philosophy in 1922.[78] For the next three years he was Cornelius's assistant. Adorno recalled the first time he saw him:

> . . . you were eight years older than I, appeared to me to be hardly a student, more like a young gentleman from a well-to-do home, who rendered to

academia a certain distant interest. You were unconsumed by that occupational deformation of the academic who all too easily confuses involvement in learned things with reality. Except what you said was so intelligent, so clear-sighted, and above all, autonomous, that I quickly enough felt you superior to that sphere from which you imperceptibly held yourself apart.[79]

In Cornelius's seminar Horkheimer read a paper on Husserl, which Adorno found "truly brilliant": "Spontaneously I went to you and introduced myself. From that time on we were together."[80]

The Frankfurt *Institut für Sozialforschung,* whose codirectors they would eventually become, was founded by Felix Weil in 1923. But Adorno was not involved in its inception, and Horkheimer only marginally, by virtue of his close friendship with Friedrich Pollock, an economist, whose role was considerable, and who was largely responsible for Horkheimer's assuming the directorship in 1931. Under Carl Grünberg's directorship (1924-1927), the Institute was avowedly "Marxist" in an orthodox sense (although free from Party affiliation), and primarily interested in historical and empirical research into the labor movement and economic conditions.[81] Adorno and Horkheimer were far more animated by questions of philosophical and aesthetic theory, and in these areas they had not yet taken a Marxist advocacy position whatever their personal political convictions may have been.[82]

In the first years of their friendship, Husserl and Kant more than Marx and Hegel were the topics of their discussions. It was from Horkheimer that Adorno acquired his deep regard for Husserl, which persisted even after his move to Marx (and longer than Horkheimer's own enthusiasm). Adorno remained convinced that Husserl more than any of his contemporaries had correctly articulated the issues and dilemmas which philosophy presently confronted, that with his phenomenology bourgeois idealism had gone as far as it could, and that precisely Husserl's failure to resolve these dilemmas was evidence of his philosophical integrity. Three times during his life Adorno was deeply involved in Husserl's philosophy. His doctoral dissertation, completed in 1924, was a critique of Husserl's theory of the object. It analyzed Husserl's dilemma of desiring a return to the objects, to the "things themselves" as the source of knowledge, while fearing that the transient, empirical objects were too insecure a basis for truth. Adorno argued in line with Cornelius that empirical things had to be the basis of knowledge, or else one was forced into metaphysics.[83] In 1934-1937, living at Oxford, Adorno again tackled Husserl, attempting through the negation of his phenomenology nothing less than the transcendence of bourgeois idealism altogether.[84] He later revised this study, publishing it with a new introduction as *Zur Metakritik der Erkenntnistheorie* in 1956.[85]

By the 1930s Adorno's analysis of Husserl was conceived within the frame of the Marxist-Hegelian dialectical tradition. But elements of Cornelius's empiricism were still visible, not only his insistence that knowledge remain immanent, that is, within the bounds of experience, and that the objects of experience were contingent, concrete, particular phenomena, but also his belief that art provided a better model for philosophy than Husserl's cognitive utopia of pure mathematics. Indeed, Adorno always considered art and philosophy complementary occupations, and his interest in music was far from preempted by his philosophical studies. In 1924 he was given the opportunity to study musical composition with Berg in Vienna. He leaped at the chance.

VIENNA

Alban Berg came to Frankfurt in spring 1924 for a premiere performance of fragments from his opera *Wozzeck,* conducted by Hermann Scherchen.[86] Adorno was in the audience:

> Overcome by the music, I begged Scherchen, with whom I had contact, to introduce me to Berg. In a few minutes it was agreed that I should come to Vienna as his student. . . .[87]

The excitement of studying with Berg was the promise of initiation into Schönberg's compositional method, which had revolutionized music by overthrowing classical tonality. Adorno's teacher in Frankfurt, Bernhard Sekles (who also taught Paul Hindemith),[88] was a moderate and provincial in comparison with Arnold Schönberg and his pupils Berg and Anton Webern, the last of a long line of music geniuses of Vienna:

> . . . the *Wozzeck* fragments, above all the introduction to the "march," and then the "march" itself, struck me as if it were Schönberg, and Mahler too, all at once, and that was then and there my image of the true, new music.[89]

Adorno had to wait to finish his doctorate in July 1924, and his move to Vienna was delayed until the next January. His stay was brief, less than two years, but the experience left a decisive impression.

The Austro-Hungarian Empire had collapsed in 1918, and Vienna in the twenties continued to exhibit the anomalies of the late empire. Baroque relics of the feudal past existed alongside fragments of modernity. The bourgeoisie, which included many Jews, had never displaced the aristocracy. Although Austria's economic structure was capitalist, the feudal prejudice for land rather than investment remained, and the social prestige of noble titles was still considerable. In Vienna, the veneer of gaiety covered a more somber reality. The froth of operettas, waltz music, and gay cafés bubbled alongside a poorly housed proletariat, its numbers swollen in the wake of agricultural depression. As Karl Kraus is alleged to have said: "In Berlin, things are serious but not hopeless; in Vienna they are hopeless but not serious."[90]

It was a city of paradoxes. The aristocracy was anti-Semitic, identified Jews with entrepreneurs and entrepreneurs with parvenus, yet Jews provided a lion's share of the cultural elite, and they identified with the German intellectual heritage. The philosophical climate was neo-Kantian,[91] which meant that metaphysics was discredited and problems of truth were equated with problems of logic and language, but it caused many, like Wittgenstein, to doubt whether the really important things could be expressed at all. Sex was unmentionable, and thus terribly important. Sigmund Freud was attacked due to the very moral repressiveness which his therapy was designed to overcome. Culturally, Austria was conservative, but still it was the home of expressionists, including Georg Trakl and Oskar Kokoschka, as well as Schönberg. Vienna "offered splendid potentialities for the highest accomplishment, as well as the most stubborn resistance to its realization."[92] As Adorno recalled, everything new was opposed, only later to be defended as the new tradition.[93]

Artistic and cultural rebellion by individuals took the place of organized political or social revolt: "The life of art became a substitute for the life of action."[94] Yet there was an awareness of the inability of words to provide through culture a new unity and cohesion for society. Wrote Hofmannsthal: "Everything fell into parts, the parts again into more parts, and nothing allowed itself to be embraced by concepts any more."[95] For many intellectual rebels the only alternative was to goad on the cultural disintegration, with the hope of transcending present reality by the demolition, not of reality (for they opposed the war and were not revolutionaries), but of the kind of consciousness which proved to be so compatible with — even enthusiastic for — war and the existing social order.

The anomalies of Vienna were personified by Karl Kraus, whose satirical journal *Die Fackel* (1899-1936) recorded the history of the Viennese society it so keenly criticized. His satire was relentless against the press: he journalized against journalism. His aim was not to "do" the news (*bringen*), but to "do it in" (*umbringen*).[96] He was a pacifist, prosocialist, yet against the socialist parties. Born Jewish, he was an archenemy of Herzl's Zionist movement, entered the Catholic Church, and left again twelve years later. He defended prostitutes and homosexuals, claiming laws governing ethics were unethical: the scandal begins, he noted (anticipating the New Left of the sixties), when the police move in to end it.[97] His defense of freedom in the private realm ruled out attraction to a revolutionary socialism which would desire more, not less, control of citizen's actions. Typical of his milieu, his rebellion remained individual (after 1911 he wrote all of *Die Fackel* himself), and it was aimed primarily against culture and consciousness rather than politics and the socioeconomic structure. Kraus saw the evils of society mirrored in the abuse of the German language,[98] and it was language which he wished to purify. In its early years *Die Fackel* supported expressionism, publishing articles by Kokoschka, Lasker-Schüler, Schönberg, Wedekind, and Werfel;[99] it defended Trakl, and even Bertolt Brecht on occasion. Yet Kraus's own language incorporated almost none of the expressionist stylistic devices. He was conservative, almost prudish, in his strict adherence to the laws of meaning and grammar. The wit, the satire of his writings was achieved by an immanent critique of language which played on double meanings and syntactical ambivalences, turning the expressions of Viennese society against itself. For Kraus the critique of language became an act of social protest.[100]

Conversely, the accurate use of language was synonymous with the representation of truth. Hence the importance of "presentation" (*Darstellung*): truth was not just *what* was said, but how; form was inseparable from content. The notion that language provided an "image" (*Bild*) of reality and the equation of this image with truth were not unique in Kraus's writings. They tied him to several contemporary intellectuals, including Arnold Schönberg.[101]

Presenting Kraus with a copy of *Harmonielehre*, his book on musical composition, Schönberg wrote the inscription: "I have learned more from you, perhaps, than a man should learn, if he wants to remain independent."[102] A decade later Berg, Schönberg's student, remained similarly impressed. Adorno wrote:

> Berg's attitude toward Kraus was that of unbounded respect; whenever I was in Vienna we went to every available Kraus lecture. . . . The relationship to Kraus was one of authority.[103]

The theory of music of the Schönberg school directly paralleled Kraus's theory of language: Schönberg considered musical composition a "representation" of truth characterized by a clarity of expression which was achieved through strict adherence to the laws of musical "language," out of the inner logic of which the composition was developed.[104]

Schönberg's was a radical departure from the nineteenth-century approach to aesthetics, when issues had been defined by the debates between Wagnerites and anti-Wagnerites. The former claimed music was a subjective expression of truth which had its source in an eternal, natural, and irrational realm of the spirit (the view was compatible with Schopenhauer's philosophy)[105] and which should be judged by its emotional and dramatic effect (*Wirkungsaesthetik*). Against this romantic view, the conservative Viennese critic Eduard Hanslick argued the classical position, claiming that music was self-sufficient; it did not need to "express" anything except the thematic material itself, which developed according to the inner logic of the composition.[106] Schönberg's originality lay in his ability to merge elements from the extremes of Wagnerian romanticism and earlier classicism in a new configuration, thus altering the whole context of the debate. Like Wagner he believed music expressed truth, but he claimed that this truth was objective rather than subjective, demanding rational articulation rather than emotional immediacy,[107] and that the effect of the composition on the audience was extraneous to its aesthetic validity. But if music was an experience of the intellect, if it unfolded in accord with its own objective, inner logic, this logic was no longer the harmonious classicism admired by Hanslick: musical logic was not governed by formal and eternal laws; it developed historically, and hence its inner dynamics necessitated going beyond the forms of the past, not their resuscitation. In this way, Schönberg used Hanslick's conservative aesthetics to justify the most radical musical means, and it was Wagner whose music appeared conservative in comparison.

Harmonielehre (1911),[108] Schönberg's handbook of composition, justified the revolutionary overthrow of tonality which had governed music throughout the bourgeois era. "Tonality," it declared, "is no eternal natural law of music."[109] Traditional theoreticians, so shocked by his music, were concerned

> . . . only with eternal things, come always therefore too late in life. . . . To the devil with all these theories, if they only serve to erect a barrier to the development of art![110]

Art developed through individual artworks, each of which was governed by its own inner logic.[111] Whereas natural law demanded that the particular case be an example of a general rule and thus "knows no exceptions, theories of art exist above all out of exceptions."[112] The composer's job was thus to transcend rather than submit to tradition.

The refusal to accept bourgeois cultural norms as absolute was a unifying characteristic of expressionism, the otherwise diverse artistic revolt of the 1910s with which Schönberg himself identified. But whereas expressionist contemporaries, like Klee in art or Trakl in poetry, retreated into a subjective, psychological realm, Schönberg focused on the material itself. He approached the teaching of music as teaching a craft, in which the knowledge of laws governing past compositions provided a technical mastery which necessarily preceded original creativity. He taught his pupils, not musical theory, but compositional practice,[113] and urged them to rely on their own aesthetic experience:

> And a false theory found through honest searching always stands higher than the contemplative security of him who opposes it because he presumes to know — to know without having searched himself![114]

Berg continued this pedagogic method. Adorno recalled an exercise Berg gave him: "to instrument passages out of the *Götterdämmerung* and then compare them with Wagner's solutions, an exceptionally instructive enterprise."[115]

According to Schönberg the creativity, the genius of the composer consisted in his ability to develop the objective potentialities within the material. These potentialities were not unlimited: they had to adhere to the logic of the musical language, just as for Kraus verbal expressions adhered to grammatical logic. But because this logic developed historically, what was called "atonality" (Schönberg did not like the term) was not so much a break with tonality as its culmination: in it the Wagnerian principle of chromaticism was carried to its extreme, so that tonality destroyed itself:

> When Schoenberg says that his music is tonal, he means that each chord has its own fundamental, independent of the context. Each chord is in a certain key. But according to Schoenberg, four successive chords, for example, will be in four different keys. The speed at which one key passes to another and the complexity of each chord do not leave the ear enough time to take in the different keys and their relationships. Since there is no continuity in establishing a given key, apparent atonality results.[116]

Adorno became quickly convinced that the transcendence of tonality and of traditional forms was a musical necessity.[117] Beginning in 1925 he wrote a series of articles for radical music journals in defense of the compositions of Schönberg and his students Anton Webern, Alban Berg, and Hanns Eisler.[118]

But Adorno was not simply an apologist for the new music. His articles were critical reflections containing the beginnings of his own theory of aesthetics, which, significantly, rested on philosophical conceptions of the dialectic not articulated by Schönberg himself.[119]

The music of Webern and Berg,[120] even more than of Schönberg, had become identified with expressionism. Adorno conceded: "Webern's music corresponds, like scarcely any other, to the claims of expressionism," due to its individualism, its "pure representation of subjective intention," and its "seemingly ahistorical, absolute lyricism."[121] Yet he claimed that the truth of the music, and hence its aesthetic validity, had to be understood dialectically: Precisely its "ahistoricity" was connected to history. "Its extreme individualism is the completion of romantic [individualism], held spellbound at that point which marks its historical reversal [*Umschlag*]."[122] There was history within Webern's music despite its apparent lack of development: "Its source is authentically dialectic, and it possesses within itself sufficient dialectical antitheses to transform itself within the narrow space which it is granted."[123]

If these articles anticipated Adorno's later aesthetic theory, they did not yet manifest an identifiably Marxist orientation. They do, however, document that Adorno's understanding of dialectical logic was influenced by his study of musical logic, and this fact accounts for much that was original in his theory. Hegel had little appreciation for music, and Schönberg was hardly a Hegelian. Yet Adorno would later acclaim Schönberg as "the dialectical composer."[124] It seems clear that Schönberg's revolution in music provided the inspiration for Adorno's own efforts in philosophy, the model for his major work on Husserl during the thirties. For just as Schönberg had overthrown tonality, the decaying form of bourgeois music, so Adorno's Husserl study attempted to overthrow idealism, the decaying form of bourgeois philosophy.[125]

Adorno's direct contact with Schönberg was limited. He wrote:

> When I came to Vienna I had an image of the Schönberg circle as rather closely knit, analogous to the circle around [the poet Stefan] George. Already by then that was no longer accurate.[126]

Schönberg had remarried and was living outside Vienna in Mödling, isolated from his old friends. Adorno recalled being introduced to him there by Berg; a more intimate meeting came only later through Rudolph Kolisch,[127] whose sister was Schönberg's new wife. But Adorno and Schönberg were never close, and the latter was not totally appreciative of Adorno's interpretation of his music.[128]

Berg, however, was most accessible. Whereas Schönberg evoked from his students a deference not unconnected with anxiety,[129] Berg was an unauthoritarian teacher, the opposite of a father figure,[130] who, using the inside of his piano as an ashtray, bubbled encouragement even when critically demolishing the student's compositional attempts.[131] Twice a week Adorno came for lessons, which consisted of going through his own compositions:

> All his corrections had an unmistakably Bergian character. . . . But if the resolutions were his, they were nonetheless confirmed as being compelled objectively, and were never grafted upon [the composition].[132]

One Bergian characteristic was an eye for detail, an articulation of nuances, which Adorno also found in Walter Benjamin,[133] and which became a canon of his own dialectical thinking. Also similar to Benjamin was a certain staticness, despite the dynamic compositional principle of thematic variation.[134] Berg used nineteenth-century musical means, but he transformed their function.[135] As with Wagner there was nihilism in his music, but Wagner glorified nihilism, while Berg's representation was a lament.[136] He juxtaposed opposites:

> For Berg, to form always meant to combine, also superimpose, to synthesize the incompatible, the disparate, to let it grow together: to *trans*form. In his music the word concrete finds its home.[137]

He avoided simplicity. Adorno commented on seeing the partitur of the march from Berg's Three Pieces for Orchestra (op. 6) that it must sound like Schönberg's Pieces for Orchestra played on top of Mahler's Ninth Symphony, and Berg was delighted.[138]

Berg introduced Adorno to his circle of friends, the dramatist Franz Werfel and his wife Alma Mahler (formerly married to Gustav Mahler); Erhard Buschbeck, who had been close to Georg Trakl;[139] the musicians Rudolph Kolisch and Eduard Steuermann.[140] Adorno went with Berg to the Berlin premiere of *Wozzeck* (December 1925),[141] where he met Hanns Eisler.[142] Berg probably introduced him to Ernst Krenek[143] and brought him into contact with the two radical musical journals, *Anbruch* and *Pult und Tactstock*, which published many of Adorno's articles.[144] Berg was a Catholic of aristocratic origin, whose personality had the uniquely Viennese combination of metaphysical pessimism and unabashed hedonism.[145] He hated German food, and had a Parisian passion for wine. Here too, Adorno was an appreciative student.[146]

Adorno had serious aspirations to become a composer. Yet he was not prolific,[147] and he had little success in getting his music performed.[148] He returned to Frankfurt after little more than a year in order to resume his study of philosophy with the hope of obtaining a university teaching position. The reasons for his leaving Vienna are unclear. It is true that Berg did not much appreciate Adorno's "philosophical ballast," which he referred to as "fad."[149] Adorno was perhaps too reflective, too self-conscious, and lacked the spontaneity necessary for uninhibited composing. He may have realized that, given his penchant for philosophy, he was better suited to musical criticism than composition. Furthermore, the "heroic era" of the Schönberg school was over; the really significant breakthrough had already been accomplished. During the period of Adorno's stay in Vienna, Schönberg was developing the twelve-tone technique, and although Adorno was an early defender of the tone-row method,[150] it was in his own terms, not Schönberg's. He may have already had the doubts which he later articulated[151] concerning the limitations and constraints of the twelve-tone schema, compared to the relative freedom of the earlier atonality.[152] He certainly rejected the propensity toward magic and superstition which existed in the Schönberg group, despite the stress on musical "logic" and composition as rational articulation: Berg was neurotically superstitious and considered 23 his magic number; Schönberg believed in horoscopes, fearing the number 13 and all its multiples. When Adorno returned to Frankfurt and philosophy, it was to Cornelius's tradition of Enlightenment. He seems to have felt the need to demonstrate that the irrational could be rationally understood. It led him first to Freud and then, almost immediately, to Marx.

FREUD AND MARX

Cornelius's philosophy had been out of the academic mainstream in the early twenties; it was even more so by the time Adorno returned from Vienna in 1926. Antirationalist tendencies were increasingly evident in philosophy and art,[153] as well as the rapidly expanding realm of popular culture.[154] Much of this spirit was intended as social revolt: it protested against the rationalization of existence (which Max Weber had defined as the developmental characteristic of modern industrialism) by protesting against rationalism in thought, along with the positivistic methodology which modernization had engendered. The argument (which still today has appeal in certain "radical" circles) was simply that if secularization, the "disenchantment" (*Entzauberung*) of the world, was the source of social alienation, what was needed was a return to myth and an affirmation of primitive immediacy, of the instinctual powers of the unconscious. Such antirationalism was what Adorno chose to attack in his *Habilitationsschrift* (the prerequisite study for a professorial position), and his method followed closely the neo-Kantianism of his mentor Hans Cornelius. There were, however, a few surprises.

Adorno's stated purpose in the study, entitled "The Concept of the Unconscious in the Transcendental Theory of Mind,"[155] was to determine whether a philosophical theory of the unconscious (which was lacking in Kant's original theory)[156] could be established in accord with Cornelius's brand of Kantianism, that is, without recourse to dogmatism (hence refusing to posit any ontological realm of the unconscious)[157] and without overstepping the limits of critical reason (hence refusing to accept the apparent irrationality of any empirical phenomena, including manifestations of the unconscious). Adorno began with an immanent critique of Schopenhauer and later *Lebensphilosophen*,[158] who accounted for the unconscious by constructing an ontological, "naturalist" metaphysics of the irrational.[159] He then spelled out the requirements for a theory of the unconscious which would accord with Cornelius's Kantianism. His next step was quite remarkable. He proceeded to demonstrate that these requirements were essentially met by the psychoanalytic theory of Sigmund Freud.

Was Adorno first exposed to Freudian theory during his stay in Vienna?[160] Was Cornelius himself impressed by Freud? Whatever originally prompted Adorno to write a philosophical justification of psychoanalysis, he seems to have studied Freud on his own, independent of academic connections.[161] And it was the theory, not the practice of psychoanalysis with which he was acquainted. The Kant-Freud study depended almost exclusively on one source for Freudian theory, Freud's introductory lectures of 1916-1917.[162] Adorno was struck by psychoanalysis as a cognitive model:[163] "Therapy strives to be nothing else but knowledge";[164] its goal was "disenchantment" of the unconscious by exposing the inner logic of its manifestations – Freudian slips, dreams, neurotic symptoms – and making them accessible to conscious, rational understanding.[165]

To defend Freudian psychoanalytic theory in an academic study during the twenties was daring enough, as Freud was not even accepted by psychiatrists, much less philosophers.[166] But Adorno did not stop here. In the closing pages of the Kant-Freud study, he articulated for the first time a critique of ideology that was identifiably, unequivocally Marxist. It was, he held, of more than academic importance to criticize the irrationalist theories of the unconscious because

> . . . we do not view these theories to be isolated, but connected to the historical situation; because of the fact that they do not originate solely out of the disposition and fantasy of their creators; but rather, they fulfill within the social reality a precisely determined function; one which is dangerous, which needs to be acknowledged, and which we believed it was necessary to counter.[167]

Adorno spelled out clearly the social function of these irrationalist theories, and hence what he felt was the reason for their dominance in intellectual circles:

> . . . the suspicion should not be dismissed that the contradiction between the philosophies of the unconscious and the ruling economic order becomes complementary in value; that theory is supposed to make up for what is lacking in reality; with other words: that it is exploited as ideology.[168]

The irrationalist theories functioned ideologically (that is, as mystifications of reality which lent support to the bourgeois status quo) in four ways:

> First, these theories want to turn away from the dominant economic mode and the supremacy of economic factors in general in that they offer evidence that outside of economic forces there are other, no less effective forces which are in every sense independent of consciousness, and are thus

removed from the economic tendencies of rationalization; that therefore there remain islands for the individual, onto which he can retreat from the flood of the economic struggle of competition.[169]

Second, encouraging people to withdraw into a private psychic sphere as a "pleasure-break from economic pressure"[170] which was the "luxury" of "a small circle of people"[171] diverted attention from social relationships, and from "the possibility of their transformation."[172] Indeed, the glorification of the unconscious functioned to defend society in that the latter's existing form appeared to be determined by "natural" drives: "the most pernicious plans of imperialism find their ideological defense as outbreaks of unconscious, vital powers of the mind which accord with nature's desires."[173] Finally, Adorno claimed that these tendencies, evident in Nietzsche and Spengler, found political expression "most clearly in the ideology of Fascism."[174] If Freud's theory was not totally free of similar tendencies,[175] if, moreover, it largely ignored the dependence of unconscious phenomena on "the material world, namely, society,"[176] and thus ignored the necessity of social as well as psychological transformation,[177] nonetheless, its present disfavor among psychological circles bore witness to its relative incompatibility with the dominant ideology.[178]

Adorno's defense of Freud's theory as the demythification, the "disenchantment" of the unconscious[179] had a political as well as an academic intent. However, Adorno readily admitted the limitations of its political effectiveness:

> We do not flatter ourselves with the hope of having done serious injury to the dominant theories of the unconscious: too many powerful interests are at play within public opinion that protect those theories. . . . Overcoming the practical consequences of false theories cannot, to be sure, be brought about by theory alone, but insight into the falseness of the theory and the constitution of more correct theory in its place is a prerequisite.[180]

This more limited goal was Adorno's intention.

In the preface to the Kant-Freud study, Adorno expressly acknowledged his debt to Max Horkheimer, who, having completed his own *Habilitationsschrift* on Kant in 1925,[181] was teaching social philosophy at Frankfurt University. It seems likely that this debt included the Marxist orientation of the concluding remarks.[182] It will be recalled that Horkheimer's close friend Friedrich Pollock was an influential member of the *Institut für Sozialforschung* during the twenties,[183] and Horkheimer's own role in the Institute had increased during Adorno's stay in Vienna. The kind of Marxism that appeared in Adorno's Kant-Freud study was similar to that of the early Institute in two respects: its relatively orthodox, almost "vulgar" Marxist approach to ideology, in that superstructure phenomena were interpreted as a direct reflection of economic interests;[184] and its nonetheless marked independence from the official line of the Communist Party (which had officially denounced Freudian analysis as "bourgeois aestheticism" in 1925).[185]

When Adorno submitted the Kant-Freud study as his *Habilitationsschrift*, it was rejected. It would not be surprising if Cornelius (who soon left Germany for Denmark) failed to appreciate the association of his philosophy with Marx. But intellectual prejudice was not necessarily the reason. In its conception, the Kant-Freud study contained an inner contradiction which justified its rejection on purely logical grounds: how could a neo-Kantian (hence idealist) justification of Freud be made compatible with a Marxist (hence materialist) critique of ideology?[186]

Adorno seems to have been aware that he was on untenable ground. Quite possibly, the shift in his method from Kant to Marx documents a shift in his own orientation during the months he was writing the Kant-Freud study. That would explain why, instead of trying to revise it (or simply dropping the final pages with their Marxist critique), he abandoned it altogether and started to work on the problem which the contradiction in his own work had made apparent.

BERLIN AND WALTER BENJAMIN

Beginning in 1927 Adorno spent much time in Berlin.[187] He visited his future wife, Gretel Karplus,[188] and their circle there included Walter Benjamin, Siegfried Kracauer,[189] Ernst Bloch,[190] Otto Klemperer, Moholy-Nagy, and, importantly, Bertolt Brecht and his friends: the composers Hanns Eisler and Kurt Weill and Weill's wife, the actress Lotte Lenya.[191]

Berlin in the twenties was the new Paris, attracting artists and literary figures like a magnet. Here *avant-garde* art and leftist political theory converged. Adorno later said the *Zeitgeist* appeared to be with his circle there.[192] If Berlin was the capital of an increasingly monopolistic economy (an economy on the verge of collapse), to him it still felt like "an open world"; recalled Lotte Lenya: "We had fun."[193] For Adorno's friends, Berlin was an experimental workshop for a new aesthetics politically committed to the goals of Marxist revolution.[194] But in opposition to the Marxism of the Party,[195] the Berlin circle considered art too important to view it as a mere economically determined epiphenomenon. Whereas the Communist Party ultimately condemned modern art as a manifestation of bourgeois decadence, Brecht believed that the new aesthetic techniques could be "refunctioned" (*umfunktioniert*), dialectically transformed from bourgeois tools into revolutionary ones which could bring about a critical consciousness of the nature of bourgeois society.[196]

Concerned with the role of art in transforming consciousness, it is not surprising that the Berlin group was attracted to a Hegelianized Marxism, which stressed the role of consciousness in the dialectic of social change, and which had been formulated in the early twenties by Karl Korsch[197] and Georg Lukács. Particularly influential was Lukács's book *History and Class Consciousness* (*Geschichte und Klassenbewusstsein*) of 1923, one of the seminal documents in the birth of Western Marxism.[198] Lukács argued that dialectical materialism was not a dogma but a "method," a "road to truth," which remained valid even if Marx's individual theses were "disproved once and for all. . . . "[199] Lukács had been the friend of Ernst Bloch before the war, when both were students of Max Weber at Heidelberg,[200] and surely Adorno discussed *History and Class Consciousness* with Bloch and the Berlin circle in the late 1920s.[201] Horkheimer, also a frequent visitor in Berlin, was extremely influenced by Lukács's book at this time, and he began studying the philosophies of Marx and Hegel in earnest, lecturing on both in his courses in political and social philosophy.[202] It was a Hegelianized, Lukács-oriented Marxism that Horkheimer brought to the Frankfurt Institute when he became its director in 1931 — with the original contribution of a Freudian approach to social psychology.[203] But when Horkheimer went to the Institute, Adorno took a different step. Instead of following Horkheimer into problems of social theory, he remained concerned with problems of philosophy and aesthetics. Like the Berlin circle, he wanted to experiment with Marxism as a method of aesthetic analysis rather than analyzing society.[204] It was here that the influence of Walter Benjamin was decisive.

In 1928 Adorno began meeting with Benjamin in Frankfurt, and they had a series of theoretical discussions. Although there is no specific documentation of the contents of these talks,[205] they clearly marked a turning point for Adorno. In his writing before this time there was not a trace of Benjamin's idiosyncratic terminology. But from 1928 on virtually everything that Adorno wrote bore the imprint of Benjamin's language.[206] To someone like Adorno, reared in the tradition of Kraus and Schönberg, who viewed language as the "representation" of truth,[207] a change in vocabulary had a theoretical importance of the first magnitude.

Their friendship, it will be recalled, dated back to 1923, when Benjamin was influenced by Scholem's scholarship in Jewish mysticism. During Adorno's stay in Vienna Benjamin had moved in two paradoxical directions simultaneously. One was toward his original goal of developing a cognitive theory on a Kantian base, which could account for religiomystical as well as philosophical experience.[208] The second was toward Marxism. Asja Lacis, a Latvian actress and director, who had participated in Moscow in the proletarianization of the arts during the early Leninist years, gave herself credit for Benjamin's making that move, and it was she who introduced him to Bertolt Brecht.[209] She met Benjamin in 1924, and they spent time in Capri and Positano.[210] Benjamin was studying Hebrew and considering joining Scholem in Palestine, but Lacis argued that the path of a progressive man led instead to Moscow.[211] Benjamin did begin to concern himself with Marx (and with Lukács's Hegelianized interpretation of Marx),[212] but he hardly took a straight road to Moscow. He was working at the time on a literary study of Baroque drama, *Ursprung des deutschen Trauerspiels* (The Origin of German Tragic Drama). Lacis complained that it was a dead topic; Benjamin countered that Baroque drama was analogous to expressionism, and that he was thus indirectly giving philosophical legitimation to contemporary drama as well.[213]

But there was more to this study. The introductory chapter of the *Trauer-*

spiel book sketched out a Kantian-based yet Kabbalist-influenced theory of cognition that accounted for both philosophical and religious cognitive experience, which had been his goal since 1918.[214] What tied this theoretical chapter to the rest of the study was an attitude toward aesthetic criticism very similar to that of Novalis and Schlegel, about which Benjamin had written in 1919,[215] that is, that the task of the art critic was to see and to articulate conceptually the truth which the artwork expressed only sensuously. As the interpreter of truth, the activity of the critic and that of the philosopher coincided.

Benjamin submitted the *Trauerspiel* study to Hans Cornelius as his *Habilitationsschrift* in 1925, and, like Adorno's later Kant-Freud study, it was not accepted.[216] Benjamin managed to publish it anyway in 1928. Meanwhile, he was identifying increasingly with the Marxist left.[217] Benjamin's intellectual dilemma was essentially the same as Adorno's: how could he reconcile his Marxist commitment with his Kantian effort in philosophy, especially when, furthermore, he considered religiomystical and philosophical experience as one?

What was remarkable about Benjamin and what made possible his continued intellectual friendship with the unlikely triumvirate of Scholem, Adorno, and Brecht (each of whom was suspicious of the others) was that in his move to Marx, rather than forsake (Kantian) philosophy or (Kabbalist) mysticism, he retained what he considered their common cognitive structure but "refunctioned" it, to use Brecht's term,[218] transforming idealist cognition into materialist cognition, and religious illumination into profane illumination. This rather incredible accomplishment needed to be demonstrated to be believed. And this is precisely what happened in the fall of 1929. In September and October Adorno was with Benjamin in Königstein, a small village outside Frankfurt in the Taunus mountains. Adorno referred a decade later to their "unforgettable conversations" there,[219] and Benjamin in 1935 recalled these talks as "historical" in their significance.[220] It was then that Benjamin first read Adorno excerpts from the *Passagenarbeit* (Arcades study)[221] which would become his major work, a study of the Paris arcades of the nineteenth century which put into practice a Marxist, materialist version of the philosophical method he had outlined in his *Trauerspiel* book. As he wrote, the *Trauerspiel* book, although

> . . . certainly not materialist, was already dialectic. But what I didn't know at the time of its formulation which soon after became clearer and clearer, was that from the very unique position of my philosophy of language there is a mediated relationship — even if still problematic and full of tension — to the observational method of dialectical materialism.[222]

This was not despite affinities between the *Trauerspiel* method and the Kabbalah, but because of them.[223] In fact, it was precisely in the structure of dialectical materialism that the cognitive experiences of philosophy and mysticism converged, resolving the problem which Benjamin had first posed in 1918.[224]

Benjamin's procedure had affinities to that of the early Lukács,[225] but also a high degree of originality[226] which may have struck Adorno as more faithful to Marx's theoretical impulse than were Marx's more orthodox disciples. It should be noted that Horkheimer participated, at least in part, in the König-stein talks (Benjamin referred to a momentous last discussion, with Horkheimer, Adorno, Asja Lacis, and Gretel Karplus around a table),[227] but although he was of one mind with many of the philosophical premises of the Königstein program, his writings reflect nothing of the strength of Benjamin's impact on Adorno. The latter was extraordinarily impressed. The language of his writing had already begun to show the influence of Benjamin's *Trauerspiel* study.[228] But, it seems, only now did he see its relevance to the intellectual conflicts with which his own move toward Marx confronted him. The effect on his work was immediate. A November, 1929, critique of Berg's *Wozzeck* demonstrated both the enthusiasm of his conversion,[229] and the still rough, still undigested form in which he incorporated the new ideas.

It was one of Adorno's first music articles with a clearly Marxist commitment.[230] Indeed, published just after the stock market crash in New York, its political message was more direct than it would ever be again.[231] And yet already here, in this interpretation of Berg's music, what distinguished Adorno's materialist aesthetics was his argument that the validity, the truth of the music did not rest on the composer's conscious political intent (Berg was no Marxist, and *Wozzeck* was an expressionist opera). Just as Benjamin discovered affinities between mysticism and materialism, so Adorno found a *structural* convergence between this music's inner logic and a Marxist critical understanding of the reality of contemporary society.[232]

Nor did he stop there. Adorno also sought in this article to articulate a convergence between the music and the cognitive procedure of psychoanalysis.[233] All this was done with the aid of concepts from the introductory chapter of Benjamin's *Trauerspiel* book.[234]

In the same year Adorno began work on a second *Habilitationsschrift* with a totally new topic: it was an implementation of the cognitive method outlined in the introduction to Benjamin's *Trauerspiel* chapter for the purpose of providing a Marxist critique of the philosophy of Sören Kierkegaard.[235]

The study (which never mentioned Marx directly)[236] was accepted by the Protestant theologian Paul Tillich, an antiauthoritarian teacher with prosocialist leanings, who was then a philosophy professor at Frankfurt University,[237] and in 1931, the same year Horkheimer became director of the Frankfurt Institute, Adorno himself joined the Frankfurt philosophy faculty. He was twenty-eight years old. His inaugural lecture outlined a program for a "dialectical," "materialist" philosophy, in Benjaminian language and based on the Königstein program, which governed his theoretical efforts for the rest of his life.

Chapter 2. Marx Minus
the Proletariat: Theory As Praxis

ADORNO'S "DIALECTICAL MATERIALISM"

Adorno's inaugural lecture, "Die Aktualität der Philosophie" (The Actuality of Philosophy), presented in 1931 to the Frankfurt philosophy faculty and officially marking his entry to its ranks, outlined a program for philosophy which claimed to be both "dialectical" and "materialist."[1] But, laden with the language of Benjamin's *Trauerspiel* chapter, it was not dialectical materialism in any orthodox sense. And although it was indebted to Marx and might even be termed "Marxist," it was not Marxism. No matter how hard one tries to defend Adorno as the true inheritor of Marx's theoretical legacy — as a result of the controversy surrounding him in the late 1960s, Adorno has had his share of "Marxist" apologists — throughout his life he differed fundamentally from Marx in that his philosophy never included a theory of political action. Although he continued to insist on the necessity for revolutionary social change, such statements remained abstract insofar as Adorno's theory contained no concept of a collective revolutionary subject which might accomplish that change. It has been noted frequently that Adorno adhered to the Jewish *Bilderverbot* by refusing to delineate the nature of postrevolutionary society.[2] But his silence on this point — which Marx to a large extent shared — was never so profound as his total refusal to deal with the problem of revolutionary praxis.

In 1966 Adorno wrote: "Philosophy, which once seemed obsolete, lives on because the moment to realize it was missed."[3] It is a mistake, however, to assume from this often-quoted introduction to *Negative Dialektik* that in the pre-Hitler years, when the realization of philosophy still had a chance, Adorno's position regarding the legitimacy of doing philosophy was anything different. Whereas Jay has written of the Frankfurt Institute in general and Horkheimer in particular that they reluctantly gave up belief in the revolutionary power of the proletariat only after Hitler's consolidation of power and still not fully until the outbreak of World War II,[4] it is impossible to document such a gradual disillusionment in the case of Adorno. This does not necessarily prove that Adorno never placed his hope in the proletariat.[5] What it does indicate is that he refused to incorporate this class within the foundation of his theory, to allow theory's validity to be in any way dependent upon the existence of a collective revolutionary subject or the possibility of its direct application to political praxis.

Adorno retained this position in the 1960s,[6] to the great frustration of the new student leftists: how could one claim to be a Marxist theorist without giving theoretical support to the proletariat, or to any other revolutionary class? Despite this apparent contradiction, Adorno's position did have an inner logic based on his intellectual experiences, which by 1931 had convinced him of three things: that any philosophy, and Marxism was certainly no exception, lost its legitimacy when it overstepped the boundaries of material experience and claimed metaphysical knowledge (this had been the lesson of Cornelius's neo-Kantianism); that the criterion of truth was rational rather than pragmatic, and hence theory could not be subordinated to political or revolutionary goals; and that *avant-garde* art, even when as with Schönberg's music it had no consciously political intent, could be progressive rather than simply bourgeois decadence, that it was not mere ideology, but, at least potentially, a form of enlightenment as well.

As has been noted, Adorno's move to Marx (like that of Horkheimer, Benjamin, and the Berlin circle) was decisively influenced by Lukács's 1923 book *History and Class Consciousness.* In order to understand Adorno's reception of Marx, the exact nature of Lukács's influence needs to be made clear. For as strong as it was, it was strictly limited. Adorno never accepted Lukács's early interpretation of Marx in its entirety.

RECEPTION OF LUKÁCS

Lukács opposed the mechanistic, deterministic, "vulgar" Marxism which had dominated the Second International, and by claiming that Marxism was essentially a dialectical "method," he returned to Marx's Hegelian roots. Lukács's understanding of dialectical materialism had two components. The first was negative. He saw it as a method for critically analyzing the dialectical relationship between bourgeois consciousness and material social conditions. As *Ideologiekritik,* it was a metacriticism of bourgeois intellectual efforts, a demonstration of the necessary limits of all bourgeois theories in their attempts to know reality. The second level was positive. Lukács moved from a social critique of bourgeois consciousness to an affirmation of the revolutionary consciousness of the proletariat class. The mediating link was a concept of the historical totality which, through a materialistic interpretation of Hegel's alienation theory, revealed the proletariat as the subject-object of history and hence the only class capable of "true" consciousness. In good Hegelian fashion, the dialectical process of knowledge was thereby "seen to be identical with the course of history."[7]

Hence for Lukács Marxism was a method of cognition *which led to a program of action.* But Adorno never took this second step. From the start, he remained unimpressed by Lukács's equation of truth with proletariat class consciousness and by the Hegelian concept of history which it implied. His debt to Lukács was clearly limited to the negative level of *Ideologiekritik,* the critical analysis of bourgeois class consciousness.

Lukács's *Ideologiekritik* proceeded by analyzing the dialectical relationship of the part to the whole: "This means that 'ideological' and 'economic' problems lose their exclusiveness and merge into one another."[8] Instead of reducing bourgeois thought to the economic conditions of its production, Lukács argued that the nature of those conditions could be found within the intellectual phenomena themselves. Indeed, each single aspect of society contained "the possibility of unravelling the whole abundance of the totality from within itself."[9] But this possibility could only be realized when the *structure* of the social totality was identified. And here lay Lukács's most original contribution.[10] He maintained that the commodity structure, whose mysteries Marx had dispelled in the first Chapter of *Kapital,* permeated every aspect of bourgeois society, including the very patterns of bourgeois thought. The problem of commodities, he asserted, was "the central structural problem of capitalist society in all its aspects"; it was the "model of all the objective forms of bourgeois society, together with all the subjective forms corresponding to them."[11]

In his famous chapter "Reification and Class Consciousness," Lukács analyzed the tradition of bourgeois philosophy, demonstrating that the antinomies which continuously appeared within it had the same structure as the contradictions of bourgeois economic production. He argued that the fundamental problem of idealism, the dualistic separation of subject and object, had its prototype in the problem of commodities, in which products appeared as objects divorced from the workers who had produced them. The concept of reification provided the key to both. Just as commodities in the realm of production took on a reified form, became "fetishes" which appeared cut off from the social process of their production, so bourgeois theory's reified conception of the "object" as an immutable "given" obscured the sociohistorical process through which it had come to be. And just as the reified commodities took on an abstract exchange value, divorced from their social use value, so the reification of bourgeois logic was manifested in its abstract separation of form from content. Hence the limit to bourgeois thought was "objective; it is the class situation itself."[12] The significance of Lukács's analysis was that instead of seeing bourgeois theory as a mere epiphenomenon, a thin veil for naked class interests, he argued and attempted to demonstrate that even the best bourgeois thinkers, in their most honest intellectual efforts, were not able to resolve contradictions in their theories, because the latter were based on a reality which was itself contradictory. Once these thinkers accepted given social reality as *the* reality, they had to come upon a barrier of irrationality which could not be overcome (and which had led Kant to posit the thing-in-itself), because that barrier could not be removed from theory without being removed from society. Conversely, if theorists could see through the reified appearances, they would recognize that the antinomies of philosophy were due not to the inadequacies of reason, but to those of the reality in which reason tried to find itself. And this, claimed Lukács, was "tantamount to observing society from a class standpoint other than that of the bourgeoisie,"[13] that is, the revolutionary class of the proletariat.

There can be no doubt that for Adorno, Lukács's insight into the manifestations of commodity structure within bourgeois consciousness was "of an importance which can scarcely be overestimated,"[14] and that the time of its impact on him occurred directly following his initial move toward Marxism. Whereas his 1927 Kant-Freud study shows no influence of Lukács's philosophically sophisticated *Ideologiekritik* (and this was precisely its weakness), the critical analysis of Kierkegaard, on which he worked from 1929 to 1933, was heavily indebted to Lukács's concepts of "reification," "commodity structure," and "fetishism." Not only did Adorno further pursue Lukács's method of analyzing bourgeois philosophy; he extended its application to the sphere of music.[15]

After World War II, with the horrors of Auschwitz and Hiroshima, Adorno identified the structure of domination as the primary evil: "As opposed to the possibility of total catastrophe, reification is an epiphenomenon. . . ."[16] But during the thirties, Adorno seems to have accepted as correct Lukács's claim that there was no solution to the problems of bourgeois philosophy "that could not be found in the solution to the riddle of the commodity-structure."[17] Indeed, in his inaugural lecture of 1931 the only illustration he gave for his philosophical program was an example borrowed from Lukács: the use of the commodity structure to unriddle the Kantian problem of the thing-in-itself. Yet Adorno did not fully identify his program with that of Lukács. He wrote that the solution to the thing-in-itself problem was not solved

> . . . in the sense that somehow the social conditions might be revealed under which the thing-in-itself problem came into existence, as Lukács even thought the solution to be; for the truth content of a problem is in principle different from the historical and psychological conditions out of which it grows. But it might be possible that from a sufficient construction of the commodity structure the thing-in-itself problem absolutely disappeared: that the historical figure of commodity and of exchange value just like a source of light laid free the form of a reality over whose hidden meaning the investigation of the thing-in-itself problem troubled itself in vain, because it doesn't have any hidden meaning which would be redeemable from its one-time and first-time historical appearance.[18]

Adorno was not disagreeing with Lukács's analytical procedure. The distinction he made related instead to the significance of that procedure. It was the philosophical validity of the approach which impressed him. It will be recalled that Hans Cornelius had rejected the Kantian doctrine of the thing-in-itself as a metaphysical residue.[19] Lukács, didn't just reject this doctrine, he explained its historical appearance. And for Adorno the real significance of this explanation, that objective reality (the commodity form of bourgeois society) was present within subjective consciousness (Kantian idealism), was that it exposed as false the Kantian premise of the duality of subject and object which had been the source of the thing-in-itself problem in the first place. Adorno was convinced of the truth of this analysis regardless of whether or not it reflected the "standpoint of the proletariat." Objective truth might indeed converge with this class's subjective standpoint, but such a correspondence between theory and proletariat self-interest was not the criterion of truth. At least in the beginning, Adorno and Benjamin seem to have been of one mind on this point, and it distinguished their reception of Marx from even their closest intellectual colleagues.[20] Benjamin wrote to a friend that same year (1931) explaining that he was a materialist because this position came nearest to "truth," and warned against

> . . . seeing me as an advocate of dialectical materialism as a dogma, but instead as an investigator of reality, to whom the *attitude* [*Haltung*] of the materialist appears more scientific and humane in all things that move before us, than that of the idealist.[21]

Adorno thus considered it possible to accept Lukács's dialectical materialism as a cognitive method only, without embracing his ontological theory of the historical process or his concept of the proletariat as subject-object of that process. That these two levels could be held separate was not Lukács's intent. He insisted on the identity between "objective understanding of the nature of society" and "the self-understanding of the proletariat class."[22] Fresh from his experience as Deputy Commissar for Education in the short-lived Hungarian Soviet Republic, Lukács's intent was to convince intellectuals to become revolutionaries. The purpose of his critique of bourgeois consciousness was to prove that what thinkers of his time had called the "cultural crisis" could not be overcome on the level of theory, but only by joining the proletariat cause.[23]

But his intention had a danger of backfiring. The very sophistication of his critique, which made dialectical materialism intellectually respectable,[24] provided Adorno with a most effective tool for continuing to do philosophy.

REJECTION OF THE PROLETARIAT

Why did Adorno limit his acceptance of dialectical materialism to the level of critical cognition? Given his almost literal following of Lukács's critique of bourgeois consciousness, why was he so unwilling to affirm the alternative, the revolutionary consciousness of the proletarian class?

In the first place, in his re-Hegelianization of Marx, Lukács's concept of the proletariat as the subject-object of history was a highly problematic construct.[25] Not only did it remain faithful to Hegel's ontological schema of the dialectic of history, and hence border on metaphysics.[26] It had to deal with the fact that the actual, empirically existing workers did not see the world from the "standpoint of the proletariat class." Well aware of this difficulty, Lukács introduced the distinction between "empirical" and "imputed" (*zugerechnete*) consciousness, i.e., what the proletariat *would* think if they had an accurate awareness of their objective position. His theory then bridged the gap between empirical and imputed consciousness by positing the Party as the embodiment of the proletariat "general will."[27] The possession of correct theory made the Party the legitimate spokesman, the "vanguard of the revolutionary class."[28] The Party was "distinguished from the rest of the proletariat by the fact that it has a clear understanding of the historical path to be taken by the proletariat as a whole."[29] It provided the mediating link, the organ in which theory and praxis converged.

This vision of the Communist Party spearheading the movement through which the proletariat, the "subject-object" of history, would realize its "historical mission"[30] was far more compelling in the early twenties than at the end of the decade. Writing in the potential-charged years immediately following the Russian Revolution and World War I, Lukács was caught up in the messianic conviction, "very much alive at the time, that the great revolutionary wave that would soon sweep the whole world, or Europe at the very least, to socialism had in no way been broken. . . ."[31] After 1924, the Third International admitted that European capitalism had entered an era of "relative stability."[32] With Stalin's consolidation of power, the goal of world revolution was subordinated to the program of building socialism in one country. The outbreak of world depression may have given new conviction to the prophecy that the contradictions of capitalist society would be "reproduced by the dialectical mechanics of history at a higher level, in an altered form and with increased intensity."[33] Yet neither the German Communist Party nor the workers themselves possessed a consciousness that could turn this crisis into a revolution. In 1928 the Communist International reversed its previous tactic of a "united front," and despite world depression and the rising power of Hitler, the Party continued to denounce the non-Communist left as "Social-Fascists," a strategy which divided the workers and benefited the National Socialists. In the September election of 1930, with more than 4 million German workers unemployed, 6.4 million votes were cast for the National Socialists, while the Communists received 4.6 million.[34] And in the next two years, the strength of Hitler's party continued to increase.

Moreover, and this was probably the decisive factor for Adorno,[35] theory, when transformed into an instrument of revolution, manipulated truth according to the needs of Party strategy. It had become clear by the end of the twenties that Party loyalty, in the name of enabling the realization of theoretical truth, demanded its submission. This dialectical reversal was already present in Lukács's book. As he admitted, within the Party "what was right today can be wrong tomorrow."[36] The criterion for correct theory was thus reduced to sheer pragmatism:

The pre-eminently practical nature of the Communist Party, the fact that it is a fighting party presupposes its possession of a correct theory, for otherwise the consequences of a false theory would soon destroy it.[37]

Furthermore, Lukács had no illusions as to the discipline demanded of Party members: "the *active engagement of the total personality.*"[38] Arguing against Rosa Luxemburg's statement (also Adorno's sentiment) that "freedom is always freedom for the one who thinks differently,"[39] Lukács countered: "Freedom must serve the rule of the proletariat, not the other way round."[40] As a result of submission to the Party, the role of consciousness in the revolutionary struggle, which Lukács's book had done so much to reinstate in Marxist theory, lost its material base, the concrete consciousness of actual human beings.

Lukács's personal history was a living example of this dialectical reversal inherent in his theory. In 1924 he demonstrated his solidarity with the Bolshevization of the Third International by writing a eulogy of Lenin, whose concept of dialectical materialism was markedly different from Lukács's early theory. Later that year Zinoviev explicitly denounced *History and Class Consciousness* as "theoretical revisionism."[41] In 1928 Lukács's "Blum-theses," which contradicted the International's rejection of the united front strategy, were branded a "right deviation."[42] Lukács again submitted to Party censure. In January 1931 (the year of Adorno's inaugural lecture outlining his own brand of dialectical materialism) a decree of the Bolshevik Party Central Committee eliminated the freedom to dispute the official interpretation of dialectical materialist philosophy. That same year Lukács began writing for the Party journal *Die Linkskurve* in support of proletarian literature and in protest against all attempts to distinguish art from propaganda.[43] Finally, in 1934, Lukács openly renounced *History and Class Consciousness* for being guilty of what Lenin had termed "materialism on the surface" but "idealism underneath."[44]

By the time of Adorno's move to Marxism, the careers of Lukács and other Communist intellectuals had made it clear that solidarity with the Party necessitated sacrificing intellectual independence, which Adorno considered not only essential for critical thinking but fully compatible with his own "Marxist" theory. The very fact that he incorporated Lukács's early method was an implicit criticism of the Party which had denounced it. At the same time, like Lukács (and like Lenin), he was fully aware of the inadequacies of the workers' empirical consciousness. It was on this point that Adorno broke with Brecht. Writing to Benjamin in 1936 and citing Lenin in his support, he criticized Brecht for addressing his works

. . . to the actual consciousness of the actual proletariat, who have nothing, absolutely nothing, over the bourgeoisie except for an interest in the revolution, but who otherwise bear all the marks of the bourgeoisie's truncated personality.[45]

Faced with the dilemma of submitting to the Party as Lukács had done or, like Brecht, appealing to the proletariat at its present level of consciousness, Adorno took a third position, one which he later termed "non-participation" (*nicht-mitmachen*). He insisted on the freedom of the intellectual from Party control, indeed from all direct concern as to the effect of his work upon the public, while at the same time maintaining that valid intellectual activity was revolutionary in itself. Adorno was arguing that theory and political praxis were nonidentical and that their relationship was a highly mediated one. He accepted as necessary the division of labor between intellectual and manual workers, and even among the intellectual disciplines: "in reified society, all progress occurs via continued specialization."[46]

Here he ran directly counter to the Lukács of *History and Class Consciousness,* who viewed division of labor as the archevil. Lukács claimed that on the level of theory, specialization led to fragmentary knowledge which prevented intellectuals as well as workers from seeing through the reified appearances of reality: "The specialization of skills leads to the destruction of every image of the whole."[47] On the level of praxis, as Breines has pointed out, Lukács's understanding of dialectical materialism necessitated the liquidation of the division of labor

> . . . in the very formation of the revolutionary forces. On the one hand, the proletariat must begin to dissolve itself as a proletariat by becoming historically and class conscious; on the other hand, philosophers, located at the other end of the social division of labor, must begin to dissolve themselves as philosophers (and begin to dissolve philosophy as philosophy) by becoming conscious of proletarian class consciousness and participants in its full emergence. Both, hand workers and mind workers, must begin to become "whole men". . . .[48]

In accepting the division between theory and political praxis, was Adorno's "Marxism" a radical deviation? Whether one's frame of reference is Marxist-Leninism or Lukács's neo-Hegelianism, the answer is clearly yes.[49]

It needs to be remembered that when Adorno first outlined his "dialectical," "materialist" theory, his frame of reference was still Kantian rather than Hegelian.[50] Whereas Lukács conceptualized the dialectical relationship between subject and object as the relationship between (proletarian class) consciousness and the sociohistorical *totality,* for Adorno the subject was the individual's consciousness, and the object referred to the particular phenomena of experience. In line with Benjamin's theoretical design, Adorno conceived of dialectical materialism as a cognitive method based on an essentially Kantian structure of experience. One could say (although Karl Kraus would have winced at the language) that if Lukács re-Hegelianized Marx, then Adorno re-Kantianized Lukács.

And yet Adorno may have been influenced by writings of the young Marx which had not been available to Lukács in 1923, specifically, the 1844 *Economic and Philosophic Manuscripts.*[51] In these early manuscripts it was not Hegel's dialectic of history which Marx considered his great contribution, but the fact that in his "dialectic of negativity as the moving and productive principle,"

Hegel "grasps the concept of *work.*"[52] But whereas "the only labor Hegel knows and recognizes is abstract mental labor,"[53] Marx argued that work — not only manual labor but *intellectual labor as well* — was concrete social praxis. In the third manuscript Marx stated:

> Even as I am *scientifically*[54] active, etc. — an activity I can seldom pursue in direct community with others — I am *socially* active because I am active as *man.* Not only is the material of my activity — such as the language in which the thinker is active — given to me as a social product, but my own existence *is* social activity; what I make from myself I make for society, conscious of my nature as social. . . .[55]

THE ARTIST AS WORKER

Whether or not Adorno was in fact inspired by Marx's early writings,[56] the notion that writers and artists were themselves productive workers, more similar to the proletariat than to their capitalist exploiters, was widespread among members of the Berlin circle. Brecht referred to intellectuals as "brain-workers" (*Kopfarbeiter*) and Benjamin wrote a theoretical article on "The Author as Producer."[57] If this attitude was aimed at demystifying the bourgeois cult of the artist, who was no longer a creator but a producer for the market, it was also an implicit protest against the conception of intellectuals as mere spokesmen for the Party, and hence against the increasing intellectual repression marked by the purges in Russia during the thirties. Stalin's communism and Hitler's fascism converged in their condemnation of modern art as degenerate.

The contrast between Lukács's practical experience in the Budapest Soviet and Adorno's discussions of Marx within his literary circle in Berlin manifests itself in their differing conception of the intellectuals' role — according to Lukács, they were the *vanguard* of the Revolution; according to Adorno, they were the revolutionary *avant-garde.* Despite the common Renaissance-military origin of these words, their meanings had diverged in history. Specifically, the military connotations of the term *avant-garde* had become purely metaphorical by the nineteenth century. It applied to literary and aesthetic rather than sociopolitical praxis. And if in the pre-1848 period the artistic *avant-garde* allied itself with political revolutionaries and after the failure of the Paris Commune that alliance was renewed,[58] the subsequent movement of *l'art pour l'art* clearly demonstrated that politics was not its essential characteristic. The *avant-garde* rejected bourgeois cultural tradition; the fact that such rejection functioned as social protest was in many cases a secondary consideration, or even totally unintentional. Lukács's notion of the Party vanguard implied that the intellectual's role was one of leadership and political instruction, whereas the model of the *avant-garde* was antiauthoritarian: the intellectual was an experimentor,[59] openendedly defying dogma; his leadership was exemplary rather than pedagogic.

In this connection, Brecht's program for "refunctioning" (*umfunktionieren*) modern aesthetic techniques was important: aesthetic creation was a sector of production, and the artist's revolutionary role was to dialectically transform the technical developments within his own profession, reversing their function from ideological tools into tools of human liberation.[60] It followed that, as Bloch wrote, "there is nothing in creative reality that does not belong to Marxism and its goals."[61] What counted was not the bourgeois *origins* of the techniques, but the *critical attitude* which the intellectual brought to them. Just this was what Adorno had in mind when he referred to the work of the artist or theorist as dialectical praxis.

There emerged out of this conception a totally new meaning of the Marxist concepts of "forces of production" and "relations of production" (*Produktivkräfte, Produktionsverhältnisse*). In Adorno's music articles of the thirties, "forces of production" referred not to the music industry, not to the production of music as an economic enterprise, but to techniques of composing and the musical material as it developed historically; and, "relations of production" meant the relations not between capitalist and worker, or even conductor and musician (there is never a mention of anything so mundane as a musicians' union), but between the composer (or conductor, musician, or audience) and the music itself. Adorno's articles were concerned with musical "production" in the sense of composition, "reproduction" in the sense of musicians' and conductors' interpretation, and "consumption" in the sense of audience reception.[62] Similarly, when Horkheimer talked about the "productive forces" of scientific theory being restricted by the "historical process," he meant that there was a tendency to repress theoretical work critical of the social order.[63] Crucial to the "Critical Theory" of the Frankfurt Institute under Horkheimer's directorship was the belief that bourgeois theoretical methods, "like a material tool of production," could be refunctioned from oppressive tools into liberating ones.[64]

But what were the criteria for such refunctioning? How could one know that the technical material of theory or of art had been "liberated"? Here was the point on which Adorno and Brecht split ranks. In 1930 Adorno could still write a favorable review of Brecht's drama *Mahagonny,* with its Marxist political message.[65] And they shared against Lukács not only an affirmation of modern art techniques,[65] but also the belief that valid art (and theory) *revealed* social contradictions rather than presenting aesthetic resolution of them; therefore intellectual work should be viewed as a series of trial experiments or "attempts" (*Versuche*) rather than the construction of holistic systems. But by the end of 1930, with the polarizing effect of economic and political crisis, Brecht wrote in justification of the artist's submission to practical imperatives: "No: neither artists nor their historians can be declared free from guilt for our conditions, nor can they be released from the duty to work at changing the conditions."[66] In the fall of that same year Adorno had made it clear where he stood by resigning from the editorial staff of a Viennese *avant-garde* music journal,*Anbruch,* when it moved close to the Communist Party and adopted the view that only intentionally political music was meaningful. He wrote to Krenek that "I have broken my contract with *Anbruch* because the publishers want to transform the sheet into a pure propaganda organ and would have taken from me even the most modest intellectual freedom. . . ."[67]

Both Adorno and Brecht agreed that the goal of intellectual work was critical enlightenment, the freeing of "consciousness" from the veil of bourgeois ideology, but the question was, whose consciousness, that of theorists and artists or that of the proletariat? Brecht opted for the proletariat, claiming that the artist had to ally himself with the workers' cause and appeal to the empirically existing consciousness of the proletariat for the purpose of political education. But Adorno insisted that the criterion for art could not be its political effect on the audience.[68] Benjamin was caught between them. Like Adorno he was initially attracted to dialectical materialism for its truth value rather than its political effects, but the influence of Brecht became increasingly apparent. In 1934 Benjamin wrote that political validity of necessity implied aesthetic validity.

> . . . that the tendency of a work of literature can be politically correct only if it is also correct in the literary sense. That means that the tendency which is politically correct includes a literary tendency.[69]

On the one hand, then, he supported Adorno's position that the writer's solidarity with the proletariat "can never be other than mediated":[70] not his attitude toward the proletariat, but his attitude toward the productive process determined his place in the class struggle.[71] On the other, he argued with Brecht that political commitment was a necessary, if not sufficient, condition for valid intellectual work.[72] He concluded that only one thing was demanded of the writer:

> . . . the demand to think, to reflect upon his position in the production process. We can be sure that such thinking, *in the writers who matter* – that is to say the best technicians in their particular branches of the trade – will sooner or later lead them to confirm very soberly their solidarity with the proletariat.[73]

But Benjamin's dismissal of the differences between Adorno and Brecht was wishful thinking.[74] The most technically innovative artists were often in fact aloof from politics, and not understood by the bourgeois public, much less the proletariat. Adorno did not delude himself on either issue, and as his letters to Benjamin with their repeated admonitions document,[75] he stood clearly on the side of the innovative artist.

The issue for him was Schönberg's music. It had no conscious political intent, and absolutely no appeal for a working-class audience. Brecht compared Schönberg's music with the neighing of a horse about to be butchered and processed for bockwurst.[76] The Schönberg-trained composer Hanns Eisler, now Brecht's collaborator, complained:

> [Schönberg] said somewhere: "the fact that listeners are there appears to be

necessary, because an empty concert hall doesn't sound good." In other words: I somehow put up with them, as material, but I could get by without them.[77]

Yet throughout the thirties Adorno not only continued to defend the new music despite its political autonomy; he interpreted Schönberg's compositional procedure as authentically dialectical.[78]

Ironically, it was Lukács who provided Adorno with a justification of his position against Brecht. Lukács had argued that correct revolutionary consciousness could not be equated with the empirically existing consciousness of the working class and therefore a Party elite was justified; Adorno used the same argument to justify an intellectual elite, claiming that if understanding of the new music was limited to an exclusive audience, "then that is the fault of the social structure and not the experimental artist."[79] More importantly, Lukács unintentionally supported Adorno's position in another way. *History and Class Consciousness* had sought to demonstrate that the commodity structure had permeated the "material" upon which the thinker or the artist worked – not only its content but also its form. Adorno's argument was essentially that if the bourgeois intellectual tradition, if its philosophy and art, reflected the commodity structure of capitalist society, then the material contained within it the problems of society translated into a different mode. When the intellectual "worker" confronted technical problems of his discipline, he was dealing in a mediated fashion with the problems of the social totality:

> [Music] fulfills its social function more accurately when, within its own material and according to its own rules of form, it brings to articulation the social problems which it contains all the way to the inmost cells of its technique. In this sense, the job of music as art bears a specific analogy to that of social theory.[80]

If the intellectual's problems (as Lukács had argued) reflected the antagonisms of the social structure, then there was no necessity to go outside the division of labor and take on an "imputed" proletarian consciousness. Indeed, the intellectual worker could paradoxically best serve the proletariat by remaining an intellectual. From this viewpoint, it could be argued that the theorist or artist who intentionally manipulated his material in order to achieve a particular political effect was in fact a psychological idealist, ignoring the objective demands made upon him by the historically developed, socially mediated material of his trade. Hence Adorno could claim that

> . . . precisely in his solitariness and isolation the composer carries out social demands; that society itself dwells in the inmost cells of the self-enclosed technical problems, and he registers its demands all the more legitimately, the less he is prompted from the outside, arbitrarily, and in constraint of the rule of form [*Formgesetz*].[81]

Schönberg's revolution in music, the "dialectical" negation of tonality which had been the bourgeois form of music, provided the model for what Adorno hoped to accomplish in philosophy, his own sector of intellectual "production." The program which he outlined in his inaugural lecture of 1931 called for the dialectical negation of idealism, the bourgeois form of philosophy:

> I am not afraid of the reproach of unfruitful negativity. . . . If philosophical interpretation can in fact only prosper dialectically, then the first dialectical point of attack is given by a philosophy which cultivates precisely those problems whose removal appears more pressingly necessary than the addition of a new answer to so many old ones. . . . Only in the strictest dialectical communication with the most recent solution-attempts of philosophy and of philosophical terminology can a real *change of philosophical consciousness* prevail.[82]

It must be emphasized that Adorno never equated theoretical praxis with revolutionary political praxis. A "change of philosophical consciousness" (or a "change of musical consciousness"[83]) would not cause a change in real social conditions. The latter could be brought about "only socially, by changing society."[84] The contribution of theory or art and its interpretation, its "change-causing gesture,"[85] was in robbing the present of its ideological justification. Adorno's goal was the "explosion of reification."[86] His critical attack aimed at tearing away the ideological veil of reification which prevented true knowledge of social reality. This conception of the role of intellectual praxis was a recognition of the limitations of theory rather than its omnipotence. Here he differed from the Left Hegelians with whom, due to the absence in his theory of a concept of the proletariat, he has often been critically compared. In 1932 Adorno wrote Ernst Krenek criticizing the "bourgeois" position which "considers the world to be the product of Mind and correctable merely by means of Mind, whereas both are entwined in one another and the correction can only be conceived in the dialectic between them."[87]

Yet it must be admitted that Adorno never fully explained the nature of the relationship between theory and social change. It seems clear that he viewed critical negativity as a creative force in itself, believed that it could, through its own strength, at least attain knowledge of the truth, and that the resulting change in "consciousness" would somehow lead to social praxis. His letter to Krenek continued:

> To this extent I would agree with Benjamin's statement concerning the scar on the body of society, namely we intellectuals: admittedly not without thinking of what Kierkegaard says of despair in *Sickness unto Death,* namely that the sickness, dialectically, is at the same time the cure.[88]

But precisely whose consciousness was to be changed? Obviously the intellectuals', yet this alone was not a sufficient condition for the revolution of society. If the intellectuals were the *avant-garde,* then whom were they leading?

THE EXAMPLE OF "REVOLUTIONARY" MUSIC

In order to illustrate this problem, as well as the elements which distinguished Adorno's notion of intellectual praxis from those of Lukács on the one hand and Brecht on the other, there is no better place to begin than his 1932 article "Zur gesellschaftlichen Lage der Musik" (On the Social Situation of Music). It was Adorno's first contribution to Horkheimer's Institute journal, the *Zeitschrift für Sozialforschung.*[89] It outlined a materialist aesthetics of music, and because compositional praxis was Adorno's model for philosophical praxis, this analysis demonstrates the nature of his reception of Marx generally, as well as the intellectual difficulties into which it led him. The article began with an unmistakably Lukácsian statement: "The role of music in the social process is exclusively that of a commodity; its value is that of the market."[90] Adorno acknowledged that music's commodity nature was not in itself new.[91] But whereas in the nineteenth century music-making formed part of the private lives of bourgeois families, now, with "the technology of radio and film which belonged to powerful monopolies, and with unlimited access to the total capitalist propaganda apparatus,"[92] it had become almost exclusively an event of the marketplace. As a specifically capitalist commodity, it had become reified. Its use value had been fully subsumed under its exchange value, and this, claimed Adorno, was the source of music's alienation from the bourgeois listening public.[93] But instead of simply lamenting this condition, Adorno found in it a positive moment: it gave music a degree of autonomy and hence of revolutionary potential, whereas if music tried to overcome its alienation by accommodating the public, it contributed only "to covering up the situation."[94] The alienation of music, then, was the mark of its nonparticipation in the bourgeois status quo. It was no use to appeal to the proletariat, whose consciousness had become as stupefied as that of the bourgeoisie: "Just as theory transcends the present consciousness of the masses, so music must do likewise."[95] Instead of attempting to reestablish the immediacy of art, music's proper concern was its own material: "here and now music can do nothing else but present the social antinomies within its own structure, which also carry the guilt for music's isolation."[96] If music, like theory, could not change social conditions, it could at least articulate those conditions rather than perpetuate a false ideology:

> Music which wishes to justify its right to exist today must in a certain sense possess the *character of knowledge.* Within its material, music must purely articulate the problems which the material — itself never purely natural but sociohistorically produced — presents to it; the solutions which music finds thereby are like those of theory: social postulates are contained in them, whose relationship to praxis may indeed be highly mediated and difficult, and which can in no way be easily realized. . . .[97]

Music, like theory, had to satisfy itself with a dialectical rather than immediate relationship to praxis. Even progressive music ought not to be viewed "as 'classless' and itself the music of the future . . . but indeed music which most accurately fulfills its dialectical cognitive function [*Erkenntnisfunktion*] ."[98] As with his program for philosophy, Adorno claimed that music's revolutionary contribution was a function of its critical negativity:

> The extraordinarily violent protest which such music confronts in the present society . . . appears nonetheless to suggest that the dialectical function of this music can already be felt in praxis, if only merely negatively, as "destruction."[99]

Analyzing certain specific trends in contemporary music, Adorno demonstrated that the relationship of music to progressive social forces was not self-evident, but needed to be interpreted in each case, and this was the function of aesthetic criticism. He strongly attacked *Gemeinschaftsmusik,* which strove to give people the sense of community (*Gemeinschaft*) denied to them by actual social conditions (*Gesellschaft*). Related to the general *Gemeinschaft* movement of Weimar (which bore many parallels to the apolitical, counterculture protest of youth in the sixties),[100] this music returned to preclassical forms because it was felt that bourgeois classicism was too individualized in its instrumentation and too "subjective" in its use of thematic development, compared with the "objectivity" of the Baroque. Musicians rearranged preclassical pieces for performance by amateur groups of *Wandervögel* who, armed with recorders and hiking back to nature, believed that they could remove social problems by removing themselves from society.[101]

Adorno challenged *Gemeinschaftsmusik* for ignoring the historical specificity of music and of the composing process. *Gemeinschaftsmusik* was "reactionary in its musical technique [*innermusikalisch reaktionär*]."[102] It rejected "as 'intellectual' or 'individualistic' the further dialectical movement of the musical material," and instead tried to restore an immediate relationship between music and society, an attempt which was premised on "an inferior, static concept of nature."[103] Adorno argued that instead of trying to return to a "primitive, pre-individualistic level," bourgeois music had to be recognized as a "necessary step in the liberation of music for men," and, therefore, that it could only be transcended dialectically, corrected from within by means of its own "immanent contradictions."[104] He maintained that Stravinsky and Hindemith, proponents of *neue Sachlichkeit* (new objectivity) in music, were guilty of a similar ahistorical treatment of the material in their assertion that the "objectivity" of musical forms enabled their use in any historical era. Although Stravinsky used modern musical means, he fused them with "old and assumedly eternal models" so that they were robbed of their historical specificity. Adorno argued that such "objectivism" was in fact subjectivism: when the artist had free access to all musical forms, past and present, the actual choice became a matter of subjective arbitrariness. He made an invidious comparison:

As in fascism where a "leadership elite," namely the monopoly capitalists, rule over the social "organism," so the sovereign composer rules freely over the so-called musical organism; when to introduce a dissonance, when a suspended note is to be resolved, is decided neither by a pre-arranged schema . . . nor by the immanence of the structure . . . but instead solely by the will, namely the "taste" of the composer.[105]

Adorno was not referring to the composer's actual political position, but to what he saw as a similarity of structure (arbitrary authority) between fascist power relations and the relation of such composers to their material. As he wrote: "the social interpretation of music is not concerned with the individual consciousness of the authors, but with the function of their works."[106]

Because dissonance and formal discontinuity reflected social antagonisms, they could function as progressive protest, compared with the traditional conciliatory harmonies and holistic forms which served only to veil these antagonisms. Yet, Adorno cautioned, the mere use of dissonances was not enough. For example, Stravinsky's ahistorical use of dissonance had the effect of affirming social antagonisms as natural and eternal. As for the works of Hindemith, they combined modern musical means with totally incompatible, traditional rules of composition, a contradiction which robbed his music of validity: the "contrast between fortuitous motif-material and proven rules of form, between the fundamental non-repeatability of the musical elements and the forms of repetition which externally bind them together" marked the "false façade . . . of *neue Sachlichkeit.*"[107]

In contrast, maintained Adorno, Schönberg avoided this undialectical imposition of the will of the composer on his material. His individualism was not arbitrary because it was controlled by the demands of the material itself. The form of his music was truly objective, "not forced on the material from the outside but drawn out from within it. . . ."[108] Thus Schönberg, despite his isolation from society and scorn of the public, could write the most socially progressive music:

> If the esoteric Schönberg is not reserved for a specialized and socially irrelevant history of music as *Geistesgeschichte,* if it is instead possible to project the dialectic in his material onto the social dialectic, then this is justified on the grounds that he found in the form of problems in the material, which he took over and further developed, the problems of the society which had produced that material and which presented in it social contradictions as technical problems.[109]

Yet Adorno was not totally uncritical of Schönberg's music. Anticipating his later critique of the twelve-tone system,[110] he explicitly challenged Schönberg's use of closed forms:

> Above all, however, it is a question of whether the ideal of the closed, balanced artwork, which Schönberg took over from classicism and which he loyally retained, can still be reconciled with the means which he crystal-

ized, whether this ideal, like totality and cosmos, can still be maintained at all.[111]

Nor did Adorno reject out of hand the possible validity of compositions which were consciously intended as social criticism. Such polemical music could indeed be positively evaluated, so long as its intent was limited to critical negativity, the exposure of society's contradictions, without any pretention that music itself could resolve them. In this connection, Adorno praised his friend Kurt Weill, composer of the music for Bertolt Brecht's *Three-Penny Opera* and *Mahagonny*. Weill's music was "unquestionably . . . today the only [music] of real socially-polemic effectiveness, as long as it maintains itself on the peak of its negativity. . . ."[112] Weill's use of musical material shocked the public out of its complacency:

> He does not present a primitivized artificial music to people for their use [*Gebrauch*]; he holds their own use-music [*Gebrauchsmusik*] before them in the distorting mirror of his artistic procedure and displays it as commodity.[113]

Weill's use of the surrealist principle of montage broke apart "the 'organic' surface form of neoclassicism":

> The shock with which Weill's composing procedure presents the customary compositional means, over-exposed, like a phantom, becomes horror over the society out of which they spring, and at the same time becomes a negation of the possibility of a positive *Gemeinschaftsmusik*. . . .[114]

But Adorno saw a danger that Weill's music could not maintain its critical negativity, precisely because of its social commitment. When music became affirmative, even if its affirmation was an expression of solidarity with the proletariat class, in its glorification of the collective it became difficult to distinguish from *Gemeinschaftsmusik*. Such, claimed Adorno, was the fate of Hanns Eisler's proletarian choruses, which affirmed proletariat consciousness "already here and now" as "positive."[115] Adorno's lumping of Eisler's music together with *Gemeinschaftsmusik* was a damning criticism, one for which he brought in Marx for support:

> Thus it is not recognized that precisely the demands toward which production is supposed to orient itself [according to Eisler], sing-ability, simplicity, collective effectiveness as such, are necessarily attached to a level of consciousness which is so stamped and bound by class domination — no one formulated it more strongly than Marx — that this level, should production one-sidedly gear itself to it, becomes a shackle on the forces of musical production.[116]

Adorno did not question the "agitational value and thus the political right of proletarian *Gemeinschaftsmusik* such as Eisler's choruses";[117] what he did question was its aesthetic right:

> However, as soon as this music steps away from the front of immediate

action . . . and sets itself up as an art form, it is undeniable that the produced forms cannot hold their own against progressive bourgeois productions, and that they present themselves as a questionable mixture composed
out of scraps of inner-bourgeois, surpassed styles of form, indeed the petty-
bourgeois mens chorus literature, and scraps of progressive "new" music
which are robbed by virtue of this mixture of the sharpness of their attack
as well as the validity of every technical formulation.[118]

But here of course was the issue. Assuming that Benjamin's optimism was
misplaced, assuming that correct political tendency and correct aesthetic tendency did not of necessity converge,[119] was the point to produce sociohistorically
valid art, or was it to change social reality? Adorno's insistence on transcending
bourgeois cultural forms from within rather than supporting their liquidation
from without, his insistence on the mediated relationship between intellectual
praxis and political praxis, may have been logically consistent. It may have
provided a critical, even politically relevant method of aesthetic analysis. It
may have allowed compelling "Marxist" insights into the structural similarities
between the relation of the composer to his material and the relations of the
social totality. But where was the link between his "dialectical," "materialist"
analyses and revolutionary political praxis?

Nowhere was Adorno more adamant than in his assertion that

> . . . one who without concern, that is, here and now, solitarily works on his
> material serves a true collective better than one who submits to the demands
> of what presently exists and thereby, despite collective appearances, forgets
> the social demands which come out of his own aesthetic sphere, namely his
> work and its problems.[120]

But even if this argument contained an element of truth, if a "true collective"
was to be more than a utopian hope, then it had to be grounded in a present po-
tentiality. Adorno wrote in 1936:

> The development of the musical forces of production as men's free disposal
> over the natural material, as the emancipation of freedom from the natural
> condition, will not be possible for those whose consciousness is itself trun-
> cated by the [social] mechanism; at first, therefore, only a few. The con-
> cept of the *avant-garde* has its meaning aesthetically as well as actually.[121]

But this again raises the question, precisely whom was the *avant-garde* leading? The answer could only be those who understood the complexities of musical
technique, that is, other intellectuals. Adorno spoke of those "few" who have
escaped the truncation of consciousness perpetrated by bourgeois class domination. In order to give this statement concrete meaning, it needs to be interpreted
by a much more mundane Marxism, perhaps the very "vulgar" Marxism which
Adorno attempted so assiduously to overcome. In reality, access to the "truth"
of Schönberg's music (or of Adorno's philosophy) was open only to the cultured
elite from the bourgeois ranks whose economic security gave them the neces-

sary means for acquiring a specialized training. The difficulty was that this group would always remain a "few" so long as the educational system of bourgeois society remained an institution for the perpetuation of its ruling class. Due to the elitist, class nature of education, then, the connection between *avant-garde* intellectual praxis and the formation of a "true collective" was effectively blocked.

It must be admitted that there was something immanently democratic in Adorno's conception of the intellectual, something *anti*elitist and antihierarchical in the notion that intellectuals acted in concert with the proletariat by revolutionizing their own production process. But this element was more ideal than real. The fact of the matter is that Adorno's talk of the mediation between intellectual praxis and political praxis remained abstract and vague, with no explication of the social medium which might serve as a conduit for this mediation, once the role of the Party was rejected. The medium for Adorno's "mediation" remained as mysterious as the medium between the spirits and the flesh of the world, and Hanns Eisler's criticism had an undeniable kernel of validity:

> This metaphysical, blind belief in the "development of music".... If Adorno would only once understand that music is made by people for people — and if it also develops, this development is not abstract but somehow can be connected with social relationships! — then he would not say this abstract nonsense.[122]

There was indeed something metaphysical in Adorno's stress on truth, and in his vision of the intellectual elite as the formulators of that truth.

Benjamin wrote in 1936 that Marxism provided "the politicophilosophic substructure" of his essays.[123] The same could be said for Adorno's writings. In Kantian idealism, the structure of consciousness provided the unity and meaning of experience, while in Adorno's and Benjamin's materialism, that unity was provided by the structure of society as Marx defined it. Adorno accepted a Marxist social analysis and used Marxist categories in criticizing the *geistige* products of bourgeois society. But the whole of his theoretical effort was to continue to interpret the world, whereas the point had been to change it.

Chapter 3. Dialectics Without Identity: The Idea of Natural History

HISTORY AND AESTHETIC FORM

The initial impulse for Adorno's concept of history did not come from the field of philosophy. His early academic training had focused on Kant and Husserl, fundamentally ahistorical thinkers, whose philosophies of history were not central, but rather appended to essentially epistemological theories. It was Adorno's study of music which first made him aware of the vital significance of the historical dimension, and his understanding of history remained indebted to this field of aesthetics which had been its source.

Music, which has often been called the most abstract of the arts, is in the historical sense the most concrete. For no art is more integrally related to the dimension of time. The composition is itself history: the sense of each transient note both determines and is determined by that which has been and that which will come. Musical sound unfolds in a continuous, transitory present. As Adorno wrote:

> Music is, as temporal art, bound by its very medium to the form of succession, and therewith as irreversible as time. Once it commences, it is obliged to go further, to become something new, to develop itself.[1]

Hence: "History is not external to the work."[2] This was true not merely in the general, phenomenological sense of music's temporality, but concretely in regard to content: the very meaning of music's material principles, of dissonance and harmony, structure and form, was historically defined. Seen through the historical present of Schönberg's atonality, classical dissonance lost its meaning, Beethoven's revolutionary strangeness became commonplace, and the once-creative discovery of thematic development degenerated into the formalized schema of popular music. There were no eternal laws of composition which could guarantee immortality. Musical forms could die. Here too, the truth of music appeared inextricably bound to its transiency.

It is no accident that Adorno's concept of history owed far more to Lukács's pre-Marxist, aesthetic writings than to *History and Class Consciousness*. In 1921[3] Adorno read *Die Theorie des Romans* (The Theory of the Novel) by Lukács who at the time of its writing (1914-1915) was influenced by Kierkegaard, Dilthey, and Hegelian idealism.[4] Here Lukács first developed the concept of reification as an expression of the historical process of decay which emptied the meaning, the inner life, from both the aesthetic forms and the ideas which they articulated. Two aspects of Lukács's analysis made a lasting impression on Adorno. One was his insight into the relationship between form and history: literary form was not an atemporal, abstract, subjective ordering principle, but was itself content, a reflection of objective historical conditions. Hence, for example, the novel was the product "of an era for which the extensive totality of life is no longer given as meaningful . . . and which nonetheless possesses the conviction of totality."[5] The second aspect was the theme of cultural disintegration (*Zerfall*), which not only threatened past art forms with extinction but characterized the present crisis in culture, determining the technical problems of contemporary artistic creation.[6]

From the time of his study with Alban Berg, Adorno was concerned with the technical implications of the problem of history as it manifested itself in the act of musical reproduction.[7] If like literary forms musical forms were not immortal, if like material nature they decayed in time, then the task of the conductor in performing a past work was to rescue its living meaning, which history threatened to obliterate. In this sense, the dimension of history formed the core of the problem of musical reproduction. In 1925 Adorno began to question "whether all works are interpretable at all times."[8] He argued that the conductor could not simply repeat the piece as it had been played at the time of its creation, since its meaning would be lost to us. Nor could he play it as a modern piece, a procedure which would violate the truth of the work, which was integrally related to its history. Instead, the conductor needed to mediate between past and present, transforming the work according to its own "inner history." In order to be faithful to the material, to draw from it its meaning, he paradoxically had to change that material, altering its tempo, its articulation and expression. Valid reproduction was therefore no carbon copy of the original: it was the result of a dialectical mediation between the present and the past, the conductor and the composition.[9]

In a sense, the role of the composer was the reverse of that process. If the reproduction of past music required the mediation of the present, then the creation of new works necessitated a mediation with the past. No composer was more aware of the historical determinacy of musical material than Schönberg, whose revolutionary break from past music was made possible only by an intimate understanding of its historical development.[10] And Adorno could well have learned from Schönberg that once the moment of transitoriness within history was recognized, concern for historical tradition became transformed from a justification of cultural conservatism into a mandate for cultural radicalism. In his *Harmonielehre*, written in 1911, Schönberg justified breaking

with tonality by arguing that there were no eternal rules which governed composition, nor was music's development determined by "natural laws." Art
developed through artworks rather than in accord with some transcendent
principle, and past laws of form could not be criteria for creations of the present.[11] This same iconoclastic spirit characterized Adorno's early music articles.
And here Adorno diverged from Lukács's *Die Theorie des Romans*. For the
tone of the latter was melancholic. Lukács lamented the modern age, with
its reified, disintegrating forms which, robbed by history of their living content,
confronted man as mere convention, "second nature."[12] It was with a sense of
nostalgia that Lukács spoke of the decay of epic form, as irrevocably lost as
the classical Greek *Weltanschauung* which it embodied, one based on the un-
questioned, immediate experience of a harmonious totality between man
and nature, thought and deed, the ideal and the real. Lukács interpreted the
nineteenth-century novel as an attempt by the artist to reinstate a sense of
wholeness by means of aesthetic form, and he questioned whether in the present
era of advanced cultural disintegration any art form at all was possible. Both
then and more so later, after he embraced Marxism, Lukács was no friend of
modern art. Not so Adorno, whose attitude toward the decay of culture could
well have born as its motto Nietzsche's statement *"Was fällt, das sollt Ihr stos-
sen"* ("If something is falling, give it a shove"). Hence Adorno's lack of nostalgia
in criticizing Strauss's recent opera *Intermezzo* for its attempt to pour new
wine in old bottles by filling the decaying Wagnerian opera form with the
"modern" theme of bourgeois family life.[13] Hence his defense of Schönberg's
music in 1925 against the charge of anarchy:

> . . . if it leads to anarchy, this is no penetrating objection, since no art has
> the right to endure when it is not genuine, and since the genuineness of
> such anarchy, even if it were itself positive, would be negative in its effect,
> in that it forced the decay of that which is ungenuine, much less [is the
> charge of anarchy valid] . . . in view of the positive fullness and incon-
> ceivable force of form which governs precisely in Schönberg's compositions,
> whose demonic revolt unmasks every natural law of music proclaimed today
> as ideology.[14]

By 1929, Adorno had identified this "ideology" as specifically that of the
bourgeois class:

> . . . disputing the decay of works in history serves a reactionary purpose;
> the ideology of culture as class privilege will not tolerate the fact that its
> lofty goods might ever decay, those goods whose eternity is supposed to
> guarantee the eternity of the class's own existence.[15]

THE LOST TOTALITY: HISTORY IN FRAGMENTS

In the case of both Lukács and Adorno, their move to Marxism entailed
a shift in the context of their theory from the realm of aesthetics to that of

the concrete, social totality structured by class and commodity production, which they now saw as mediating all *geistige* phenomena. But their earlier differences showed up again in the way they interpreted Marx. The thrust of Lukács's thought remained holistic, moving in the direction of reconciliation, of closing the circle, just as the classicists had done in art; whereas Adorno's thinking, like the expressionist movement which spawned modern art, moved in the opposite direction, toward the negation, the explosion of given forms. When he became a Marxist, Lukács began to interpret the alienation of man in a reified world as a specifically bourgeois problem: the crisis in culture became a sign of the bankruptcy of bourgeois society: "This ideological crisis is an unfailing sign of decay. The bourgeoisie has already been thrown on the defensive. . . . *Its power to dominate has vanished beyond recall.*"[16] If the artist was no longer able to create a unity between subject and object, Lukács now placed his hopes in the proletarian class. In viewing alienation as a moment within the total historical process, one which was ultimately moving toward a reconciliation of antagonisms, criticism of the present became transformed into a messianic hope for the future: the proletarian revolution would reestablish the lost totality whose passing had been the source of Lukács's earlier cultural despair.

This vision of history moving in the direction of synthetic unity, of resurrecting the lost totality, was an aspect of Lukács's Marxism which Adorno categorically rejected. In his 1931 inaugural lecture, "Die Aktualität der Philosophie," he wrote (in language otherwise reminiscent of *Die Theorie des Romans*) that the very concept of totality was irrevocably lost in the passing of history:

> The adequacy of thinking about Being as totality . . . has decomposed itself, and therewith the idea of existing being has itself become unaskable: The idea which could only stand over a round and closed reality, as a star in clear transparence, and which perhaps fades from human eyes for all time, ever since the images of our life are guaranteed through history alone.[17]

Adorno insisted that if truth was relative to history, then the idea of history, itself the discovery of the bourgeois era, could not in turn be counted upon to provide the absolute, secure truth which it had robbed from phenomena. If consciousness of historical time had emptied the concept of totality of meaning, then only by stepping into metaphysics could one hope to rediscover that lost meaning in history itself. He was fond of the formulation "History is in the truth; the truth is not in history."[18] What he meant by this rather cryptic statement was simply that although all truth was historical, although there was no truth above time, the actual process of history was not identical to truth in any metaphysical or ontological sense.

In 1932 Adorno criticized Lukács's *Die Theorie des Romans* because it could conceive of transcendence of the alienated, reified world only in metaphysical terms, "under the category of theological reawakening, under the eschatological horizon";[19] this statement can be seen as an indirect criticism of *History and Class Consciousness* as well. Not by interpreting the historical process as an irresistible power pressing toward a messianic break with the present, but by focusing on the breaks, the gaps within the present — here was where Adorno saw the hope of a new future, but never its guarantee. Lukács's concept of the proletariat as the subject-object of history was an attempt to bring consciousness and the objective forces of history into identity with each other. When he described the "total process" of history as "the authentic higher reality,"[20] when he spoke of the proletariat as "entrusted by history"[21] with a revolutionary mission which it "cannot abdicate,"[22] he came very close to a Hegelian metaphysics of history as the rational unfolding of truth, the progressive realization of freedom.[23] It could be argued that in fact, he had no option. Without a belief in history as progress, the proletariat consciousness upon which his theory rested would have been condemned to mere relativism. For if the meaning of objective history did not substantiate the proletariat's view as correct,[24] what prevented this class's standpoint from being merely another perspective of reality, another Diltheyan *Weltanschauung*?[25]

But Adorno neither identified correct consciousness with the subjective viewpoint of a collective revolutionary class nor accepted any overarching concept of the objective course of history as a totality. History formed "no structural whole."[26] Instead, it was "discontinuous,"[27] unfolding within a multiplicity of divisions of human praxis through a dialectical process which was open-ended. History did not guarantee the identity of reason and reality. Rather, history unfolded in the spaces *between* subjects and objects, men and nature, whose very nonidentity was history's motor force. It is in this sense that Adorno's criticism of the identity theory of Hegel can be interpreted:

> History is the demarcation line of identity. It is not that man is the subjectifying subject-object of history, but instead the dialectic of the diverging moments between subject and object is again and again drawn out by history.[28]

This total rejection of the Hegelian concept of history as the identity of subject and object, the rational and the real (indeed, skepticism regarding all progress-interpretations of history) was a fundamental point of agreement between Adorno and his closest intellectual colleagues. It defined the limits of their willingness to see Marx through Hegelian glasses. In his inaugural lecture, Adorno's opening statement was unequivocal: "No justifying reason could rediscover itself in a reality whose order and form quashes every claim to reason."[29] One year earlier (1930), Horkheimer had argued: "History *has* no reason. . . . The pantheistic granting of autonomy to history, of a uniform, substantial essence, is nothing but dogmatic metaphysics."[30] The legacy of Horkheimer's and Adorno's training with Hans Cornelius was certainly a source of their suspicion of history as a metaphysical category.[31] But their position was not motivated merely for philosophical reasons. They were aware that the glorification of history as higher truth functioned to justify the suffering which its course had brought upon individuals, the violence it had done to humans as natural, physical beings.[32] The importance of the category of nature as a corrective to the ideological implications of history as progress had been lost by Lukács. When in *History and Class Consciousness* he argued that nature was subordinate to the historical process, that it was a mere "societal category,"[33] he justified the tyranny of theory and praxis over individual human existence. The brutality of discipline which was thereby required from Party members, the subordination of the individual's "total personality" to Party demands,[34] bore witness to this fact.

The danger of rationalizing suffering, inherent in all progress-theories of history, had already been articulated by Nietzsche:

> The significance of German philosophy (Hegel): to evolve a pantheism through which evil, error, and suffering are not felt as arguments against divinity. This grandiose project has been misused by the existing powers (state, etc.), as if it sanctioned the rationality of whoever happened to be ruling.[35]

It was with Nietzsche in mind that Horkheimer wrote:

> That history has realized a better society out of a worse one, that it can realize an even better one in its course, is a fact; but it is another fact that the path of history leads over the suffering and misery of individuals. Between these two facts there are a number of explanatory connections, but no justifying meaning.[36]

And Walter Benjamin later[37] argued that the crest of history was ridden by conquerors; its process was a "triumphal procession," in which the rulers stepped "over those who are lying prostrate."[38] Hence he claimed:

> There is never a document of civilization which is not at the same time a document of barbarism. And just as such a document is not free from barbarism, neither is the process of transmitting it from one generation to another. A historical materialist therefore dissociates himself from it as far as possible. He regards it as his task to brush history against the grain.[39]

To "brush history against the grain," to fight against the spirit of the times rather than join it, to look backward at history rather than forward – this was a program Adorno held in common with Horkheimer and Benjamin, and the rejection of history as progress became an increasingly dominant theme in their writings after the outbreak of World War II,[40] marking their uniqueness within the tradition of radical thought. Hence Adorno was able to find a moment of validity in Spengler's analysis of the decline of the West.[41] Hence Horkheimer's continued fascination with Schopenhauer, and Benjamin's adherence to the Old Testament motif of history's origin in the Fall and the resultant suffering of a silent nature.[42] Yet it would be completely incorrect to assume an unequivocal affinity between their position and the concept of history found in Judaism, Schopenhauer, or Spengler. For it was one thing to point out the irrationality and destructiveness within history, and it was quite another thing to raise the inadequacies of history to the level of ontological truth. Adorno and his colleagues did not view irrationality as "natural" and hence eternal; they considered it no more the essence of reality than they did reason. For to do so would have been to replace the myth of historical progress with an equally mythical concept of constant "nature." As Adorno wrote: "A nature . . . which hardens oppressively and gloomily in itself and shuns the light of illuminating and warming consciousness, ought justly to be mistrusted. . . . What is unchangeable in nature can take care of itself. Our task is to change it."[43]

NON-IDENTITY AND HISTORICAL RELATIVITY

We are close to the crux of Adorno's argument, and it was prototypical of his approach generally. It is accurate to say that Adorno *had* no concept of history in the sense of an ontological, positive definition of history's philosophical meaning.[44] Instead, both history and nature as its dialectical opposite were for Adorno *cognitive* concepts, not unlike Kant's "regulative ideas,"[45] which were applied in his writings as critical tools for the demythification of reality. At the same time, each provided a critique of the other. Nature provided the key for exposing the nonidentity between the concept of history (as a regulative idea) and historical reality,[46] just as history provided the key for demythifying nature. Adorno argued, on the one hand, that actual past history was not identical to the concept of history (as rational progress), because of the material *nature* to which it did violence. At the same time, the "natural" phenomena of the present were not identical to the concept of nature (as essential reality or truth), because as Lukács had argued in *Die Theorie des Romans*, they had been historically produced. By insisting on their dialectical interrelationship, their nonidentity and yet mutual determinacy, Adorno refused to grant either nature or history the status of an ontological first principle (*prima philosophia*). His purpose was to destroy the mythical power which both concepts wielded over the present, a power which was the source of a fatalistic and passive acceptance of the status quo. This demythifying process relentlessly intensified the critical tension between thought and reality instead of bringing them into harmony. In the space, which he later called the "force-field" generated by this process, Adorno placed his hope for the future realization of freedom, which Hegel had prematurely attributed to the history of the past.

There was no dialectical "law" of history or nature which functioned independently of men's actions and guaranteed progress toward a rational, classless society. Instead, history emerged from the dialectic of human praxis, a process between men and material reality. Whether this process was merely the reproduction of given social conditions or the production of something qualitatively new depended both on material reality and on men's critical consciousness. So long as the latter simply yielded to what existed, hence reproducing the same irrational social relations despite the fact that the bourgeois order showed unmistakable signs of decay, the word "progress" could not be applied to present history. Instead, it had validity only as the struggle to free consciousness from submission to the given, that is, as "progress in demythification."[47]

Of course, this demythification was itself a dialectical process, a dialectic of mental labor which, it will be recalled,[48] Adorno saw as the intellectual's specific kind of social praxis: the thinker or the artist needed to critically negate the (reified, bourgeois) material of his trade, which functioned ideologically yet contained in a mediated form the antagonisms of that society whose historical development had been the source of its production. If Adorno rejected Hegel's metaphysical conception of history as an overarching totality, he was still convinced that the "material" of intellectual activity developed in history dialectically in accord with its own inner logic, its own "immanent laws,"[49] and he equated such development with "progress." In 1930 he wrote: "Progress [in music] means nothing else but persistently grasping the material at the most advanced level of its historical dialectic."[50] Such statements might seem to imply a faith in history's development which would contradict Adorno's rejection of any concept of history meaningful in itself. Indeed, it can be argued that without some faith in historical development, the whole thrust of his efforts to negate intellectual "material" would have been simple nihilism, a position whose political implications were anarchism.[51] Nonetheless, Adorno's language was often more idealist, more metaphysical, than his intent. For when Adorno spoke of musical material's "historical dialectic," he was not referring to a transcendent principle of its development, but simply to the dialectical process of compositional innovation as it developed in empirical history. As Schönberg had noted, art developed through artworks,[52] and, Adorno would have added, these in turn were the product of dialectical praxis, the artist's ability to elicit the new out of the potentialities of the present material. In this context, "advanced level" did not imply a teleological unfolding of art. As he himself clarified: "It is not being suggested that one can compose better today or, thanks to historical Grace, produce better works. . . ."[53] Instead, "advanced" simply meant most recent, the *most present*, and indeed, in an era of bourgeois decline, the present was "progress" only in the sense of progressing disintegration.

Adorno's focus on the present was a crucial point. He seems to have felt that by keeping the present as his point of reference, he could avoid not only a metaphysics of history but also the problem of historical relativism which had created such difficulties for Dilthey and his followers. I suggested earlier that Lukács's concept of proletariat consciousness needed the support of a teleological theory of history if it was to have more validity than a mere *Weltanschauung*. Now Adorno rejected all metaphysical theories of history (as well as the notion of proletariat consciousness), and at the same time he accepted the historicization of truth, the fact that neither the thinker nor the material could transcend the historical specificity of its existence. But whereas Dilthey had found the very concept of truth threatened by such historicity, Adorno turned this problem into a virtue. For if the present was the unavoidable point of reference, then it was in the present that the concept of truth found its concrete meaning. For Adorno, the present did not receive its meaning from history; rather, history received its meaning from the present. Not a transcendent and absolute idea, but the "present objective situation of truth"[54] was the goal of his critical inquiry. To use an expression of Baudelaire which Adorno quoted often: *"Il faut être absolutement moderne"* – in the sense, not of following the demands of the time,[55] but of criticizing the modern, and hence rubbing history against the grain. The "inner logic" of intellectual and artistic material strained against the course of history, instead of identifying with it in a Hegelian synthesis.

The critical process of demythification was fruitful only in its relation to the present. This explains Adorno's intense interest throughout the thirties in Husserl as the most "advanced" idealist philosopher, even though his own position indicated a great debt to the century-old philosophies of Hegel and Kant.[56] It also explains his preoccupation with Schönberg, Berg, and Webern, despite his deep understanding and personal appreciation of early bourgeois composers like Beethoven.[57] It is perhaps the reason for his greater interest in the more recent Marxism of Lukács's *History and Class Consciousness* than in Marx's own standard works. Even if the object of his interpretation was a past phenomenon (for example, a musical composition), the historical present provided his focus. Past works were mediated through time in which their meaning threatened to disappear: "indeed, the truth character of the work is bound precisely to its decay."[58] The future also found expression in the critical reflection upon what now existed: "The power of that which is to come reveals itself much more in the construction of the present."[59]

For Adorno historical relativism, instead of robbing the phenomena of meaning, precisely determined it. Only if the goal was a transhistorical, eternal truth, a goal which Adorno rejected, did historical relativism become a threat to truth:

> The problem of relativism exists only so long as one discusses the relation of a supposed "consciousness in general" to a supposed "object in general." It disappears in the concrete process in which subject and object mutually determine and alter each other.[60]

Whereas historicists relativized the present by situating current phenomena within a general historical development, Adorno's procedure was the reverse: the present relativized the past. History became meaningful only as it manifested itself as "inner history" within the present phenomena.

This focus on history as it appeared in concrete configurations within the phenomena was a unique aspect of Adorno's method, and it bore the imprint of Benjamin's thinking more than that of Horkheimer and the Institute.[61] When Benjamin attempted to articulate the present truth of a past literary product (Baroque tragic drama, Goethe's *Wahlverwandtschaften*), he faced the same philosophical problems which Adorno confronted with regard to the reproduction of past musical works. These phenomena were doubly determined by history, both in the moment of their conception by the artist out of the material in its historically developed form, and in their existence after creation, when they acquired a life of their own.[62] Adorno wrote that "history enters into the constellation of truth,"[63] and therefore the truth of any phenomenon needed constant rearticulation. The vulnerability of phenomena, and hence the precariousness of truth, was without compensation, for history had no grand meaning which could provide a permanent salvation:

> In this remains the great, perhaps the everlasting paradox: philosophy persistently, and with the claim of truth, must proceed interpretively without ever possessing a secure key to interpretation; nothing more is given to philosophy than fleeting, disappearing traces in the riddle-figures of that which exists and their astonishing entwinings; thus so few "results" are given to it; thus it must always begin anew. . . .[64]

History was constructed backwards, like Proustian remembrances, or Freudian screen-memories. As Benjamin wrote:

> The Copernican Revolution in the historical mode of viewing is this: one used to consider the "past" [*Gewesene*] as the fixed point, and saw the present as attempting to lead knowledge gropingly toward this firm ground. Now the relationship is to be reversed, and the past becomes the dialectical turning, the dawning of awakened consciousness.[65]

In making the present his point of reference for critical analysis, both Adorno's application of the concept of history and his uses of history's empirical contents took on a polemical character. He would not have winced at the charge of rhetoric. If intellectual activity was indeed social praxis, then "partisanship," to use a term of Horkheimer,[66] was not only justified, it was inevitable. The only choice was whether one perpetuated the myths of the present by accepting the "given" world immediately as truth, or one employed dialectical, critical negation to articulate its truth as untruth, applying consciousness against the grain of history in order to demythify it and break its spell.[67]

NATURAL HISTORY AND HISTORICAL NATURE

Adorno formulated his conception of history very early, in a speech delivered in July 1932 to the *Kantgesellschaft* at Frankfurt. As was true of his 1931 program for philosophy, this speech was never published by Adorno,[68] but its lasting significance for his theory is substantiated by the fact that he incorporated its argument (and even quoted from it directly) in his 1966 study *Negative Dialektik*.[69] Although the language of the document represents Adorno at his most obscure, it provides no insurmountable obstacle to understanding in view of the points that have already been clarified. Indeed, it serves to illustrate those points through concrete documentation.

The *Kantgesellschaft* speech was Adorno's contribution to the "Frankfurt discussion," part of the debate on historicism which had been going on at the university since Max Scheler and Karl Mannheim taught there in the twenties and worked to establish a sociology of knowledge. At that time Adorno and Walter Benjamin took part in a seminar analyzing Ernst Troeltsch's newly published book on historicism.[70] Troeltsch tried to justify the existence of a transcendental realm of truth and ethics despite the historical relativity of ideas, and this was essentially the premise of Scheler's "materialist ontology" as well.[71] In contrast, Mannheim took an "immanent" position, totally rejecting the concept of a realm of eternal absolutes transcending history, and hence denying the possibility of an ontology of being.[72] The issue was hotly debated by Adorno's intellectual mentors. Scholem recalled that Benjamin took him to visit Kracauer in the hospital, where the two had a heated debate over the question of ontology, and Adorno, then barely twenty, was in the room.[73] Educated in the Kantian tradition, where questions of "meaning" related to objects of empirical experience (*seiende*) rather than to the ontological category of being (*Sein*),[74] Adorno was more disposed by training toward the "immanent" position of Mannheim, with whom he was "for years in constant contact."[75] Yet by disposition he was impervious to the alleged perils of radical relativism into which this position led. He wrote in a 1947(?)[76] critique of Mannheim:

> Ever since puberty, when it is customary to get excited about such questions, I have never again really understood the so-called problem of relativism. My experience was that whoever gave himself over in earnest to the discipline of a particular subject learned to distinguish very precisely between true and false, and that in contrast to such experience the assertion of general insecurity as to what is known had something abstract and unconvincing about it. Let it be that confronted with the ideal of the absolute, everything human stands under the shadow of the conditional and temporary — what happens when the boundary is reached at which thought must recognize that it is not identical to being, not only allows the most convincing insights, but forces them.[77]

It is perhaps then no surprise that when in 1928 his writings broke from Kantian idealism, Adorno flirted briefly with concepts like "ontology" and "being," using them in ways he later found embarrassing.[78] Yet during the Königstein talks of 1929,[79] Adorno agreed with Benjamin that "dialectical," "materialist" theory required that they take seriously a radical relativism which ruled out ontology and all philosophical first principles in favor of an "immanent" method with its focus on the present as the mediation for all statements of "truth" and "meaning."[80] They were consequently unable to accept Martin Heidegger's attempt in

Sein und Zeit (1927) to resolve the dispute between the ontological and historical positions by positing historicity itself as the ontological essence of existence.
Heidegger's "resolution" was the most acclaimed in the "Frankfurt discussion"
of 1932, and Adorno's *Kantgesellschaft* speech was a conscious criticism of it,
one which suggested that the whole attempt at "resolution" be abandoned.[81]

The title of the speech, "Die Idee der Naturgeschichte" (The Idea of Natural
History) signaled the dialectical character of Adorno's approach. For, as we have
already seen, the concepts of nature and history were for Adorno not exclusive,
but mutually determining: each provided the key for the demythification of the
other. The fruitfulness of both concepts for dialectical analysis rested on their
multidimensional meanings. Indeed, each was itself dialectical; each had a
"double character." Nature had a positive, materialist pole: it referred to concrete, individual, existing being which was mortal and transitory — for Adorno,
the material products of men's labor as well as their own corporeal bodies.
Natural matter "embodies history; in it appears what is substantial in [history]."[82]
At the same time, nature had a negative meaning. It referred to the world not
yet incorporated into history, not yet penetrated by reason, hence outside of
human control. In this sense, nature was "the mythical . . . that which is eternally there . . . as the fateful construction of pre-given being."[83] This was
nature's static side, perpetuated by the unchanging rituals of the people who
submitted to its domination.

History, too, had a positive and negative meaning. Adorno defined the former as dialectical social praxis:

> . . . that mode of human behavior, that transmitted social behavior which
> is characterized above all by the fact that the qualitatively new appears in
> it . . . it is a movement which does not run its course in pure identity, the
> pure reproduction of such as already was there, but in which something new
> emerges. . . .[84]

The double character of the concept of history, its negative pole, was determined
by the fact that the actual history of actual human praxis was *not historical* insofar as it merely statically reproduced the conditions and relations of class rather
than establishing a qualitatively new order.[85]

Whenever theory posited "nature" or "history" as an ontological first principle, this double character of the concepts was lost, and with it the potential
for critical negativity: either social conditions were affirmed as "natural" without regard for their historical becoming, or the actual historical process was
affirmed as essential; hence the irrational material suffering of which history
was composed was either dismissed as mere contingency (Hegel) or ontologized
as essential in itself (Heidegger).[86] In both cases, the result was the ideological
justification of the given social order. Adorno insisted on the "concrete unity"
of nature and history within any analysis of reality. For only in specific, dialectical relationship to each other could a critical perspective be maintained. It
was necessary *"to grasp historical being in its most extreme historical deter-*

minacy, there where it is most historical, as itself natural being, or . . . to grasp nature there where it appears to harden most profoundly within itself, as historical being."[87]

For the purpose of exposing the historical dimension in that which appeared as natural, Adorno found the concept of "second nature" a valuable tool. "First nature" referred to the sensual world, including the human body, whose physical well-being was the proper concern of the materialist. This was the concrete, particular nature to which the course of history did violence. "Second nature" was a negating, critical concept which referred to the false, mythical appearance of given reality as ahistorical and absolute. Adorno cited Lukács's *Die Theorie des Romans,* in which "second nature" was used to describe the alienated world, emptied of meaning, "created by man yet composed of things which have become lost to him, . . . the world of convention."[88] Lukács saw that "ossified history is nature, or ossified natural life is merely what has become historically."[89] These hollow conventions wielded a mythical power over men reminiscent of primitive societies in which "first nature" dominated as an inexplicable force. Like primitive fetishes, their historical origins had been forgotten; hence men submitted to them as if they were fate: "An archaic anxiety descends over all where the apparent world [*Scheinwelt*] of convention confronts us."[90] But instead of reacting to this anxiety by turning inward, instead of rejecting "first nature" and retreating to a "false spiritualism"[91] as existentialists from Kierkegaard to Heidegger had done, Adorno wanted to rob the conventions of their mythic power by penetrating through their alien appearance without which reality "cannot be described."[92] The conventions of second nature presented themselves as "ciphers" of the truth, but they needed to be interpreted. Adorno wrote: "Lukács already saw this problem in its strangeness and riddle-character."[93]

In fact, Lukács did not originate the concept of "second nature." Hegel had originally used the term to expose the eternality of forms as mere appearance.[94] Further, Lukács later altered his understanding of the significance of this concept in *History and Class Consciousness,* where he used "second nature" synonymously with Marx's concept of "fetish" in his analysis of bourgeois conventions in terms of the commodity structure. That Adorno was implicitly referring to the term in this latter sense is clear.[95] But he must have been well aware that his audience was more disposed to consider the merits of a concept from Lukács's pre-Marxian period than from Marx himself. As Adorno employed the term in his own writings, "second nature" was one of a constellation of critical concepts together with "fetish," "reification," "enchantment," "fate," "myth," and "phantasmagoria,"[96] which were used to see through the mysterious "natural" appearance of objects in their "given" form to the historical dimension of their production.[97] The purpose of such an analysis was to destroy the mythical aura of their legitimacy.

But Adorno felt that Lukács had seen only part of the problem, the relationship of the reified phenomena to outer history, to the general historical process. There was, continued Adorno, "another side of the phenomenon."[98]

The outer history was no abstract teleological structure, and it did no good to demythify "second nature" only to replace it with another myth, that of a meaning-filled historical totality. To avoid "the *enchantment* of history,"[99] the historical had to be interpreted in terms of the concrete "first nature" which passed away within it. In this connection Adorno cited Walter Banjamin's pre-Marxist study *Ursprung des deutschen Trauerspiels* (Origin of German Tragic Drama). Whereas Lukács had an eschatological view of history which envisioned the reified world brought back to life by the resurrection of the lost totality, Benjamin read history within the individual phenomena, bringing them "back to life" in the sense that his cognitive process released their concrete, living meaning. In the *Trauerspiel* book, Benjamin brought nature and history "out of infinite distance and into infinite proximity" and made them "the object of philosophical interpretation,"[100] applied in this case to seventeenth-century allegorical dramas. The "truth" which Benjamin had discovered in this literary form, one which had been lost in the history of its interpretation, was that allegory was not an arbitrary representation of the idea which it portrayed. It was instead the concrete expression of that idea's material foundation. Specifically Benjamin had demonstrated that "the theme of the allegorical is decisively history,"[101] expressed in the form of ruins, concretely, as the decay and suffering of "first nature." The seventeenth-century allegorists had "a notion of nature as eternal passing in which alone the saturnine gaze of that generation recognized history."[102] Allegory was the "mundane exposition of history as the history of world suffering [*Leidensgeschichte der Welt*] ."[103] Classical art portrayed a harmonious totality (the source of its appeal to Lukács), using nature symbolically for the ahistorical representation of the ideal. Its *schöner Schein* (beautiful appearance) covered up the antagonisms and contradictions of reality. But the contemplative mode of the allegorists was dialectically opposed to classicism. To quote Benjamin: "the false appearance of totality withers away."[104] In its place was a critical representation of concrete history as the "unfreedom, the imperfection and brokenness of the sensual."[105] The allegorical mode of portraying truth was meaningful only in times of historical decay;[106] hence its greater relevance for the present than the lost classicism lamented by Lukács. The similarity between Baroque allegory and modern expressionism was not lost on Benjamin, for as he noted, both were expressions of the collapse of a historical era.[107]

The demythifying thrust of the allegorical concept of history was essentially the same as that of "second nature" when used as a critical cognitive concept. The truth of both was their revelation of the transitoriness of material reality. This moment of transitoriness, wrote Adorno, was "the deepest point in which history and nature converge."[108] When material reality took on the appearance of a mythic permanence, recognition of its historical becoming and therefore of its transiency pierced through this myth. When history appeared in the mythic form of a "structural totality,"[109] its translation back into concrete, particular "first nature" revealed history not as a systematic unity, but as "fully *discontinuous,* not only insofar as it contains disparate facts and evidence, but also in that it contains disparateness of a structural nature."[110] In the gaps and ruptures of history, which the demythifying consciousness articulated and intensified, lay the hope of a historical progress that would be no mere myth.

Hence history and nature were not abstract "invariant concepts," but "arrange themselves around the concrete historical facticity,"[111] forming a constellation which released in the phenomena the moment of transitoriness which might break their mythic spell over the present:

> Nature itself is transitory. It thus contains within it the moment of history. Whenever the historical appears, it refers to the natural which passes away within it. Conversely, where "second nature" appears, whenever that world of convention confronts us, it is deciphered by the fact that its meaning becomes clear precisely in its transitoriness.[112]

The "sublation [*Aufhebung*] of the traditional antithesis of nature and history"[113] occurred in this moment of transitoriness, this "one-time-ness" (*Einmaligkeit*) of the phenomena, to use a term which Adorno borrowed from Georg Simmel.[114] In his study on Kierkegaard, Adorno wrote that "precisely what comprises real history" was "the irreversible one-time-ness of the historical fact"[115] – that is, concrete, particular, transitory nature. But to affirm transitoriness as the essential factor in both nature and history was ontology only in a negative, *antiontological* sense. It was in itself dialectical: for that which is transitory, the one-time, particular, material facticity, cannot be held onto, cannot be possessed. As Horkheimer wrote Benjamin: "The injustice, the terror, the pains of the past [are] irreparable."[116] History was irreversible, a "one-way street."[117] The transitoriness of nature was the source of suffering, but at the same time, because its essence was change, it was the source of hope. This perhaps provides the key to Benjamin's cryptic statement, which Adorno quoted with affirmation, "Only because of the hopeless is hope given to us."[118]

THE DOUBLE CHARACTER OF CONCEPTS

I have argued that Adorno had no ontological concept of history as meaningful in itself. He used history, in connection with nature as its dialectical opposite, as a critical congitive concept, a theoretical tool to demythify sociohistorical phenomena and rob them of their power over consciousness and action. He applied history and nature as mutually determining, mutually corrective concepts. Each in itself had a dynamic and static pole (transitoriness – myth), and their precise meaning depended upon the way in which they needed to be grouped around the particular object analyzed so that its significance could be released.

What appeared as "natural" was exposed as "second nature," hence historically produced. And what appeared as "historical" was exposed in terms of the material "first nature" which passed away within it. But the process of demythification might proceed on another axis: the archaic could be made to appear meaningful in the light of the present; or the very newness and modernity of the present could be made to suddenly release its significance when seen as archaic. To a large extent, Walter Benjamin's writings revolved around this axis. As Adorno noted:

> The totality of his thought is characterized by what may be called "natural history." . . . He is driven not merely to awaken congealed life in petrified objects — as in allegory — but also to scrutinize living things so that they present themselves as being ancient, "ur-historical" and abruptly release their significance.[119]

Adorno also used this cognitive technique, particularly the procedure of identifying archaic elements within the most modern phenomena.[120] Whatever the axis of the analysis, the critical procedure remained the same: dialectically opposed concepts were used as tools to demythologize the world and open it up to critical understanding.

To understand this procedure is to grasp the essential mechanism of Adorno's method of criticism as a process of dialectics without identity. It will be recalled that he accepted Lukács's argument that the antinomies of bourgeois thought reflected a reality in itself contradictory; they could not be reconciled in theory so long as social reality remained unchanged.[121] Given the premise of an essentially antagonistic, contradictory reality, it is clear why Adorno felt that knowledge of the present demanded the juxtaposition of contradictory concepts whose mutually negating tension could not be dissolved.

Not only the antithetical concepts of history and nature but also, for example, the concepts of individual and society were used in this way by Adorno as critical tools of cognition: whenever bourgeois theory posited the primacy of the autonomous individual (e.g., the *autonome ratio* of idealism), Adorno demonstrated the way in which the individual reflected the social totality. But where the social collective was given essential priority (e.g., the left's concept of a collective revolutionary subject, the right's concept of *Gemeinschaft*, Hitler's concept of *das Volk*), Adorno countered with the charge that the modern individual was in fact as isolated and monad-like in his existence as bourgeois theorists like Husserl maintained. Or, that which appeared as rational order in bourgeois society was shown by Adorno to be irrational chaos; but where reality was posited as anarchic and irrational, Adorno exposed the class order which lay beneath this appearance.[122] Still another example: where nature confronted men as a mythic power, Adorno called for the control of that nature by reason; but where rational control of nature took the form of domination, Adorno exposed such instrumental reason as a new mythology. The fluctuating meanings of Adorno's concepts, their purposeful ambivalence, is a major source of the difficulty in interpreting his works. But it was precisely his intent to frustrate the categorizing, defining mentality which by the twentieth century had itself become "second nature." Only if thought remained fluid and avoided dogma could it be the ally of history as it ought to unfold. In Adorno's essays, dialectically opposed pairs of concepts, each of which in itself had two opposed levels of meaning, were juxtaposed to reveal the truth of a contradictory social reality.

The discussion so far has been documented with the early, pre-Institute writings of Adorno, in keeping with the focus of this study on the origins of his theory. Yet although it is discussed again in a later chapter and a different context, the book *Dialektik der Aufklärung* (Dialectic of Enlightenment), which Adorno wrote with Max Horkheimer during World War II, cannot be left out of a consideration of Adorno's conception of history, even at the risk of repetition.[123] *Dialektik der Aufklärung* presented a historical dialectic of reason, originating in the negation of myth, only to reverse in modern times into myth itself. Because this notion was far removed from Marx's description of history as class struggle, the study has been commonly interpreted as a turning point in the theory of the Frankfurt Institute when, as Jay has argued, "the Frankfurt School travelled the last leg of its long march away from orthodox Marxism."[124] It seems clear that what Jay observed as a new direction of the Frankfurt "School" was due far less to its own organic development than to the shift in power among its members after Adorno joined, and especially after he moved to California in 1941 and began working closely with Horkheimer.[125] For *Dialektik der Aufklärung* was not a radical departure from Adorno's earlier methodology. It could in fact be seen as a concrete working out of the idea of "natural history" which he outlined in his 1932 speech. In the book the moments of dynamic history and static myth were juxtaposed in order to give critical meaning to the present: reason was criticized as "myth," while historical progress was seen as the return of the "ever-identical" (*Immergleiche*) because of the violence which it did to material "first nature"; the most recent history (mass culture and anti-Semitism) was exposed as archaic barbarism, while the archaic, the epic poem of the *Odyssey,* was read as an expression of the most modern, with Odysseus the "prototype of the bourgeois individual."[126] There was a constant use of antithetical concept-pairs (magic-science, enlightenment-myth, morality-barbarism, progression-regression) converging in constellations which demystified both the concepts and the reality they attempted to define.

Adorno's 1932 speech was openly indebted to Benjamin's *Trauerspiel* study; *Dialektik der Aufklärung* showed just as clearly the influence of Benjamin's *Geschichtsphilosophische Thesen* (Theses on the Philosophy of History), the last piece he wrote before committing suicide in 1940.[127] This short and very enigmatic document was one of Benjamin's most significant philosophical statements. It was intended as the theoretical introduction to his major, never-completed work the *Passagenarbeit,* on which he worked throughout the decade of the thirties.[128] Significantly, whereas the *Trauerspiel* book was not intended to be dialectical and materialist, the *Passagenarbeit* was. Yet in these theses on history Benjamin returned[129] to the radical relativism to which he and Adorno had committed themselves at Königstein in 1929: the truth of any past phenomenon was not static, not outside of history, but immanent and hence mediated by a constantly changing present.[130] The historian who heeded this

> . . . stops letting the sequence of events run through his fingers like a rosary. He grasps the constellation which his own era enters into with a very specific earlier one.[131]

The articulation of historical origins was not the discovery of something in the past, as in Ranke's famous formula *"wie es eigentlich gewesen ist"*[132] (as it actually was). To identify the historical "source" (*Ursprung*) or historical prototype (*Urbild*) or historical development (*Urgeschichte*) was to construct it from the perspective of the present, and for the purpose of criticizing the present. *Dialektik* was precisely this kind of construction, *der Aufklärung* the *"Urgeschichte* of subjectivity."[133] And when the first "Excursus" interpreted Odysseus as the prototype (*Urbild*) of the bourgeois individual, the purpose was not to challenge the Marxist paradigm of history as class struggle,[134] but to read this archaic image as a configuration of modernity so that it became the occasion for a critical comprehension of the present. If the method was not new for Adorno, what had changed was the nature of the "present." Objective conditions in 1944 were not what they had been at the time of Adorno's speech to the *Kantgesellschaft*. When in 1932, with the bourgeois order in ruins, an objective potential for revolution existed, the greatest cognitive obstacle to its realization seemed to be the reification which made reality appear as "second nature" rather than historically produced. By 1940, it was less the static appearance of reality that needed demystifying than the appearance of historical progress. The revolutionary situation had led to totalitarianism rather than liberation, and this was true not only of Hitler's Germany but Stalin's Russia as well. Shocked by the Nazi-Soviet Pact of 1939[135] (so much so that he saw the necessity for the retreat of revolutionary vision into theology, now that all earthly homelands had proven unsafe),[136] Benjamin claimed that the major stumbling block to revolutionary consciousness had shifted from the acceptance of a static "second nature" to the belief in history as progress: "Nothing has corrupted the German working class so much as the notion that *it* was moving with the current."[137] Marxist theory needed to be reinterpreted within this present constellation. Benjamin noted in a rough draft of the *Geschichtsphilosophische Thesen*:

> Marx says, revolutions are the locomotives of world history. But perhaps it is really totally different. Perhaps revolutions are the grasp by the human race travelling in this train for the emergency brake.[138]

Dialektik der Aufklärung was an attempt by Adorno and Horkheimer to fulfill precisely the cognitive task which Benjamin had identified in 1940 as the most pressing, that is, to dismantle the myth of history as progress. To do this they built upon the work of the Institute on authority,[139] and demonstrated that what Max Weber had identified as the increasing rationalization and "disenchantment" of society did not lead progressively to a rational social order, but instead to new structures of domination in the forms of monopoly capitalism and political totalitarianism. It was within this configuration that Adorno and Horkheimer reconstructed the historical dialectic of reason: reason originated as the tool for the domination of nature, but, intimately connected with self-renunciation and bourgeois asceticism, it had turned "against the thinking subject himself."[140] Rational control of inner and outer nature was reflected in the very form of Enlightenment thought: logical abstraction led not only to the reification of cognition but also to the domination of the content of thought by the concepts; such conceptualizing legitimated doing violence to "first nature." The authors concluded: "Enlightenment is totalitarian."[141]

   Dialektik der Aufklärung was not a self-contained philosophy of history, and to read it as a positive if gloomy statement of the essence of history is to miss the point. The book was a *critical negation* of that rationalist, idealist, progressive view of history which in bourgeois society had itself become "second nature." This critique was made *for the sake of* the Enlightenment and the rationality which it promised. The words Adorno used to describe Walter Benjamin's method apply perhaps with equal accuracy to his and Horkheimer's negation of the bourgeois view of history:

> He viewed the modern world as archaic not in order to conserve the traces of a purportedly eternal truth but rather to escape the trance-like captivity of bourgeois immanence.[142]

The polemical, iconoclastic intent of the study is the reason why it focused on two sacred cows of bourgeois rational thought, the harmonious age of ancient Greece[143] and the eighteenth-century Enlightenment. These moments of an idealized past were juxtaposed to the most barbaric, most irrational phenomena of the present in order to demythologize the present and the past's hold over it. As an attack on progress, the book should be interpreted less as proof of the authors' growing pessimism (a subjective-psychological explanation) than as documentation of the shift in *objective* conditions. For when Hitler caught the wave of history, revolutionary hope found itself pitted against the historical tide.

   Was this position really so far removed from Marx? Jay has claimed that in *Dialektik der Aufklärung* class conflict, "that foundation stone of any truly Marxist theory," was replaced "with a new motor of history. The focus was now placed on the larger conflict between man and nature both without and within. . . ."[144] The importance of the concept of class for any "truly Marxist" theory cannot be disputed; neither can the fact that this emphasis represented a change in the focus of the "Frankfurt School," insofar as such a "school" can be said to have existed. What seems clear, however, is that at least Adorno never considered the theory of class struggle as the essential element of dialectical materialism, that from the very beginning he rejected the concept of dialectical development as an immutable law of history or nature, that he conceived of the dialectic in accord with Marx's paradigm of the dialectic of labor rather than the history of class struggle,[145] as a process between man and nature, consciousness and reality, present knowledge and past history. The critical tension which this nonidentity generated was the potential for the actual development of reason in history.

In "Die Idee der Naturgeschichte," Adorno stated that his argument was derived "from certain fundamental elements of the materialist dialectic."[146] It is true that the term "natural history" was used by Benjamin in his 1925 study of Baroque tragic drama, and that he had not then borrowed it from Marx. But Adorno in 1932 was certainly aware that Marx too had used this term. The phrase "natural history" (*Naturgeschichte*) appears in Marx's 1844 *Economic and Philosophic Manuscripts,* that document to which, as was noted in the preceding chapter, Adorno most assuredly had access even before it was first published in Germany in 1932.[147] Not only did Marx state that "history is an actual part of *natural history,*" rather than positing history as an ontological first principle.[148] He also used the terms "nature" and "history" as critical, intercorrective concepts in much the same manner as Adorno, and attacked Hegelian idealism because it totally subsumed nature within the historical unfolding of absolute spirit.[149] He criticized vulgar materialism for speaking of human activity as mere nature, thereby neglecting its social, noneternal (i.e., historical) character.[150] Finally, when Marx defined society's goal as "the true resurrection of nature, the fulfilled naturalism of man and the humanism of nature,"[151] this was not far from Adorno's and Horkheimer's hope in *Dialektik der Aufklärung* for the realization of a "reconciliation [*Versöhnung*] with nature."[152]

It is not our task here to consider at length Marx's own concept of history. Surely he shared the bourgeois belief in progress, and there was much in Marx's later writings to justify Engels's understanding of dialectics as a natural law of historical development, as well as Lukacs's teleological understanding of history, with its sanctioning of the domination of nature.[153] If there were Marxist elements in Adorno's understanding of history, his was not Marx's understanding.

Nonetheless, on a deeper level than simply common vocabulary, *Dialektik der Aufklärung* had an affinity to Marxism which, it could be argued in the case of Adorno, marked a turn *toward* Marx rather than away from him. For if the book was more than a critical negation of bourgeois philosophies of history, then its positive message was that when dialectical change takes place within the superstructure alone and leaves the class structure untouched, it falls back on itself and repeats itself like a cycle of nature. The book thus attested to the inadequacy of revolution within "reason" when what was needed was a revolution within society.[154] But the same, it implied, was true of a dialectic within the substructure alone.[155] And Adorno was not ready to give up philosophizing.

Chapter 4. A Logic of Disintegration: The Object

THE ORIGINS OF NEGATIVE DIALECTICS

In the preceding chapter, Adorno's approach to the problem of history provided a concrete illustration of his dialectical procedure. By juxtaposing antithetical concepts (nature-history) and by exposing the irreconcilability of concepts with the reality which they were supposed to describe (the idea of history or nature versus its reality), Adorno was engaged in a double task of seeing through the mere appearances of bourgeois reality and the alleged adequacy of bourgeois concepts used to define it. As with Hegel, contradiction, with negation as its logical principle, gave this thinking its dynamic structure and provided the motor force for critical reflection. But whereas Hegel saw negativity, the movement of the concept toward its "other," as merely a moment in a larger process toward systematic completion, Adorno saw no possibility of an argument coming to rest in unequivocal synthesis. He made negativity the hallmark of his dialectical thought precisely because he believed Hegel had been wrong: reason and reality did not coincide. As with Kant, Adorno's antinomies remained antinomial, but this was due to the limits of reality rather than reason. Nonreconciliatory thinking was compelled by objective conditions: because the contradictions of society could not be banished by means of thought, contradiction could not be banished within thought either.

Adorno affirmed neither concept nor reality in itself. Instead, he posited each in critical reference to its other. Put another way, each was affirmed only in its *nonidentity* to the other. Indeed, the "principle of nonidentity," which Adorno was to develop with increasing richness, became the foundation of his philosophy, that is, of "negative dialectics."

Adorno did not speak of a "principle" of nonidentity until after he joined the Institute,[1] and "negative dialectics" was an even later formulation,[2] although the substance of both was already evident in Adorno's theory by the early thirties. At that time he called his philosophical method a "logic of disintegration,"[3] a phrase which not only indicated the nonholistic character of the approach but also implied the reason for its necessity. For as we have seen,[4] Adorno believed that the lost sense of wholeness of his own time was a symptom of the decay of the bourgeois era. Present history was the chronicle of its disintegration. Bankruptcy faced not only the bourgeois economic system but its efforts at ideological hegemony as well. Economic crisis and the widely acknowledged "crisis in culture" which had anticipated it were hence two sides of the same inflated coin. As Walter Benjamin wrote: "With the upheaval of the market economy, we begin to recognize the monuments of the bourgeoisie as ruins even before they have crumbled."[5] The fragmentation of intellectual disciplines, the fact that philosophy had lost its early bourgeois position as the synthesizer and systematizer of all knowledge, was one manifestation of such disintegration. Accepting the division of intellectual labor as an unavoidable condition of present production yet convinced that the technical problems of *geistige* praxis manifested the antagonisms of the social structure,[6] Adorno considered that his task as a philosopher was to undermine the already tottering frame of bourgeois idealism by exposing the contradictions which riddled its categories and, following their inherent logic, push them to the point where the categories were made to self-destruct. It was this goal, the accomplishment of a liquidation of idealism from within, which Adorno had in mind when he formulated the current demands of philosophy as necessitating a "logic of disintegration."

What separated Adorno's goal from sheer nihilism was his belief that a new logic could be educed out of the very contradictions of idealism. To use a phrase which Adorno borrowed from Brecht, he felt the decaying categories could be "refunctioned" (*umfunktioniert*)[7] into tools of dialectical materialist cognition. The sublation of idealism might be induced to generate out of its own ruins a "dialectical," "materialist" philosophy, the historical and logical necessity of which was thereby demonstrated. In good Hegelian fashion,[8] Adorno made no distinction between theory and method: the process of arriving at such a philosophy was itself the new philosophy in action.

Such was the philosophical program which Adorno outlined in his inaugural lecture "Die Aktualität der Philosophie." It must be admitted that his procedure had a certain *ex post facto* character. He already had an idea of what the categories of the new materialism would look like. Most of them had been articulated by Walter Benjamin during the 1920s. But whereas Benjamin simply posited the categories, Adorno, far better versed in the problems of contemporary philosophy, attempted by means of a critique of Kierkegaard's existentialism (written 1928-1933) and a critique of Husserl's phenomenology (written 1934-1937) to educe them systematically out of these late forms of idealism. Nonetheless, Adorno's almost intuitive conviction of the validity of Benjamin's approach predated his efforts to prove its logical and historical necessity.

The origins of "negative dialectics" are therefore to be found in Benjamin's early works and the intellectual dialogue between him and Adorno, which began in 1929 when they formulated a common program at Königstein, and which bore fruit in Adorno's writings during the early thirties. An analysis of these origins provides a key to Adorno's philosophy, even in its later, mature form. The next two chapters will present the first formulations of his philosophical categories, demonstrate their indebtedness to Benjamin's early work, and analyze them as a response to the technical problems confronting the philosophy of his own age, problems which the traditional bourgeois methods seemed incapable of resolving.

Before proceeding, however, one point needs clarification. During the 1960s Adorno's method of "negative dialectics" became identified with the "Critical Theory" of the Frankfurt Institute, of which he had become the most illustrious member. Yet in tracing the origins of Adorno's method, I have purposely avoided equating it with "Critical Theory," a term which lacks substantive precision. Critical Theory was never a fully articulated philosophy which members of the Institute applied in an identical fashion. It was far more a set of assumptions which they shared, and which distinguished their approach from bourgeois, or "traditional," theory.[9] Within this common frame, methodology of individual members could and did vary. Furthermore, the term lacks historical precision, referring generally to the Institute's theoretical orientation during the thirty-odd years of Max Horkheimer's directorship, and although Adorno later clearly felt comfortable with the term, he first outlined the distinguishing characteristics of his own method in the inaugural lecture written seven years before he became an Institute member. At that time (May 1931), Horkheimer had been the Institute's director for only a few months, and the new orientation in critical methodology which he brought to it was just beginning to take shape. Of course, even then Horkheimer's ideas had much in common with Adorno's, due to their close personal and intellectual friendship. Their move toward Marxism in the late twenties had been a shared experience, and Horkheimer had been present at the Königstein talks. But the impact of dialectical materialism on their thinking was not identical and it led them in different directions. Horkheimer turned toward the social sciences, while Adorno, instead of joining his friend at the Institute, chose to accept an academic position.

The young Adorno saw himself as a philosopher and an artist,[10] not a social scientist, and he was then clearly more excited by the literary criticism of Walter Benjamin than by the empirical social research projects of the Institute. As for the Institute's evaluation of Adorno, it is worth noting that two articles which he submitted to the Institute journal in the thirties failed, repeatedly, to pass the review board.[11] And although the articles by Adorno which were accepted — "Zur gesellschaftlichen Lage der Musik" (1932) and "Über Jazz" (1936) — were of lasting importance to his intellectual development,[12] his major works of these years were the more strictly philosophical studies of Kierkegaard and Husserl. The themes of jazz and the social condition of music reflected the Institute's primary concern with the ideological content of cultural phenomena, the question of how *geistige* products functioned to support or challenge the societal status quo. This was, of course, something quite distinct from Adorno's self-prescribed task of fostering the liquidation of idealist philosophy.

Horkheimer believed as firmly as Adorno that bourgeois philosophy was in a state of decay,[13] but he seems to have concluded that if metaphysics was no longer possible, then the philosopher had to look to the aid of the social sciences in order to find truth. Although those sciences, in turn, needed a critical, speculative awareness, philosophy as a separate discipline was eliminated — liquidated from without as it were.[14] For Horkheimer, the problem of "the object" tended to dissolve into (Marxian) sociology, the problem of "the subject" into (Freudian) psychology,[15] and Critical Theory attempted to explain their interrelationship. In his inaugural lecture as Institute director, he referred to a dialectical interaction between theory and empirical research.[16] Adorno, however, discerned a dialectical process *within philosophy itself.*

Indeed, Adorno had an almost Hegelian faith in the immanent logic of philosophy, in its historical development as the unfolding of truth, even if, in very un-Hegelian fashion, he believed that truth critically challenged the course of history rather than merged with it. Convinced that social contradictions appeared within the material of philosophy in a mediated form, and that the philosopher, like the artist, had to be "absolutely modern," had to grasp these contradictions in their most current and (in an age of disintegration) their most antagonistic manifestation, Adorno took up the struggles bequeathed by the preceding generation of philosophers, placed himself within their ranks, and from this fifth-column position pressed the antinomies of their theories to the point where the dialectical negation of idealism might be achieved.[17] This argumentation from within, on the basis of philosophy's own inherent, historically developed logic, in order to break out of bourgeois idealism and into revolutionary materialism, was Adorno's meaning of "immanent criticism," and it constituted the substance of his idea of a "logic of disintegration."

This program bound Adorno to Benjamin more than Horkheimer.[18] Although Horkheimer, too, claimed that if bourgeois theory was to be effectively challenged, it had to be from "within," to him this meant simply that such theory could not be dismissed externally by adapting some metaphysically transcendental, antibourgeois viewpoint, that instead one had to expose the gap between bourgeois theory and its own reality. In his essays Horkheimer would confront bourgeois concepts (of justice, reason, individualism) with the actuality of bourgeois society (its injustice, irrationalism, monopoly capitalism), or he would point to the discrepancy between the potential affluence of present productive forces and the existing scarcity, or he would demonstrate that, e.g., *Lebensphilosophie* betrayed its own intent of protest because, functioning as a support for the societal status quo, it converged with precisely the positivism it attacked.[19] But unlike Adorno, Horkheimer did not get deeply involved in the technical controversies of contemporary philosophy.[20] Hence, although almost all his articles in the Institute's journal, the *Zeitschrift für Sozialforschung,* during the thirties were critiques of bourgeois philosophy, they were not themselves "philosophical" in the strict sense of the term. Keeping one foot outside the discipline, he traced themes and concepts descriptively through the history of the bourgeois era (his factual knowledge of history was far superior to Adorno's) so that their social function might be revealed.[21] Horkheimer moved between theory and society, pointing out corresponding structures in consciousness and reality in a manner more similar to the early Lukács (and hence Lukács's teacher Wilhelm Dilthey, whose work Horkheimer appreciated considerably).[22] In contrast, Adorno used "immanent criticism" not merely as a method of *Ideologiekritik*, but as a means of discovering truth. He attempted quite literally to make the structure of bourgeois society visible within the very words of the bourgeois texts – it was a kind of dialectical exegesis, *Spachkritik* rather than *Ideologiekritik*, more critical *interpretation* than theory.[23]

The difference between Adorno's and Horkheimer's methods implied a different ground for judgmental validity. Horkheimer's arguments rested on principles of moral rectitude,[24] indeed, principles developed by the very bourgeois society that he was attacking. As he explained:

> If we take seriously the ideas by which the bourgeoisie explains its own order – free exchange, free competition, harmony of interests, and so on – and if we follow them to their logical conclusion, they manifest their inner contradiction and therefore *their real opposition to the bourgeois order.*[25]

The transcendent element of idealism which allowed a moral distinction to be made between what is and what ought to be remained essential to Horkheimer despite his advocacy of empirical research. Adorno would later recall, "With you the primary thing was indignation over injustice," and he noted that Horkheimer was indebted to the Judaic ethics of his family as well as bourgeois Enlightenment principles for this impulse.[26] At the same time he observed that their early experiences "did not run parallel. Far more, they converged."[27] If the impulse for Horkheimer's social criticism was an ethical, quasi-religious humanism, Adorno was primarily concerned with the problem of truth. For him, not issues of right or wrong, but judgments of true or false were the necessary ground for theory's validation. In an era when metaphysics had lost all legitimacy, Adorno kept asking the metaphysical question, just as in an era which had proclaimed God dead, Horkheimer refused to dismiss the moral problem of good and evil.[28]

Adorno, the metaphysician with no faith in metaphysics; Horkheimer, the moralist without belief in divine providence – to describe them thus may in fact articulate what held their intellectual paths apart in the thirties, and indeed throughout their lives.[29] The difference accounts for Horkheimer's greater concern with the gap between "imputed" and empirical proletariat consciousness,[30] for he considered that in the modern era, moral praxis was necessarily political praxis. The failure of the proletariat to achieve revolutionary consciousness became the focus of the Institute's research during the first decade of his directorship,[31] whereas Adorno's overriding interest in the questions of the truth of theory, or the validity of art, as issues totally separate from the problem of proletariat consciousness, caused the whole notion of a collective revolutionary subject to fall out of his theory.[32]

Still, the polarity between metaphysician and moralist should not be stressed too strongly, as it was never categorical.[33] Their work was essentially complementary, and became increasingly so after 1938. Even if Adorno's original choice was to teach within the traditional discipline of philosophy rather than to join Horkheimer's Institute, he acknowledged from the first the dependence of his kind of philosophizing on the findings of social science research,[34] just as Horkheimer considered speculative theory indispensable to the process of research. The former was doing sociological philosophy; the latter, philosophical sociology. Furthermore, Adorno early incorporated Horkheimer's concern for the injustices of human suffering, as we saw in his critique of the concept of history.[35] And Horkheimer shared Adorno's interest, if not his preoccupation, with the task of establishing a new ground for dialectical, materialist theory.[36] In fact, Adorno's correspondence makes it clear that hope of collaborating with Horkheimer on this task was one reason why Adorno in 1938 finally decided to join the Institute in the United States. As he wrote Benjamin in June of that year:

> Furthermore, the literary plans of Max and me are now taking on a very concrete form. It is as good as set that we will first of all write a long essay together on the new open-ended form of the dialectic. We are both totally full of the plan. . . .[37]

With the outbreak of war, however, this essay, part of a "proposed great materialistic logic,"[38] was put aside in favor of *Dialektik der Aufklärung*, the theme of which more adequately expressed their shock at the barbarism of Auschwitz and Hiroshima. When Adorno finally wrote his essay on the new form of the dialectic in 1966 (*Negative Dialektik*), it was as the sole author.[39]

It is interesting that the description of Critical Theory which appeared in the Institute's journal in 1941 (in the first English issue) reflected Adorno's more rigorous conception of immanent criticism,[40] as well as a very Benjaminian kind of induction as the method of arriving at truth,[41] indications that the change in the Institute's theory at that time was as much the result of a power shift following Adorno's arrival as it was a response to world events, while Adorno's own position remained remarkably consistent over time.[42]

This is not to suggest that Adorno had no new ideas after the age of thirty. The theme of domination which became central in his writings after 1940 was heavily indebted to the Institute's theoretical and empirical work during the thirties on the problem of authority,[43] work which Adorno carried further in his contribution to *The Authoritarian Personality*.[44] Nor did those ideas which remained constant in his theory emerge full-blown like Minerva out of his youthful head; one has the sense from his early writings that his formulation of concepts preceded his own full understanding of their potentialities. Only after years of working with them was he able to develop out of their abstract possibilities a clear, concrete meaning.

The goal of transcending idealism by leading its concepts via their own immanent logic to the point of self-liquidation was one to which Adorno kept returning. As he wrote in the preface to *Negative Dialektik:*

> To use the strength of the subject to break through the fallacy of constitutive subjectivity — this is what the author felt to be his task ever since he came to trust his own mental impulses. . . .[45]

This was the impetus for his major study on Husserl, *Zur Metakritik der Erkenntnistheorie,*[46] and it was the task which he first proposed for philosophy in his inaugural lecture. Indeed, it is tempting to suggest that Adorno may have had this latter document before him when he was writing the introduction to *Negative Dialektik,* so great is the affinity of their philosophical intent.[47] "Die Aktualität der Philosophie" is therefore a key document for introducing the concepts of Adorno's "logic of disintegration" and the "negative dialectics" into which it evolved.

In the following discussion of those concepts in their original formulation, attention will be given to the way in which each embodied a specific configuration of the idea of nonidentity.[48] In the process of demonstrating the extent of Adorno's indebtedness to Benjamin (as distinct from Horkheimer and the Frankfurt Institute)[49] I shall document the consistency of Adorno's theory over time by noting parallel passages from *Negative Dialektik.*[50]

THE CONCRETE PARTICULAR AND THE DILEMMA OF BOURGEOIS PHILOSOPHY

> Philosophy, in view of the present historical situation, has its true interest where Hegel, at one with tradition, registered his disinterest: with the nonconceptual, the singular and the particular; with that which since Plato has been dismissed as transitory and insignificant, and upon which Hegel hung the label of "foul existence."[51]

If, in his inaugural address, Adorno was not yet attempting a systematic eduction of a materialist logic out of the ruins of idealism, he nonetheless made it clear that the problem of "Die Aktualität der Philosophie" could not be detached from the history of philosophy. He began by summarizing briefly the problems encountered by current philosophical schools, and concluded:

> I have discussed the most recent history of philosophy not for a general intellectual history [*geisteswissenschaftliche*] orientation, but because only out of the historical entanglement of questions and answers does the question of philosophy's actuality emerge precisely.[52]

Adorno's point was that his program for "the dissolution of that which has long been termed philosophy"[53] (i.e., bourgeois idealism) was not an arbitrary choice of subjective fancy, but that it emerged out of the "demands of the philosophical material in its present stage of development." "Actuality" referred to:

> . . . whether, after the failure of the last great efforts, there exists an adequacy between the philosophical questions and the possibility of their being answered at all: whether the actual results of the most recent history of these problems is more, the essential inanswerability of the cardinal philosophical questions. The question is in no way rhetorical, but should be taken very literally. Every philosophy which today does not depend on the security of current intellectual and social conditions, but instead upon truth, sees itself facing the problem of a liquidation of philosophy.[54]

Adorno used terms of *natural* decay in his speech to describe idealist concepts and tenets of philosophy, treating them like material objects with a life and a death of their own, and thereby conveying their *historical* character, that is, their transitoriness.[55] He argued, in critical reference to Heidegger's then popular ontology of being:[56] "The idea of being has grown feeble in philosophy; it is no more than an empty form principle whose archaic value helps to adorn any contents whatever."[57] And he used language of decay to describe what he saw as the crux of philosophy's present difficulties, the dissolution of the premise of identity between subject and object, considered by bourgeois idealism to be the prerequisite for knowledge of truth, which it assumed was necessarily both absolute and total: "The adequacy of thought and being as totality . . . has decomposed. . . ."[58]

> The *autonome ratio* — that was the thesis of all idealist systems — was supposed to be capable of developing the concept of reality, and all reality, from out of itself. This thesis has disintegrated.[59]

Horkheimer, in the more pedestrian, less metaphorical language of *Ideologiekritik*, described the death of the identity principle upon which bourgeois metaphysics had been founded in terms of a change in the social relations of production:

> The idea of unbroken harmony between reality and reason belongs to the liberalist phase. It corresponds to a social economy marked by a plurality of individual entrepreneurs.[60]

The correspondence had historical validity. The building of great metaphysical systems did in fact coincide with the pre-1848 period of bourgeois liberalism, before the events of that year placed the bourgeoisie on the defensive. No longer advocates of revolution, they thenceforth became protectors of their own status quo, now threatened by a growing industrial proletariat. Since the 1860s the slogan "back to Kant"[61] had articulated the disillusionment among philosophers with all metaphysics. Yet neo-Kantianism, the product of new historical conditions, never really did go "back." Whereas Kant's critique of metaphysics had been radical in its social implications, these new Kantians turned critical reason into an ideology of resignation, a positivism that was really defeatism, the passive acceptance of the world in its given form. According to Adorno, concurrent to the growing "crisis of idealism" the "given" world of the bourgeois social order became increasingly difficult to justify.[62] As reason and reality lost touch with each other outside of philosophy, they lost touch within philosophy as well, and the relationship of subject and object became the most urgent technical problem confronting modern philosophy, threatening, in fact, its very existence.

Adorno claimed that no matter what their class allegiance, philosophers could not avoid acknowledging this problem if they heeded the philosophical material itself,[63] even if their adherence to idealist premises prevented them from resolving the issue — for it didn't occur to them that the subject-object relationship could be philosophically grounded in the very nonidentity which appeared so problematic. Contemporary bourgeois philosophers felt instead compelled to opt for either (formal, absolute) reason or (historical, relative) reality as the foundation of theory. At one pole, the Marburg neo-Kantians held onto the idealist concept of reason as universal, but paid dearly for this by sacrificing (historical and social) content:

> [The Marburg School] renounces every right over reality and withdraws into a formal region in which every determination of content is condemned to virtually the farthest point of an unending process.[64]

At the opposite pole, *Lebensphilosphie,* by accepting the historical relativity of truth, as well as the necessity of philosophy's dealing with empirical content (lived experience),

> . . . has admittedly maintained contact with reality, but in so doing has lost every claim to make sense out of the empirical world which presses in upon it. . . .[65]

Edmund Husserl, whom Adorno considered the most progressive of current bourgeois philosophers, tried to hold onto both reason and reality. Phenomenology was a stubborn attempt to reach knowledge of the object, the "things themselves" (*"zu den Sachen"* was Husserl's slogan) without letting go of the traditional idealist concept of reason as universal and absolute.[66] Husserl failed, but according to Adorno his failure was precisely his success, for it brought the dilemmas and inner antagonisms of idealist philosophy to their fullest articulation.[67] Protesting against abstract formalism, Husserl maintained that knowledge was always knowledge *of something,* yet at the same time he shied away from empirical existence because, as transient and contingent, it could not afford a base for absolute knowledge. He therefore tried to distinguish between the material, "natural" object and its presence within thought, hoping to establish a transcendental realm of "thought objects" which could be analyzed by a pure logic uncontaminated by empirical heterogeneity. He used the following example: In thinking of the apple tree in the garden, the object of one's thought, while particular, is not the same as the actual, "natural" tree. The latter can be "bracketed out" in phenomenological analysis, because even if it burns up, the "meaning" of the tree remains as the "intention" of the thinking act.[68] Adorno had already protested against this distinction in his thesis for Cornelius in 1924, arguing the empiricist position that the fact that the real tree could burn was precisely the point — *"particular things can burn up"*:[69] the meaning of the tree, the truth that it could change, resided in just that heterogeneity which Husserl had tried to eliminate.

It is important to realize that what was being debated as a philosophical problem was of more than scholastic concern. At stake was the very possibility of rational understanding. For if reality could not be brought into identity with universal, rational concepts, as idealists since Kant had claimed, then it threatened to splinter into a profusion of particulars which confronted the subject as opaque and inexplicable. These intractable, ineluctable "things," which Hegel, from the macroscopic perspective of a rational totality, had been able to dismiss as "foul existence," suddenly lost their easy familiarity and loomed upon the human horizon as alien and threatening, the source of overwhelming anxiety. Testifying to the historical specificity of this experience of anxiety was its frequent recurrence as a theme in the literature of the twenties and thirties.[70] It was perhaps nowhere more vividly expressed than in Jean-Paul Sarte's novel *Nausea* (1938). His description of a chestnut tree in the park (it might just as well have been in Husserl's garden), experienced as a totally "unintentional" object, with none of its material contingency bracketed out, merits quoting:

> The roots of the chestnut tree were sunk in the ground just under my bench. I couldn't remember it was a root any more. The words had vanished and with them the significance of things, their methods of use, and the feeble points of reference which men have traced in their surface. I was sitting, stooping forward, head bowed, alone in front of this black, knotty mass, entirely beastly, which frightened me. . . . And then all of a sudden, there it was, clear as day: existence had suddenly unveiled itself. It had lost the harmless look of an abstract category: it was the very paste of things, this root was kneaded into existence. . . . All these objects . . .[71] how can I explain? They inconvenienced me; I would have liked them to exist less strongly, more dryly, in a more abstract way, with more reserve. The chestnut tree pressed itself against my eyes. . . .
>
> *In the way*: it was the only relationship I could establish between these trees, these gates, these stones. In vain I tried to *count* the chestnut trees, to locate them by their relationship to the Velleda, to compare their height with the height of the plane trees: each of them escaped the relationship in which I tried to enclose it, isolated itself, and overflowed.[72]

Adorno, whose high regard for Sartre the artist was not extended to Sartre the philosopher,[73] might have recognized the validity of this description, but not the philosophical conclusions which Sartre drew from it. The latter argued that the impossibility of subsuming particular phenomena under general, abstract categories was proof that existence was absurd.[74] To Adorno it proved only the absurdity of the whole classificatory process, and the equation of such pigeon-holing with knowledge. In his 1931 speech he stated:

> If philosophy must learn to renounce the question of totality, then it implies that it must learn to do without the symbolic function, in which for a long time, at least in idealism, the particular appeared to represent the general. . . . [75]

This philosophical mandate was in agreement with Sartre's experiential observation. But where Adorno felt existentialism (as well as phenomenology and *Lebensphilosophie*) made its mistake was in accepting "natural" phenomena as "given" immediately in experience. Hegel had already demonstrated the illusory nature of such attempts at "concreteness" in the opening pages of *Phänomenologie des Geistes,* arguing that the immediately given "this" or "here" was in fact the most abstract. Adorno made use of Hegel's argument (although he couched it in the language of Walter Benjamin) in his critique of the founder of modern existentialism, Sören Kierkegaard:

> It may be said that abstraction is the seal of mythical thinking. The ambiguity of the guilty connection with nature, whereby everything communicates with everything without differentiation, knows no true concretion. Here the names of the created things are confused, and in their place remains the blind matter or the empty sign. The wide-spread custom of ascribing to mythic − archaic − thought the highest degree of concreteness, due to the conceptually immediate perception of the "this-here," leads to error. [76]

For Adorno, "concreteness" necessitated grounding the particular in its dialectical, mediated relationship to the totality. The object was thus *more* than itself, and knowledge of it was more than the tautological A=A. But only by the mediation of conceptual reflection could this relationship be understood, precisely because it was not immediately "given" in experience.

Of course, the "totality" which Adorno had in mind was not that of Hegel's closed metaphysical system, but the Marxian meaning of the total socioeconomic structure of relations which characterized the bourgeois order. [77] Abstracted from this whole, looked at as an isolated, "natural" entity, the object "congeals . . . into a fetish which merely encloses itself all the more deeply within its existence." [78] The fallacy of existentialism and (Husserl's) [79] phenomenology was that by stopping with the immediately given object, they did not see past this fetish-like appearance, whose reified form Lukács had analyzed as "second nature." [80] (Both Sartre's and Husserl's blindness to the *social* nature of objects was clear from the start in their very choice of a tree, a "first nature" object, to illustrate the essence of the cognitive problematic.)

But (as might be anticipated with Adorno's penchant for juxtaposing opposite positions) there was another side of the issue as well. If the existentialist view needed the corrective of dialectical mediation, then dialectics, in turn, in abandoning closed, metaphysical systems, needed to confront the particular phenomena of everyday life, Hegel's "foul existence," to which *Lebensphilosophie* and existentialism had justly drawn philosophical attention. Wrote Adorno, philosophy "must give up the great problems, the size of which once hoped to guarantee the totality, whereas today between the wide meshes of the big questions, interpretation slips away."[81] What distinguished Adorno's approach was not only his Hegelian assertion of the dialectical relation between the particular and the general, but the fact that, unlike Hegel, he found the general within the very surface characteristics of the particular, and indeed, within those that were seemingly insignificant, atypical or extreme. At the crossroads of two seemingly contradictory positions, insisting on the dialectical relationship of the phenomenon to the totality and, at the same time, on the necessity for microcosmic analysis, Adorno grounded his concept of the "concrete particular."

There can be no doubt that it was Walter Benjamin who convinced Adorno of the validity of this approach. Although the rejection of holistic theories and a respect for the individual and particular formed a common theme among the diverse early influences on Adorno, no one, in his opinion, had made this concern more methodologically fruitful than Benjamin.

All those who knew Benjamin were impressed by his acute sensitivity for the "minutiae," (das Kleinste), the seemingly insignificant detail. Ernst Bloch wrote:

> Benjamin had something, which Lukács so frightfully lacked;[83] he had an extraordinary eye . . . for the unusual and unschematic, the disruptive, individual being (Einzelsein) which doesn't fit into the mold. . . .[84]

Benjamin's "microscopic gaze," as Adorno often called it, through which the most common objects appeared remarkable, was a uniquely personal characteristic, but it was more. As a tool for philosophical cognition, it provided a means for making the very particularity of the object release a significance which dissolved its reified appearance and revealed it to be more than a mere tautology, more than simply identical with itself. At the same time, the knowledge it released remained bound to the particular, instead of sacrificing material specificity by moving to a level of abstract, ahistorical generalization.[85]

In order to clarify precisely what was unique about Benjamin's approach, it will be helpful to draw a comparison. In his inaugural address Adorno made critical reference to Georg Simmel because of the "irrationalistic" and "psychologistic" orientation of his Lebensphilosophie.[86] Yet on several other occasions he acknowledged Simmel as a precursor of his own intellectual circle.[87] Significantly, Simmel also focused his analytical eye on particular phenomena, and also had a gift for interpreting the minutiae of existence.[88] Lukács, who had studied with Simmel in Berlin before the war, described his former teacher by referring to

> . . . the lightening-like grasp and the strikingly meaningful expressions of as yet undiscovered philosophical evidence, the ability to view the smallest and most inessential appearances of everyday life so intensively sub specie philosophae, that they become transparent, revealing behind their transparency a relational pattern of eternal philosophical meaning.[89]

The above description is remarkably similar to Bloch's of Benjamin, except for the word "eternal." That this one exception, however, provides the key to the critical difference in their respective methods of dealing with the "particular" is apparent in the following illustration.

Simmel's short essay "Sociology of Mealtime" was an interpretation of this common human activity inspired by an insight into the essential paradox of meals: what all men shared in common, "that they must eat and drink," was at the same time the most individualistic, ego-centered activity:

> . . . what I think I can let others know, what I see I can let them see, what I speak can be heard by hundreds – but what the individual person eats can under no circumstances be eaten by another.[90]

Precisely this fact, he argued, provided the key to interpreting the social rituals surrounding meals. Regularity of time and place, the use of utensils and of identical dishes, aesthetics and table manners – these ceremonial details symbolized the necessity of socializing individual wants, which in their "natural" form threatened the cohesiveness of the community.[91]

Now consider this short statement from Walter Benjamin's *Einbahnstrasse*:

> The way a dinner party has gone can be told at a glance by whoever stays behind to view the placement of dishes and cups, of wine glasses and food.[92]

It is clear that whereas Simmel's analysis of the meal points toward an eternal verity of (subjective) human existence,[93] the observation encouraged by Benjamin remains bound to the particular (objective) historical event: "His philosophical interest was not at all directed at the ahistorical, but instead at precisely the most temporally determined, the irreversible."[94] At the same time these minutiae, the "remains of the physical world" (*Abhub der Erscheinungswelt*), as Adorno, citing Freud, referred to them,[95] lack the absurdity of mere existence which characterized Sartre's chestnut tree. Benjamin was able to educe a meaning which was more than tautological, which transcended the immediately "given" objects without transcending their particularity. The uncleared dinner table does not bear witness to some general principle concerning the nature of society; but it might indeed reveal the nature of that particular society whose members have left their traces behind them in the dining room.[96]

It should be noted that microscopic analysis was an early characteristic in Benjamin's writings, predating his move to Marxism, at a time when he was influenced by German romantic theories of literary criticism (especially Novalis and Schlegel)[97] and by the Kabbalah, the tradition of Jewish mysticism to which Gershom Scholem had introduced Benjamin in the 1910s. An outline of this method in its pre-Marxist form was provided by Benjamin in *Ursprung des deutschen Trauerspiels* (1927), where he applied it to the task of literary criticism.[98] Here the phenomena were historical texts rather than natural objects: the "idea" of Baroque tragic drama was "decoded" out of the arrangement, not of dishes and cups, but of the extreme and often contradictory elements which the texts of those dramas contained. It was as a method of textual analysis (but placed within the frame of Marxist theory) that Benjamin's approach appeared to Adorno as such a potentially fruitful tool for his own project, the liquidation of idealism. A microscopic analysis which could identify the general (i.e., the bourgeois social structure) within the particular (the details of bourgeois philosophical texts) could indicate more than the social function of ideas (*Ideologiekritik*); it promised to make possible statements of objective truth, albeit historically specific. Instead of simply demonstrating the ideological implications of philosophical schools, the way in which general positions (positivism, irrationalism, and the like) acted as supports to the status quo, this method took Adorno deep into the particulars of the philosophical texts, so that the very words and their arrangements, apparently insignificant details, became meaningful, releasing a significance not even intended by the author. Indeed, "unintentional truth" was precisely the object of Adorno's critical inquiry. But before examining more closely this idea of unintentional truth (which was also Benjamin's originally), it may be helpful by way of summary to make explicit the aspects of "nonidentity" contained within the concept of the "concrete particular."

The particular was not "a case of the general"; it could not be identified by placing it within a general category, for its significance lay in its contingency rather than its universality.[99] Further (and this was what separated the theory from nominalism), the particular was not identical to itself. It was more than the tautological "rose is a rose" because of its mediated relationship to society.[100] Like Leibniz's monads,[101] each particular was unique, yet each contained a picture of the whole, an "image of the world,"[102] which within a Marxist frame meant an image of the bourgeois social structure. Because this general social reality was also not absolute, but a particular moment within the historical process,[103] instead of being ontologically and eternally valid, it was itself "sedimented history."[104] There was also a utopian dimension to nonidentity as it related to the concrete particular. The transitoriness of particulars was the promise of a different future, while their small size, their elusiveness to categorization implied a defiance of the very social structure they expressed. Reading the nonidentity of the particular as a promise of utopia was an idea Adorno took from Ernst Bloch.[105] Insisting on recognition of the "not-yet-existing" (*Nochnicht-seiende*),[106] Bloch grounded hope for the future in those nonidentical "traces" (*Spuren*)[107] of utopia already experienced within the present. In his inaugural lecture, Adorno echoed this thought: "only in traces [*Spuren*] and ruins" was there "hope of ever coming across genuine and just reality."[108] That the locus of utopian hope was in the small things, in details which slipped out of the conceptual net, was an idea Adorno had already expressed in his philosophy of music, and it remained important in his aesthetic theory. As he wrote in 1928 in regard to Schubert's music:

> . . . change succeeds only in the smallest thing. Where the scale is large, death dominates.[109]

UNINTENTIONAL TRUTH

> Interpretation of the unintentional through a juxtaposition of the analytical-
> ly isolated elements, and illumination of the real by the power of such
> interpretation: that is the program of every authentically materialist knowl-
> edge. . . .[110]

Crucial to "negative dialectics" was not only the object's nonidentity with
itself, but its nonidentity with the knowing subject, the mind and its logical
processes. In Adorno's inaugural lecture, this level of nonidentity found expression in the term "unintentional truth," and Adorno's choice of words was not
without significance. At the time, Horkheimer and his colleagues at the Institute
were also insisting that subject and object were not identical.[111] But the notion
of "the unintentional" said more. If the Institute's *Ideologiekritik* essays exposed
the untruth of identity (of the Hegelian claim that the real was rational), Adorno
was stating the converse as well: nonidentity was the locus of truth.[112]

In the strange and singular theory of cognition which Benjamin outlined in
his *Trauerspiel* book[113] (which brushed up against materialism far more intimately
than its own, Kabbalist-inspired author first intended), the idea of "the unintentional" played a central role:

> Truth never enters into a relation, and particularly not an intentional one.
> The object of knowledge as something determined within conceptual inten-
> tion is not truth. Truth, built out of ideas [rather than appearing within
> them], is unintentional being. The procedure which adequately conforms
> to it is therefore not an intending within the knowing process, but an enter-
> ing into [truth] and disappearing. Truth is the death of intention.[114]

Benjamin's argument was a critical reversal of the "doctrine of intentionality"
which, formulated by the medieval Scholastic Duns Scotus, had been revived by
Franz Brentano[115] and incorporated into the phenomenology of his pupil Edmund Husserl.

We are back in Husserl's garden. For the purpose of the doctrine of intentionality was to distinguish empirical objects (e.g., the actually existing apple
tree) from *intentional* objects (the tree as it existed in the thought of it) whose
objectivity did not reside in empirical existence. (That such "objects" as unicorns
or mermaids could be thought about was seen to demonstrate the necessity of
this distinction.) What appealed to Husserl, of course, was that this doctrine
could be used to justify his "bracketing out" process: if judgments of truth
could be made about objects whether or not they actually existed, then phenomenology could avoid resting its case on the shaky, uncertain ground of
empirical beings — just those transitory particulars which Adorno and Benjamin
considered crucial.

Benjamin's rejection of intentionality may have had its source in a mystical impulse; yet it converged with materialism in its claim that the object was the source of truth.[116] The subject needed to go to the object, to *enter into* it, whereas to stop short at the "thought objects" was to discover nothing more than the subject's own reflection as "intention." Benjamin had not so much proved the unintentionality of truth as asserted it in the *Trauerspiel* study. Later Adorno, in his lengthy study on Husserl, demonstrated how Husserl's method led him unavoidably back into the circle of idealism which he had tried to escape, and used this criticism to validate his own materialist premise of unintentionality.[117]

It should be noted that this notion was "materialist" not so much in the Marxian sense as in the simpler sense of pre-Kantian materialism.[118] Except it was even more extreme: Adorno insisted that philosophy recognize not only natural objects as "matter" but *geistige* phenomena as well (including Husserl's notion of "thought objects"). Like physical matter, the "material" of ideas, theories, concepts, of novels and musical compositions, lived, grew old, and decayed. Not even the products of thought, then, were mere subjectivity, and this meant that they too were the locus of "unintentional truth."

Describing phenomena as if they had a life of their own,[119] as if they expressed a truth of which their human creator was unaware, was a unique feature of Benjamin's writings. It was a kind of anthropomorphism, a modern expression of the archaic, which surfaced in Adorno's works as well. But instead of robbing nature of its otherness by identifying it with the subject, this anthropomorphism had the inverse effect of increasing the nonidentity, the strangeness of the object. Benjamin called this strangeness "aura,"[120] and it was a mystical motif in his writings.

Precisely this orientation of Benjamin and Adorno distinguished their method from the bourgeois approach to *Geisteswissenschaft*. The latter found its most conscious articulation in the writings of Wilhelm Dilthey. Once again, a comparison is instructive. Like Adorno, Dilthey was concerned with concrete, historically particular phenomena[121] whose structural forms bore the imprint of a specific social era. Cultural "objects" — texts, documents, artworks, and the like — demanded *interpretation,* and, according to Dilthey, this interpretive, hermeneutic approach was what distinguished the method of *Geisteswissenschaft* from that of the natural sciences. Adorno made a similar distinction between philosophy and science in his inaugural lecture: "Plainly stated: the idea of science is research; that of philosophy is interpretation."[122] But despite the fact that Adorno's negative dialectics was clearly a hermeneutic procedure, it diverged radically from Dilthey's hermeneutics, and the notion of "unintentionality" provides the key to that difference: Dilthey treated *geistige* phenomena as psychological expressions; his aim in interpreting them was to recapture the original subjective meaning, the original intention behind the written word or other form of cultural expression.[123] In contrast, Adorno wanted to know what the cultural objects were saying *despite* their creators' intent: "ascribed to the basic assumptions of philosophical interpretation" was "construction out of small, unintentional elements"[124] within *geistige* phenomena. For Dilthey, it was the artist which hermeneutics tried to understand; for Adorno it was the artwork.

A study of Goethe's novel *Die Wahlverwandtschaften* (Elective Affinities), which Benjamin wrote in 1921–1922, before he met Adorno, had protested against the Diltheyan approach to literary history. He argued that the truth of the novel did not depend on the interpreter's ability to empathetically identify with the sentiments expressed in the novel[125] or with the author's intent;[126] instead, truth lay within the novel itself. This truth was not immune to history, and perception of it was in fact enhanced by the temporal distance separating the interpreter from his object.[127] Adorno's early experience with the reproduction of music, his awareness of the difficulties in trying to recapture the truth of a past composition within a present interpretation, had led him to the same conclusion.[128] For a part of the problem was that, as he later expressed it, "great works can be recognized in the difference between that which stands out in them and their own intention."[129] But not until Benjamin and Adorno articulated the problem within the frame of a Marxist theory of society did they name the source of the "unintentional" elements: the socioeconomic structure mediated all *geistige* production and hence expressed itself within cultural artifacts alongside (and often in contradiction to) the subjective intention of their creators. *Geistige* phenomena were therefore not exhausted by an analysis of subjective psychology. But they were also not reducible to the substructure alone, as the "copy theory" of orthodox Marxism maintained. Against both psychological and economic reductionism, Benjamin argued:

> The question is namely: if the substructure determines the superstructure to a certain degree, its thought and experience material, yet this determination is not one of simple copying or reflection, how is it then – totally apart from the question of its causal origins – to be characterized? As its expression [*Ausdruck*]. The superstructure is the expression of the substructure. The economic conditions under which society exists come to expression in the superstructure.[130]

Once again, a literal affinity with the language of Diltheyan hermeneutics illuminates the nonidentity of the two positions. For Dilthey, cultural phenomena were "expressions" (*Ausdrücke*) of "life," the articulation of conscious reflection upon past subjective experience. But if that which the phenomena "expressed" was the objective social structure and this occurred despite conscious intent, then the focus of interpretation shifted to the opposite (the objective, materialist) pole. In this light, cultural objects became "a medium for the unconscious history-writing of society."[131]

It was this aspect of "unintentional truth," of course, which enabled Adorno to argue that the artist could best serve society by ignoring politics and concentrating on his material, just as it allowed him to call Schönberg's music revolutionary in not just a cultural but a political, Marxian sense, despite Schönberg's own lack of sympathy for Marxism. Unlike more orthodox Marxists, Adorno could maintain that bourgeois art and also bourgeois philosophy were not simply ideology, and that they should thus be interpreted as more than false consciousness.[132] Ideology was exposed by demonstrating the historical character of premises which were accepted as "second nature"; to quote Lukács: "what philosophy does *not* find problematic."[133] But the truth content of bourgeois thought lay in the opposite direction, in the "breaks" (*Brüche*) in its logic, the gaps of its systematic unity. Indeed, because truth revealed itself in the non-identity between psychological intent and its concrete objectification, the bourgeois thinker was most likely to express truth when he felt himself farthest away. Paradoxically, then, his theory gained in truth in proportion to its admission of failure, for this failure bore witness to a reality whose real contradictions could not be resolved on the level of thought alone.

The bourgeois thinker expressed truth in spite of himself; or rather, like Freudian slips of the tongue, truth surfaced in the inconsistencies of his theory, now more than ever, because of philosophy's "disintegration." Here was an important corollary to the principle of unintentional truth, one which was specifically Adorno's contribution.[134] Ever since his first exposure to philosophy, when at age sixteen he read Kant together with Kracauer on Sunday afternoons, he had been struck by the significance of logical breaks:

> If later, in regard to the traditional philosophical texts, I not so much let myself be impressed by their unity and systematic coherence as I concerned myself with the play of opposing and conflicting forces which goes on under the surface of every self-contained theoretical position, and which codified philosophy sometimes accounts for as force-fields, then it was certainly Kracauer who gave me the idea. He made the *Critique of Pure Reason* present to me not simply as a system of transcendental idealism. Much more, he showed me . . . how the most eloquent parts of the work are the wounds which the conflict in the theory leaves behind.[135]

The fractures, the ambiguities and contradictions, were the philosophical details upon which Adorno focused his interpretive efforts.

Although Adorno was convinced that truth lay in the object, not in the mind which strove to know it in thought, even there it was not intentional. "Given" reality was not somehow in accord with divine intention, or with that of Hegel's absolute reason: "it is not the task of philosophy to portray reality as meaningful in a positive sense and to justify it."[136] Philosophy

> . . . does all the more justice [to the materialist procedure] the more it distances itself from every "meaning" of its objects and the less it relates itself to an implicit, quasi-religious meaning.[137]

Adorno agreed with Goethe, who cautioned: "Do not look behind the phenomena; they themselves are the truth."[138] Yet in their mere "givenness" they were as absurd as Sartre's anguished hero had supposed. This was the difficulty which plagued positivists as well as existentialists.[139] Against both positions Adorno argued that "the world in which we live . . . is otherwise constituted than out of mere perceptions of reality. . . ."[140] The interpretive process necessitated more than immediate experience of the "given"; it required the active intervention of the thinking subject.[141]

Here the focus shifts from consideration of the concrete particular as the source of unintentional truth to the role of the subject in interpreting that truth. It is a crucial shift, for, like Husserl, when faced with the merely "given" world, Adorno returned to the subject as the source of knowledge, but *not at the cost of giving up the nonidentity between subject and object.* Instead, he saw them as necessary codeterminates: neither mind nor matter could dominate the other as a philosophical first principle. Truth resided in the object, but it did not lie ready at hand; the material object needed the rational subject in order to release the truth which it contained.

Chapter 5. A Logic of Disintegration: The Role of the Subject

THE INDIVIDUAL AS SUBJECT OF EXPERIENCE

Adorno's aversion to the idea of a collective subject has already been considered.[1] It was the source of his refusal to join the Communist Party and the reason why he avoided resting his theory on either the concept or the reality of the proletariat class. Adorno criticized Stalin's purges of dissenting individuals no less than Hitler's. The persecution of deviation, of the *nonidentical* view, he condemned as totalitarian regardless of its motivation. Against the Nazi slogan "The individual is nothing, the people everything,"[2] but equally against Brecht's line "The party has a thousand eyes, the individual but two,"[3] Adorno stubbornly and continuously held on to the concept of the individual, insisting that it could and should be salvaged from the wreckage of the bourgeois liberalism which had been its origin. In *History and Class Consciousness* Lukács had argued: "The individual can never become the measure of all things. . . . Only the class can relate to the whole of reality in a practical revolutionary way."[4] But for Adorno, the point was still to *interpret* the world – not as a substitute, but as a precondition for change, and as a preventative against false praxis. In his "dialectical," "materialist" theory the Marxian conception of class consciousness as a political experience was lacking, and in its place Adorno developed a conception of individual consciousness as the subject of cognitive experience.[5]

On this point Adorno was really falling behind not only Marx but Hegel (whose absolute *Geist* was the quintessence of collective subjectivity)[6] and returning to Kant.[7] He echoed Ernst Bloch's earlier appeal "to let Kant burn through Hegel: the 'I' must always be maintained."[8] But even as Adorno reaffirmed the Kantian notion of an individual, spontaneous, knowing subject, he transformed radically its philosophical function. Kant had maintained that the subject could not experience the object as it was in itself, but only as structured by subjective forms and categories – only, that is, as something essentially identical to the subject. Adorno's concept of experience reversed the polarity of the relation between subject and object, gave, as he later worded it, Kant's "Copernican Revolution an axial turn,"[9] so that nonidentity became the very basis of knowledge.

Far from considering the Kantian subject too individualistic, Adorno maintained it was not individualistic enough. Like the exchange principle of bourgeois commodity production, Kant's conception was formal and abstract, the least common denominator of human thought. The universality of the transcendental subject ignored historical particularity and implied the interchangeability of every subject; it was really not individual at all. In his inaugural lecture Adorno protested against Kant that the subject

> . . . is not ahistorically identical and transcendental, but assumes with history changing and historically revealing forms.[10]

Horkheimer worded it more concretely:

> There is no "thought" by itself, but always only the particular person, in which to be sure the entire social situation plays a role.[11]

The subject of philosophical experience was the empirically existing, material and transitory human being — not merely mind but a sentient human body, a "piece of nature" (*Stück Natur*).[12] This was a Feuerbachian theme (although in Marx and Lenin as well) which both the Institute and Adorno began to emphasize in the late 1930s, along with the notion that the goal of society was "sensual happiness" (*sinnliche Glück*).[13] For Adorno this meant not only, as Horkheimer emphasized, that cognition had to acknowledge the reality of human suffering but also that the act of cognition itself had a somatic character.[14] Here his mentor was Benjamin, in whose writings "thought presses close to its object, as if through touching, smelling, tasting, it wanted to transform itself."[15]

On this point, as elsewhere, Adorno's "materialism" was more akin to the Enlightenment than to Marxism, or even Left Hegelianism. Horkheimer gave deference to a more orthodox Marxism by at least mentioning the significance of class in his description of the subject as

> . . . a definite individual in his real relation to other individuals and groups, in his conflict with a particular class, and, finally, in the resultant web of relationships with the social totality and with nature.[16]

And class as a determining variable in subjective experience was a focus of the Institute's research during the thirties.[17] But Adorno's statements about the subject were remarkably unconcerned with considerations of class origin or the particular subject's position within the social relations of production.[18] He considered bourgeois and proletariat equally susceptible to the ideology which produced false consciousness. It was not that he denied the role of class in the socialization of the subject — he explicitly rejected Karl Mannheim's notion of a "free-floating" (*frei-schwebende*) intelligentsia.[19] But his acknowledgment of class bias even here was peripheral to the major thrust of his argument.[20] That thrust, as might be anticipated, was in the direction of nonidentity. For if the subject as concrete and particular was determined by sociohistorical circumstances, it was also true that his particularity (in opposition to the exchange principle) made him unique and irreplaceable. Moreover, the subject did not remain identical with himself over time. Philosophical experience as a dialectical process of social praxis did not leave the subject untouched. This view was, as Adorno noted, in marked contrast to bourgeois theory, where

> The subject is conceived as a fixed point of arrest in cognition, as unchangeable, existing once and for all time, and thus all movement is mistakenly accorded only to the object. Should then contradictions become evident in the course of the cognitive process, because the subject itself is entwined in that process, is itself a moment in the movement, is itself also moved, then all panic breaks out.[21]

It will be recalled that Adorno insisted on the necessity of the thinker or artist being "absolutely modern," in the sense not of swimming with the tide, but of brushing current history "against the grain."[22] The individual's capacity for refusing to identify with the status quo, while at the same time dialectically acknowledging his own dependence upon the present and its determining conditions, was the prerequisite for true philosophical experience. In short, instead of judging the correctness of consciousness by its *identity* with the interests of the proletariat (Lukács's "imputed" class consciousness), Adorno had as his criterion the individual subject's *nonidentity* with the world, the object of his reflection, in its present "given" form.[23] In the Marxian concept of class consciousness, cognition meant knowledge of one's own socioeconomic position and consequent historical role, but in negative dialectics cognitive experience meant something quite different: it was in fact synonymous with intellectual nonconformity.[24]

Not accidentally, Adorno's intellectual heroes were "outsiders,"[25] men like Schönberg, Freud, Benjamin, Kafka, Trakl, who dared single-handedly to defy the traditions of their trades. None, of course, were from working-class backgrounds, none except Benjamin were even armchair Marxists; yet Adorno judged the critical posture they took toward their own bourgeois cultural heritage as both truly revolutionary and revolutionary in its truth. However, Adorno's theory never squarely faced the problem of the relationship between cultural revolt and political revolution. These things were, after all, nonidentical, as had been documented by the failure of the expressionists before Adorno to transform their outcry of cultural protest into political praxis.[26] Furthermore, it was not at all clear that every human being was capable of the kind of intellectual experience Adorno was describing. For if nonconformity was a criterion of correct consciousness, then the inner logic of the very word meant that only a minority could possess it.[27] Adorno in fact conceded the "privileged" nature of intellectual experience. Yet he was careful to point out that in contrast to the Establishment intellectuals (those whom Ringer has described as Germany's "mandarin class"),[28] this elite was at odds with the ruling class, whose hegemony it threatened.[29] Yet in failing to articulate the connecting link between the individual experience of intellectual revolt and the transformation of social reality, Adorno here again[30] leaves us with the question, precisely whom were the *avant-garde* leading?

Perhaps Adorno could ignore this question because his concept of experience did not include or even imply a theory of intersubjectivity.[31] As he wrote in *Negative Dialektik*: "Truth is objective, not plausible."[32] It was not dependent on subjective consensus.[33] What gave knowledge its consistency was not the universality of the subject, but the uniform (commodity) structure of the object, "the affinity which objects have for each other."[34] The uniquely individual experiences of critical subjectivity ran parallel because they focused on particulars which reflected the same objective reality, and it followed that collaboration was possible among intellectuals even when they worked alone. Nothing pleased Adorno more than when a friend came to similar insights independently, for he considered it a validation of their correctness. As Benjamin enthusiastically exclaimed after reading the manuscript of Adorno's Kierkegaard book: "There is still something like collaboration after all. . . ."[35]

EXACT FANTASY: MIMETIC TRANSFORMATION

The hallmark of the Kantian subject was its "spontaneity," that is, its active role in the cognitive experience. If Adorno claimed Kant didn't take the individual character of the subject seriously enough, he argued similarly in regard to its active participation in cognition. Kant's subject was creative only in the sense that it molded the objects in accord with the *a priori* forms and categories of rational understanding: the mind had a preformed, permanent structure to which the objects of experience conformed. But Adorno, in giving Kant's Copernican revolution a turn, argued that the object, not the subject, was preeminent: it was the preformed, historically developed structure of society which made things what they were, including Kant's reified categories of consciousness. As he wrote Benjamin in 1935:

> The fetish character of commodities is not a fact of consciousness, but dialectic in the eminent sense that it produces consciousness.[36]

Adorno argued that the autonomous, spontaneous moment of cognition lay in refusing to acquiesce to the resulting fetishization of thought in which subject was split from object, mind from matter. The subject had to get out of subjectivity's box by giving itself over to the object, *entering into it*, as Benjamin had stated in his *Trauerspiel* book.[37] This "immersion in particularity"[38] did not lead to the subject's rediscovery of itself,[39] but to a discovery of the social structure in a particular configuration. Whereas Hegel, also arguing against Kant that the subject needed to immerse itself in the object, claimed the structure of reality was ultimately identical to rational subjectivity, Adorno considered the object simply not rational, although it was rationally understandable. But only a dialectical logic could grasp the inner contradictions of phenomena which reproduced in microcosm the dynamics of the contradictory social whole.

Marx stated in his critique of Hegel's *Rechtsphilosophie* that philosophy was not a "matter of logic" (*Sache der Logik*), but the "logic of the matter" (*Logik der Sache*), and Adorno incorporated this phrase into his own vocabulary. Yet he really altered its meaning, connecting it with a pre-Marxian philosophical tradition. In his inaugural lecture he wrote:

> One may see here [in Adorno's own program] an attempt to reestablish that old concept of philosophy which was formulated by Bacon and passionately contended around the time of Leibniz, a conception which idealism derided as a fad: that of the *ars inveniendi*.[40]

The term *ars inveniendi* was well chosen: it meant literally the art of coming upon something, invention in the sense, not of making something up, but of discovering it for the first time. Yet against the passive receptivity and observer posture of the positivist, "scientific" subject to which Bacon's natural philosophy had led historically, Adorno insisted: "The organon of this *ars inveniendi*, however, is fantasy."[41] Instead of simply taking in reality as it was immediately given (and being taken in by it), the subject's "fantasy" actively arranged its elements, bringing them into various relationships until they crystallized in a way which made their truth cognitively accessible. Even as the subject "entered into" the object, then, it was not swallowed up but maintained the distance necessary for critical activity.[42] And at the same time, what separated this fantasy from mere dreamlike fabrication was its strict adherence to the facts. It was:

> An exact fantasy; fantasy which abides strictly within the material which the sciences present to it, and reaches beyond them only in the smallest aspects of their arrangement: aspects, granted, which fantasy itself must originally generate.[43]

"Exact fantasy" was thus a dialectical concept which acknowledged the mutual mediation of subject and object without allowing either to get the upper hand. It was not imagination in the sense of subjective projection beyond the existing world either into the past[44] or into the future;[45] it remained "immanent," within the material phenomena, the factuality of which acted as a control to thought. "Exact fantasy" was scientific in its refusal "to step out of the perimeters of the elements."[46] Yet like art, it rearranged the elements of experience, the "riddle-figures of empirical existence,"[47] until they opened up to cognitive understanding. It was this interpretive rearrangement which brought to light what Adorno meant by the "logic of the matter." The subject yielded to the objects, yet it did not leave them unchanged. Instead of being merely duplicated in thought, they were transformed within a verbal representation.

In his *Trauerspiel* study Benjamin had differentiated between knowledge (in the sense of collected data) and the philosophical experience of truth:

> Knowledge is an acquisition. . . . In it there remains the character of property. Presentation is secondary to its possession. It does not exist from the start as something which presents itself. This, however, is precisely what applies to truth.[48]

In Marxist terms, knowledge as "possession" was a commodity (the medium of language might be seen as the truck that took it to market, where the "exchange" of ideas meant simply the transmission of information). But philosophy, according to Benjamin, was revelation, the *presentation of truth*, and here language didn't transport, but *transformed* the objects from matter into words. In themselves, the objects were mute. They needed to be "brought to speech" by the exact fantasy of the subject which expressed their inner logic in a verbal translation. Language thus expressed the "logic of the matter" in a new modality.

It was in this connection that the term "mimesis" appeared in Adorno's writings, and here again, his debt to Benjamin was manifested. Benjamin's experience translating Baudelaire and Proust[49] paralleled Adorno's early concern with the reproduction of music.[50] Both were mimetic activities. Literary translation and musical performance did not simply copy the original; they maintained the "aura" of the original by *transforming* it, precisely so that its truth might be preserved.[51] To mime the original in a new modality thus required "exact fantasy." As Tiedemann has noted in Benjamin's case, translation provided the model for his theory of truth because it was "simultaneously reception and spontaneity: the translator needs the model, the original, and his task is to produce a new version."[52]

Jay writes that with Adorno's and Horkheimer's first collaborative study, *Dialektik der Aufklärung* (1947), "the Frankfurt School introduced a new term into its vocabulary: mimesis."[53] (It may have been new for the Frankfurt "School," but not for Adorno.) Jay suggests a connection between their use of the term and its appearance in sociological and psychological writings of the nineteenth century.[54] Adorno documented its connection with a far older tradition: *Dialektik der Aufklärung* itself explains that mimesis had its origin in primitive magic, in the shaman's imitation of nature.[55] When magic disintegrated, mimesis survived as a principle of artistic representation.[56] Since Plato and Aristotle the concept of mimesis was integrally tied to the history of aesthetic philosophy, and, as Benjamin noted in an early essay, even its primitive, shaman-like form had been preserved in ontogenetic development: "The child imitates not only shopkeeper or teacher, but windmill and railroad train as well."[57] Benjamin viewed the development of language as an advanced level of this capacity: words imitated nature as "non-representational correspondence" (*unsinnliche Ähnlichkeiten*).[58] He regarded this ability as one of the highest human talents, and considered mimesis an "ineluctable moment in cognition."[59]

The transformational character of the mimetic moment in Adorno's theoretical method must be taken quite literally. The "inner logic" of objects (jazz music, a theater seat) was transformed into words; and conversely, words (of a popular song, of a Kierkegaard text) were transformed into "images."[60] Unlike that mere duplication of the "given" world which was the signpost of bourgeois theory, exact fantasy performed a metamorphosis, which, for all its enlightened reason, retained the faint image of a magic trick, and Adorno not accidentally could imagine his friend Benjamin in a magician's three-cornered hat.[61]

Mimetic transformation can be seen as a reversal of Kantian subjectivity. The creativity of the latter consisted in the subject's projecting onto experience its own *a priori* forms and categories, absorbing the object into itself. But Adorno's subject let the object take the lead; it formed the object only in the sense of *trans*forming it into a new modality. The language of philosophical expression was thus neither subjective intention nor an object to be manipulated, but "a third thing"; it expressed truth through configurations "as a dialectically entwined and explicatively undecipherable unity of concept and matter."[62] Truth as mimetic, linguistic representation meant calling things by their right names.

THE NAME

In Benjamin's thought the notion of the "name" played a paramount role, and its original inspiration was mystical rather than Marxist.[63] His very early writings interpreted the story of Genesis as the source of the problem of knowledge: God called the world into being with his Word; creating man in his image, he gave man the power of speech.[64]   As the name-giver of God's creatures, Adam, not Plato, was the father of philosophy.[65] But the language of Paradise was wounded by the Fall, and the babble of human language, in which words *intended* objects,[66] could not recapture the concrete knowledge of the particular provided by the name. Words lost their adequacy vis-à-vis content.[67] Although even before the Fall, nature, unlike man, was mute:

> Now her other speechlessness begins . . . . It is a metaphysical truth that all nature would begin to lament if language were granted her. . . . [A]nd where even only plants are rustling, with it is the sound of a lament. It is because she is mute that nature mourns.[68]

This theme later surfaced in Adorno's writings as well, but transformed into a Marxist frame. The statement "Language reflects the longings of the oppressed and the plight of nature"[69] and the claim "The need to lend a voice to suffering is a condition of all truth"[70] were secularizations of the Genesis myth: the source of nature's suffering was understood no longer in terms of the Fall of Man, but in terms of the rise of class oppression.[71] In late bourgeois society words had become fetishes, indifferent to the objects they signified: "It is a sign of all reification resulting from idealist consciousness that the things can be named arbitrarily. . . ."[72] True naming, in contrast, was mimetic in that it demanded precision of referents: the verbal representation of phenomena really yielded to the particularity of things, forming a one-time-only configuration.

As *critical* configurations, the constructs of Adorno's exact fantasy were polemical: they were meant to break the spell of second nature and to liquidate reified consciousness. In this sense, Marx had provided a model in *Capital*, calling commodities by name and thereby dissolving their "mystical character."[73] Adorno considered it the essence of art to provide a similar function. In 1930 he praised Brecht's play *Mahagonny* because it broke through reified concepts and *named* social truth:

> It is that [truth] of violence as the source of the present order, and of the ambivalence in which order and violence stand opposed to each other. The essences of mythical violence and mythical law are startled in *Mahagonny*. Brecht names their paradoxical simultaneity.[74]

With Benjamin the notion of the "name" was not merely polemical. It retained, even after his move to Marxism, traces of its theological origin: utopia, the return of the lost Paradise, implied the reestablishment of the divine language of names. Benjamin's focus on the overlooked art form of Baroque tragic drama, or on the seemingly insignificant historical details which come alive in his *Passagenarbeit*, reflected the hope for rescuing the phenomena from temporal extinction by redeeming them within the name. This notion of a profane redemption of things in their particularity was a constant theme in Benjamin's writing, one which, according to his most knowledgeable critic, "binds the early metaphysical phase of his thought with the later Marxist one."[75] As Adorno recalled:

> Just as his thought sought again and again to free itself of all impulse to classify, the prime image of all hope for him was in the name, of things and of men, and it is this that his reflection seeks to reconstruct.[76]

It was questionable whether the negating, polemical procedure of "naming" things was compatible with the use of language to rescue the phenomena.[77] During his dispute with Benjamin in the thirties, Adorno criticized the redemption theme in Benjamin's writings for its tendency to slip into positive theology.[78] But Adorno reintegrated Benjamin's ideas into his theory after the latter's death in 1940, and the utopian elements of mimesis − the idea of redemption and the image of utopia as the restitution of the language of names − began to emerge in his own writings in connection with the new concept of "reconciliation" (*Versöhnung*).[79]

True, the utopian future could not be affirmatively defined. However, the cognitive process which served that future could be, and it was the lack of domination and violence which the mimetic restoration of the "name" promised on the level of cognition which became so attractive to Adorno. The "name" paid attention to the object's nonidentity by identifying it as particular and unique; it imitated nature, whereas the concept subordinated it.[80] Where Benjamin had lamented the inadequacy of human language compared with the paradisical name, Adorno agreed, yet in keeping with his own "negative" theology he argued that the nonidentity implied in that inadequacy was necessary to maintain the critical tension between subject and object upon which the hope for utopia depended:[81]

> . . . the words we use will remain concepts. Their precision substitutes for the thing itself, without ever quite bringing its selfhood to mind; there is a gap between words and the things they conjure.[82]

Words as concepts could never be particular enough on their own. Yet philosophy could not do without the conceptual moment. Hence philosophy's representations of truth relied upon clusters of concepts, on continuous combinations and arrangements of words. Adorno called these cluster patterns "constellations":

> The determinable flaw in every concept makes it necessary to cite others; this is the font of the only constellations which inherited some of the hope of the name.[83]

CONSTELLATIONS

The concept of "exact fantasy" was designed to avoid the undialectical positions of subjective idealism, on the one hand, and "vulgar" materialism, on the other: strict adherence to the material guaranteed the priority of the objects; yet the active arrangement of their elements, the verbal articulation of their inner logic, rescued philosophical experience from simple duplication of the given. But this program was easier stated than achieved. The problem was how to yield to the object "exactly" without copying it, and how to arrange and transform its elements through "fantasy" without resorting to fiction.

In his 1931 speech Adorno described philosophy's task as the construction of "changing constellations," extricating this term from its astrological connotations.[84] Benjamin had originated the philosophical use of the term, even arguing that astrology itself had been progress over primitive magic: he claimed it was a nodal point in the development of the human mimetic ability, for like language, its principle was "non-representational similarity."[85] "Constellations" were a central image in the theory of knowledge which Benjamin outlined in the opening chapter of his *Trauerspiel* study.[86] Again, despite the fact that this essay was not Marxist (and not even Hegelian), it provides the key for explaining why the construction of "constellations" should be defined as the task of a "dialectical" and "materialist" philosophy.

Benjamin began his study of German Baroque tragedy with an essay which, fusing elements of Kant and Plato, sought to articulate the philosophical experience of truth. Already in 1918 he had outlined the direction of this theory, in the then unpublished piece, "On the Program of the Coming Philosophy" (*Über das Programm der kommenden Philosophie*). Here Benjamin praised Kant for being the only philosopher since Plato to concern himself with the justification of knowledge; yet he criticized the limited nature of Kant's concept of experience, its "religious and historical blindness,"[87] and thus its inadequacy when confronted with the transitoriness of the phenomena, on the one hand, and their "religious" or noumenal truth, on the other. Exposed through Scholem to the mystic's idea of experiencing matter as revelation, and claiming the "virtual unity of religion and philosophy,"[88] he believed this inadequacy could be corrected "on the ground of the Kantian system,"[89] and this was precisely what he attempted in the first chapter ("Erkenntniskritische Vorrede") of the *Trauerspiel* study. In a remarkable inversion of Platonism, Benjamin presented a theory of "ideas" which he referred to as "constellations" that was compatible with Kantian empiricism. The theory was abstruse, and aspects of it were wedded to a religiomysticism which Adorno never incorporated,[90] yet certain other aspects of it in fact cannot be ignored if Adorno's theory is to be understood properly. At the risk of oversimplification and in full awareness of the difficulties of the text,[91] an interpretation of Benjamin's *Trauerspiel* theory of ideas must be attempted.

The *Trauerspiel* essay distinguished between the Kantian concept of experience as "knowledge" (*Erkenntnis*), the cognitive method of which was adequate for science, and what he called philosophical "experience" (*Erfahrung*), which was concerned with the revelation of truth. In the former case, the subject constituted the world in accord with its own conceptual structures; in the latter, the subject constituted "ideas" whose structure was objective, determined by the particular phenomena themselves, by the "elective affinities" of their elements, to use Goethe's term;[92] in Adorno's language, by their "inner logic." Kantian knowledge was "possession";[93] it entailed breaking reality apart so that it could be subsumed under the concepts which "issue from out of the spontaneity of understanding."[94] But philosophical experience was the "representation of ideas" (*Darstellung der Ideen*)[95] from out of empirical reality itself. And yet concepts played a role here, too, as mediators between the empirically given phenomena and their ideas:

> The phenomena, however, do not enter whole into the realm of the ideas, not in their raw empirical existence, mixed as it is with mere appearance (*Schein*), but they are redeemed alone in their elements. . . . In this partitioning of them, the phenomena stand under concepts. It is the concepts which carry out the unravelling of the phenomena into their elements.[96]

The conceptualizing subject acted as mediator in arranging the phenomenal elements (or, perhaps more correctly, provided the linguistic medium through which their arrangement was transmitted) so that the relationships between them became visible to the intellect, so that they formed an "idea" which could be mentally perceived. It was the fate of the phenomena in the hands of the concept, rather than conceptualizing *per se*, which marked the crucial difference between cognitive knowledge and the philosophical representation of truth.[97] The former was achieved by means of abstraction: the particular entered into the concept and disappeared. But in truth's representation, the particulars, although conceptually mediated, reemerged in the idea; or more accurately, they *became* the idea in the conceptual arrangement of their elements.[98] The role of the subject,[99] to draw connections between the phenomenal elements, was not unlike that of the astrologer, who perceived figures in the heavens: "Ideas are related to the phenomena as constellations to the stars."[100]

The ideas were nothing but the empirical phenomena, and at the same time, as "constellations," they were more. This was where Plato and Kant converged in Benjamin's theory, what gave his theory of ideas a unique, Kantian twist. For if Platonic ideas were absolute, transcendental forms whose likeness appeared within the empirical objects as a pale reflection of their own eternal truth, Benjamin constructed the absolute from out of the empirical fragments themselves. The smallest, most transitory particulars were the stuff and substance of the ideas. Adorno wrote in an essay on Benjamin:

> The later Nietzsche's critical insight that truth is not identical with a timeless *universal*, but rather that it is solely the historical which yields the figure of the absolute, became, perhaps without his knowing it, the canon of his practice. The programme is formulated in a note to his fragmentary main work, that "in any case the eternal is more like lace trimmings on a dress than like an idea" [in the traditional Platonic sense].[101]

In Plato the ideas as truth appear in the phenomena. Benjamin's theory was an inversion of Plato: the phenomena appear as truth in the ideas, so that the "dignity"[102] of the transitory particulars is maintained. More, they are immortalized. Benjamin intended nothing less than their "redemption" (*Rettung* – the word was intentionally religious) by catching their elements up in the structure of an idea as an "eternal constellation."[103] Thus the two things, "the redemption of the phenomena and the representation of the ideas,"[104] were to occur simultaneously.

Adorno was less concerned with the fate of the phenomena than he was intrigued by the originality of Benjamin's method and its usefulness for his own program. For without positing a metaphysical realm beyond the historically transient, behind or above physical existence in some noumenal or ideal being, Benjamin's theory confronted the metaphysical question as to the truth, the essence of reality, attempting to read its answer in the empirical elements themselves. To use Kant's language, the *phenomenal* realm was made to yield *noumenal* knowledge – precisely what Kant had claimed was impossible. Avoiding the pitfalls of speculative dogmatism, but also those of positivism and historicism, Benjamin's *Trauerspiel* theory provided a groundwork for nothing less than nonmetaphysical metaphysics.[105] Small wonder that Adorno, metaphysician in an antimetaphysical age, was so struck by the *Trauerspiel* chapter.

Moreover, even if mystical elements were undeniably present in the *Trauerspiel* study, Benjamin (who had been introduced to Marxism by Asja Lacis before its publication) was quite aware that the radicality of his theory lay in its antiidealism. Benjamin criticized the metaphysical systems-builders (he mentioned specifically Plato, Leibniz, and Hegel) for undervaluing the empirical realm and viewing truth and being as nonempirical absolutes:

> Common to all these attempts is, namely, that they retain their meaning even when, indeed they are often first developed to a higher power only when, in place of being related to the empirical world, they are related to the world of ideas.[107]

Beginning in the late twenties, Adorno as well as Benjamin[108] worked to develop the *Trauerspiel* theory within a Marxian context as an alternative to bourgeois idealism. Adorno's inaugural lecture clearly documents this attempt.[109] It virtually equates materialism with the construction of ideas as constellations:

> Interpretation of the unintentional through the juxtaposition of elements isolated by analysis and the illumination of reality by the power of such interpretation; that is the program of every genuine materialist knowledge. . . .[110]

Adorno could appreciate the fact that Benjamin's *Trauerspiel* method was "immanent," not only in its refusal to transcend the realm of phenomenal elements (hence its "exactness") but also in its dialectical relationship to the history of philosophy. For its originality was achieved not by ignoring the past, but by altering traditional concepts, dialectically reversing their relationships and challenging "second nature" shibboleths. When Benjamin treated the phenomenal elements as absolutes while viewing the ideas, and hence truth, as historically specific and changing, he was inverting the long-established Platonic conception; when he used empirical reality in constructing a metaphysics, he fused the "intelligible" and empirical realms which Kant saw as unalterably opposed. As for the term "constellation," he had brought it down to earth, turning a prescientific concept into a tool for materialist enlightenment. Against Heidegger, who felt a radical reorientation of philosophy permitted, even necessitated, a new philosophical vocabulary, Benjamin argued that "the introduction of new terms" was a "dubious" procedure; instead, the old language ought to be "renewed."[111] That philosophy could not "start from scratch" was, as we have seen,[112] a cardinal point in Adorno's inaugural speech. And, in an unpublished essay of the same period, he echoed Benjamin's criticism:

> Heidegger's language takes flight from history, yet without escaping it. . . . The traditional terminology, no matter how shattered, is to be preserved,

and new words of philosophers arise today solely out of changing the configuration of the words which stand within history, not by inventing a language. . . ."[113]

Where Adorno attempted to "redeem" elements of the past, it was in the dialectical sense, as "sublation" (*Aufhebung*), Hegel's notoriously untranslatable term which means simultaneously "preservation" and "negation." Adorno's use of the philosophical past against itself, his immanent criticism of traditional concepts to foster the liquidation of tradition, was distinct from the theological desire of Benjamin, literally to resurrect the phenomena by bringing them to speech, rescuing them through the name from historical obliteration.[114] It was not because it resurrected German tragic drama that Adorno in a 1934 letter to Benjamin praised the *Trauerspiel* study, but because "you have in the Baroque-book redeemed induction."[115] Benjamin's method was indeed inductive at the same time that it was not the old induction which, as he explicitly noted in the *Trauerspiel* chapter, built general concepts by abstracting similarities from diverse phenomena rather than constructing the general from out of the disparate particulars themselves. Traditional induction, like deduction (its only apparent opposite), assuming a "pseudo-logical continuum"[116] between the particular and the general, proceeded by classification and systematization, both of which were incompatible with Benjamin's approach. In his theory each "idea," each construction out of the particular, was self-contained. As a "monad," each contained the totality, a "picture of the world," yet each differed from every other idea.[117] Constellations were "discontinuous."[118] Like atoms, like cells, like solar systems[119] they each had their own center: without hierarchy, they stood next to each other "in perfect independence and unimpaired."[120] It followed that in constructing ideas it was continuously necessary to return to the phenomena themselves,[121] the more so as the ideas were not eternal but historically specific constellations. Hence philosophical description "begins anew with every idea."[122] Such a fragmental approach fulfilled the technical requirements of philosophy as a "logic of disintegration," and it determined the form of philosophical representation. Adorno in 1931 wrote that the essay, the self-contained, undogmatic "attempt" to extrapolate significance from the one-time-only particular or detail, needed to be reinstated from its present debasement as a lesser aesthetic form[123] and made the medium for the new philosophy.

That for Adorno "redemption" meant sublation, not just preserving elements of the past but transforming them through negation, is important to keep in mind here where the *Trauerspiel* origins of his theory are being discussed. For if Benjamin had to change the meaning of "induction" in order to redeem it, Adorno had similar plans for redeeming the *Trauerspiel* theory. This fact is a primary source of the difficulties in interpreting Adorno's 1931 speech, as it uses language identical to that of the Kabbalah-influenced *Trauerspiel* chapter to express a *non*identical content: By changing the configuration of the words Adorno translated Benjamin's mystic-influenced theory into a "dialectical," "materialist" one.

Adorno in his inaugural lecture made the same distinction as Benjamin between knowledge as the collection of data and philosophy as the representation of truth: "Plainly put: the idea of knowledge [Wissenschaft] is research; that of philosophy is interpretation."[124]

> He continued: "The task of philosophy is not to search for concealed and manifest intentions of reality, but to interpret the unintentional reality in that, by the power of constructing figures, images, out of the isolated elements of reality, it negates [*aufhebt*] questions whose exact articulation is the task of knowledge.[125]

Knowledge gathered through research was science, conceptualizing the "given" in a way which made its philosophical interpretation possible. But Adorno transformed Benjamin's original conception of the latter by "refunctioning" it with the aid of Marxist theory: now the idea, the "essence" of a phenomenon, was its historically specific *social* content. As Adorno later wrote:

> The [Marxian] theory of society arose out of philosophy, while at the same time it attempts to refunction [*umfunktionieren*] the latter's formulations of questions by defining society as its substratum which in traditional philosophy is called eternal essences or spirit [*Geist*].[126]

Chapter 6.   The Method in Action: Constructing Constellations

PRINCIPLES OF CONSTRUCTION

Each of Adorno's essays articulates an "idea" in Benjamin's sense of constructing a specific, concrete constellation out of the elements of the phenomenon,[1] and it does so in order that the sociohistorical reality which constitutes its truth becomes physically visible within it. The fact that social "essence" (*Wesen*) emerges from the appearance (*Schein*) of the phenomena sounds dialectical in the Hegelian-Marxist sense. But Adorno's meaning was really closer to the phenomenological notion of cognitive experience developed by Husserl in which essence appeared under the intellect's gaze. When Marx set out to "decipher" the mystery of commodities, he noted explicitly that their true nature was "imperceptible," that it had "absolutely no connection with their physical qualities."[2] And consequently, in order to understand them it was necessary to analyze the relations and forces of production behind the commodities. Adorno's interpretations were only marginally concerned with economic determinants of production. His central effort was to discover the truth of the social totality (which could never be experienced in itself) as it quite literally *appeared* within the object in a particular configuration.

As the phenomena interpreted by Adorno in each case differed, so did the construction process; "to regroup" (*umgruppieren*)[3] the elements was a continuously renewed attempt to picture the essence of society. Although Adorno's method of construction was not a formal one which can be divorced from its specific application, it is nonetheless possible to discern certain components in the process and principles governing the assembly of constellations. Adorno, understandably, only hinted at these in his philosophical program,[4] yet his works during the thirties embodied their concrete application. If overschematization, inimicable to Adorno's thinking, is to be avoided, it is at least possible to clarify the compositional principles of his theory by seeing them in action. Indeed, it is necessary if Adorno's idiosyncratic use of terms is not to acquire a fetish character of its own.

The phenomenal "elements" presented themselves in the "riddle-figures of that which exists"[5] as components of the concrete particulars. Adorno referred to them as "codes" or "ciphers" (*Chiffren*)[6] of social reality, which contained the bourgeois social and psychological structure in monadological abbreviation, but which needed philosophical interpretation so that their perplexing, given form could be "deciphered" (*dechiffriert*). The particular phenomena were seemingly insignificant (jazz, a popular song), the fleeting event (a concert performance), the easily overlooked details (a fragment of a philosophical text, a musical transition). The elements of these phenomena, the "ciphers," were their structural components — for jazz the specific musical material, technical elements of form and rhythm, performance; for a concert the particulars of place, the relationship between players and audience; for a text the individual words, phrases, images, and their juxtapositions. The phenomena first needed to be broken up, their relevant components isolated and conceptualized, and here philosophy depended on the humanistic and social sciences, whose task it was to research and analyze the empirical data in a way that made them accessible to philosophical deciphering. Philosophy's success was thus dependent upon the adequacy of this process, through which were developed what Adorno called "key categories": "Interpretive philosophy depends on the construction of keys before which reality springs open. But the size of the keys is specially made to order."[7] Not just any categories would do: some were too large to fit the lock; others too small to open it.[8] But if Adorno's language echoed the familiar fairy tale, the real meaning of his message was clear: the keys necessary for "igniting the illuminating power of philosophy"[9] were not the classificatory categories of bourgeois sociology (of, e.g., Karl Mannheim), but the critical[10] categories of Marxist theory: its concepts of class,[11] ideology, and commodity structure (fetish character, exchange value, reification). And, although psychoanalytic categories were not mentioned as "keys" in the 1931 lecture, Adorno's writings in the thirties also (and increasingly)[12] made critical use of Freud's concepts (ego weakness, anxiety, anal character, sadomasochism) to illuminate the psychological aspects of a society based on class and commodity structure.

Adorno's simultaneous use of categories from Freud and Marx was dialectical in that the categories affected each other, resulting in the modification of both. He thus demonstrated the sociohistorical particularity of psychological phenomena conceptualized by Freud, at the same time making visible the psychological determinants of social conditions. Such a juxtaposition, despite the fact that Freud and Marx were in many ways incompatible theorists, was characteristic of Adorno. For his aim was not to develop a theoretical synthesis, but to decipher a contradictory reality. Consider the following:

In decoding a musical phenomenon, the familiar C sharp minor Prelude by Rachmaninoff, Adorno focused on two elements: it sounded grandiose, yet it was childishly easy to play. With the aid of Freud, he interpreted the great appeal of this "constellation of heavy bombardment [*schweres Geschütz*] and easy performability":[13]

> Psychoanalysts have discovered the Nero complex. The Prelude has antici-
> pated its gratification. It allows delusions of grandeur to have their fling,
> without being caught. . . . Daring and security are mixed together in this,
> one of the most glaring cases of daydreams in music.[14]

At the same time, Adorno made the piece's social function perceptible within
the musical material itself. The entire prelude was "one single closing cadence."[15]
The closing cadence, a romantic gesture, functioned in music to affirm what
came before it. Here, where it was the whole of the compositional material, the
affirmation was "fully emancipated from all musical content and thrown onto
the market as a commodity."[16] Thus fetishized, the cadence repeated itself like
a "relentless commercial."[17]

Similarly, in his book on Wagner, Adorno saw the musical production of
leitmotifs as an anticipation of the production of commercial advertisements.[18]
And alongside this sociological insight, he introduced a Freudian category: the
repetitious *leitmotif* was obsessive-compulsive.

> One cannot break free from it. . . . It is the external projection of that
> which is secretly subjective and thereby alienated from the ego, [a projec-
> tion] in which, as in its own foolish fancy, the ego loses itself. The Wag-
> nerian leitmotif remains imprisoned in this source. . . . What psychology a
> hundred years later christened ego-weakness, is already taken into account
> in the Wagnerian method of composition.[19]

In all of these cases, instead of being *subsumed under* a Marxian or Freudian
category, the phenomena were interpreted as themselves concrete and physical
representations of the categories. This means that while the concept (the subject's input) was unlocking the riddle, the "riddle-figure," the object itself, was
providing an image of the concept. This notion of the phenomenon as an
"image" rather than a symbol[20] or example of the concept, including the idea
of their dialectical, reciprocal interrelationship (paralleling the polar relationship
between exactness and fantasy, or mimesis and transformation), had its own
history, threading (not without snags) through the fabric of his friendship with
Benjamin. But before looking at it more closely,[21] we need to illustrate concretely the principles by which Adorno's constellations were assembled.

The structure of Adorno's essays was the antithesis of commodity structure.
The form of commodities, as Marx had explained in the first chapter of *Capital*,
was governed by principles of abstraction (of exchange value from use value),
identity (of all commodities with each other through the medium of money),
and reification (ossification of the object as a mystifying fetish by splitting it off
from the process of its production).[22] Adorno's constellations, in contrast, were
constructed according to principles of differentiation, nonidentity, and active
transformation. Differentiation as a compositional procedure meant articulating
nuances which pinpointed the concrete, qualitative differences between apparently similar phenomena.[23] Adorno asserted that "nowhere do essences
separate more sharply than where they come closest to each other."[24] This

principle is the source of much apparent ambiguity in Adorno's writings, for it implied that phenomenal "elements" had no absolute value, no constant meaning, if torn out of the context of their particular manifestations. It was thus impossible to speak in the abstract of what made, e.g., "good" art or "progressive" theory, as if a set of attributes could be capsulized in a definition and then found either present or lacking in any particular case. Conversely, the fact that Adorno judged specific qualities positively in one constellation and negatively in another makes it impossible, in turn, to capsulize his own thinking and is a cause of the elusiveness, the resistance of his writings to categorization within any particular intellectual pigeonhole. A small example will illustrate this point: a childlike quality in music was not interpreted uniformly as progressive or regressive. Discussing this same element in the music of three composers, Adorno clarified the difference:

> Debussy's child-likeness was a game of the man who knows himself and his own limits; Stravinsky's is an oblique attack on the grown-up world; Ravel's alone was the aristocratic sublimation of sorrow.[25]

In the first case, the childlike quality connotes the cynicism of bourgeois self-consciousness; in the second, the powerlessly rebellious perspective of youth; in Ravel's "aristocratic" music it is the constellation of play and grief, an interrelation of opposites which, Adorno implied, in its embodiment of contradiction came closest of the three representations to an awareness of truth.[26]

A variation of this principle of differentiation was turning a word or concept against the phenomenon it was intended to signify. We have already encountered this dialectical device in Adorno's speech on the "idea" of natural history (— the reason for his choice of words should now be clear): "nature" was seen to be not at all natural, and history as it actually unfolded was no "history" in any meaningful sense.[27] Such negations of tautological truths appear frequently in Adorno's essays ("life does not live";[28] gratification is the enemy of gratification[29]) where they function to set the constellation and critical thinking in motion.

If one of the fulchrums of Adorno's dialectical argumentation was to break apart the apparently identical by means of specific differentiation, a second was the reverse of this principle: to juxtapose seemingly unrelated, unidentical elements, revealing the configuration in which they congealed or converged. Construction of similarities out of opposites by a "juxtaposition of extremes" had been advocated and applied by Walter Benjamin in the *Trauerspiel* study:

> And indeed, those elements whose release from the phenomena is the task of the concept are most accurately manifested in the extremes. The idea is transcribed as a relational configuration in which the one-of-a-kind stands among its own ilk.[30]

When Adorno introduced nature in order to give history, its polar opposite, true representation, when he pointed to their convergence in the moment of transiency,[31] he was following Benjamin's inspiration. The assumption which underlay this principle (assumed also in Marx's notion of social antagonisms and the Freudian concept of ambivalence) was that reality was itself contradictory, that its elements formed no harmonious whole, not even within one particular phenomenon. Constellations were constructed to make this essentially contradictory character visible: in his "representation of the sociohistorical phenomenon of jazz,"[32] a phenomenon he called "the utterly alienated [appearing] as the utterly familiar,"[33] Adorno interpreted its "origin"[34] in a configuration of the extremes of salon music (the sentimental intimacy of the strolling violinist) and the military march:

> The former represents an individuality, which in truth is no such thing, but rather its socially produced appearance; the latter is an equally fictional collective, which is constructed by nothing else but using force to line up atoms in a row.[35]

"Juxtaposing extremes" meant discovering not only the similarity of opposites but also the connecting links (the "inner logic") between seemingly unrelated elements of a phenomenon. To illustrate: Adorno saw three apparently unconnected components of Wagner's operas, "envy, sentimentality and destructive impulse," congeal in a "configuration" which he interpreted as a "pre-form" of the bourgeois personality's "transformation in the totalitarian era."[36] Further, these elements were themselves contradictory; in each of them was a convergence of extremes which revealed that Wagner's "radicalism" was really conservative: "envy" of bourgeois supremacy was the proper name for Wagner's social protest; his sentimentality glorified the beggar but also the ruler; his destructive impulse turned sexuality into the death instinct — "physical desire and death become one."[37] Adorno located Wagner's anti-Semitism in the extremes of sadism and masochism: "the contradiction between derision toward the victim and self-denunciation."[38]

A favorite technique of Adorno, which, like the juxtaposition of extremes, illuminated truth as contradictory instead of eliminating contradictions as untrue, was to turn ideological statements into critical ones by transposing the sequence of their "elements," i.e., the words themselves: for example, his statement "The truth is not in history; history is in the truth."[39] The special appeal of this technique was that it satisfied concretely the demand that critical interpretation remain "immanent," adhering strictly to the elements under scrutiny.

The meat-and-potatoes principle of dialectical logic was, of course, that what appeared to be one thing was essentially its opposite, and Adorno's writings contain their fair share of this Hegelian staple. His 1936 analysis of jazz was structured largely by such arguments: jazz's "individualism" was shown to be stereotyped, its "improvisation" standardized; its use value was really exchange value; its syncopation was repetitious uniformity; its "objectivity" (*Sachlichkeit*) was in fact ornamentation; jazz appeared democratic but was really totalitarian; its eroticism was a new repression; masked as the future collective, it was in fact a return of the primitive, "the music of slaves."[40] This dialectical technique was most in keeping with the approach of the Frankfurt Institute (in whose journal the jazz essay appeared). But where Adorno demonstrated his unique capacity for analysis, as well as the intensity of Benjamin's influence, was in interpreting the very smallest phenomena, extracting like splinters from their most specific components recognizable fragments of the bourgeois social structure.

It is often in his minor writings that this skill appears most strikingly. In "Especially for You,"[41] a short article Adorno wrote in the thirties, the "phenomenon" was an American hit song. Adorno noted two contradictory elements: its existence as a commodity of mass culture and the personalized message of its title. The paradox could be seen within the words of the song themselves:

> *Especially for you* that's what a moon's for
> *Especially for you* that's what a June's for[42]

More than mere ideology, the lie of the lyrics unintentionally spoke a social truth: of course neither moon nor June was there especially for the individual, and the same was true of the relation between a popular song and its audience. The song producers had no more concern for the customer's real interests than "that moon interests the dog that howls at it . . ."[43] (while the consumer had no real choice but to howl along in unison). In the apparently unrelated juxtaposition of elements on the sheet music itself, Adorno again read social content: the song title was followed by the U.S. copyright law warning of criminal prosecution for the violation of private property:

> The man who might get it into his head that something is there especially for him and therefore bought the song in the first place will thereafter no longer fall into the mistake of thinking it belongs to him.[44]

Now Adorno reversed the words, echoing Marx's analysis of commodities "He belongs to the product, not vice versa," and concluded with another reversal, showing the law-abiding individual as himself imprisoned: "If he wanted to change something he would be locked up, that is, if he were not locked up already."[45]

Adorno didn't write essays, he *composed* them, and he was a virtuoso in the dialectical medium. His verbal compositions express an "idea" through a sequence of dialectical reversals and inversions. The sentences develop like musical themes: they break apart and turn in on themselves in a continuing spiral of variations. The phenomena are viewed as Freud viewed dream symbols: They are "overdetermined," so that their contradictory complexity needs to be disentangled through interpretation. But there is no affirmation, no "closing cadence." The contradictions are unraveled; they are not resolved.

HISTORICAL IMAGES

There were two moments in the dialectical process of constructing constellations. One was conceptual-analytical, breaking apart the phenomenon, isolating its elements, and mediating them by means of critical concepts. The other was representational, bringing the elements together in such a way that social reality became visible within them. In the analytical process, the phenomenal elements were viewed as a code language, "ciphers" of sociohistorical truth, whose translation into the conceptual language of Marx and Freud provided their interpretation, making it possible to "transform" them into a readable text.[46] Here visibly "given" objects were translated into the terms of a nonvisible social process. But in the moment of representation, the reverse occurred: the elements "fall into a figure";[47] they congealed into a visible image of the conceptual terms. In constructing "trial combinations" of the elements, this moment brought the dialectical motion to a standstill, but not, as with Hegel, because the antagonisms had been overcome. The images illuminated contradictions rather than negating or sublating them; the procedure was one of mimetic representation rather than synthesis. I spoke earlier of the arranged elements of the object providing an "image" of the concept. Adorno meant by this, simply, that as the visible world was interpreted analytically by Marxian and Freudian concepts, these concepts themselves became visible in the world. In this sense, constellations were not unlike hieroglyphs, uniting the perceptual and conceptual; the phenomena became rebuses, riddles whose qualitative elements, juxtaposed, were the concepts translated into picture form.[48]

The notion of the "visibility" of truth, which does not show up in the writings of Horkheimer[49] (or the members of his Institute), must be understood quite literally: the "images" were not symbols of the concepts, not poetic analogies for the social totality, but the real, material manifestation of both of them. "Images" were empirical, perceptible evidence of the mediated relationship between the particular and the bourgeois social structure. This conception might appear esoteric in its convolutions, and, paradoxically, childlike in its concreteness. In fact, like many of Benjamin's inspirations, it was both.

Already in the *Trauerspiel* chapter Benjamin had spoken of ideas as monadological "images" (*Bilder*) of the world, a "stage" (*Schauplatz*) for the representation of reality. Images resembled allegories; indeed, they were like the very Baroque tragic dramas Benjamin was interpreting, in which "the temporal motion of events is caught up in a three-dimensional picture and analysed."[50]

In his 1931 address, Adorno christened them "historical images" (*geschichtliche Bilder*), so that there was no doubt as to their predominantly objective nature and their sociohistorical specificity.[51] At the same time Benjamin was working on his own revision of the original conception, for which he coined the term "dialectical images." As a tool for analysis, the promise of these constructions lay in their potential for avoiding "vulgar" Marxist reductionism on the one hand and pseudo-Marxist idealism on the other: the images were objective, they really existed; but they needed the activity of subjective fantasy to be discovered. Adorno described them in his inaugural lecture:

> These images are not simply self-given. They do not lie organically ready in history; no gaze [*Schau*] and no intuition [both Husserlian terms] are

required to become aware of them; they are not magically sent by the gods to be taken in and venerated. Rather, they must be produced by human beings. . . .[52]

Yet promise was one thing and realization another. The dialectical "production" of "objective" images was problematic, and its actualization became a central point in Adorno's dispute with Benjamin in the thirties.[53]

At birth, however, Adorno's "historical" and Benjamin's "dialectical" images were close fraternal twins. They often combined philosophical subtlety with a certain playfulness, a delight in those double entendres and unexpected juxtapositions which were the source of humor in puns, or picture puzzles like "Spot the Object." These optical puzzles are called *Vexierbilder* in German, which was how Benjamin described the fragments he published as *Einbahnstrasse* (1928).[54] Adorno used the term in his own writings: interpreting Dvořák's "Humoresque," Adorno recalled a *Vexierbild* on the newspaper puzzle page picturing an empty house on an empty street in the rain, with the question, "Where is the burglar?"

> One had to keep turning the thing around, on its sides, on its head, until one discovered that somewhere the line of rain with a rough-built chimney portrayed a grimace which let itself be apprehended. The memory of these *Vexierbilder* is preserved in Dvořák's example of the musical genre. Where is the humor?[55]

Adorno answered that it had fled the scene of the music and was hiding as a barely perceptible grin in the title alone. The piece was an image of bourgeois false consciousness:

> Quaint: the piece was written somewhere in America, and a memorial was placed on the spot. But the knowing flicker at the corners of the mouth, as the memorial of which the Humoresque itself survives, is the readiness once again to understand all presently existing vileness, in order all the better then to be able to excuse it.[56]

Analogies and metaphors only pretended likeness, but historical images were authentic replications. Like translations,[57] they were mimetic transformations; they *named* where the analogy signified, where the concept only "intended." Hence the "whimpering vibrato" of the jazz instrumentalist *was* the bourgeois subject's helplessness;[58] the social irrationality which determined the fate of a popular song *was* the irrationality of the stock market.[59] Vividly, in the layout of the bourgeois theater, Adorno claimed one could *see* the structure and attributes of class relations: the physical arrangement of seats provided a perceptible image. In the orchestra sat the bourgeoisie,

> . . . all placed on the same slanted [*schief*][60] level, and each carefully separated from the other by armrests. Their *liberté* is that of open competition: to interfere with the others and hog the best view of the stage. Their *fraternité* emanates from the long rows of seats where each seat looks like the other and yet all remain secluded and unperturbed within the order of

things. Their *egalité* is bounded by the hierarchy of place and price. But it is invisible. The seats in the first and second row don't look any different.

The seats are folding chairs. With their red cushion covers they preserve the recollection of the private boxes: for the orchestra dwellers advance to the ruling class of the world.[61]

The private boxes were reserved for the nobility, the ruling class of the feudal era, now obsolete, peripheral to economic production and the resulting class structure. Yet [like the Prussian Junkers around Hindenberg — the year was 1932] they still exerted power behind the scenes:

> The boxes are inhabited by ghosts. They have lived there since 1880, or since the *Ringtheater* burned down. They haven't bought tickets, but possess pre-historic subscriptions, gilded patents of nobility, consigned to them by God knows whom. Like true ghosts they are confined to their place. They can sit in no other seat: either they remain here, or disappear. They are separated from all the living in the theater. But a concealed door leads from them into the machinery caverns behind the scenes. Sometimes, they still give the great prima-donna a champagne supper between the acts, and no one sees it. True boxes are dark.[62]

Was Adorno's theater image meant to transform Plato's allegory of the cave into a socially specific, historical image? The contemporary audience watched the illusion of reality on the stage, just as the cave inhabitants viewed their own shadows on the wall. But in the top tier of the balcony, farthest away from the stage and hence least taken in by its illusions, sat not only Plato's "philosophers," the intellectuals who understood the performance, but the lower class. For these were the cheapest seats in the house, close to the eaves, where the occupants

> . . . know all the better that the roof above them is not tightly fastened, and await whether or not they will one day explode it and bring about a union between stage and reality. . . . Today, when the stage is bound by the text and the audience by bourgeois morality, the balcony remains the only place in the theater of true improvisation: it has entrenched itself on the outermost borders of the theater-space, builds its barricades out of the wood of the folding chairs.[63]

The theater, then, *was* society in its historically present form. The audience was urged to look away from the illusions performed on the stage and see the theater itself as a stage for the performance of social reality.

Similarly, under Adorno's interpretive gaze, the jazz performer became the "stage" for a dramatic documentation of the individual's relation to society. An analysis of the historical figure of the "jazz-subject" culminates Adorno's article on jazz for the *Zeitschrift für Sozialforschung* (written 1936, published 1937). When the article was republished in 1964[64] this section was set apart at the close of the essay (which uses more standard dialectical principles of argumentation to lay bare the ideological content of jazz), marking his own uniqueness among the critical theorists of the Frankfurt Institute.[65] When the jazz performer, the "subject," made temporary "breaks" away from the chorus-like repetitions of the music, he portrayed the reality of the constraints society imposed upon him. Thus the jazz subject

> . . . falls out of the collective like syncopation out of the respectable measured beats; out of protest or incompetence, he does not wish to become a member of the given majority which exists prior to and independent of him, until, in the end, he is received by special grace of the collective, or better, is fit into it; indeed, until the music, concluding with a rounding-off phrase, ironically gives evidence that he was in it from the beginning; that he is himself a piece of this society and actually can't fall out of it at all; in fact that his apparent bungling is actually the virtuosity of adapting; that his inability in every sense, and certainly the sexual only to begin with, means precisely being able to, means that he can also adapt; indeed, can do it better.[66]

Adorno claimed that the "eccentric" was the origin,[67] the historical archetype of the jazz subject. The clown (a closely related figure) refused by the immediacy of his gestures to conform to the bourgeoisie's "reified life," becoming laughable but making the latter appear laughable as well.

> . . . the eccentric, of course, falls just as much out of the goal-oriented regularity — the "rhythm" — of bourgeois life. . . . But his falling out discloses itself at once: not as impotence, but as superiority. . . . The rhythm of his arbitrariness fits smoothly into a larger, legitimate one . . . : being obedient to the law and nonetheless different.[68]

Adorno interpreted this constellation of contradictory elements: obedience and superiority, protest and conformity, within the musical material itself (with the felicitious aid of a Freudian key category). The syncopation, the rhythmic category of the "eccentric,"

> . . . is not like that of Beethoven, its opposite, which rises up against the existing law until it produces from out of it a new one. It is purposeless; it leads nowhere, and is arbitrarily revoked through a dialectical, mathematical conversion of time-counts which leaves no remainder. It is merely coming-too-early, just as anxiety leads to premature ejaculation, as impotence expresses itself in premature and incomplete orgasm.[69]

The apparent superiority of the jazz subject's improvisation was thus only proof of his impotence. Jazz was not merely ideology: the "decisively radical tendency of jazz" was that its own inner logic expressed a real social contradiction:

> . . . that this weak subject, precisely because of his weakness, indeed, as if in reward for it, fits exactly that collective which made him so weak, and whose norms his weakness cannot satisfy.[70]

The relationship between solo "break" and refrain *was* the relationship between bourgeois individual and the social totality. This social truth was precisely what the form and content of jazz whispered in the ear of an interpreter whose exact fantasy could succeed in bringing it to speech.[71] Adorno concluded with a description which spelled out the logic of fascist submission:

> Psychologically, jazz accomplishes the squaring of the circle. The arbitrary individual, as a member of the bourgeois class, is himself essentially forfeited to blind social law. To the degree that he now learns to fear social judgment, experiencing it as a threat of castration — in its immediate form, as anxiety over impotence — he identifies himself with the judgment he must fear, thus, however, belongs to it himself and is allowed to dance in unison. The sex appeal of jazz is a [military] command; follow orders, and then you yourself can give them; and the dream thought, as full of contradictions as the reality in which it is dreamt, becomes: When I allow myself to be robbed of my manhood, only then do I become potent.[72]

The original inspiration for interpreting historical "figures," like the jazz performer or eccentric, as a "stage" upon which images of social reality appeared seems to have been Benjamin's. Certainly he carried the whole notion of "images" the farthest. His first conception of the *Passagenarbeit* (1928) involved educing from the figure of the gambler images which "were to decipher historically-philosophically the phantasmagoria of the nineteenth century as the figure of hell."[73] In Benjamin's *Einbahnstrasse* (1928), a collection of "thought-images,"[74] the fragmentary thoughts, memories, even dreams of the author himself became the stage for images of impersonal, objective reality.[75] And if here subjective experiences were dialectically interpreted for their objective content, in the Proust-like remembrances of *Berliner Kindheit* (1930) Benjamin also reversed the process: objects (telephone, crooked street, lectern) were dissolved so that their "inner history," the subjective experience congealed within them, was released. In 1930 Benjamin wrote that what distinguished the Enlightenment thinker from the dialectical materialist was that the latter not only pointed out contradictions (as had Kant), but was able to show the point at which thesis and antithesis converged. "Dialectical images" were meant to illuminate this point.[76] Benjamin's images functioned like switches, arresting the fleeting phenomena and starting thought in motion or, alternately, shocking thought to a standstill and setting the reified objects in motion by causing them to lose their second-nature familiarity.

Increasingly, he began to rely on them alone in his writings. In the thirties, exiled in Paris, Benjamin revised his plan for the *Passagenarbeit*. It was to be a "panorama of dialectical images"[77] elicited from figures of the collector, the prostitute, the *flâneur,* the conspirator, as well as the gambler, and from the historical phenomena of fashion, photography, iron construction, glass architecture, the bourgeois *intérieur.*[78] As a kaleidoscope of constellations, they were to illuminate not the heavens beyond, but the world of the past: Paris, the capital city of the nineteenth century, and of course, one could add, the city of capital. Out of the fragments of its history (which he unearthed as an inveterate frequenter of the *Bibliothèque Nationale*), Benjamin "intended to construct the idea of the epoch in the sense of an ur-history of modernity."[80]

The term "ur-history" (*Urgeschichte*)[81] appears interchangeably with "natural history" (*Nat-urgeschichte*) in Benjamin's *Trauerspiel* study. By the time of the *Passagenarbeit*, he used the former term almost exclusively.[82] And yet its meaning closely paralleled Adorno's 1932 interpretation of history as nature (i.e., as repetition, hence not "history" at all).[83] But whereas the staticness of bourgeois society was adequately expressed by the notion of (second) nature, reference to the modern as "archaic" suggested more: that present "civilization" pressed dangerously close to being barbarism itself. Benjamin's "ur-history" of the nineteenth century

> . . . was designed not somehow to uncover archaic rudiments in the most recent past,[84] but to define the most modern itself as a figure of the most archaic.[85]

Against the reality of Hitler's consolidation of power, the theme of the modern as archaic was not merely a polemical one; increasingly it became a description of the empirical course of events.[86] But if bourgeois culture, like bourgeois commodities, revealed all the attributes of myth and mystification and if Hitler's own myth of the Führer made use of the psychological impotence which resulted, then these were still to be understood as historical phenomena, not expressions of a constant human nature. Likewise, dialectical images were intended as historically specific constructions, not Jungian archetypes. As Adorno wrote in regard to Benjamin's *Passagenarbeit:*

> . . . the dialectical image was meant objectively, not psychologically: the representation of the modern as the new, the already past, and the ever-identical [*Immergleiche*] in one, was to be the central philosophical theme and the central dialectical image.[87]

The fragmentary *Passagenarbeit* thus clearly anticipated Adorno's and Horkheimer's *Dialektik der Aufklärung.* Their critique of the history of enlightenment, their argument that reason had reversed itself and become a new form of myth, was based precisely on such an interpretation of the modern as archaic.

The approach was new for Horkheimer, but Adorno had been experimenting with its application since the early thirties; "the 'momentarily new,'" he wrote in 1932, "that which is dialectically produced in history, presents itself in [the constellation of] truth as *archaic*,"[88] and his interpretive essays illustrated this conviction. Specifically, Adorno wanted to demonstrate that the commodity structure of present phenomena bore the distinguishing characteristics of myth; resurfacing within modernity was the structure of a primitive era.[89] In a series of short pieces (written 1931-1933)[90] Adorno used images of the archaic to make visible the fetishization of culture. The reification of cultural events, their relationship to the audiences as "a commodity that can be bought," reduced culture to a "ceremonial function":

> Applause is the last form of objective communication between music and listener. . . ; the activation of the listener is now an illusion;[91] only in the blind execution of applause do they [listener and music] meet each other. The procedure could refer to the ancient, long-forgotten sacrificial ritual. Perhaps, we might surmise, men and women once thus clapped hands when priests slaughtered sacrificial animals. . . .
>
> The virtuoso is accorded applause above all, because he most clearly preserves the characteristics of the priests of sacrifice. . . . Often we no longer know what it is that is being sacrificed here: the music, the virtuoso, or in the end, we ourselves.
>
> As a ritual act, applause places a magic circle around the performer and those who are applauding, which neither are able to penetrate. Only from outside does it let itself be understood.[92]

It was one thing to read the elements of a theater performance as an unintentional expression of commodity fetishism; it was another to discover such changes within the musical material itself. Adorno's article on jazz educed images of the archaic (of myth, magic, the tyranny of the collective) out of an analysis of the technical elements of the music in order to demonstrate, not that jazz music was authentically primitive,[93] for it was "a commodity in the strict sense,"[94] but that precisely as commodity, precisely in those elements which determined it as a modern phenomenon of mass culture, it possessed qualities which bore the name of the primitive: "The modern archaic of jazz is nothing else but its commodity character."[95] Adorno argued that the laws governing the composition of jazz music, those same laws which guaranteed its marketability as a cultural commodity, gave it a structural identity to primitive myths:

> . . . the rigid, almost timeless immobility in the [music's] movement, the mask-like stereotypy of a fusion between a wild agitation which appears to be dynamic and an inflexibility of process which rules over such agitation. Above all, however, the law, which is one of the market just as much as of myth: it must always be the same, and simultaneously feign being always the new.[96]

Jazz's tendency to "demythify" the dance by transforming its ceremonial movements into secularized "steps" reversed dialectically into a "new magic": the rhythmic spell of the military march.[97] In the improvisational "breaks" of jazz music which pretend to be individualistic, hence progressive, Adorno saw the image of archaic ritual. The musical alteration of verse and refrain, the solo breaks followed by thematic repetition, paralleled the primitive dancer performing for the collective,[98] and this in turn was an image of the relationship between the modern individual and society in which the former, powerless, made a "sacrifice to the collective";[99] he was, like archaic man, really no individual at all: he "sacrifices an individuality which he doesn't possess. . . ."[100]

Adorno's jazz critique was written in England in 1936, before he had decided to join Horkheimer's exiled Institute in the United States, the mass-culture mecca. In reading the music and its performance as a "sociohistorical cipher," the translation of which exposed its modern commodity form as archaic, in applying concepts of both Marx and Freud to an interpretation of the musical material itself, in making social reality visible within the surface features of the phenomena, his analysis of jazz provided a model for all Adorno's later critiques of mass culture — of popular music, radio, television, and horoscopes, to name a few. It was from the foundations laid in this article[101] that Adorno, collaborating with Horkheimer in the United States, developed the theory of "culture industry" in the 1940s.[102]

Edward Shils, the most vocal American critic of this theory, argued in 1957 (from a liberal rather than a Marxist standpoint) not only that such a "Leftist" criticism of mass culture was untenable, but that Adorno, Horkheimer and other immigrants failed, because of European intellectual hubris, to appreciate the democratic essense of American mass culture.[103] Regardless of the merits of mass culture, Shils's argument missed the point as far as Adorno was concerned. As his jazz article clearly demonstrates, far from belittling mass culture, Adorno took it extremely seriously, applying to its phenomena the same sophisticated analytical method, the same intellectual spleen, which he used in interpreting Husserl, Kierkegaard, and Stravinsky. Nor did he suggest that the distinction between critical consciousness and mass consciousness paralleled differences in education or in class.[104] Adorno may indeed have been an intellectual snob, but an argument *ad hominem* won't do as a criticism of his theory. The latter was fundamentally concerned with the relationship between subject and object, and by granting the trivia of modern existence philosophical dignity rather than retreating into the aristocratic chambers of the abstract "big questions" of philosophy or deifying the subject's domination of matter, Adorno's conception of the subject-object relationship was "democratic" in a very real sense.

Adorno, then, did not dismiss jazz, or claim that as "low-brow" culture or "ideology" it was insignificant. He insisted on the contrary that appearance — phenomenal, ideological *Schein* — was precisely the locus of truth;[105] it was precisely here that he riveted his philosophical gaze, under which appearance was dialectically "redeemed," transformed from ideology into social truth. Jazz was revealed as a stage for social reality. As unintentional truth, it gave *itself* away. Its performance was thus "the static ritual of revelation of its social character."[106]

But only a critical attitude toward jazz (or any other phenomenon), a refusal to identify with it, could discover this truth. The uncritical affirmation of jazz was "pseudo-democratic."[107] Jazz was "static" indeed in both meanings of the English word: it was mythically repetitive, and also a garbled message: "interference"[108] which needed deciphering. This deciphering did not leave the object (or the subject) untouched: it was praxis, *intervention,* knowledge which altered the phenomena so that, like *Vexierbilder,* they could never be viewed in the same, mystifying way again:

> If jazz were only really listened to, it would lose its power. Then people would no longer identify with it, but identify it itself.[109]

Chapter 7. The Method in Action: Liquidating Idealism

MATERIAL PROOF

Adorno's method was remarkably versatile. It could be applied to any kind of bourgeois[1] social phenomenon. Whether it was jazz, atonality, a play by Beckett, listening to radio, a sociological concept, an aesthetic principle, or a philosophical text, his interpretive procedure followed those principles which I have attempted to describe and to illustrate. In all cases, whatever the discipline to which these phenomena traditionally belonged, his goal was the development of critical consciousness and knowledge of social truth so that the world of objects, not identical to reason, became accessible to rational understanding. Yet when the object was bourgeois philosophy, the procedure yielded a unique result: insofar as the method was successful, it not only revealed the ideological implications of that philosophy; it proved it wrong by negating the idealist tenets upon which it rested. Here was the method's real revolutionary potential, and because these tenets, in turn, provided the foundation of all bourgeois intellectual inquiry, Adorno made it the central focus of his work. Here he hoped not only to heighten critical awareness of philosophy's ideological, social function, but to make a positive contribution: to articulate the logic inherent within the material of philosophy itself, which led by its own dynamics to the disintegration of its bourgeois, idealist, commodity form. This negation at the same time *redeemed* philosophy by transforming ontology, epistemology, metaphysics, ethics, and aesthetics[2] from self-enclosed, idealist systems into dialectical, materialist activities of thought which participated self-consciously in the process of social change.

The qualitative distinction of the results of Adorno's method when applied to the phenomenon of bourgeois philosophy is an important point, so let me be quite specific. In Chapter 2 I cited the only concrete illustration which Adorno gave in his 1931 program for philosophy, a constellation, organized according to the "key" concept of commodity structure, which was capable of interpreting and simultaneously negating Kant's problem of the thing-in-itself. Here I noted that what Adorno found so exciting about this interpretation (which was Lukács's originally) was not simply that it demonstrated the historical relativity of Kant's thinking, but that it proved by "immanent" criticism that Kant's premise of the duality of thought and reality was absolutely wrong,[3] that subject and object were inextricably bound, reflecting one another, and that the problematic elements of bourgeois commodity production were precisely the problematic elements of Kant's idealism: the "indifferent" relationship between Kant's subject and object was the reified relationship between worker and product; the abstractness of Kant's formalism was the abstractness of exchange value; the irrationality of the thing-in-itself was the resulting opacity of commodities; the acceptance of the "given" world of experience was the acceptance of class relations as second nature. The distinguishing characteristics of the Kantian subject, of the *autonome ratio* upon which all idealism was based, were its independence from the object, its historical and formal universality, and its ordering[4] of the empirical world. Now if it could be demonstrated that these elements were reflections of social reality, if, like those glass paperweights which, when turned upside down, snowed upon a world within,[5] these elements, when turned on their heads and made transparent, revealed an image of social reality in "monadological abbreviation," then the very claims of the *autonome ratio* — its ahistoricity, its separation from the object, its universality — were proved wrong, negated, liquidated. As a result, the riddle of the thing-in-itself problem (which had only become problematic because of the assumption of an autonomous subject in the first place) was solved, not because an answer had been found, but because the question itself was meaningless, because it "absolutely disappeared."[6] Adorno's program of philosophy as the liquidation of idealism was thus defined as a process of "riddle-solving":

> And just as riddle-solving is constituted, in that the singular and dispersed elements of the question are brought into various groupings for so long until they close together in a figure out of which the solution springs forth, while the question disappears — so philosophy has to bring its elements, which it receives from the sciences [*Wissenschaften*], into changing constellations . . . until they fall into a figure which can be read as an answer, while at the same time the question disappears.[7]

When constellations were constructed in order to solve the riddles of idealist philosophy, the phenomena, the "objects," were philosophical texts, and their "elements" were the disparate, fragmentary, seemingly insignificant details: thought particles, turns of phrase, specific words and images. The "riddles" were located in the antinomies, the logical breaks of the texts, because here, where the subjective intention of the philosopher faltered, where, faced with contradiction, he himself felt he had failed, he succeeded, unintentionally, in making social truth visible. The juxtaposition of seemingly remote elements in the particular one-time-only arrangements whose structures correspond to the "key" categories of Marx and Freud, created "historical images" of these categories. The philosophical texts thus interpreted became transparent, a stage for objective social reality, just when, as *idealist* texts, they intended to be speaking about a subjective, autonomous, absolute realm. Idealism, by means of immanent criticism, was made to contradict its own tenets, and Adorno's constellations thus promoted the self-liquidation of idealism:

> I am not afraid of the reproach of unfruitful negativity. . . . If philosophical interpretation can in fact only prosper dialectically, then the first dialectical point of attack is given by a philosophy which cultivates precisely those problems whose removal appears more pressingly necessary than the addition of a new answer to so many old ones.[8]

This was written in 1931. In 1966 Adorno could still argue that "philosophy is obliged ruthlessly to criticize itself,"[9] that

> Though chained to the questions of traditional philosophic problematics, we certainly must negate those problematics.[10]

There was thus a remarkable persistence in Adorno's conception of the task of philosophy. And yet his description of the riddle-solving process did change in a way which reflected a shift in the balance of factors which went into the construction of constellations. Adorno's 1931 program, reflecting Benjamin's influence, stressed the crucial role of "historical images." The illumination of these "images" formed the climactic moment: they lit up the problem "like lightning":

> Authentic philosophical interpretation does not meet up with a fixed meaning which already lies behind the question, but lights it up suddenly and momentarily, and consumes it at the same time.[11]

Adorno's light imagery evoked several historical traditions simultaneously: it conjured up Platonism,[12] but also the eighteenth-century Enlightenment; as illumination, it was associated with the revelatory experience of mysticism[13] and of poetic intuition,[14] but also the most modern technology: an electric shock,[15] an atom exploding,[16] or a camera flash capturing a picture of the real.[17] In his inaugural speech Adorno, speaking of historical images, stated that their validity was guaranteed by the fact that "reality congeals about them in striking evidence [*in schlagender Evidenz*]."[18] Soon, however, Adorno developed reservations about this illuminative moment. Perhaps it was too reminiscent of Husserl's concept of *Anschauung*, of the "intuitive gaze" to which the object's essence became phenomenologically "evident," and which Adorno attacked in his critique of Husserl, written 1934–1937. In 1938 Adorno began to recognize the same invocation (*Beschwörung*) of truth in Benjamin's writing, whereby reality was intuitively revealed rather than theoretically interpreted. When Benjamin began to rely on a "montage" of objective data to provide "images" of truth without any interpretive mediation by the subject, Adorno wrote him:

> The "mediation" which I miss, and find hidden by materialistic-historio-graphic invocation [*Beschwörung*] is in fact nothing other than just that theory which your work bypasses.[19]

Historical images never disappeared from Adorno's writings. But they became more clearly one pole of his constellations, or "thought models,"[20] rather than their culmination, held in suspension by dialectical, theoretical argumentation.[21]

DECODING KIERKEGAARD: THE IMAGE OF THE BOURGEOIS *INTERIEUR*

Adorno's *Habilitationsschrift*, with which he fulfilled the requirements for a position on the Frankfurt philosophy faculty,[22] was a critique of Kierkegaard. In this study, written in 1929–1930 and published in 1933,[23] Adorno applied the philosophical method outlined in his inaugural lecture. The book, *Kierkegaard: Konstruktion des Aesthetischen*, which Adorno republished without revision in 1962,[24] illustrates how a historical image functioned in Adorno's early writings and how his interpretive philosophy solved the "riddles" of idealism by fostering their self-liquidation.

In attacking Kierkegaard, then highly admired in philosophical circles,[25] Adorno was challenging the whole tradition of existentialism, including its latest proponent, Martin Heidegger, whose influential book *Sein und Zeit* had appeared in 1927.[26] Kierkegaard's critique of Hegel was the bourgeois alternative to that of Marx. Although both rejected Hegel's identity theory because it lost sight of lived reality, Kierkegaard rested his case on the reality of individual existence, whereas for Marx existence was a social category. For Kierkegaard, the riddle of philosophy was ontological: the meaninglessness of human existence. The problem of existence, less critically formulated,[27] pre-occupied twentieth-century existentialists as well. When Adorno used his riddle-solving procedures to illuminate and explode the ontological question, his purpose was twofold: to rob current existentialism of its validity, and to justify simultaneously a (modified) Marxist alternative. But this was not all. As the subtitle, "Construction of the Aesthetic," indicated, Adorno had a further purpose: to argue against the view, found in Kierkegaard and in other more contemporary thinkers, that aesthetics was the realm of subjective immediacy and irrationalism, and to validate in its place the Hegelian conception of aesthetics as a medium for knowing objective truth (a higher medium for truth than either Kierkegaard or Hegel had supposed).[28]

With all this going on in one short study, clarity of purpose was not its strongest asset.[29] The full intricacies of Adorno's argument cannot be followed here. The book concerns us specifically as an early demonstration of his philosophical method.

It will be recalled that for Kierkegaard the aesthetic sphere marked the lowest stage in the dialectic of spiritual development. As the starting point for the process of transcendence, its construction crystallized the form of the existential problem. The characters in Kierkegaard's writings embodying the aesthetic attitude were depicted as hedonists whose actions were dictated by the sensual immediacy of their "situation," rather than by moral choice. Kierkegaard deprecated this sphere for its "creaturely immediacy," compared with the higher realms of ethics and religion. But Adorno argued that in this, the most concrete stage of his theory, Kierkegaard came closest to truth.[30] He noted that when Kierkegaard described the alienation of men's existential situation, he showed an acute awareness of the realities of capitalist society:

> . . . he indeed took note . . . of the relationship between reification and commodity structure in a simile which needs only to be taken literally for it to correspond with Marxist theory.[31]

But in rejecting Hegel, Kierkegaard overreacted and tried to avoid the problem of objective history altogether: "He analyses neither the necessity or justice of reification, nor the possibility of its correction."[32] Instead of attempting to remove reification from the world, Kierkegaard tried to remove the world, arguing that if material reality was reified (*verdinglicht*), then truth was not in matter (*dinglich*).[33] Kierkegaard turned to the interior world of individual religious experience: "With the category of the 'person' and his inner history [Kierkegaard] would like to repress external history from his circle of thought."[34] Kierkegaard reduced the historical dimension of existence to historicity (an abstract, anthropological concept), and he robbed social reality of its specific content by referring to it generally as the existential "situation." Instead of seeing alienation as the product of his own bourgeois era, Kierkegaard gave the latter philosophical sanction by raising it to the level of an ontological principle,[35] while the relationship between subject and object was characterized not by mutual transformation, but by "indifference."[36] Concrete reality

> . . . falls away. It provides for the subject a mere "occasion" for action, mere opposition for the act of faith. In itself [the world of things] remains arbitrary and fully undetermined. No part in "meaning" is granted to it. There is in Kierkegaard as little subject-object [relationship] in the Hegelian sense as there are content-rich objects: only isolated subjectivity, closed up inside, secluded from the dark otherness.[37]

Through the "superior strength of the otherness"[38] Kierkegaard's subject was thrown back on itself. His dialectic was thus inner-subjective, an "objectless dialectic" which "can be thought of, in Kierkegaard's sense of philosophy, as the movement in contradictions of the individual person's consciousness."[39] The result was that Kierkegaard, who had charged Hegel with abstractness because he had ignored the lived existence of the individual, sacrificed the very concrete content he intended to rescue: "Kierkegaard's theory of existence can be named Realism without Reality."[40]

But it was also subjectivism without a subject. For once objective reality was dismissed and left behind, in order to give life meaning Kierkegaard's individual ended up sacrificing itself, its own (first-nature) body as well as its critical consciousness, through a blind leap into a realm of mythic spirituality and submission to God.

The contradictory moments of Kierkegaard's theory, of the subject, the object, and the riddle of meaning, "remain entwined within one another. Their figure is called inwardness."[41] Adorno was not satisfied with demonstrating the logical difficulties of this configuration or even its ideological implications, the reasons why it promoted bourgeois, or "false" consciousness. He wanted more, to prove Kierkegaard's idealist premises incorrect, by showing that precisely where Kierkegaard thought he had escaped the objective world, he remained caught in it: "real history makes its way into his philosophy. Even the objectless subject with its inner history is tied to historical objectivity."[42] Indeed, Kierkegaard's errors were expressions of "unintentional" historical truth: the inner realm into which the logic of his theory led was itself a historical manifestation, marking the passing of the bourgeois era; Kierkegaard's realm of the spirit was inhabited by the ghosts of earlier bourgeois idealism. As Benjamin noted in a review of Adorno's book for the *Vossische Zeitung* in 1933:

> Wiesengrund's [Adorno's] question is, then, if one will, historically posed. . . . It leads to a critique of German idealism, the unriddling of which begins in its old age. For Kierkegaard is a late arrival. . . . In, namely, the aesthetic idealism of romanticism, absolute idealism's mythic elements really come to be illuminated.[43]

The philosophical "unriddling" of Kierkegaard did not involve giving an answer to the apparent meaninglessness of life, but demonstrating the meaninglessness of the existential question, which was not absolute, but limited to "its one-time and first-time historical appearance."[44] If Adorno could prove that the existential riddle was historically specific, he could destroy the ahistorical, ontological, idealist claims of that riddle, which had led Kierkegaard, incorrectly, into seeking a solution in pure spirituality rather than social reality: the "answer" was not the negation of self, but the negation of the social conditions which gave rise to the problem in the first place. Attacking Kierkegaard from within, using his own words against their intent, Adorno needed to demonstrate that the "configuration of inwardness" which appeared at all points of contradiction in Kierkegaard's philosophy was permeated by the external world. Existential inwardness had to be translated out of conceptual abstraction into sociohistorical concreteness. To achieve this, Adorno constructed a "historical image" using the elements of a metaphor supplied by Kierkegaard himself: the interior of a bourgeois flat of the mid-nineteenth century. Adorno argued that the image of the "bourgeois *intérieur*,"[45] when taken literally, revealed the historical truth of Kierkegaard's philosophy and at the same time contained its own "immanent" criticism:

> The name suitable for the "situation" as the powerlessly immediate indifference between subject and object is not the knight's castle with which, romantically, Kierkegaard compares inwardness. And it does not need to be sociologically established in mere "association" [*Zuordnung*] to Kierkegaard, but lies present pragmatically in his work itself. Specifically, in the metaphors of the apartment interior. . . . It is the bourgeois *intérieur* of the nineteenth century before whose arrangement all talk of subject, object, indifference, situation, pales to abstract metaphor even if, for Kierkegaard, the image of the *intérieur* stands itself as a mere metaphor for the connection between his basic concepts. The relationship reverses itself as soon as interpretation gives up the identity compulsion. . . .[46]

The bourgeois *intérieur* was a seemingly insignificant detail in Kierkegaard's writings, overlooked by "philosophically trained authors,"[47] which Kierkegaard intended as a symbolic representation of his philosophical concepts. Under Adorno's interpretive gaze, this historical image represents unintentional social truth and demonstrates that these concepts are false (while the Marxist concepts are proved to be true).

The image appears frequently in Kierkegaard's works. Adorno cites an early example: father and son, at home, walk back and forth across the floor, pretending they are strolling past exciting places in the outside world. Adorno comments: "Thus the *flâneur* goes for a walk in the room; reality appears to him simply as reflected out of mere inwardness."[48] Unlike the Paris *flâneur*, who at least observed the empirical, urban surface of social reality,[49] Kierkegaard's reflective man reflects at home. He is the *rentier*, living off the rents of the buildings he owns (as was Kierkegaard in fact), excluded from the productive process which does not even enter his field of vision.[50]

The imagery of reflection is a part of the *intérieur*. Kierkegaard *intends* the reflecting mirror as a symbol for the seducer: "But with it, an image is posited in which is condensed, against Kierkegaard's will, social and historical content."[51] Mirrors known as "spies" (a word Kierkegaard used to describe himself)[52] were standard furniture in the bourgeois flat of the nineteenth century. They were positioned ". . . to reflect the endless streetlines of such rental apartments into the secluded bourgeois living space."[53] The external world was thus subjugated to the *intérieur* at the same time it defined its limits, just as in Kierkegaard's philosophy the "situation" is "subjugated to subjectivity and yet confines it as well."[54]

"Space does not fall into the *intérieur*. It is solely the latter's boundary."[55] The mirror testifies to the objectlessness of Kierkegaard's dialectic. It brings only the appearance of things into the individual's private world. But even the objects inside the *intérieur*, the pieces of furniture, are reduced to mere appearance, without concrete content. Kierkegaard's seducer describes Cordelia's living room — filled with the foreign imports of an imperialist economy — as an ornamental, decorative arrangement. The furniture objects receive their meaning

> . . . not from the substance out of which they are manufactured, but out of the *intérieur*, which assembles the illusion of the things as a still-life. Here the forfeited objects are conjured up in an image. The self is overtaken in its own domain by commodities and their historical essence.[56]

Yet enclosed in his private space, the bourgeois subject cannot grasp the actuality of the objects as commodities of capitalist production:

> Their appearance-character [*Scheincharakter*] is historically-economically produced through the alienation of the thing from its use value. But in the *intérieur* the things do not persist in appearing alien.[57]

Instead, "the mute objects speak as 'symbols'":[58] by interpreting them as subjectively meaningful, Kierkegaard blots out their historical specificity and accepts them as second nature: "thus objects which appear historically are arranged to appear as unchanging nature."[59]

The bourgeois *intérieur* has no room in which to unfold. It exists, once and for all, frozen in the still-life of a furniture arrangement, and thereby provides the concrete image of the "indifference" between subject and object. But the *intérieur* is also the "living image" of Kierkegaard's indifference to historical change, his fusion (and confusion) of temporally specific existence with eternal nature. Instead of presenting themselves as dialectically interrelated, as mutual, nonidentical mediators, "in the apartment eternity and history merge together."[60] Kierkegaard's philosophy refers to an existential "point," which neither extends in space nor develops in time, but is rather "a complete simultaneity of all moments":[61]

> In the point, however, reality is not allowed to extend, but only to appear in optical illusion, just as in a peephole. In the appearances [*Schein*], however, historical reality presents itself as nature.[62]

The symbol of mirrored reflection perpetuates this confusion, mystifying the existentialist despair. Kierkegaard speaks of father and son as mirror images of one another: the son, like the father, will spend his days in doubt. The reason for melancholy (*Schwermut*), the "captivity of mere spirit by itself,"[63] while actually a *historical* constellation,[64] takes on the ontological appearance of "archaic and persistent nature."[65]

When phenomena from the outside world do enter into the configuration of inwardness, Kierkegaard transforms them into religious symbols. Utterly specific historical technologies become representations of a timeless and abstract spirituality: the train passenger becomes a symbol of the sinner; machine imagery conjures up the demonic and magical; a rising air balloon, "the strangest image of the technology of his day," becomes the inverse symbol of sinking into doubt.[66] All these Kierkegaardian symbols "circle about the bourgeois dwelling as their place of social realization and as their powerful cipher."[67]

Inside, the subject experiences twilight as the Day of Judgment and seeks comfort in the illumination of the gaslight, but "the consolation of this light is also appearance [*Schein*]":[68]

> Out of the twilight of such melancholy emerge the contours of the "domesticity" [*Häuslichkeit*] which for Kierkegaard constitutes the place of existence. But therewith, the place of his existentialism as well. Inwardness and melancholy, [mere] appearance of nature and reality of [divine] Judgment, his ideal of concrete, individual human life and his dream of hell which the despairing individual inhabits like a house during his lifetime — the models of all his concepts are bound in the deceptive light of the room in late day into a wordless tableau, out of which it is worth extricating them if one wishes to see what is truth in them and what is illusion.[69]

But this is precisely what Kierkegaard doesn't do. Instead, he takes flight in the opposite direction, abandoning the bourgeois *intérieur* (which at least bordered on the external world) and retreating into a "second inwardness," i.e., the existential subject himself, who now becomes merely the "stage" for a religious dialectic of self-abnegation. And as Kierkegaard flees through the ethical sphere into the realm of pure spirituality, Adorno follows in pursuit, armed with the tools of dialectical criticism to shoot holes in existentialism by exposing simultaneously the logical contradictions of its content and the social content of its logic: Kierkegaard's abstract, "objectless" ethics is "false and deceptive class morality."[70] Kierkegaard's attempt to transcend what he calls the "myth" of immediate appearance, motivated by a hostility to nature [*Naturfeindschaft*],[71] leads him to sacrifice the subject's own body (his first nature), and traps him in an inner realm of the spirit more mythical than the first.[72] His internalized dialectic forms a closed system,[73] a mythic circle controlled by fate, where the subject relinquishes both body and critical reason to an unknown and unknowable God.[74] Like the mirror reflections in the bourgeois flat, this realm is characterized by repetitive duplication.[75] The existentialist dialectic is really static: the dialectic "stays in place," becoming what it already is, and thus it corresponds "precisely to the image of the *intérieur* in which in fact the dialectic comes to a stop."[76]

Adorno does not rely solely on the power of the bourgeois *intérieur* to "unriddle" Kierkegaard's philosophy. Even in this early study where its role is central, the historical image never takes the place of philosophical and logical argumentation. The bourgeois *intérieur* illuminates the elements of the riddle, providing a frame in which its fundamental contradictions can be seen in a flash:

> . . . in it the moments of his [Kierkegaard's] theory of archaic, fixed nature present themselves without mediation as those of the historical constellation which presides over them.[77]

It thus sets the critical philosopher off on the right track, but it remains his task to demonstrate specifically that Kierkegaard's fusion of the archaic and the historical, of nature and spirit, of myth and reality, is a case of mistaken identity; that these dialectically paired concepts need to be unraveled by theory and held apart as mutually determining, mutually critical ones; that otherwise, theory succumbs by its own inner contradictions to self-liquidation. Adorno concludes that Kierkegaard's intent of avoiding Hegel's abstraction and identity theory is a failure: Hegel is "turned inside" by Kierkegaard,[78] but he is not overcome:

> both of them [Kierkegaard and Hegel] remain idealistic: Hegel, with the definitive thought-determination of Being [*Dasein*] as meaningful, as "rational"; Kierkegaard, with its negation, which rips existence apart from "meaning" just as completely as Hegel forces them together. In Kierkegaard, ontological and idealistic elements cover each other up, and their intermingling is what makes his philosophy so impenetrable.[79]

In the image of the *intérieur*, Kierkegaard is turned on his feet: Adorno argues that Kierkegaard comes nearest the truth where he thought himself furthest away, in the aesthetic sphere where the metaphor of the *intérieur* most persistently appears, and where the object at least has a sensual existence outside subjectivity, despite the undialectical "indifference" of the subject-object relationship. Implied in this criticism was, of course, a defense of the Marxian perspective. But Adorno was also attacking Martin Heidegger, as anyone familiar with *Sein und Zeit* (1927) — and Adorno's intellectual peers certainly were — could not help but be aware. For in attempting to define being, Heidegger had employed a strikingly similar illustration — the objects in the interior of his study, which, like those of Kierkegaard's *intérieur*, could be perceived only in their immediacy. For Heidegger objects were "equipment" (*Zeuge*), owned and manipulated by the [domesticated, bourgeois] subject: their use value was personal rather than social. Their being-in-the-world was merely being-at-hand; their "meaning" had nothing to do with their socio-economic production, but was determined, like Kierkegaard's still-life of furniture pieces, by their physical arrangement in the interior:

> Equipment is essentially "something in-order-to . . ." ("*etwas um-zu . . .*"). A totality of equipment is constituted by various ways of the "in-order-to," such as serviceability, conduciveness, usability, manipulability.
> In the "in-order-to" as a structure there lies an *assignment* or *reference* of something to something. . . . Equipment — in accordance with its equipmentality — always is *in terms of* (*aus*) its belonging to other equipment: ink-stand, pen, ink, paper, blotting pad, table, lamp, furniture, windows, doors, room. These "Things" never show themselves proximally as they are for themselves. . . . What we encounter closest to us . . . is the room, and we encounter it not as something "between four walls" in a geometrical spatial sense, but as equipment for residing. Out of this the "arrangement"

emerges, and it is in this that any "individual" item of equipment shows itself.[80]

Heidegger's "room" does not even allow for the reflection of the external to shine into it. Through an extension of the lines of Adorno's argument (and hence between the lines of his Kierkegaard study), Heidegger's purportedly "materialist" phenomenology, as outlined in *Sein und Zeit*, appears not at all the most progressive of current philosophies (Husserl at least looks outside at the apple tree; Sartre gets as far as the park bench).[81] Indeed, Heidegger "falls behind" Kierkegaard, by Adorno's criteria, since the latter's critical perception of social reality led him at least to pose the ontological question negatively. As Adorno wrote in a later article:

> All Kierkegaard's gloomy motives have good critical sense as soon as they are interpreted in terms of social critique. Many of his positive assertions gain the concrete significance they otherwise lack as soon as one translates them into concepts of a right society.[82]

Hence Adorno's liquidation of Kierkegaard's idealism (legitimated by its own logical dynamics) at the same time redeems his writings as an unintended expression of social truth.

If Benjamin's original theory of ideas was an inversion of the Platonic one, the bourgeois *intérieur* (be it theater or house) can indeed be seen as similarly related to Plato's myth of the cave, on whose walls only the reflection of reality appeared, chaining the consciousness of its inhabitants to illusion. What made this relationship an inverse one was the historical specificity of Adorno's image. Leaving the *intérieur* meant entering concrete social reality, while leaving Plato's cave meant entering an ahistorical realm of ideal truth. Plato's myths, like Kierkegaard's metaphors, were symbols, establishing relationships of identity between thing and concept, meaning and intention. Adorno's historical image aimed at *de*mythification by transforming the symbolic relationships established by Kierkegaard's words into dialectical ones. By bringing Kierkegaard's philosophical concepts into *critical* juxtaposition with symbols from the historical reality which had been their source, Adorno transformed Kierkegaard's eternally fixed images (which ruled over the individual with the fatalism of an astrological sign) into dynamic, *historical* constellations: he set their elements in motion so that they negated the very concepts they were intended to symbolize.

Chapter 8. Theory and Art: In Search of a Model

THE AESTHETIC EXPERIENCE

Thickness of texture, complexity of composition, inversion and variation of thematic motif — these were qualities which Adorno's writing had in common with a work of music. *Kierkegaard: Konstruktion des Aesthetischen* was itself an aesthetic construction. It wasn't that Adorno favored transforming philosophy from a scientific inquiry into an art form.[1] Rather, he rejected the dichotomy between science and art, which he considered not necessary, but the product of a particular historical era.

Ever since the seventeenth century, in the wake of the Newtonian revolution in science, the realms of art and knowledge, "mere" fiction and factual "truth," had been split into two opposing camps. In the context of this dualism, Enlightenment reason took the side of science. The *philosophes* were hostile to art, which, secularized and hence robbed of its aura as a theological symbol, was no longer considered a form of truth in itself but rather a pedagogic tool, a means of moral persuasion.[2] In the bourgeois revolutions art became a platform for political propaganda. It can be said that the Marxian aesthetics of Lukács and Brecht were still within this Jacobin tradition insofar as they were committed to art as a means of political instruction (although they differed radically in their definition of the kind of art that met this requirement).[3]

In protest against the Enlightenment, nineteenth-century romanticism championed art as a source of truth in its own right, but it remained within the existing paradigm by accepting without question the notion of a dichotomy between reason and art. Hence, for example, music was glorified by Schopenhauer and Wagner as the expression of a subjective, irrational will. Adorno, siding with neither the romantics nor the rationalists, challenged the basic dualistic assumption. He wrote in 1939 in regard to aesthetic criticism:

> It is my conviction that . . . a rationality [which can judge the truth or falsity of artworks] is today not a matter of "science" concerned with art,

122

but of art itself. That is to say, that every art which deserves serious attention approaches the aim of rationality by its very structure, and tends more
and more toward "knowledge."[4]

Of course, in the Hegelian system art was granted a rational cognitive function,
but it was relegated to a lower sphere in comparison with philosophy, just as
Kierkegaard had condemned the aesthetic mode of lived experience to a lower
level in comparison with spirituality. Opposed to both rationalist and existentialist idealism, Adorno argued that aesthetic experience was in fact the more
adequate form of cognition because in it subject and object, idea and nature,
reason and sensual experience were interrelated without either pole getting the
upper hand – in short, it provided a structural model for "dialectical," "materialist" cognition.

Such a position was to a certain degree anticipated by Kant, who recognized the mediating position of art between thought and praxis, and this theme,
developed in Kant's third critique, was the subject of Horkheimer's *Habilitationsschrift* for Hans Cornelius in 1925.[5] But Adorno's appreciation of the cognitive
value of aesthetic experience came first-hand, through the composition and
performance of music. His mentor Schönberg was a romantic in some ways but
not in his conception of the creative process. Schönberg rejected the notion of
artist-as-genius and replaced it with the artist as craftsman; he saw music not as
the expression of subjectivity, but as a search for knowledge which lay outside
the artist, as potential within the object, the musical material. For him, composing was discovery and invention through the practice of music-making.[6] Its
goal was knowledge of truth, and if Schönberg believed that the mimetic elements
of the process had affinities to magic, then this was not to negate the rational,
"logical" moment of music, but rather, to emphasize its material, objective side,
not identical (and therefore not reducible) to the subject.

In arguing that aesthetic production was not the expression of (either rational or irrational) subjectivity, Schönberg's procedure in fact paralleled science.
At the same time, scientists contemporary with Schönberg, theorists of the new
scientific revolution, were recognizing that their own activity bore little affinity
to the present-day rationalism of scientific positivism and logical formalism, but
instead, as an objective and true "construction" of reality, converged with art.[7]

Scientific positivism had become the hallmark of official Marxism. But by
1931 Adorno had access to Marx's newly discovered *Economic and Philosophic
Manuscripts,*[8] and he must have been struck by the similarity between the young
Marx's conception of the dialectic of labor as a cognitive experience and Schönberg's conception of the aesthetic experience of composing. In both, the processes
of creativity and cognition, production and reflection, were one and the same.
Thus when Adorno based his Marxist philosophy on aesthetic experience, his
aim was to "aestheticize" neither philosophy nor politics, but instead to reconstitute the dialectical relationship between subject and object which he believed
to be the correct structural basis for all human activities – knowledge, political

praxis, and art. In this sense, both philosophy and art *had* a moral-pedagogic function, in the service of politics not as manipulative propaganda, but rather as teaching by example. In comparison, the positivist, "scientific" notion of social engineering, which held that an elite group first acquired knowledge and then attempted through manipulation of the others to recreate the world in accord with that knowledge, was far more guilty of "aestheticism," in the negative sense connected with political totalitarianism, than was Adorno's own position.[9]

SURREALISM AS MODEL: THE EXPERIENCE OF HASHISH

Walter Benjamin was also convinced that the aesthetic experience was fundamental to correct philosophical understanding, but his intellectual development and the place where it led him were not identical to Adorno's. Impressed in his early years by the tradition of theological and mystical experience, to which his friendship with Gershom Scholem had exposed him, he was first attracted to the aesthetics of Friedrich Schlegel, Novalis, and other early German romantics who were the self-conscious heirs to these traditions. His dissertation, *Der Begriff der Kunstkritik in der deutschen Romantik* (1920),[10] had interpreted the concept of aesthetic *criticism,* particularly as it was developed in the fragments of Friedrich Schlegel's writings. Benjamin argued that the two operations of critical philosophy, thought (consciousness) and thought about thought (critical reflection, or self-consciousness), had their parallel in Schlegel's aesthetics in the creation of the artwork on the one hand and its critical interpretation on the other. It followed that the act of interpretation was the necessary completion of the artwork,[11] because only in this second operation did the truth of the artwork, its "idea," become manifest.[12] Literary criticism, or *Sprachkritik,* was thus itself cognitive revelation. For the early romantics, noted Benjamin, criticism was "a totally esoteric concept," one "which in regard to knowledge rested on mystical premises. . . ."[13] Novalis viewed poetic texts – indeed, all of nature as well – as "hieroglyphs" and "codes," whose interpretation depended on a sacred language which only the few could read.[14] The conception was very different from that of Goethe and the French *philosophes,* for whom criticism was exoteric and inessential, having a limited, instructive function. But for the early romantics art, brought to completion by criticism, converged with philosophy (Schlegel) and religion (Novalis) as revelation of truth. This conception clearly influenced Benjamin's philosophical theory first outlined in *Ursprung des deutschen Trauerspiels,* which in turn made such a major impression on Adorno.

It will be remembered that by 1926, in the midst of working on the *Trauerspiel* book, Benjamin had found himself in the paradoxical position of espousing a philosophy influenced by mysticism at the same time that he became politically committed to Marxism. At this crucial intellectual juncture he read Louis Aragon's surrealist text *Le Paysan de Paris.* He later recalled his extreme excitement: "evenings in bed I could never read more than two or three pages before my heartbeat got so strong that I had to put the book down."[15] The book used sacred language to portray sensuous love, and glorified the profane as the source of revealed truth, combining elements of the extremes of mysticism and materialism which now formed the poles of Benjamin's thinking. As an aesthetic model, surrealism appeared far more compatible with his purposes than the romanticism of the early bourgeois period, and Aragon's book became the inspiration for his study of nineteenth-century Paris, the *Passagenarbeit,* on which Benjamin worked for the rest of his life. In 1927 he began spending time in Paris, the center of the surrealist movement.[16] Two years later, the same year he read the first fragments of the *Passagenarbeit* to Adorno at Königstein, Benjamin wrote that surrealism demonstrated "the true, creative overcoming of religious illumination," its transformation into "a profane illumination of materialist, anthropological inspiration. . . ."[17]

It is thus no accident that many of the elements of their Königstein program were at home in the discourse of surrealism. André Breton, who founded surrealism in 1924, was himself influenced by the Kabbalah, and he enthusiastically endorsed Freudian theory at the same time that he embraced Marxism. In 1926 Breton proclaimed surrealism's solidarity with the Communist Party,[18] yet like Adorno and his friends, he remained independent of actual affiliation. A nonconformist and a tactical anarchist whose aim was to make art explosive in order to clear away the old world for the new, Breton identified progress with man's "unlimited capacity for refusal."[19] In this sense he saw art as critical knowledge that implied a demand for action: " 'Transform the world,' Marx said; 'change life,' Rimbaud said. These two watchwords are one for us."[20] Not content to remain in the isolated sphere of *l'art pour l'art,* Breton's goal was the reconciliation of dream and reality "into a kind of absolute reality, a *surreality,*"[21] and his volitional politics called for a transformation of society in accord with human desires. It can be said that the surrealists took literally Marx's statement "the world has long since possessed something in the form of a dream which it need only take possession of consciously, in order to possess it in reality."[22]

It was the artistic technique of surrealism that fascinated Benjamin. Surrealist art portrayed everyday objects in their existing, material form (in this literal sense surrealist fantasy was "exact"), yet these objects were at the same time *trans*formed by the very fact of their presentation as art, where they appeared in a collage of remote and antithetical extremes.[23] Prototypical of Benjamin's "dialectical images," surrealist artworks illuminated unintended truth by the juxtaposition of "two distant realities" from which sprang "a particular light . . . , the *light of the image,*" as Breton wrote in the first Surrealist Manifesto.[24] In *Les Vases communicants* (1933) Breton maintained:

> To compare two objects as remote as possible from each other or, by any other method, to place them together in an abrupt and startling manner, remains the highest task to which poetry can aspire.[25]

This was the method of montage, the technique developed in the new film medium of using single frames rather than scenes as the basic unit of construction.[26] Film montage made possible the rapid succession of seemingly disconnected images, and its inner logic was radically different from the conceptual, linear logic of the traditional print medium. To Benjamin the principle of montage appeared precisely adequate for his study of nineteenth-century Paris. Urban experience was composed of shocks, of collage-like fragments that bombarded the senses: "no face is more surrealist than the true face of a city."[27] The way transitory material objects, the smallest, seemingly insignificant fragments of human existence appeared in his *Passagenarbeit* — smokestacks, fashions in clothes, turtles taken for a stroll in the shopping arcades — paralleled "the shock-like flashes of obsolete elements from the nineteenth century in surrealism."[28]

Not only did Benjamin use dreams, the surrealist material *par excellence,* in his writing.[29] Like the precursor of surrealism Charles Baudelaire (whose works he translated), Benjamin experimented with consciousness-transforming drugs — hashish primarily, but also opium and mescalin. Benjamin was prompted by reading *Steppenwolf,* Hermann Hesse's 1927 novel,[30] to record his experiences both under the influence and afterward.[31] These records of sessions dating from 1927 to 1934 were found in his estate and recently published. They reveal that although he recognized drug-taking as a liberating act, he considered its relationship to political liberation problematic:

> Since Bakunin no radical conception of freedom has existed any longer in Europe. The surrealists have it. . . . But are they successful in uniting this experience of freedom with the other revolutionary experience which we must recognize since we have had it: with the constructive and dictatorial [aspect] of revolution: in short — in uniting revolt with revolution?
>
> To win for the revolution the powers of being high: surrealism revolves around this in every book and endeavor. That can be called its most particular task.[32]

Drugs did not themselves provide the "profane illumination" that Benjamin was seeking: "The true, creative transcendence of religious illumination . . . does not really lie in narcotics":[33]

> . . . the most passionate examination of hash-smoking will certainly not teach half as much about thinking (which is an imminent narcotic) as the profane illumination of thinking about hash-smoking. The reader, the person thinking, the person waiting, the *flâneur,* are just as much types of *Illuminati* as the opium-eater, the dreamer, the intoxicated, and they are profaner.[34]

Nonetheless, "hashish, opium and whatever else" could "provide the introductory course" for profane illumination,[35] and the recordings of these sessions make it clear that the insights induced by drugs were not insignificant to Benjamin's theoretical endeavors. His notion of the subject-object relationship which lay at the heart of his theory of knowledge bore the stamp of these sessions and characterized the particular nature of his empiricism, in which concentration on the objects' appearance did not result in a mere reflection of the given. Under the gaze of the hashish smoker the object transformed itself so that the very details of its surface appeared in changing configurations:[36] "the first rush loosens and entices things out of their familiar world; the second places them very quickly into a . . . new one."[37]

The drug experience was especially significant for Benjamin's secularized theory of the "aura" of objects.[38] Emanating from the surface of the phenomena and revealing their inner essence, this aura became visible within the "image-zone" of drugs,[39] and could be reproduced on the artist's canvas: "Perhaps nothing gives a more correct concept of authentic aura than the late pictures of van Gogh, where – so one might describe these pictures – the aura is painted into all things."[40] The goal of Benjamin's writing as a series of dialectical images was to capture this aura in the written word as well.

CRITICISM OF SURREALISM: ATONALITY AS MODEL

There were difficulties in Benjamin's choice of surrealism as a model for philosophy. The essentially static nature of his "dialectical images" (Benjamin called them "dialectics at a standstill"[41] and spoke of a "Medusan gaze"[42]) became the focus of Adorno's criticism in the thirties, manifesting to him the ultimate inadequacy of the surrealist model.[43] At the outset, however, in the early days in Berlin, Adorno was not lacking in enthusiasm. In a 1930 review of Brecht's *Mahagonny* Adorno praised this "first surrealist opera"[44] for its use of shock, scandal, and montage to construct the "ur-images of capitalism"[45] not only within the dramatic action but in Kurt Weill's music as well.[46] Adorno considered the form legitimate for a critical representation of the fragmentation and decay of bourgeois reality, and claimed that it promoted "the disenchantment of the capitalist order. . . ."[47] In 1932 Benjamin could count on Adorno's positive reaction when he said of the latter's Kierkegaard study: "since the latest verses of Breton (the *'union libre'*) nothing has so cultivated me in my particular fields as your map showing the way through the land of inwardness. . . ."[48] In completing the overthrow of bourgeois art forms which had been begun by expressionists at the start of the century, the surrealists were involved in a project which clearly had Adorno's sympathies. But decipherable within the surrealist techniques there were impulses of the movement and its reception of Marx and Freud that were bluntly incompatible with Adorno's conception of his and Benjamin's Königstein program. Specifically, in violation of their early commitment to demystification, surrealism affirmed the irrational: it was intentionally in complicity with enchantment, and this was technically manifested in the immediacy of representation in its artworks. Surrealist montages were random assemblages of existing objects in their immediately given, hence reified form. If their fortuitous juxtaposition was interpreted at all, then this was not in

Marxian terms, that is, as manifestations of sociohistorical reality, but in terms of meanings projected onto them by the subject. Yet these meanings themselves were reproduced immediately in surrealist art as a "photography of thought."[49] Following the Freudian principle of free associations, the surrealist project was to "write quickly, without any preconceived subject [matter]; fast enough so that you will not remember what you're writing and be tempted to reread what you have written."[50] But Freud himself saw this as only half the process in illuminating the truth. Not the dream image and its associations, but the *interpretation* of this configuration of elements, in connection with the subject's waking experiences, was necessary to reveal a latent logic within the manifest absurdity. As Adorno wrote in a 1956 essay criticizing surrealism:

> Every analyst knows what pains and struggle, what will it takes to become master of the unintentionally expressed [dream] material which is already taking shape in the analytical situation by virtue of such struggle, but this is much less so in the aesthetic [situation] of the surrealists. In the world debris of surrealism the in-itself of the unconscious does not come to light.[51]

Surrealism "regrouped" the dream elements without liquidating them, and thus, claimed Adorno, its images were "fetishes — commodity fetishes — in which at one time subjective libido became fixed," and for which the true model was pornography.[52] Insofar as efforts at interpretation were made, then they were attempted only by imposing ready-made categories, like the Oedipus complex, mechanically from the outside.[53]

In crucial ways, then, surrealism was undialectical. (Breton was a great appreciator but poor interpreter of Hegel, to whom he referred as the "inventor" of "the dialectical machine.")[54] Surrealism fused subject and object in the art image rather than, as Adorno attempted, making manifest the antagonisms characterizing their mutual mediation. Breton's famous dream image of a man cut in two by a window[55] might indeed have lent itself to interpretation within the constellation of the bourgeois *intérieur,* but such interpretation was hindered by that immediacy of aesthetic representation which was the outspoken goal of the surrealists. In Breton's conception, the role of the artist as subject was reduced to the passive reception of images: "we, who have made no effort whatsoever to filter, who in our works have made ourselves into simple receptacles of so many echoes, modest *recording instruments*. . . ."[56] The danger was that their art would not achieve the materialist objectivity they desired, but would provide only the magical reflection of the world of appearances. As Brecht noted critically, the objects of surrealism "do not return back again from estrangement";[57] and in using surrealist techniques in his own epic theater he insisted on their "refunctioning." For Brecht this meant transforming them into didactic tools as a means for political education. For Adorno, of course, the external criterion of effect on the audience could not redeem the techniques, the validity of which would have to exist internally — "immanently" — or not at all.[58] To him the problem was whether the inner structure of surrealist procedures was so contaminated by irrationalism that redemption was impossible.

At least by 1934, Adorno was skeptical. In a letter to Benjamin he called attention to André Breton's recently published *Les Vases communicants*, which

> . . . directs itself against the psychological interpretation of the dream and replaces it with one composed of objective images, and appears to attribute to the latter the character of historical keys. The whole thing lies too near to your theme not to make necessary perhaps a radical reversal precisely at the most central point.[59]

That same year Adorno published an essay on Schönberg as a "dialectical composer,"[60] describing Schönberg's method with the same terms he had used to define his own philosophical project in 1931. It elaborated and made explicit the philosophical significance which Adorno had long sensed in Schönberg's compositional procedure. The article can be read as a counter to Benjamin's efforts to work with surrealism as a model for dialectical, materialist philosophy. For if the surrealist artist attempted to fuse subject and object by becoming the passive medium through which the material of the unconscious was expressed in empirical reality, if as a result surrealist images were reified and hence "undialectical," then, so Adorno claimed, Schönberg as composer was not merely the medium but the active mediator in a dialectical process between the artist and his material.[61] Adorno wrote that it was the "absolutely new" contribution of Schönberg that this dialectical relationship between artist and material achieved its "self-consciousness" in a Hegelian sense.[62] He was referring to the logic of the music's technical construction. The musical technique functioned "as the stringent locus of decisions concerning the musical contents."[63] Schönberg, he wrote, worked neither as a "blind craftsman" nor with the "arbitrariness and optional choice of a subjectively unrestrained artist."[64] Instead, the composition emerged out of an unresolved contradiction between the subjective freedom of the composer and the objective demands of the material, "if one may express it in philosophical vocabulary, between subject and object — compositional intention and compositional material."[65] Using the Benjaminian terminology of his 1931 inaugural lecture, he described this procedure as "exact fantasy."[66] In surrealism an anarchistic, arbitrary fantasy converged with the seemingly opposite tendency of passive duplication of the given, intensifying mystification rather than dispelling it. But Schönberg, it will be recalled,[67] developed the material to the point of a dialectical reversal: tonality carried to its extreme resulted in atonality, which demystified music by demonstrating that the tonal "laws" were not natural and eternal. In his 1934 article, Adorno argued that this reversal enabled the self-conscious repossession of the means of musical "production," precisely the goal of the Marxist project.[68]

Adorno's positive evaluation of Schönberg's music played a major role in his intellectual estrangement from Brecht.[69] This explains why he failed to send a copy of the Schönberg article to Benjamin for his comments,[70] as the article appeared in Vienna on September 13, 1934, and Benjamin was with Brecht in Denmark from July to October of that year. Yet there is no doubt as to the seriousness with which he viewed the potential applicability of Schönberg's procedure for his project, the original conception of which had owed so much to Benjamin. That same year he began a critical study of Husserl, his major work of the thirties. Building on the Kierkegaard book, Adorno hoped to transcend bourgeois philosophy conclusively by means of an immanent dialectical critique of idealism in this, its most historically advanced form. The opening pages of the Husserl manuscript refer to "the model-character of musical logic," particularly Schönberg's, for his endeavor.[71] Significantly, his criticism of the subject-object relationship in Husserl paralleled his critique of surrealism: the immediacy of objects as "given," the passivity, the arbitrariness of the subject, and the essentially static, undialectical relationship between subject and object.[72] In contrast, Adorno described as the "idea" of his investigation

> . . . the task, in the interior of the matter, thus without presupposition of an anticipated process of its production which would be merely external, to disclose . . . the moment of production, i.e., the dialectic congealed within [the matter]. This procedure is synonymous with the deciphering of dialectical images.[73]

The structural relationship between subject and object in this procedure paralleled that of Schönberg's composing. Adorno had already defended this method as inherently revolutionary,[74] arguing that Schönberg's overthrow of bourgeois tonality, a transformation *within* music, carried with it a reversal of music's external, social function as well, transforming it from an ideological function into a critical one. He expressed the exemplary character of such music for theory in a 1934 letter to Ernst Krenek:

> It is . . . the task of a true theory not to conceal and "mediate" reality's ruptures by means of harmonious thought-forms, but precisely to expose them and through knowledge of them to contribute to overcoming them. And I indeed believe that Schönberg distinguishes himself from other music in that through the conception and resolution of its antinomies he goes as far beyond the structure of present society as the most progressive social theory.[75]

Not only had Schönberg changed the social function of music from ideology to critical knowledge. The very structure of his compositions provided the "image of a liberated music,"[76] and Adorno came to see in this image a utopian vision of society. He continued to Krenek: "Doesn't this [Schönberg's] music (I want to express myself carefully) have something to do with that which in Marx is called the 'association of free men'?"[77] Adorno meant of course Schönberg's liberation of the twelve tones from the domination of the lead tone, which led him not to anarchy, but to the construction of the twelve-tone row in which each note had an equally significant yet unique role in the musical totality,[78] analogous to the equal yet nonidentical, individual citizens in the hoped-for classless society. Schönberg's music was nonrepresentational, and thus the utopian image it provided was structural rather than pictorial or descriptive.[79] Yet Adorno here was at the brink of breaking the *Bilderverbot* in regard to delineating the nature of postrevolutionary society. To argue that the correct structure of *geistige praxis* could provide the model for a new social structure was to go well beyond the intentions of *Ideologiekritik,* and it clearly separated Adorno's Husserl project from the work of Horkheimer's Institute during the thirties. Not yet disillusioned as to the potential of Schönberg's twelve-tone techniques,[80] Adorno went radically far in transposing Schönberg's method from the musical to the philosophical mode. There was a parallel between his own abandonment of philosophical first principles and Schönberg's abandonment of tonal dominance, also between his aversion to harmonious totalities and Schönberg's use of dissonance and rhythmic irregularity.

Moreover, Schönberg's development of musical ideas, which Adorno described as a "movement between extremes"[81] comparable to "riddle-solving"[82] or "deciphering,"[83] was structurally analogous to Adorno's development of philosophical ideas. Adorno's prototypical 1932 essay "Die Idee der Naturgeschichte" (discussed in detail in Chapter 3) developed its analysis from the paradoxical constellation of the extremes of "history" and "nature." It would not be forcing the analogy to argue that the structure of this essay bore a distinct correspondence to the rules of twelve-tone composition, i.e., (1) the *statement* of the tone row: "all history is natural" (hence transitory); (2) retrograde, or *reversal* of the row: "all nature is historical" (hence socially produced); (3) *inversion* of the row: "actual history is not historical" (but merely the reproduction of second nature); and (4) *retrograde inversion*: "second nature is unnatural" (because it denies nature's historical transitoriness). Following a similar procedure in his Husserl study, Adorno unraveled the "paradoxical constellation" of rationalism and empiricism in phenomenology,[84] demonstrating how each of these extremes tended to negate itself (inversion) at the same time that it converged with the other (reversal). And if Adorno developed philosophical ideas the way Schönberg developed musical ideas, if each of his essays was constructed out of all the possible permutations of polar extremes,[85] showing the identity of contradictions (history is natural) and the contradictoriness of identities (history is unhistorical), then it was also true that in his unwillingness to allow any one aspect of the paradox to dominate, the structure of his essays could be read as a mimesis of a social structure free of domination.

Is this perhaps the hidden, positive moment in Adorno's "negative dialectics"? Is each essay, precisely because of its unrelenting negativity, in fact a utopian emblem, a secret affirmation? Indisputable at least is the significance for Adorno of correct cognitive procedure understood as a structure, or "model," which could be translated into different modes and different realms of intellectual discourse. Hence, for example, he could see parallels between the structure of Schönberg's composing and Freudian analytical procedure.[86] Or he could discern echoes of Schönberg in the structure of Benjamin's writing:

> Just as the new music in its uncompromising representation tolerates no "execution," no distinction between theme and development, but instead every musical thought, indeed every tone stands equally close to the center, so Benjamin's philosophy is likewise "athematic."[87]

THE AESTHETIC MODEL AND ITS LIMITS

The notion of equivalences between different modes of experience – between philosophy and image for Benjamin, philosophy and music for Adorno – was far from new. In literary history it had a clear precedent in Baudelaire's theory of correspondences, itself the secularization of an older mystical conception (*Gematria* in the Kabbalist tradition,[88] of which at least Benjamin, through discussions with his close friend Gershom Scholem, must have been familiar). What was new, however, was their discovery of such equivalences between aesthetic experience and dialectical materialism, which at least in its orthodox (non-Hegelian) Marxist form adhered strictly to that paradigm of bourgeois science which opposed itself irreconcilably to art, and which Adorno and Horkheimer later so devastatingly attacked in *Dialektik der Aufklärung.* [89] Whereas within the scientific paradigm dialectics was viewed as an objective law of history and nature, which could be known and described by the detached subject in a totally *un*dialectical fashion, the aesthetic paradigm was based on a subject-object relationship in itself dialectical. At the same time, it avoided the speculative, metaphysical representation of the dialectic in which Hegel had expressed his philosophy, and which rested on the potential for synthesizing antagonisms both within and between the realms of reality and thought: surrealist art and Schönberg's music expressed contradictions negatively, without resolving them into harmonious totalities.

To base philosophy on aesthetic experience thus understood was to retrieve that which had been lost by the ideological preeminence of the subject in bourgeois philosophy in both its Enlightenment-rational and romantic-irrational forms. In this new form of "negative dialectics," the subject retained contact with the object without appropriating it. The thinker reflected on a sensuous and nonidentical reality not in order to dominate it, not to butcher it to fit the Procrustean beds of mental categories or to liquidate its particularity by making it disappear under abstract concepts. Instead the thinker, like the artist, proceeded mimetically, and in the process of imitating matter transformed it so that it could be read as a monadological expression of social truth. In such philosophy, as in artworks, form was not indifferent to content – hence the central significance of representation (*Darstellung*), the manner of philosophical expression. Aesthetic creation itself was not subjective invention so much as the objective discovery of the new within the given, immanently, through a regrouping of its elements.[90]

Implied in this cognitive model was a transformation of the idea of knowledge. No longer was it a search for causal laws which would make possible manipulation and prediction of the future. Now knowledge meant "seeing," a kind of secular revelation (the influence of Husserl as well as theology was clear here) by means of critical interpretation. In line with the Kantian distinction in the third critique, this kind of knowledge was not empirical information which one possessed, but judgment which provided the capacity for action.

Throughout his life, Adorno insisted on the parallels between philosophical and aesthetic experience. His major work on aesthetics, published posthumously,[91] made continuous reference to the similarities between art and theory. *Negative Dialektik*, his mature philosophical work, explicitly noted the structural analogies between critical thinking and musical composition.[92] There exists in his estate the manuscript of a book-length study comparing the development of the "concept" in Hegelian logic with compositional development in Beethoven's music (although as contemporaries, Hegel and Beethoven themselves never appreciated the connection).[93]

Yet it would be wrong to conclude that in Adorno's theory art and philosophy were one and the same. From the start and repeatedly, he insisted that if they converged in their "truth content," they were nonetheless nonidentical. In his inaugural lecture of 1931 he insisted:

> . . . it would be better just to liquidate philosophy conclusively and dissolve it into the particular disciplines than to come to its aid with a poetic ideal which means nothing more than a poor ornamental cover for faulty thinking.[94]

His Kierkegaard study (1933) stated: "Even with a view to the final convergence of art and philosophy, all aestheticizing of philosophical procedure ought to be avoided."[95] And in *Negative Dialektik* (1966) he wrote: "Philosophy that imitated art, trying to turn itself into a work of art, would cancel itself out."[96]

Perhaps the clearest expression of his position was in a 1935 letter to his friend Ernst Krenek. Here Adorno criticized what he called Krenek's "idealist" attempt to discover the cognitive character of art through "relativizing the difference between art and science [*Wissenschaft*]."[97] The division between them, historically produced, was a "historical necessity"[98] which could not be wished away. Science should not be "aestheticized," nor art made scientific. Instead, argued Adorno dialectically, it was precisely as separate activities, both true to their own particularities, that they converged.[99] As subjective "experiences" of the object, art, science and philosophy had a similar dialectical structure. However, as cognitive processes, each remained distinct. As he wrote elsewhere, ". . . most bitterly irreconcilable is that which is similar but which feeds on different centers. . . ."[100] The cognitive value of art, which was by definition *other* than given reality, depended upon the adequacy of aesthetic form to the content or idea which it expressed; the value of science, which gazed at reality head-on, depended on the adequacy of the theoretical concepts used to describe its objects.[101] Philosophy was "a third thing."[102] Its task was to speak the truth, and it did so by the critical interpretation of both art and science, showing how their adequacy demonstrated the *in*adequacy of reality.[103]

Adorno believed that Benjamin allowed the tension between cognitive modes to collapse. This lay at the heart of their intellectual dispute during the thirties, which is discussed in detail in the next chapters, and hence takes us ahead of our story. Here we may simply note that much of the problem was implicit in Benjamin's choice of surrealism as a philosophical model. Surrealism fused science and art by eliminating what made them different (theory and concept in science, the logic of form in art), and Benjamin tried to fuse art with philosophy in much the same manner. Adorno wrote:

> It was Benjamin's intention to renounce all open explanation and to allow the meanings to emerge solely through the shock-like montage of the material. Philosophy was not only to catch up with surrealism, but become surrealistic itself.[104]

The result was that Benjamin's work lost the critical negativity which for Adorno lent philosophical interpretation its value as truth, and lapsed back into that positive theology which his choice of surrealism as a model had been an attempt to overcome.

In the sense which Adorno criticized, surrealist aesthetics was actually less adequate than the early romanticism of Schlegel and Novalis, who insisted that the truth content of art did not emerge until it was critically interpreted. Music as a model did not pose quite the same problem. Its modality was distinct from that of the art image.[105] The latter condensed the material, whereas music unraveled it. In art images, contradictory elements converged, superimposed on one plane, but music brought them to articulation by extrapolating them and extending them in time.[106] Moreover, while the art image existed ready-made, music had to be reproduced, translated from written text into sound, and this meant that it had to be thought through, *interpreted* in order to exist at all.[107]

The fact that the very existence of music necessitated its critical interpretation, that in the performance or (nonmechanical) reproduction of music the two moments of creation and interpretation fell together, whereas the immediate appearance of the art image and its interpretation were separate and self-contained activities, made music intrinsically more analogous to Adorno's conception of philosophy. He clearly found his own experience producing music to be prototypical of cognitive experience in general.[108] The limitation of music as a model lay elsewhere, however. The medium of philosophy was language, and its practice was "language criticism."[109] Like language, music was composed of "the temporal succession of articulated sounds that are more than mere sound"; and "the succession of sound is related to logic: it can be right or wrong."[110] But because musical "language" lacked concepts, its interpretive procedure was different: "Interpreting language means understanding language; interpreting music means making music."[111] In the first case, conceptual analysis was crucial; in the second, imitation, or mimetic representation.[112]

Aesthetic models, whether music or art image, could not carry the whole weight of philosophical practice. Criticizing Benjamin's overestimation of the illuminative power of "dialectical images," Adorno wrote in 1966:

In fact no philosophy, not even extreme empiricism, can drag the *facta bruta* by the hair and present them like cases in anatomy or experiments in physics; no philosophy can paste separate particulars into the text, as many paintings would falsely seduce it into believing.[113]

Aesthetics provided a corrective for the positivism and pseudo-scientific rationalism which did violence to the object by consuming it within a reified conceptual schema. But philosophical interpretation could not get beyond immediate appearances of reality without the theory and concepts developed by the sciences, by Marxian sociology and Freudian psychology specifically. Science and art, concept and image, analysis and expression — these formed the two poles of philosophical activity. Philosophy didn't sublate their differences in a false synthesis. Rather, it existed within the tension between them and made that tension fruitful in order to speak the truth about the world.

Chapter 9. The Adorno-Benjamin Debate

Part 1: The Issues

EMIGRATION

In reviewing Adorno's Kierkegaard book, Walter Benjamin wrote:

> . . . much is packed into a small space. Quite possibly the later books of the author will spring forth from this one. In any case it belongs to the class of those rare first works in which, out of the cocoon of criticism, a winged thought emerges.[1]

Benjamin was correct in sensing the seminal nature of the study. But his suggestion of an organic, unbroken literary development proved indefensibly optimistic. Already the shattering experience of intellectual emigration had begun. The Kierkegaard book was published on January 30, 1933, the date Hitler took power. Benjamin's review appeared in the *Vossische Zeitung* on April 2, one day after the boycott against Jews was announced. Benjamin himself was already on foreign soil, having emigrated to Paris in mid-March. The Frankfurt Institute for Social Research, which had been explicitly Marxist since its founding, was forced to close just after Horkheimer and the Institute staff had fled for safety to Geneva.[2] Adorno's teaching position was not renewed for the summer semester. He officially lost his *venia legendi* (permission to teach) on September 11, the date of his thirtieth birthday, not because of his dialectical materialist theory,[3] but because of his Jewish name.[4] In the spring of 1934 he emigrated to England. Adorno described the period in a revealing letter to Krenek:

> The events in Germany, which I followed for the most part in Berlin, *Unter den Linden*, struck me dumb at first and threw me back totally into my own affairs. . . . Then in Berlin I came in contact with the *Vossische Zeitung* through Gubler,[5] concerning whose strange fate you have surely heard more than I, who haven't seen him since January. I wrote a great deal for the paper; by far the largest part did not appear, including some, in my opinion, really important things – I had hopes of getting the position of [music] critic, but the death of the paper took this hope away with

it,[6] and I think it was fortunate, although I clung desperately to the possibility, as I was trying to stay in Germany *at all costs* [italics mine]. But then when it became totally impossible, and when one possibility after another was taken away from me, including the most unassuming – I wasn't even allowed to give music lessons to "non-Aryans" – I decided to go nevertheless, and managed in the spring to get to London.[7]

Yet Adorno's emigration can hardly be considered a flight. He was still free to travel and made frequent visits until 1938 to his family in Frankfurt and his future wife Gretel Karplus in Berlin. In the same letter he commented:

. . . (incidentally, I would have been able to hold out perfectly well financially in Germany, and *also would have had no political objection* [italics mine]; except that every possibility for effectiveness would have been cut off from me, including that of [my music] being performed, and that was why I left; I spend my vacations at home or in the South [Italy]).[8]

Adorno's lack of concern, his misreading of the potential dangers, and his poor judgment in desiring to remain in Germany under Hitler's regime seem remarkable in retrospect. Certainly his circle of friends were less blind to the realities of the situation. Horkheimer had planned in advance for the extrication of the Institute staff and funds from Germany.[9] Clearly he advised that Adorno leave too, and promised financial support from the Institute's journal.[10] Not only Benjamin but also Kracauer, Bloch, and Brecht left Berlin before April 1933.[11] Benjamin wrote Scholem in March that it had become "scarcely possible to breathe the air" in Berlin.[12] Not only was it impossible to work, but the threat to life was already very real. Benjamin wrote to Scholem March 20, 1933:

Without doubt there are numerous cases in which people have been hauled out of bed and beaten or murdered. Perhaps more important still, but more difficult to expose, is the fate of prisoners. The most horrible rumors are circulating about them.[13]

Why should Adorno have had no fears of remaining, and more, why "at all costs" should he want to? Youth and intellectual self-importance perhaps provide much of the answer. Having never identified with his father's Judaic heritage or with any Marxist political organizations, he was preoccupied with his own intellectual career, concerning the potential brilliance of which he was never in serious doubt. Adorno saw himself as an artist and a philosopher, and still had dreams of success as a musical composer.[14] Not surprisingly, once he saw that emigration would be necessary, his first choice was to return to Vienna. His letter to Krenek explained:

I also want to tell you that I naturally made an effort to transfer my *Habilitation* to Vienna; but without success, because Mr. Gomperz[15] who handled the thing in fact found in my Kierkegaard book only the quotations interesting, and that it could not be considered an above average accomplishment – and thus Vienna was closed to me.[16]

In fairness to Adorno it must be noted that like so many of the leftists at this time who had opposed the Weimar Republic, he very much miscalculated the significance of the Nazi phenomenon. His tolerance was clearly based on a belief that Hitler's regime would be short-lived. On April 21, 1934, he wrote Benjamin (who had himself sublet his Berlin apartment in hopes of returning after a year) that the situation "for non-Aryan authors (including myself)" in regard to publishing required simply "the confirmation of the regular declaration" of national loyalty and that this could be "received without difficulty, although final confirmation could be postponed indefinitely."[17] Nonetheless, editors would accept the temporary confirmation, and Adorno suggested that Benjamin say he had left Germany for economic rather than political reasons. He continued:

> The declaration of loyalty is fully unobjectionable – from our point of view, it has no more to it than the civil servant obligation toward this republic. I won't hide from you the fact that I am beginning to question nonetheless whether the Nazi state will endure for all that long a time. . . . For although I am free from optimism, and expect for the future some kind of Rightist-anarchy and fulfillment of Bronnenist pipe dreams, if not simply military dictatorship or a kind of Dollfus regime, still the symptoms of disintegration [Verfall] are beginning to accumulate so that one no longer needs to ignore them out of fear that the wish is father of the thought.[18]

It is not clear just how and why Adorno went to Oxford. Horkheimer had connections at the London School of Economics. He sent Friedrich Pollock there in February 1934 to investigate establishing the Institute in England (before deciding on New York after his visit there in May),[19] and his contacts may have been helpful for Adorno. Positions at English universities were difficult for German emigrants to obtain, and Adorno, who had no proficiency in the language[20] and little appreciation of the British intellectual tradition, had to return to the status of a student. His original plan was to work two years for a British Ph.D. But his proposed doctoral study, the dialectical criticism of Husserl whereby Adorno hoped to negate and transcend bourgeois idealism once and for all, was so ambitious an undertaking that he was still working on it four years later when he left to join Horkheimer and the Institute in the United States.[21] The refined academic atmosphere at Oxford satisfied Adorno's cultural conceits, yet he seems to have remained largely isolated from the university community and had difficulty communicating his ideas to his colleagues. He wrote to Krenek with some pride:

> Merton College here, the oldest and most exclusive at Oxford, has taken me in as a member and "advanced student" [orig. English] and I live here now in indescribable peace and under very pleasant external working conditions; with regard to the material, there are of course difficulties, as making my actual philosophical things comprehensible to the English counts among the impossibilities; and to a certain extent I have to screw

back my work to a child's level in order to remain intelligible — which entails a fission in all my work between the academic and the real things, a situation for which I actually consider myself too old — but I have to simply take that and be happy that I am able to work undisturbed. . . .[22]

Although Sidney Webb lent his name in support of the Frankfurt Institute when it was forced to emigrate,[23] Adorno seems to have had no contact with him or others in the Fabian Society. He never joined the pacifist movements then so strong in English universities, and one searches his writings in vain for even a mention of the Spanish Civil War. His most important intellectual relationships remained the same; and again, his friendship with Benjamin was central.

Their dialogue was not without strong disagreements. Adorno found himself in the paradoxical position of defending Benjaminian orthodoxy against Benjamin himself. The geographical separation caused by emigration clearly increased the possibility for differences to develop between them. Yet the fact that they were forced to communicate by letter has allowed that debate to be preserved, and their correspondence is one of the most significant documents in the history of neo-Marxist literature.

ORIGINS OF THE DEBATE

In the late 1960s, when Adorno was the leading theoretician of the German New Left, his debate with Benjamin was viewed through the smoke of political battles then going on. More orthodox Marxists wrote to discredit Adorno by accusing him of having pressured a reluctant Benjamin to conform to the Frankfurt Institute's "revisionist" position and, as editor of Benjamin's works after his death, of suppressing the republication of his more openly Marxist texts.[24] Although documentation of their debate is still not complete,[25] the most recently published material makes it clear that this interpretation is misleadingly one-sided.[26]

Previous chapters have dealt with Adorno's theory analytically, demonstrating its consistency through time by tracing its origins, and showing the extent of Benjamin's influence in shaping those origins. But in anticipation of protests against the central thesis that the points of identity in their thinking were decisive, the *non*identities, the theoretical divergences which surfaced repeatedly in their friendship during the thirties, require more systematic attention. A discussion of the Adorno-Benjamin debate will not necessitate abandoning the main thesis, but only demonstrate the dialectics of their friendship. Addressing this theme means shifting from a synchronic frame to a diachronic one, which allows a continuation of the biographical account of Adorno begun in Chapter 1.

It will be recalled that when Adorno and Benjamin spoke together at Königstein in 1929, Benjamin was struggling to reconcile his early theological thinking with his more recent, Marxist political orientation.[27] Both poles of his thought were intellectual reflections of personal relationships: on the one side, his lifelong friendship with Gershom Scholem, and on the other, his friendship with Bertolt Brecht, which was just beginning at the time of the Königstein talks. Neither person appreciated manifestations of the opposing pole in Benjamin's writings. Scholem recalled that "the theological element in Benjamin visibly upset Brecht,"[28] who wrote in his journal critically of Benjamin's mysticism and persistent Judaism.[29] Scholem himself, a non-Marxist socialist, was no advocator of dialectical materialism. He resisted Benjamin's shift away from theology, doubting the possiblity of a real synthesis. Commenting on his friend's essay on Karl Kraus (1931),[30] he claimed Benjamin was deceiving himself to think that the introduction of a few Marxist terms in fact transformed his observations into dialectical materialism. He warned Benjamin lest he become, not the last, "but perhaps the most inexplicable sacrifice to the confusion of religion and politics."[31]

Unique among his friends, only Adorno really supported Benjamin's efforts to incorporate both poles,[32] at least by 1929, when Benjamin had found in surrealism an aesthetic model for his theological impulse which he now understood as "profane illumination."[33] Adorno referred to such profane illumination as "negative," or "inverse" theology, equating it with aesthetic experience.[34]

It is difficult to overestimate the intensity of Adorno's commitment to Benjamin's thinking at the time of their Königstein talks. Benjamin, eleven years older, was satisfied that he had found a disciple in Adorno. More, he was ready to bequeath the task of developing the program to Adorno alone. One of the most surprising disclosures of Scholem's recently published memoirs is that Benjamin's suicide in 1940 was preceded by several earlier plans to take his own life. Perhaps the earliest of these was in the summer of 1931 when, with the collapse of not only his thirteen-year marriage to Dora Pollak but also his relationship to Asja Lacis, which had been a cause of the divorce (a drawn-out and painful procedure), Benjamin began a journal "from August 17, 1931, until the day of death," with the words "This diary promises not to be very long."[35] Adorno had just presented his inaugural lecture containing their common philosophical program, an event which gave Benjamin no little satisfaction and made him feel that his work had found a successor.[36] The following year, on his fortieth birthday, Benjamin again came to the edge of self-destruction.[37] He was discouraged with his own work, with its "victory in small things" but "defeat in the large ones,"[38] in particular the long-planned *Passagenarbeit.*

Adorno, who was never as close personally to Benjamin as he was intellectually,[39] clearly was not aware of these attempts. Their correspondence was "not free from tensions,"[40] and Adorno at least was prepared for a continuing debate with his mentor. Very soon, the "whole 'disputed complex'" became connected "with the figure of Brecht,"[41] who had a growing fascination for Benjamin,[42] perhaps precisely because of their differences. For Brecht was as commonsensical in his writings as Benjamin was esoteric. Benjamin spent more time with him than with either Adorno or Scholem during the thirties.[43] Yet it would be totally erroneous to interpret Benjamin's closeness to Brecht as a rejection of his earlier ties (the mistake of anti-Adorno Marxists in the late 1960s).[44] Scholem is accurate in his insistence on the continuity of Benjamin's theological orientation throughout his life. Despite the Marxist "turning point" in 1929, Benjamin maintained a genuine theoretical interest in Scholem's research, particularly into the mystical literature of the Kabbalah.[45] The difficulty was that, instead of really integrating the two poles of theology and Marxism, Benjamin's writings tended to present them side by side — sometimes not in the same essay, but in essays upon which he worked simultaneously, each of which, as a self-contained work, appeared to stand clearly in one camp or the other. Benjamin was aware of this duality, and he often referred to the "Janus-face" of his theory.[46] His intellectual schizophrenia repeatedly exasperated Adorno, whose own notion of profane illumination was to extrapolate out of the extremes of theology and Marxism to the point where they could be shown to converge,[47] rather than simply to present these two poles in unmediated juxtaposition.

Increasingly during the thirties Adorno found himself in the middle of a tug-of-war between the two sides of Benjamin's intellectual personality. On the one hand, he considered it his "task" to keep Benjamin's "arm steady until the Brechtian sun once again sinks into exotic waters. . . ."[48] On the other, he resisted any manifestation of positive theology in Benjamin's writings, considering the theological motif valid only in its inverted, secularized form.[49] During all of their disagreements Adorno's persistent goal was to rescue Benjamin from what he considered the Scylla of Brechtian materialism on the one hand and the Charybdis of Judaic theology on the other.

BENJAMIN'S JANUS-FACE

In 1934 Benjamin completed an essay on Kafka, which he considered extremely important from a methodological standpoint. The problem of the essay, he wrote Scholem, was "indicated by the image of an arc: here I am dealing with the [two] ends simultaneously, namely the political and the mystical."[50] The essay challenged current interpretations of Kafka: "There are two ways to miss the point of Kafka's works. One is to interpret them naturally, the other is the supernatural interpretation."[51] As opposed to either the "naturalist" (empirical) or "supernatural" (theological) interpretation, Benjamin's argument moved dialectically between these two. His method was to construct a series of dialectical images meant to "illuminate" what he called "cloudy" passages of Kafka's texts, employing supernatural elements — mystical, mythical, theological — to interpret the empirical level of Kafka's texts, and employing "natural" elements — social and material — to interpret the supernatural levels.

This took the form of juxtaposing archaic elements with the most modern: Benjamin identified Kafka's bourgeois, bureaucratic-legal officialdom with the Czarist Russian, historical figure of Potempkin, with the trials of Ulysses, with *gandharvas* from Indian mythology, and legends from the Talmud. At the same time he insisted that in the mythical passages in Kafka, in his allegories and animal stories for example, the "doctrine" which they interpreted was "in every case . . . a question of how life and work are organized in human society."[52] The hunchback, "prototype of distortion," was an image of the distorting effects of social organization;[53] Kafka's animals were "receptacles of the forgotten," an image of man's alienation from nature: "the most forgotten alien land is one's own body. . . ."[54] Finally, instead of interpreting *The Trial* as a modern rendition of the Biblical Last Judgment, Benjamin read the Last Judgment as itself a metaphor for class revolution.[55]

Benjamin communicated with Scholem by letter while working on the Kafka piece, and he discussed it with Brecht during a three-month visit with him in Denmark (July-October 1934). Both his friends were admirers of Kafka, but for antithetical reasons. Scholem claimed Kafka's writings were the "linguistic paraphrase of a divine judgment";[56] Brecht called Kafka "the only truly bolshevik author."[57] Not surprisingly, both were sharply critical of Benjamin's essay: Scholem considered it not theological enough;[58] for Brecht's tastes it was too much so.[59] Adorno, however, was most enthusiastic. He wrote to Benjamin on December 17, comparing the Kafka piece with his own Kierkegaard book: "Please don't take it as presumptuous if I begin by saying that I was never so completely conscious of our central philosophical agreement as here."[60] The complexity of Benjamin's interpretation, the whole conception of affirming Kafka, like Schönberg an apolitical individualist, within the context of a dialectical and materialist interpretive framework and the esoteric language of the presentation which shunned Marxist jargon were clearly in harmony with Adorno's own work. The theological motifs of the Kafka essay functioned in a secular way, as "inverse" theology – for example, Benjamin's definition of prayer as "attentiveness to the objects," to which Adorno referred, exclaiming, "I might know of nothing more important by you – also nothing that could give a more precise elucidation of your most inward motives."[61] Nonetheless, he already began to have reservations about the surrealist-inspired way in which Benjamin juxtaposed the archaic with the most modern in constructing his dialectical images: "The relationship between *Ur*-history and modernity is not yet raised to a conceptual level. . . ."[62] Adorno missed a mediation between these two poles, and he mentioned Hegel in this connection as a more adequate model than Judaic theology.[63] Adorno was quite right in noting that Benjamin's interpretation of Kafka didn't unfold, at least not in the Hegelian sense. An idea typical of Benjamin in the essay was the observation

> The word "unfolding" has a double meaning. A bud unfolds into a blossom, but the boat which one teaches children to make by folding paper unfolds into a flat sheet of paper.[64]

Benjamin's images "unfolded" in this second sense, in which, he claimed, "it is the reader's pleasure to smooth it out so that he has the meaning in the palm of his hand."[65] But despite the vividness of the images produced, his juxtaposition of opposite extremes might as easily leave his readers with the feeling of clutching at air.

Adorno suggested, in place of Benjamin's attempt to "illuminate" the "cloudy" sections of Kafka's texts, that these be more "thoroughly articulated" (*durchartikulieren*) and "thoroughly dialectized" (*durchdialektisieren*),[66] language evoking his own aesthetic model, the process of musical composition. He had just finished his article on Schönberg as the "dialectical composer" (which Benjamin had not seen), in which, it will be recalled, he argued that Schönberg's method was dialectical not merely because it illuminated contradictions in the material, but because it developed them to the point of dialectical reversal.[67] But Benjamin, in line with surrealism, defined the dialectical image as "a flash of light";[68] it corresponded to mystical revelation on the one hand, and to the distancing "gesture" of Brecht's epic theater on the other.[69] The result was that instead of avoiding the extremes of positive theology or vulgar materialism, Benjamin's dialectical images had a tendency to be guilty of both.

This difficulty was not yet fully apparent in the Kafka essay, in part itself "clouded" by Benjamin's esoteric presentation. That same year Benjamin delivered a lecture on the author as producer ("Der Autor als Produzent") to the Paris *Institute pour l'étude du fascisme*. It was a Communist front organization,[70] and Benjamin's flattering reflections on Soviet authors were admittedly geared to his audience. Yet there is too much of Benjamin's individuality in the speech to judge it simply a piece of political opportunism. Benjamin argued that aesthetic validity was itself the criterion for political validity, that these of necessity converged,[71] and this was not out of line with his own evaluation of Kafka. But the lecture went farther, saying in language as simple as the Kafka essay was obscure that even if the original impetus for producing revolutionary literature lay in the relation between the author and his material rather than his conscious political intent (which was Adorno's position), sooner or later, "*the writers who matter*" would be led to "confirm very soberly their solidarity with the proletariat."[72] Benjamin's explanation of how the writer might best demonstrate this solidarity was modeled after Brecht's epic theater: the writer needed to "refunction" the techniques of literary production from values of the bourgeois marketplace into "revolutionary use value."[73] In the process, the author would become less and less distinguishable from the technical expert. He would be "an engineer who sees his task in adopting [the literary production] apparatus to the ends of the proletarian revolution."[74]

Benjamin had the good sense not to send this lecture, which showed only one side of his Janus-face, to either Scholem[75] or Adorno. Only Brecht received a copy when Benjamin visited him that summer. The following year Benjamin was commissioned to write a memorandum, ("*exposé*") on the *Passagenarbeit* for the Institute, which was considering funding him to write it. It gave him the occasion to rethink the conception of the *Passagenarbeit*, which, he reported to Adorno, came suddenly to a new crystallization.[76] He feared that the study was only tangentially related to the major interests of the Institute, and he expressed hope to Adorno that the latter would be able to convince Horkheimer to accept the *Passagenarbeit* project despite its literary rather than socioeconomic focus.[77] In fact, Horkheimer had an "unqualified positive reaction" to the *exposé*.[78] It was Adorno who was disturbed. Writing from Hornberg in the Black Forest where he and Gretel Karplus were vacationing, Adorno criticized Benjamin sharply.[79] Once again, he claimed that the simple juxtaposition of contradictory elements made the dialectical images merely reflect contradictions instead of developing them through critical argumentation.[80] He sensed Brecht's influence in the lack of "negative theology" in the new proposal, saying that whereas he himself endorsed sacrificing this impulse insofar as it was unable to capture the "social movement of contradiction," here its absence made the presentation less dialectical and less materialist rather than more so.[81] Adorno argued paradoxically that a restitution of the theological impulse would strengthen the Marxism of the conception:

> A restoration of theology, or better, a radicalization of the dialectic into the very glowing core of theology, would at the same time have to mean an utmost intensification of the social-dialectical, indeed economic, motifs.[82]

His letter contained a long, detailed list of reservations, and Benjamin clearly felt rebuffed. He replied, through Gretel as mediator, insisting that he hadn't strayed from their common program, that this plan for the *Passagenarbeit* and the one with which Adorno was already familiar were not mutually exclusive, but the "thesis and antithesis of the work."[83] They had a "polar relationship," the dialectical nature of which he had perhaps not yet been able to demonstrate convincingly: "Now I have both ends of the arc — but not yet the strength to bridge them."[84]

It had been Benjamin's belief (expressed in a letter to Scholem several months earlier) that his new plan for the *Passagenarbeit* granted concessions "to no side": "if I know anything about it at all then this, that no school will be in a hurry to lay claim to it."[85] And in fact the plan described in the *exposé* did not put into practice the kind of Brechtian didactic program which he supported in his 1934 speech, "The Author as Producer." It implicitly cast doubt on the correctness of totally subsuming art under use value, revolutionary or otherwise, an aspect of the draft which Adorno was quick to praise.[86] But the 1935 *Passagenarbeit* conception did follow the line of "The Author as Producer" on the crucial political point: Benjamin expressed solidarity with the working class (and with the Communist Party) by affirming the concept of a collective revolutionary subject. Behind the whole question of whether Benjamin's images were sufficiently "dialectical," the real issue by 1935 between

Adorno and Benjamin was a political one. The influence of Brecht was not so much to eliminate the theological components of Benjamin's writing as to change their direction from critical negation to revolutionary affirmation. Benjamin didn't abandon the Königstein philosophical position for Brecht's theory of epic theater. But Brecht (who supported the Party without actually becoming a member) had a decisive effect on Benjamin's political position, one which did not remain external to Benjamin's mode of presentation, and which was indeed pulling him away from Adorno. For the latter's whole conception of dialectical materialism (precisely the point on which he split with Brecht in 1932) was that the dialectical, materialist method could and in fact must be validated immanently, without depending on either the theory or the reality of a collective, revolutionary subject.[87]

In the 1935 *exposé* Benjamin cited Michelet, "'Every epoch dreams its successor,'" and wrote:

> The form of the new means of production, which at first is still dominated by the old (Marx), corresponds to images in the collective conscious in which the new is intermingled with the old. These images are wish-images (*Wunschbilder*), and in them the collective seeks both to sublate (*aufzuheben*) and transfigure (*verklären*) the incompleteness of the social product and also the inadequacies of the social order of production. . . . The [dream] experiences [of a classless society], stored in the collective unconscious and intermingling with the new, create those utopias which leave their trace in a thousand configurations of life, from permanent buildings to ephemeral fashions.[88]

Adorno attacked Benjamin heavily for this notion of a nineteenth-century collective subject with its dream of a utopian future — significantly, by trying to outflank his Marxism: "It should be clear and sufficient warning that in a dreaming collective no differences remain between classes."[89] But Benjamin's affirmation of a collective unconscious was a gesture of solidarity with the proletariat, not a regression to Jung (as Adorno charged).[90] Ironically, however, and here Adorno's criticism was justified, this led him to a less critical presentation of the bourgeois era, skewing the dialectical balance away from the original conception of the *Passagenarbeit*, which was to show the nineteenth-century commodity world as an image not only of utopia but also of hell.[91] When Adorno wrote on nineteenth-century phenomena in, for example, his 1937–1938 series of essays on Richard Wagner, his dialectical hermeneutics demonstrated how the promise of utopia in Wagner's music reversed into ideology, and made that ideology in turn transparent as an image of social truth: in a constellation with the present, Wagnerian music became legible as an anticipation of fascism.[92] The *Passagenarbeit exposé* promised a very different representation, not a critical polemic, but a redemption of the past, a religious motif, here at the service of profane illumination. Benjamin wrote to Scholem:

The work presents the philosophical realization of surrealism – and thereby its sublation – as well as the attempt to portray the image of history in the most unpretentious fixations of life, its refuse as it were.[93]

Benjamin proposed in the *exposé* that the *Passagenarbeit* provide a visual reconstruction of past history in fragmentary details. They would shimmer before the reader like the flash thoughts of a memory, and the ghost that haunted their ruins in the present was the ghost of a failed revolution, the unfulfilled dream of a classless society. Here his hermeneutics moved toward a positive philosophy of history which hypostatized the progressive emergence within capitalist society of transcendent possibilities whose realization remained the unfinished task of the present. In this conception of history, which Adorno disparaged as "almost developmental,"[94] transient nature attested to history's dynamics, instead of providing for its demystification.

Both Adorno and Scholem were skeptical of Benjamin's newly manifested "solidarity" with the proletariat because it went so deeply against the grain of his personality. Scholem remembered that three difficulties of being friends with Benjamin were his need for solitude, his dislike of talking about daily politics, and his secretiveness, which included keeping the people he knew (for example, Scholem, Adorno, and Brecht) separate from one another.[95] Adorno described how little Benjamin fit into any group, recalling the latter's admission in *Berliner Kindheit* that he would have been incapable of building a front with his own mother.[96] Yet, with Brecht the only one of the triumverate whom he saw during this period, the affirmative character of his political position intensified.

POLITICS AND ART'S TECHNOLOGICAL REPRODUCTION

In 1935 Benjamin completed an essay, "Das Kunstwerk im Zeitalter seiner technischen Reproduzierbarkeit" (The Artwork in the Age of Its Technological Reproducibility), which, he wrote to Horkheimer, "made a thrust in the direction of a materialist theory of art."[97] Horkheimer read the essay when he saw Benjamin in Paris at the end of the year, and he agreed to publish it in the Institute's journal.[98] Benjamin was clearly excited about the piece, believing it would be an important theoretical contribution to the debate on Marxist aesthetics going on among artists and literary figures both inside and outside the Communist Party in Europe during the thirties.[99] Furthermore, although its material was "totally unrelated" to the *Passagenarbeit*, the two works, he claimed, were "methodologically most intimately connected."[100] Benjamin wrote to Adorno that his discussions with Horkheimer had been "friendly" and "fruitful," and he implied Adorno would react favorably to the piece.[101] But he delayed sending a copy to Adorno for several months, and the response when it came was critical. It is difficult to see how Benjamin could have expected otherwise. The themes of the essay touched too closely to Adorno's own work for the points of difference not to be abrasive. In fact, Adorno had already informed him of his "misgivings" in the formulation of the piece, having heard about it from Horkheimer.[102]

The original impulse of the aesthetic theory Benjamin outlined in the artwork essay was not foreign to Adorno's thinking. Opposed to orthodox Marxist aesthetics which made reductionist analyses in terms of socioeconomic modes of production external to the artwork itself, Benjamin took Marx's critical cognitive method and applied it within the art superstructure itself. In the opening section of the essay (which, against heavy protests from Benjamin, had to be omitted in the published version),[103] he described Marx's method of criticizing the capitalist mode of production as going "back to the fundamental relations of capitalistic production and through his presentation show[ing] them in such a way that they revealed what one could expect of capitalism in the future."[104] There was, he claimed, a parallel development in art, as a separate process necessitating its own analysis. Lagging half a century behind the transformation of the substructure, but "no less noticeable," a dialectical transformation had occurred out of "the developmental tendencies of art under present conditions of production."[105] Adorno, of course, did not disagree as to the separateness of art's development, even if he tended to see superstructure phenomena as anticipating socioeconomic change rather than lagging behind it. But whereas he saw art's transformation brought about by the dialectical praxis between the artist and the historically developed techniques of his trade,[106] Benjamin situated the dialectic solely within the objective forces of the superstructure, that is, within the mechanical technologies of art's reproduction.[107] Furthermore, he judged their effects positively. He argued that the new technologies of audiovisual production – photography, sound recording, and film – had on their own accomplished the dialectical transformation of art, in a way which led to its self-liquidation. Specifically, the possibility of the artwork's unlimited duplication robbed it of its "aura," that very uniqueness which in Benjamin's original philosophy had been the source of its cognitive value.[108] Now he claimed that the liquidation of art's aura had a positive effect, and art had acquired a new use value:

> . . . for the first time in world history, mechanical reproduction emancipates the work of art from its parasitical dependency on ritual. . . . Instead of ritual, it begins to be based on another practice: politics.[109]

Benjamin argued that film, which was a synthesis of the revolutionary technologies, was politically the most progressive new art form because it was the least auratic: the camera man, the polar opposite of the magician, penetrated reality like a surgeon.[110] Whereas the audience for painting or books was the individual, for film it was the collective, and Benjamin affirmed its potential for "mobilizing the masses"[111] through the effects of shock and critical distancing. Finally, he claimed the liquidation of art was prophetic, programmatic of the future, in that its collectivist production process transcended the division of labor between artist and technician, brainworker and handworker.[112] Benjamin used the term "negative theology" *critically* to describe the *art pour l'art* of the late bourgeois era,[113] which, he claimed, was not immune to being used for fascist purposes:

> Its self-alienation has reached such a degree that it can experience its own destruction as an aesthetic pleasure of the first order. This is the situation of politics which fascism is rendering aesthetic. Communism responds by politicizing art.[114]

Benjamin's argument managed to tread on all ten of Adorno's intellectual toes, and the shocked outcry in his letter of response was not surprising.[115] It was he who had worried that Benjamin was guilty of aestheticism, due to the problems of surrealism as a model.[116] Now, aping the official line of the Communist Party, Benjamin was claiming that the *art pour l'art* which Adorno had judged positively as an alternative to mass culture was the aesthetic parallel to fascism. It was bad enough that art's disenchantment was supposed to occur automatically out of the revolutions in technological reproduction rather than through the active efforts of the artist as subject negating the bourgeois forms:

> . . . it disregards an elementary experience which becomes more evident to me every day in my own musical experience – that precisely the utmost consistency in the pursuit of the technical laws of autonomous art changes this art, and instead of rendering it into a taboo or fetish, approximates it to the state of freedom, as something that can be produced and made consciously.[117]

But more, Benjamin explicitly ruled out the possibility that autonomous art could be progressive. Adorno rightfully considered this a betrayal of their earlier position:

> In . . . your earlier writings, the great continuity of which, it seems to me, your present essay dissolves, you differentiated the concept of the work of art as an image from the symbol of theology as well as from the taboo of magic. I find it questionable, then – and here I see a very sublimated remnant of certain Brechtian motifs – that you now effortlessly transfer the concept of magical aura to the "autonomous work of art" and flatly assign to the latter a counter-revolutionary function.[118]

Where Benjamin brought autonomous art into a constellation with fascism, Adorno countered that *l'art pour l'art* was "as much in need of redemption" in light of "the united front which exists against it and which to my knowledge extends from Brecht to the [protofascist] Youth Movement. . . ."[119] Adorno was startled by Benjamin's uncritical affirmation of film, the medium of mass culture which had taken the place of traditional, "autonomous" art. He warned

Benjamin against "romanticizing" the laughter of the proletariat in the movie house. Bringing Lenin to his defense, he called his friend's politics "anarchistic" for its affirmation of the workers' empirically existing consciousness.[120] Film, claimed Adorno, was highly auratic, whereas Schönberg's music was not.[121] As for film entertainment providing an image of the utopian future, Adorno did not find the argument convincing, if "only for the simple reason that in the communist society, work will be so organized that the people will no longer be so tired and so stupefied as to need diversion."[122]

Adorno was just finishing his essay on jazz (discussed in Chapter 6), which criticized jazz's claim to be democratic and spontaneous as mere appearance. Benjamin's analysis, suggested Adorno, should at least include this negative moment in all mass culture, and that meant the analysis needed to be more "thoroughly dialectized": autonomous art and mass culture, as *Schein* (appearance), were simultaneously both ideology and truth:

> Both bear the scars of capitalism, both contain elements of change (naturally never and in no way the mid-point between Schönberg and the American film). Both are torn halves of full freedom, to which however they do not add up. . . .[123]

When Benjamin saw Adorno's jazz essay several months later, he wrote comparing it to his own artwork essay: "Would you be surprised if I told you that I am tremendously pleased by so deep and so spontaneous a communication in our thinking?"[124] Adorno no doubt was surprised, as he had brought up the jazz critique as an illustration of his disagreements with the artwork essay.[125] Benjamin continued: "our studies are like two spotlights which are directed at the same object from opposite sides. . . ."[126]

Benjamin gave a later version of the artwork essay to Brecht in 1938.[127] His critical response to it was ironic, in view of Adorno's criticism of its "Brechtian" motifs. Brecht wrote in his journal:

> benjamin is here. . . . he says: when you feel a gaze directed to you, even behind your back, you return it (!). the expectation that what you look at looks back at you, provides the aura. the latter is supposed to be in decay in recent times, together with the cultic. b[enjamin] discovered this through the analysis of film, where aura disintegrates because of the reproducibility of artworks. it is all mysticism mysticism, in a posture opposed to mysticism. it is in such a form that the materialistic concept of history is adopted! it is rather ghastly.[128]

But when Benjamin sent the essay to Gershom Scholem, the person who should have appreciated its "mysticism" criticized its Marxism instead.[129] Benjamin expressed disappointment and surprise that Scholem couldn't find the terrain of thought in which they were earlier both at home, blaming it on the French language of the copy.[130] When they later discussed the essay in Paris in 1938, Benjamin defended himself against Scholem's criticism by claiming, according to Scholem, that in this essay, as always, his Marxism was "not of a dogmatic nature but a heuristic, experimental one."[131] Scholem recalled him insisting that

> . . . the transferal of metaphysical, indeed theological trains of thought which he had developed in our years together profited precisely within a Marxist perspective, because there they could unfold with greater vitality, at least in present times, than in the one for which they were originally intended.[132]

But if Benjamin considered the Marxism of the piece only a heuristic device, this did not prevent him from sending the first German version to Moscow in early 1936 with the hopes of getting it published in the literary journal *Das Wort*[133] and writing: "From the standpoint of the materialist dialectic I foresee no objection to my method."[134]

Despite the diversity of interpretations which the artwork essay evoked on a theoretical level, there was political coherence in Benjamin's position. The essay was a gesture of solidarity, not first and foremost with his intellectual friends, but with the working class. It must be recalled that for Benjamin as for Adorno, truth was relative to the historical present.[135] This meant that Benjamin's interpretation of the dialectical development of art was a construction of the past as it formed a constellation with existing conditions. In his words, the artwork essay was conceived "as an indication of the precise location in the present toward which my historical construction [the *Passagenarbeit*] is drawn as toward its vanishing point."[136] The problem was that in the mid-thirties, Benjamin and Adorno had very different evaluations of the historical present. Specifically, Benjamin, like Brecht, continued to support the USSR as the leader of a world proletariat movement, while Adorno decidedly did not.[137] Unlike Adorno and the Institute members, Benjamin was

> . . . for a long time prepared to endorse the politics of the Soviet Union; and here in a certain sense he went very far. Then the Moscow trials found him for the first time somewhat at a loss.[138]

The summary executions of Zinoviev and Kamenev, which occurred August 24, 1935, shook Benjamin but did not change his affirmative evaluation of Soviet foreign policy, which still appeared to be anti-imperialist. As late as June 24, 1939, he wrote to Horkheimer that he saw the USSR "as agent of our interests in a future war,"[139] at which time it might be expected to lend revolutionary support to the German workers. Scarcely two months later, however, the signing of the Nazi-Soviet Non-Aggression Pact profoundly disillusioned Benjamin.[140] Corresponding to this alteration in his sense of the historical present, the theological motifs in Benjamin's writing would once again become dominant over the Marxist ones.

Chapter 10. The Adorno-Benjamin Debate

Part 2: Political Differences

ADORNO JOINS THE INSTITUTE

The political rift between Adorno and Benjamin was clear by 1935. While Benjamin's expression of solidarity with the workers' empirical consciousness reflected the time he was spending with Brecht, Adorno was being drawn more closely to Max Horkheimer, whose Institute had set up headquarters in exile in New York two years earlier. The Institute's journal published Benjamin's art-work essay in May 1936; but in the next issue there appeared a long essay by Horkheimer, "Egoismus und Freiheitsbewegung" (Egoism and the Development of Freedom)[1] which struck a receptive chord in Adorno for several reasons. While the essay endorsed the emancipation of the masses from capitalist oppression (more explicitly, indeed, than any of Adorno's writings), the fact that Horkheimer understood such oppression in psychological as well as economic terms made him strongly critical of mass culture, which he called the "entertainment industries" (*Vergnügungsindustrien*),[2] because it gave the false, subjective appearance of overcoming alienation while leaving the objective, social reality of alienation intact. He claimed that as a compensatory and illusionary gratification, mass culture was a new form of bourgeois asceticism, and hence a continuation of the betrayal of the true interests of the masses which had been going on since the dawn of the bourgeois era. Horkheimer's point was to demonstrate that bourgeois asceticism had an ideological function, developing not only the psychological preconditions for the emergence of the capitalist class (as Max Weber had argued) but also those necessary for the persistent submission of the masses to class domination. Moreover, whatever its bourgeois source, such asceticism had not been overcome by Stalin's Russia. As prototype for the authoritarian character of the present working class (which had been the focus of the Institute's first empirical research project)[3] Horkheimer traced in the essay the structural relationship between leaders and led in cases of demagogy from Savonarola and Luther to Robespierre, analyzing the repression on which it was based and the resulting spiritualization — even more so in the "secular" bourgeois era — of the mass's desire for real social change:

> Bourgeois leaders attempt to idealize and spiritualize the crude desires for a better life, for the abolition of property differences, and for the introduction of a true community which was espoused by popular religious leaders and theological utopians of those [prebourgeois] centuries.[4]

Horkheimer, influenced by Freud, defined social utopia in terms of that material, sensual, individual happiness which bourgeois asceticism repressed, and he included as a component of that asceticism the hostility to art and to creative intellectual activity which had developed concomitant to the rationalization of society.[5] On all these points, in particular his critical attitude toward the liquidation of art by mass culture and the replacement of the active, questioning individual by mass man, Horkheimer supported Adorno's position in the latter's debate with Benjamin.

In June 1937, Adorno made his first trip to the United States. He wrote to Benjamin enthusiastically about his reception, implying that he was somewhat surprised by the compatibility between the thinking of the Institute's inner circle (in particular Leo Lowenthal and Herbert Marcuse)[6] and what he still referred to as his and Benjamin's common philosophical program.[7] The enthusiasm was reciprocated on the part of Horkheimer who had written "jubilantly" to Lowenthal the year before that Adorno finally "really belongs to us."[8] Yet even in 1937 such a statement was premature. Adorno was still reluctant to leave Europe to become a resident member of the Institute in New York, and one reason was his desire to remain in contact with Benjamin and in fact work more closely with him. In October 1936 Adorno visited Benjamin in Paris on a trip financed by the Institute. Benjamin wrote to Horkheimer in thanks:

> Our exchange of views, which had in fact been delayed for years, made possible the recognition of a communality in regard to the most significant theoretical intentions, which was very gratifying, indeed life-giving. This accord, in view of our long separation, had on occasion an almost marvelous quality.[9]

They had the chance to discuss Adorno's long study of Husserl, which attempted through immanent criticism to transcend idealism and which illustrated the implications of Schönberg's music as a cognitive model, as opposed to surrealist art. They discussed Benjamin's artwork essay, Adorno's jazz essay, the 1935 *Passagenarbeit exposé* and Adorno's criticism of it.[10] Bearing witness to the extent of their intellectual reconciliation, Adorno wrote Benjamin in November concerning the possibility of his permanent resettlement in Paris.[11] Even after his 1937 trip to the United States he wrote to Benjamin that he planned to delay moving to New York for another two years.[12] Meanwhile, Horkheimer showed himself most receptive to Benjamin's work. He visited Benjamin in Paris that year, and later wrote to Adorno that Benjamin was really "closest to us,"[13] and

Benjamin wrote to Horkheimer August 10, 1937, that he had read the latter's essay describing the Institute's theoretical position, the seminal article "Traditional and Critical Theory,"[14]

> . . . as you can imagine with total agreement. The way in which you characterize the atmosphere in which our work proceeds and the causes which you give for its isolation strike me particularly.[15]

For whatever reasons, whether Horkheimer was wooing Adorno through Benjamin or whether Benjamin was wooing Horkheimer because of financial concern, they were both exaggerating. While it is true that Horkheimer genuinely appreciated Benjamin's work and was most consistent in providing at least a minimum of financial support to Benjamin throughout the years of his emigration, even when he took issue with the content of Benjamin's work,[16] as intellectual personalities they were quite far apart, and Scholem's observation was surely accurate:

> My distinctive impression was that he [Horkheimer] – and that means his Institute – recognized Benjamin's intellectual potency, but were totally incapable of producing any real relationship with [Benjamin] himself. And still, many years later, years after Benjamin's death, the several times I met Horkheimer only strengthened this impression.[17]

Benjamin on his part felt a "deep sympathy" for the theoretical direction of the Institute,[18] but despite the flattering tone of his letters, Horkheimer's essays do not seem to have been significant in his own intellectual development.[19]

In September 1937 Adorno married Gretel Karplus, whom he had known for years and who had been a close friend of Benjamin during the Berlin days of the early thirties. Despite their original plan to stay in Europe for at least two years, quite suddenly in November Adorno informed Benjamin that they were moving to New York right away.[20] Horkheimer had telegraphed Adorno that there was an opening for him as music director of the Princeton Radio Research Project headed by Paul Lazarsfeld, and Adorno made the decision to take it.[21] But before leaving for the United States, at the turn of the year 1937–1938, Adorno and Gretel were with Benjamin in San Remo for what they were not then aware would be their last time together. The mood was congenial. Adorno read to Benjamin the study of Wagner on which he was working, which interpreted Wagner critically as a prefiguration of Nazism. Because the essay attacked "serious" music rather than popular culture, it did not entangle them in a quarrel on the political issue. And although the analysis was polemical, lacking Benjamin's impulse for rescuing and thereby redeeming nineteenth-century phenomena,[22] although it borrowed from Horkheimer's theoretical elaboration of bourgeois aestheticism whereby the repression of sensual happiness converged with the repression of class consciousness, there was much in the essay with which Benjamin could closely identify. Specifically, he could appreciate Adorno's ability to make social reality visible within the phenomena themselves, as Benjamin wrote to Horkheimer, to make "musical facts, which could not be more remote from anyone than myself, . . . socially transparent";[23] and Benjamin found "one tendency in this work particularly interesting: establishing the physiognomic immediately in the social sphere, almost without psychological mediation."[24] This one tendency, to which Benjamin here referred as social "physiognomics,"[25] was of course the methodological stress on "immanent" interpretation, educing directly out of a constellation of the smallest, surface details of cultural phenomena an image of the social whole. It distinguished Adorno's and Benjamin's approach most markedly from that of Horkheimer and his Institute with their Hegelian stress on mediation, whereby the phenomena were related analytically to a Freudo-Marxist theoretical frame.[26]

However, after Adorno arrived in New York in February, he was not immune to Horkheimer's influence. He reread Hegel, in preparation for a collaborative study with Horkheimer on "the new, open form of the dialectic."[27] He wrote to Benjamin that summer, 1938, from Bar Harbor, Maine: "I busy myself with a renewed study of Hegel's *Logic,* a truly remarkable work that presently speaks to me in all its parts."[28] Still, Adorno did not abandon his earlier method. He was also working on an essay which reflected his experiences at the Princeton Radio Research Project, and which was published later that year in the Institute's journal with the title "Über den Fetischcharakter in der Musik und die Regression des Hörens" (On the Fetish Character of Music and the Regression of Hearing).[29] He said later that the piece reflected an advance over the jazz essay because of its greater "consideration of institutional and social mechanisms."[30] Yet one searches in vain for a real change in Adorno's methodology. There was greater use of the theoretical categories developed by the Institute in its analysis of fascism; for example, instead of the aesthetic representation of the "jazz figure," he made use of the theoretically grounded "sado-masochist character" as the interpretive key to the anthropology of mass culture. But the essay still bore the hallmarks of Adorno's immanent criticism. In an argument that moved through a complex of dialectical reversals, Adorno made the characteristics of fetishism, reification, and exchange visible "inside" the phenomenon of listening to music.[31] The essay was closely related to Benjamin's artwork essay as if conceived as its dialectical counterpart. It affirmed the thesis that art had been liquidated, but disagreed as to the source and implications of this change. Adorno claimed that "serious" and popular music converged not simply because of the revolutions of technological reproduction, but because of the transformation in the relationship between the audience as subject and the music as object, which determined the form of the new technologies as well as being determined by them. The liquidation of art had its correlate in the "liquidation of the individual" who could have experienced that art; hence (and here was a Hegelian negation of Benjamin) Adorno claimed that the "positive," that is, technological progress in the mass production of music, was in fact "negative," the development of regression in listening: the mass audience, instead of experiencing music, consumed it as a fetishized object, the value of which was determined by exchange.[32] Adorno concluded:

Music is not spared the liquidation by collective forces of that individuality which is irredeemable; but only individuals are capable of consciously representing, in opposition to those forces, the real interests of collectivity.[33]

In sum, the essay indicated that the Institute, rather than changing Adorno's orientation, was giving him a more solid theoretical and logical ground to continue defending his Benjaminian method against tendencies in Benjamin himself.

THE FIRST BAUDELAIRE ESSAY: EXTINCTION OF THE COGNITIVE SUBJECT

The harmonious atmosphere during Adorno's last visit with Benjamin in San Remo had given cause for optimism that the really divisive disputes were behind them, and Adorno was most anxious for Benjamin to come to New York. But the *Passagenarbeit,* which in 1938 again preoccupied Benjamin, necessitated detailed historical research which could only be done in Paris.[34] As the next step, Benjamin was preparing an essay on Baudelaire, commissioned by the Institute, which would be a "miniature model" for the whole.[35] Yet his research was not the only reason for his reluctance to come to New York. Scholem visited Benjamin in Paris in February 1938, and recalled him saying that despite his deep sympathies with the Institute, "there were reservations and potential points of conflict which had several times made themselves evident."[36] He noted that Benjamin spoke of these points of conflict with "a strong tone of continuous criticism, indeed bitterness which in no way corresponded to the reconciliatory attitude of his letters to Horkheimer";[37] at the same time, the Institute's financial support of the *Passagenarbeit* was crucial.

If Adorno assumed correctly in San Remo that Benjamin's intellectual schizophrenia had reached a dialectical balance compatible with his own, then that balance was a delicate one. In trying to draw Benjamin to New York, Adorno was tugging not only against Paris ties, but against the old ones that still pulled in the contradictory directions of Denmark and Palestine. After a decade of alternately planning and postponing a move to Palestine, Benjamin again broached the possibility with Scholem. During the latter's February visit in 1938, Benjamin spoke of breaking relations with the Institute and going to Palestine to work on Kafka again if Scholem could get his good friend and publisher Salman Schocken to finance the study for two years.[38] Yet Scholem was not sure of where Benjamin's theoretical loyalties really lay. Benjamin wrote that during his visit, the

. . . long due philosophical confrontations proceeded in good form. If I am not mistaken, they gave him a picture of me as a man who has made himself at home between the jaws of a crocodile which he holds apart with iron struts.[39]

When Scholem returned to Paris that summer (after a lecture trip to the United States), plans to see Benjamin again were disappointed, as the latter had gone to visit Brecht in Denmark and work there on the Baudelaire essay. But by then, Benjamin also had reservations about his relationship with Brecht:

> Despite my great friendship with Brecht, I must take care to carry out my work in strict solitude. It contains certain specific moments which for him are unassimilatable. He has been friends with me long enough to know that and is insightful enough to respect it.[40]

Yet the mere fact that Benjamin was in Denmark to write the Baudelaire essay (increasingly overdue) was enough to make Adorno nervous. Gretel Adorno sent Benjamin a plea for the speedy conclusion of the piece,[41] and when Benjamin finally telegraphed September 6 that the manuscript was on its way, she wrote again to encourage him to come to New York.[42] She, Adorno, and Horkheimer all assured Benjamin that the Institute anticipated the arrival of the manuscript with great excitement. But for a month after they received it he heard nothing. Finally on November 10 Adorno wrote a letter that made clear the reason for their silence. They were frankly disappointed. Adorno reported that he had "literally gobbled up" the manuscript when it arrived, expecting it to represent the grand *Passagenarbeit* in microcosm.[43] Instead he found only a prelude: "Motifs are gathered together but not developed."[44] Adorno realized it was not accidental or due to lack of time: "As a true connoisseur of your writings I know very well that your *oeuvre* does not lack precedents for your procedural method."[45] Specifically, the method was surrealist in a way that Adorno had already criticized in regard to the 1935 *Passagenarbeit exposé.*[46] Instead of reconstructing social reality through an immanent, dialectical analysis of Baudelaire's poetic images, Benjamin juxtaposed images from the poet with data particles from objective history in a visual montage, adding the barest minimum of commentary, like captions under pictures. "Redeeming" documentary fragments from the past, Benjamin illuminated their meaning through direct reference to the class structure of nineteenth-century society. Those fragments were the minute facts of social history: a worker who hung himself in Eugène Sue's apartment, the origins of mandatory street numbers in Paris addresses, the funereal blacks and grays of bourgeois fashions. The *exposé* made immediate associative connections between superstructure and substructure (Baudelaire's image of the drunken ragpicker and Marx's comments on the urban wine tax; the Lesbian as Baudelaire's heroine and the masculinization of women through factory work; the literary image of the crowd and the proletariat as revolutionary class), and this was supposed to be sufficient to spark dialectical, materialist revelation. Once again, Benjamin was trying to "bridge both ends of the arc" between the poles of theology and materialism.[47] Once again, Adorno accused him of falling back into both:

> I regard it as methodologically unfortunate to give particular manifest features from the realm of the superstructure a "materialist" turn by relating them immediately and indeed practically causally to corresponding features of the substructure. . . . One might express it this way: the theological motif

of calling things by their names has a tendency to reverse into the astonished presentation of simple facts. If one wished to speak very drastically, one could say that the study has settled at the crossroads of magic and positivism. That spot is bewitched. Only theory could break the spell — your own determined, good, speculative theory.[48]

Without "theory," that is, without the mediation of conceptual, critical reflection, theology degenerated into "magic," and Marxism into "positivism." Both, by positing the absolute priority of the given phenomena, were a lapse into that *prima philosophia* which Adorno and Benjamin had renounced in the Königstein program of 1929. It seemed to Adorno that Benjamin employed statements partisan to the proletariat as a substitute for the real philosophical task of *interpreting the truth* of the phenomena, and on this point he clearly lost his patience:

> There is in God's name only the one truth. . . . Ultimately there is more of that one truth in Nietzsche's *Geneology of Morals* than in Bukharin's *ABC*.[49]

Adorno was calling once more for Benjamin to return to Benjaminian orthodoxy as Adorno understood it,[50] only this time with the weight of the Institute behind him:

> I speak not only for my own incompetent self but equally for Horkheimer and the others when I tell you that we are all convinced it is not only advantageous to "your" production . . . but that it is also most beneficial to the cause of dialectical materialism and the theoretical interests represented by the Institute if you give in to your special insights and conclusions without obstructing them with ingredients which it obviously makes you so uneasy to swallow that I cannot really regard them as a blessing.[51]

Benjamin was stung by Adorno's criticism, although he might have expected it, given the history of their disputes. He responded a month later, writing Adorno that the letter "dealt me a blow."[52] Although he was "far from considering [the criticism] unfruitful, much less incomprehensible,"[53] he felt Adorno had mistakenly equated the lack of an esoteric and elaborately dialectical commentary with a lack of any theoretical interpretation whatsoever. In the first place, the piece was only a fragment of what he hoped to develop as a full book on Baudelaire. But even so, Benjamin insisted, he was still pursuing their common program of dialectical, materialist exegesis. He admitted:

> It is true that the indifference between magic and positivism, as you so pertinently formulate it, needs to be liquidated. In other words: dialectical materialists need to sublate [*aufzuheben*] the philological interpretation of the authors [quoted in the essay] in a Hegelian manner.[54]

But he claimed that the "astonished presentation" of the textual data was not antithetical to this, citing Adorno's own statement in his Kierkegaard study that "astonishment . . . registers 'the deepest insight into the relationship between dialectic, myth and image.' "[55] At the same time, he continued, the fact that quotations from the past evoked astonishment in readers of the present was itself the source of insight.[56] Dialectical, materialist revelation did not arise from the philological moment alone, which as the "inspection of a text which advances by detail" was static, "magically fixating the reader," but out of the construction of the details as they made a constellation with the present.[57]

Benjamin's theoretical justification had all the dialectical subtlety which to Adorno appeared to be lacking in the essay itself. Yet although he could still justify his position in the esoteric *Trauerspiel* vocabulary of the original Königstein program, Benjamin had indeed removed that esotericism from the presentation, and, as was the case with previous essays, his motive was political. He conceded that it might be objectively necessary due to the historical reality which one experienced to "swallow ingredients," in Adorno's words, which went against one's private intellectual disposition. But such ingredients, like a bitter pill, were not against his own true interests. Benjamin's letter recalled their discussions in San Remo earlier that year (and made it clear that at that time they had both seen the Institute's position as more traditionally Marxist and less innovative than their own original program):[58]

> If I there refused to adopt an esoteric intellectual development just for the sake of my own productive interests, [if I refused] to treat as unimportant the interests of dialectical materialism and of the Institute, then not only solidarity with the Institute or mere faithfulness to dialectical materialism was involved, but rather solidarity with the experiences, which we all have made, of the last fifteen years. Thus, here as well, it concerns the productive interests most my own; I won't deny that they may occasionally do violence to my original [interests].[59]

Benjamin admitted that Adorno's letter had saddened him, adding, not without sarcasm perhaps, that he found it "somewhat" encouraging "that your objections, no matter how solidly in agreement the [Institute] friends may be, are not to be taken as a rejection."[60] Yet those objections did mean that the Institute expected Benjamin to rewrite the piece, and he had little choice but to acquiesce. Here Adorno's behavior is open to criticism − not for overestimating the theoretical difficulties of the Baudelaire essay (for they were real),[61] but for underestimating the personal difficulties of his friend. It was fall 1938, the time of the Czechoslovakia crisis. Benjamin wrote to Pollock in August that "the danger of war appears very great."[62] He mailed the manuscript to Horkheimer only days before Chamberlain and Daladier capitulated to Hitler at Munich, writing to Adorno October 4 that finishing the essay "was a race against the war," conditions in Paris were stifling, and he was making plans to get his books out of the city.[63] Adorno's long, critical letter of November 10 made no reference to these historical events. Benjamin voiced his despondency concerning them, in his next letter:

> For one thing it is the situation of the Jews in Germany, from which none

of us can insulate ourselves. In addition there is the serious illness of my sister, who was found to be suffering from hereditary arteriosclerosis at the age of 37. She is practically immobile and thus unable to work (although at present she probably still has modest means). The prognosis is almost hopeless. Apart from all this, it is not always possible to be here without oppressive anxiety. Understandably, I am making every effort to accomplish my naturalization. Unfortunately the necessary *démarches* cost not only much time, but some money as well.[64]

Benjamin was worried (although unnecessarily) that the Institute might cut off its funding of him in Paris. The possibility of going to Palestine and being financed by Schocken to write a book on Kafka had not materialized.[65] Benjamin wrote to Scholem that the winter of 1938–1939 was "a period of protracted depression," and not the least of reasons was Adorno's "minutely grounded rejection" of the Baudelaire piece, which he was now revising with a feeling of "alienation from the present subject of my work" and a sense of intellectual isolation.[66]

Adorno, for his part, continued to encourage Benjamin's work on the Baudelaire revision, sending another letter of detailed commentary.[67] He was also not insensitive to Benjamin's financial needs, and Gretel wrote him May 5:

Teddie and I will do everything we can for you (it also depresses us that we unfortunately are no longer financially solvent enough to simply do it privately), and Max also knows the situation. Your work simply cannot be *allowed* to be disturbed by it as well.[68]

Ultimately, with the continued support of the Institute, Benjamin finished the new Baudelaire essay in July.[69] Shortly after sending the manuscript to New York, he wrote to a friend of Brecht: "My Baudelaire chapter is completed and I now await the thunderclouds that *this* text will gather over my head."[70]

THE SECOND BAUDELAIRE ESSAY: EXTINCTION OF THE HISTORICAL SUBJECT

When it came, the thunder was applause. Gretel wrote in English: "I am fully enthusiastic about the new version of your Baudelaire";[71] Adorno concurred: "my enthusiasm about the Baudelaire increases steadily. . . ."[72] This was not surprising, for in fact Benjamin had heeded Adorno's earlier criticisms. In this version the interpretive moment was fused with the philosophical one in a way that paralleled Adorno's work on Husserl. Benjamin's critical analysis of the poet's images illuminated them as an expression of the altered relationship between subject and object in the nineteenth century, and hence as an unintentional expression of social truth. Specifically, he brought the nineteenth-century literary theme of the crowd to conceptual clarification demonstrating how it revealed the disintegration of the capacity for experience (that is, in a philosophical sense, the capacity for subjective knowledge of objective reality). In the essay the concepts of alienation and reification were presented in the most visual, concrete terms within a historical, materialist theory of the transformation in perception characterizing urban existence. Benjamin argued that Baudelaire's writing represented "a change in the structure of experience,"[72] manifested in the experience of the crowd, where reality was perceived by the senses in a series of shock-like collisions. In the crowd, tactile sensations became discontinuous, like striking a match, switching on a machine, or snapping a photograph.[73] In the crowd, visual images were as fragmented and as senselessly juxtaposed as articles in a newspaper. Accompanying this disruption of spatial continuity was a transformation in the experience of time. Time lost the "aura" it has possessed as a calendar of rituals, and became empty:

> The man who loses his capacity for experiencing feels himself set outside the calendar. The big-city dweller learns to know this feeling on Sundays; Baudelaire has it *avant la lettre* in one of the *Spleen* poems.[75]

The city transformed sexuality: "The rapture of the urban resident is love not at first sight, but at last sight."[76] The excitement was not eros, but "the kind of sexual shock that can overcome a lonely person."[77]

As a defense against shock, the urban individual insulated himself by sealing himself off. He simply endured the colliding stimuli rather than respond to them, so that mere existence (*Erlebnis*) replaced active, reflective experience (*Erfahrung,* in the Kantian sense of the unity of perception). Benjamin linked this structural transformation with the transformation in the conditions of labor from that of the craftsman, whose work was a learning experience, to the disjointed, repetitive motions of the assembly-line worker: "The shock-existence [*Chockerlebnis*] which the passer-by has in the crowd corresponds to the 'existence' of the worker at the machine."[78] Baudelaire himself did not make the connection. Benjamin "deciphered" it, making use of the mediating figure of the gambler which appeared in Baudelaire's works, and illuminating the configuration in which the extremes of factory work and gambling converged:

> The jolt in the movement of a machine is like the so-called *coup* in a game of chance. The hand motion [*Handgriff*] of the worker at the machine has no connection to the preceding motion, precisely because it represents its exact repetition. Since each motion at the machine is just as sealed off from the preceding one as a *coup* in a game of chance is from the one that preceded it, the drudgery of the laborer is, in its own way, a counterweight to the drudgery of the gambler. Both kinds of activities are equally devoid of content.[79]

Benjamin argued that not only time lost its aura but also perceived objects, including other human beings;[80] and significantly, while he had judged the loss of aura positively in his artwork essay (against Adorno's protests), here he described it critically as a symptom of the disintegration of the capacity for experience. Rather than affirming the empirical consciousness of the worker, he was presenting an image of the historical "origin" of that consciousness and an explanation of why it was necessarily false: If the proletariat could not experience reality, if it could not interpret the social truth that reality contained, then it could not become aware of its own objective position. Benjamin maintained that Baudelaire provided an insight into "what is actually meant by the masses. One cannot speak of them in terms of a class or a structured collectivity. They are nothing other than the amorphous crowd of passers-by, the man on the street [*Strassenpublikum*]."[81] Urban existence thus worked against the development of class consciousness.

Benjamin's analysis of the changes in visual and tactile perception was really an extension of Adorno's theory of the regressive change in aural perception, which he had developed in his article on the fetish character of music. It marked an abandonment of Benjamin's earlier insistence (in the artwork essay) that the revolution in optic perception was progressive. Benjamin no longer saw the technological developments of camera and film as a self-contained, purely objective process, but described them as already anticipated by the disintegration inherent in urban experience: photography registered the auraless optic sensation of the crowd, while in film, "perception in the form of shock is raised to a formal principle."[82] It should be noted that there was no lack of esotericism in Benjamin's presentation. Theological motifs became visible in profane, "inverse" form to any connoisseur of Benjamin's writings.[83] Finally, because the experience of urban industrialization was not limited to capitalism, the critical implications of Benjamin's analysis in no way made an exception for the USSR.

There is no doubt that this second version of the Baudelaire essay contained changes which reconciled it successfully with Adorno's own position. In fact their production hadn't been so close since Adorno first articulated their common philosophical program in 1931. Adorno wrote to Benjamin:

> I believe it is no exaggeration to describe this work as the most consummate that you have published since the Baroque book [*Ursprung des deutschen Trauerspiels*] and the [Karl] Kraus [essay, 1931]. If at one time I had a bad conscience because of my nagging insistence, then this bad conscience has been transformed into nothing but pride, and for that you yourself are guilty — so dialectical indeed is our production.[84]

It must be conceded that this second version of the Baudelaire essay was more "dialectical" and "materialist" than the earlier one — in fact it was more "Marxist" — in that it was more in line with the epistemological model provided by Marx's famous interpretation of commodities in the opening pages of *Capital*.[85] What Benjamin had omitted, of course, was the political gesture of solidarity with the working class and the theoretical repercussions of that gesture. Just how much the omission of this Brechtian stand was motivated by a desire to placate Adorno and the Institute is a question the available documents do not answer. However, more incriminating that Adorno's "nagging insistence" on theoretical questions was the continued overimportance he attached to those questions in view of the constellation of objective historical conditions which hovered over Benjamin and threatened his very existence. Benjamin completed the second Baudelaire version in late July. In August the Nazi-Soviet Non-Aggression Pact was signed. The event shocked Benjamin, who had placed his hopes in the USSR's support of German workers in case of war.[86] The following month the war began with Hitler's *Blitzkrieg* against Poland, and Benjamin, not yet a French citizen, was confined to a work camp in Nièvre. It was here that the telegram from New York reached him with its enthusiastic response to the Baudelaire essay.[87] Through the intercession of Adrienne Monnier, a friend of Paul Valéry, Benjamin was released in November. At the end of the year he was back in Paris, facing the bleak prospect of a European war. The Institute urged him to come immediately to the United States, but visiting visas were difficult to obtain, and Benjamin's work still bound him to Paris.[88] During this period he wrote the *Geschichtsphilosophische Thesen,* eighteen theses on the concept of history which marked a retreat from political commitment and a return to the language of theology as the only remaining refuge for the ideal of the revolution. He sent a copy of the theses to Scholem, but not the Institute, worrying (mistakenly, at least in Adorno's and Horkheimer's case)[89] that its members would be critical.[90] When German troops invaded France and marched on Paris, Benjamin had no choice but to abandon the city. He left most of his work on the *Passagenarbeit* behind in the care of friends. He still lacked the proper travel papers, and wrote to Adorno from Lourdes on August 2:

> The total uncertainty as to what the next days, the next hours will bring has dominated my existence for many weeks. I am condemned to read every newspaper (they appear here on only one page) as a writ published against me and to hear in every radio report the voice of bad tidings.[91]

In September, in the company of a small group, he reached the Spanish border with what he assumed to be the proper papers, but they were told at the last moment that they couldn't proceed. That night, September 25, 1940, in a hotel in Port Bou, Benjamin took a lethal dose of morphine. The next day the border guard, not unmoved by the suicide, allowed the rest of the group to cross over the frontier.

Benjamin's decision to go through with the act of self-destruction which he had first contemplated nine years earlier was no momentary response to the immediate situation.[92] Nor should it be interpreted as a purely subjective expression, an individual act of resignation. Rather, it was the only remaining possibility for resistance. A passage from the first Baudelaire essay provides a key:

> The oppositions which modernity sets up against man's natural productive spirit are out of proportion to his powers. It is understandable if he grows tired and takes flight into death. Modernity must stand under the sign of

that suicide which places its seal upon a heroic will, one which concedes nothing to a way of thinking hostile to it. It is *the* conquest of modernity in the realm of passion. . . . Suicide could very well appear to Baudelaire as the only heroic deed which remained for the *multitudes maladives* of the cities in reactionary times.[93]

Chapter 11. The Adorno-Benjamin Debate

Part 3: Requiem

THE ISOLATION OF THE IMMIGRANT

Benjamin's suicide shocked Adorno, and he received the news at a critical time. Sorrow connected with historical events began to touch him the previous year when his seventy-three-year-old mother and ailing father were arrested and detained in Frankfurt by the Nazis. His father "received an injury during the pogrom in his already suffering eye; his office rooms were demolished, and shortly thereafter he lost the rights to his entire assets."[1]

Yet as late as then, in February 1939, Adorno expressed doubt that war would break out, believing with striking Marxist orthodoxy that England, whose "ruling class . . . cannot afford to risk anything," would continue to capitulate to Hitler, because German plans ultimately coincided with the interests of British imperialism.[2] Although therefore unprepared for the outbreak of war, his intellectual orientation was not upset by it, still less by the signing of the Nazi-Soviet Non-Aggression Pact. Unlike Benjamin, he had since the purges ceased looking to the USSR as the model for social transformation. But when historical events manifested themselves in a personal, individual constellation resulting in the loss of his friend, Adorno was deeply shaken.

Twice before he had felt the loss of death intensely. His Aunt Agathe, who had lived with him and taught him music as a child, died in 1935. Adorno wrote to Krenek at the time:

> I am totally stricken by it, and come around only very slowly even to imagine that somehow I can go on living. That sounds insanely exaggerated, but you can believe me that there is not an ounce of exaggeration or sentimentality in it.[3]

The second blow was the death of Alban Berg that same year.[4] Predictably, Adorno considered it not just a personal tragedy, but a critical statement on society:

164

. . . one thought unbearably distresses me: that material relations are responsible for Berg's death. One only has to think of it concretely: had he not wanted to spare the expense of a doctor, then he would have surely seen one, if with anxiety. The fact that he didn't attempt it and had to think about money brought about his death. The consideration that the existence of people with Berg's productive power is dependent on such things is in itself sufficient [to lead one] to the most radical consequences with regard to the status quo.[5]

How much more Adorno must have seen Benjamin's suicide as an expression of objective conditions.[6] Eleven years his senior, the vulnerable and withdrawn Benjamin was no father figure in the personal sense for Adorno, but he was an intellectual authority of the first order. Surely on one level, their theoretical debates during the thirties expressed Adorno's attempts to establish himself on equal footing with this man whose disciple he had become in 1929. Now at thirty-seven he was precisely the age that Benjamin had been then.

The intensity with which Adorno viewed this loss of one individual could not be matched by sheer numbers of victims. The war, the horrors committed against Jews in Germany,[7] the loneliness of emigration, combined with the dissipation of potential for revolution, were all expressed in Benjamin's gesture of suicide. As the literal acting out of the "liquidation of the individual," it was a tragic allegory of the contradictions inherent in the historical present. As an act of intellectual responsibility in recognition of intellectual impotence, Adorno might well have recognized the contradiction as his own. In the United States the appearance of democracy was a protection against physical extinction. Jewish immigrant intellectuals were not denied the right to work. Precisely because of this, however, "the burden of conformism, to which the native population submits as well, was particularly difficult."[8] In America "'Adjustment' was still a magic word," recalled Adorno,[9] cementing what was in fact a nation of immigrants. He was as unwilling to submit to this conformism as he had been to submit to any collective norms. The punishment, if not physical harm, was intellectual isolation and the sense of impotence which such isolation imposed — of working without effectiveness and writing without an audience. As he wrote in an essay dedicated to Benjamin:

> The individualist and the person who fits into the organization are both in danger of succumbing to the status quo; the former through his impotence which installs itself deceptively as its own tribunal but in fact cedes justice to the enemy powers, the latter through the powers to which he belongs and which carry the same injustice that they are supposed to be opposing into the ranks of the oppressors. For both must live in a world of universal injustice.[10]

Adorno had agreed to come to the United States as music director of the Princeton Radio Research Project in response to a telegram from Horkheimer, without even knowing what a "radio project" was: "I simply thought that my friend would not have made the proposal unless he was persuaded that I, a philosopher by calling, could handle the job."[11] In fact he was completely unprepared. Paul Lazarsfeld, the Viennese sociologist who was general director of the project, recorded his first impression of Adorno: "He looks exactly as you would imagine a very absent-minded German professor, and he behaves so foreign that I feel like a member of the Mayflower Society."[12]

Adorno commuted part-time from his Greenwich Village apartment to the offices at the Radio Research Project in Newark, which were located, he later recalled, "in a somewhat pioneering spirit, in an unoccupied brewery":[13]

> When I travelled through the tunnel under the Hudson I felt a little as if I were in Kafka's Nature Theater of Oklahoma. . . . My first impression of the researches already in progress there was not exactly marked by any great understanding. At Lazarsfeld's suggestion, I went from room to room and spoke to colleagues, heard words like "Likes and Dislikes Study," "success or failure of a program," of which at first I could make very little. But this much I did understand: that it was concerned with the collection of data, which were supposed to benefit the planning departments in the field of the mass media, whether in industry itself or in cultural advisory boards and similar bodies.[14]

In short, Adorno was being asked to subordinate his intellectual activity to the interests of the mass-media industry, composed, then as now, of capitalist monopolies. This was hardly a more appealing alternative to him than subordination to the line of the Party. The project was funded by the Rockefeller Foundation, and its charter required expressly that the research be conducted "within the limits of the commercial radio system" then in existence: "It was thereby implied that the system itself, its cultural and sociological consequences and its social and economic presuppositions were not to be analysed."[15] Adorno admitted: "I cannot say that I strictly obeyed the charter."[16] The result was that insofar as his writings for the project were understood at all, they were not accepted. Lazarsfeld wrote memos to his associates to explain "the brilliance and importance of Adorno's ideas"; he had Adorno himself write an explanatory memorandum,[17] but the paper that resulted obfuscated, Lazarsfeld feared, more than it clarified, so that "the distribution of this text would only have made the situation more difficult, for in English his writing had the same tantalizing attraction and elusiveness that it had in German."[18] According to Lazarsfeld, the project's funders "probably felt that my efforts to bring Adorno's type of critical research into the communications field were a failure."[19] As a result, "The renewal of the Rockefellar Grant in the fall of 1939 provided no budget for continuation of the music project."[20] Adorno lost his job, and that winter he moved to Los Angeles to join Horkheimer, who had gone there to live for reasons of health.[21] Despite their leaving, the Institute for Social Research retained its headquarters in New York, with Leo Lowenthal and Friedrich Pollock as acting directors.[22] Political and financial strains had begun to dissipate the Institute's productivity, however. Publication of the

Zeitschrift für Sozialforschung, the journal which had supported the theoretical work of Institute members since 1932, had to be discontinued after an initial attempt to produce it in the United States (under the English title *Studies in Philosophy and Social Science*) proved too expensive.[23]

Insofar as the Institute had a Los Angeles "branch," it really consisted of Adorno and Horkheimer, although they had visitors from New York, for example Pollock and Marcuse in the summer of 1942 (Pollock finally moved to the West Coast after the war). The two friends joined the community of exiled German writers and artists (including Heinrich and Thomas Mann and Alfred Döblin) who had gone there partly because of work opportunities provided by the Hollywood film industry.[24] If the Institute's affiliation with Columbia University had recreated the academic atmosphere of Frankfurt, the Los Angeles group was more reminiscent of Adorno's earlier circles in Vienna and Berlin. In some cases its members were the same. Ironically, Adorno again found himself in the company of Bertolt Brecht. Did each hold the other responsible for Benjamin's death? The available sources are silent, but they do indicate that the tension between Brecht and Adorno had far from dissipated. Brecht invented the word "Tui," the abbreviation of "tellect-ual-in," to refer to inside-out (or upside-down) intellectuals, and had plans from the early thirties on for a novel about them.[25] According to Hanns Eisler, the Tuis were those "who wanted to fix the economic problems and social ones related to them 'purely mentally' through all sorts of remedies, instead of pressing to the root of the evil – the question of the relations of property. . . ."[26] Eisler, it will be recalled, was Schönberg's student[27] and the musical collaborator of Brecht, whose "proletarian choruses" Adorno had so scathingly attacked in his 1932 article "Zur gesellschaftlichen Lage der Musik."[28] Now with Brecht in California, Eisler suggested after one lunch with Horkheimer that the Tui novel be based on the story of the Frankfurt Institute:

> A wealthy old man [Felix Weil] dies, disturbed by the suffering in the world. He leaves in his will a large sum of money establishing an institute to search for the source of misery – which is of course he himself. . . .[29]

So Brecht recorded in his diary in May 1942, adding several months later: "Adorno here. This Frankfurt Institute is a gold-mine for the Tui novel."[30] The fact that they were not infrequently together, however, was a silent admission that despite their theoretical differences, as radicals they shared a sense of intellectual impotence, and as immigrants in need of work they all made their compromises. Eisler himself had a grant from the Rockefellar Foundation for a "film music project," including a study of "Fourteen Ways to Describe Rain" which evoked some good-humored chastising from Brecht.[31] As part of this project, Adorno and Eisler actually collaborated on a book, *Komposition für den Film*,[32] which trod gingerly on the issues that separated them, combining theoretical elements from Schönberg, Brecht, Benjamin, and Horkheimer and providing practical suggestions for using music to heighten the critical impact of the film.[33] Adorno's diminished rigidity with regard to intellectual camps should surely be seen as tolerance rather than opportunism, a protest against the fanaticism of the age. It was based on the recognition that no one could survive the social contradictions unscathed. As he wrote during this period: "In a false life there is no right way to live."[34]

BENJAMIN'S THESES ON HISTORY

In June 1941, Adorno and Horkheimer first received a copy of Benjamin's *Geschichtsphilosophische Thesen* (Theses on the Philosophy of History). As Adorno was aware from previous correspondence, it was the last written draft completed by Benjamin before his death and a document of central theoretical importance, because it was intended as the methodological introduction to the *Passagenarbeit*.[35] Adorno, who in 1929 had been literally converted by the methodological introduction to Benjamin's *Trauerspiel* book, surely gave his utmost attention to this cryptic and remarkable text, composed of eighteen short theses. I have already discussed them in Chapter 3, in connection with Adorno's concept of history which was that history had no meaning in itself, but only in reference to the present, and then only as a critical concept which demystified the present. Although Benjamin's politically committed essays of the mid-thirties implied an affirmation of historical development as meaningful because they affirmed the objective development of technology, in these theses he returned to his earlier understanding,[36] which Adorno had never abandoned. The nature of the historical present had changed, however. In the early thirties, revolution still appeared possible, and the greatest obstacle to correct cognition seemed to be that reification of reality which gave the present the appearance of existing externally, as "second nature." But now, when precisely a sense of historical destiny had lured people into the catastrophes of fascism and war, it was, argued Benjamin in the theses, the myth of history as progressive change that needed dismantling: "Nothing has corrupted the German working class so much as the notion that *it* was moving with the current."[37] The image of the working class as the "redeemer of future generations" had cut

> . . . the sinews of its greatest strength. By this teaching the class is miseducated regarding hatred and the willingness to sacrifice. For both are nourished by the image of enslaved ancestors rather than that of liberated grandchildren.[38]

Whether Benjamin's theses were the source or merely lent support to a previous disposition, nothing that either Adorno or Horkheimer wrote after 1941 violated Benjamin's last charge, the mandate to negate the idea of history as progress. This meant a total transformation of the image of social revolution. Its goal, wrote Horkheimer, "is no longer the acceleration of progress, but rather the jumping out of progress."[39]

In the theses on history, the theological pole of Benjamin's thinking was strongly evident, not so much alongside the materialist pole as *within* it. The first thesis presented an image of this relationship, a "puppet in Turkish attire with a waterpipe in its mouth" playing chess at a large table, while "a hunchbacked dwarf who was an expert chess player sat inside and guided the puppet's hand by means of strings."[40] The image (which alluded as well to the "profane illumination" of drug-taking) suggested a "philosophical counterpart":

> The puppet, which is called "historical materialism," is to win all the time. It can take everyone on without difficulty if it takes theology into its service, which today as everyone knows is small and ugly, and moreover, can't allow itself to be seen.[41]

In what followed, Benjamin described how a "historical materialist" should approach the material of history, yet the language and imagery were consistently and explicitly theological: salvaging human experience from historical oblivion was compared with religious redemption; the revolution was described as the coming of the Messiah. It will be recalled that Adorno had criticized Benjamin's first Baudelaire essay because he felt that in it the theological and materialist poles collapsed into one. In that case, it seemed to Adorno, Benjamin incorporated the elements of both which were most deficient, that is, least critical. In his anxiousness to develop a nonidealist, truly Marxist method, Benjamin had simply pasted scraps of material from nineteenth-century Paris into the text with the barest minimum of interpretive commentary, as if by their mere recitation, in what Adorno described as a kind of religious "incantation" (*Beschwörung*), they would reveal their truth content. Adorno claimed, it will be recalled, that as a result the study landed on "the crossroads between magic and positivism."[42] Now in this new methodological introduction Benjamin had stressed precisely the opposite moment, in which truth emerged only by the setting up of a critical distance between the material and the interpreter, and that meant standing at the present edge of history, on the dividing line between "now-time" (*Jetztzeit*)[43] and the possibility for a radically different future. From this perspective history could not be affirmed or rationalized. As an expression of this critical, negating moment in both theology and Marxism, Benjamin interpreted in his ninth thesis a picture by Paul Klee (which was his prize possession):[44]

> There is a picture by Klee called "Angelus Novus." An angel is presented in it who looks as if he were about to move away from something at which he is staring. His eyes are wide open, his mouth is agape, his wings are spread. The angel of history must look like that. His face is turned toward the past. Where a chain of events appears to *us*, *he* sees one single catastrophe which relentlessly piles wreckage upon wreckage, and hurls them before his feet. The angel would like to stay, awaken the dead, and make whole that which has been smashed. But a storm is blowing from Paradise; it has gotten caught in his wings, and it is so strong that the angel can no longer close them. The storm drives him irresistibly into the future to

which his back is turned, while the pile of debris before him grows toward the sky. That which we name progress is *this* storm.[45]

It is true that Adorno tended to view art rather than theology as the refuge for that utopian impulse which could find no home in present reality.[46] But he had never opposed the theological pole of Benjamin's thought as long as it remained "negative." In full accord with Benjamin's theses he wrote in 1947:

> The only philosophy which can be responsibly practiced in face of despair is the attempt to contemplate all things as they would present themselves from the standpoint of redemption.[47]

Yet if Adorno's acceptance of the theological impulse was not new, there was nonetheless an intensification of it in his writings after Benjamin's death. It was a change more in tone than in concept, a new solemnity, which gave to his work the character of a philosophical requiem. It was as if the fate of the Jews had placed a taboo on his earlier language of "liquidating" idealism, as if the daily bombings and the final catastrophe of Hiroshima had made it impossible to speak of "exploding" the reified forms. There was, if one will, a new pacifism in Adorno's critical attacks. He took more seriously what he had always claimed was the "double character" of phenomena, arguing not only that a kernel of truth appeared in the shell of ideology, but that even the shell might be redeemed through the efforts of interpretation. It was as if all of profane existence took on an intensified sanctity, now that its ineffable fragility was illuminated by the fire of a war which consumed it so mindlessly.

In his first published statement on Benjamin's legacy, Adorno asserted that his philosophy would survive because it was true: "It will unfold within time because even its most private concerns are the concerns of all."[48] Yet the theses on history which he received that winter reminded him of the transiency of phenomena.[49] In them Benjamin criticized Gottfried Keller's remark that "the truth will not run away from us," claiming instead that each image of the past "threatens to disappear with every present moment which does not recognize in it its own concerns."[50] Now Benjamin was himself a part of that past, and to Adorno was bequeathed the task of redemption. This meant in the first instance rescuing his friend's work from historical oblivion, which, as editor of Benjamin's writings (1955) and letters (1966), Adorno did much to achieve.[51]

But in the spirit of their common project, the texts themselves were not to become an uncritically revered and reified dogma. Along with the exoteric redemption of the texts was an esoteric one. More strongly than ever, Adorno internalized Benjamin's philosophy in an act of *Aufhebung*, in all three senses (preserving, negating, going beyond) of this Hegelian term. It meant that he preserved his friend's work in his own so that nothing he wrote was untouched by Benjamin's personal language and unique epistemological method. But it also meant that he redeemed by means of this method the very problems in Benjamin's work which he had criticized in their correspondence. Beginning with his 1938 article on the fetish character of music,[52] what Adorno had seen as Benjamin's theoretical mistakes he began to interpret as reflections of what was wrong with society. Just as in the case of Kierkegaard or Husserl, precisely within the failures, the ruptures (*Brüche*) of Benjamin's philosophy, Adorno deciphered *unintentional* social truth. The constant theme of Adorno's criticism had been that Benjamin tended to eliminate the role of the active, critically reflective subject in the cognitive process. It was manifested in Benjamin's affirmation of the empirically existing consciousness of the proletariat, as well as in the surrealist methods which he borrowed, with their stress on the subject's passivity. It was behind Adorno's warning that citing facts without commentary caught Benjamin at the crossroads between magic and positivism. Adorno interpreted this "extinction of the ego" (*Erlöschung des Ichs*) within method as a reflection of modern man's incapacity for experience, which in turn was the cause of his political impotence (*Ohnmacht*). Adorno's subsequent work in social psychology was largely a demonstration of this problem as it manifested itself in the individual's passive conformism, his consumption of mass culture,[53] and his simultaneous reverence for positivist "facts" on the one hand[54] and for the magic of demagogues[55] and horoscopes[56] on the other. The problem, expressed in philosophical terms, meant that the subject was incapable of sufficient distance from the object to experience it dialectically, that is, critically as a nonidentical other, and identity itself became synonymous with the impotence of the subject and his domination by the social system.[57]

As a first step in the exoteric redemption of Benjamin's work, Adorno and Horkheimer published Benjamin's theses on the philosophy of history in 1942, in a mimeographed, limited "special edition" of the by then defunct *Zeitschrift für Sozialforschung*, under the title "Über den Begriff der Geschichte" (On the Concept of History). The issue also contained two essays by Horkheimer and one by Adorno. Horkheimer's contributions were seminal theoretical articles, very much in the spirit of Benjamin's theses on history. In fact, it could be said that they grounded the theses in theoretical substance, building on the analysis of contemporary capitalism developed by Horkheimer's lifelong friend Friedrich Pollock, who was then acting director of the Institute in New York. At the same time, Benjamin's criticism of the myth of historical progress because of its adverse political effect on the working class, and his radical concept of freedom that went far beyond the rationalization of economy and hence implied criticism of the USSR, gave political justification to Pollock's work, then the source of a divisive debate among the Institute's members.[58] Pollock's position was essentially that monopoly capitalism, instead of leading to collapse, had entered a new, relatively stable stage, which he called "state capitalism."[59] It was distinguished not so much by the mode of economic ownership as by the structure of authoritarian domination that characterized its institutions — monopoly corporations, mass political parties, and government and trade-union bureaucracies as well. The USSR marked no "progress" in overcoming this "command structure," in which the profit motive had been replaced by the power motive, while fascism, despite its apparent chaos, had resulted in that structure's intensification.[60] One of Horkheimer's essays appearing in the special issue in tribute to Benjamin, "Autoritärer Staat" (Authoritarian State), argued that just this structure of domination was at the source of what Benjamin referred to as the recurrent "barbarism" in history.[61]

Of course, progress in the control of nature there had been: Benjamin wrote in the theses that "progress in the domination of nature" and "the regression of society" formed the dialectical poles of historical development.[62] He, as well as Adorno and Horkheimer, lacked the consciousness of many ecology-minded radicals of the present in that they still considered at least the potential of technology in positive terms. Horkheimer wrote:

> Problems which a few decades ago were considered insurmountable technical or organizational barriers have been broken for all to see. . . . When stockings can be made out of air, only by clutching at some eternal element in man, namely, misinterpreting psychological essences as invariants, can the eternity of domination be rationalized.[63]

Nonetheless, the structure of the new technology, based on the domination of nature, had served only to reinforce the social relations of domination, the elimination of which was the sole criterion for real human progress, and in this light history appeared as the ever-identical (*Immergleiche*) despite changes in the material base. Adorno claimed (in a 1956 essay) that it was Marx's

> . . . deep presentiment, that the existential elements of history are domination and dependency, and that in spite of all progress in rationality and technology nothing really decisive has been changed.[64]

The continued existence of this condition was not inevitable. Benjamin stated in his theses on history: "As with every generation that preceded us, we have been endowed with a *weak* Messianic power. . . ."[65] This meant that although the objective course of history was not progress, "every second of time was the tiny gate through which the Messiah might enter."[66] Horkheimer argued similarly in "Autoritärer Staat" that although "as long as world history follows its logical course, it fails to fulfill its human destiny,"[67] nonetheless "For the revolutionary, the world has always been ripe."[68] Indeed, the alternative depended only on human will: "With the experience that their political will in fact changes their own lives through changing society, the apathy of the masses will disappear."[69] But it was precisely this kind of critical "experience" which mass culture now threatened with extinction — hence the vicious circle in which history repeated its archaic pattern of domination.

Benjamin's theses veered from the official Communist position not only in his rejection of history as progress. They criticized the resurrection of the Protestant work ethic (which, pointing to Marx's *Critique of the Gotha Program*, Benjamin claimed Marx did not share) and rejected the idea that economic socialization was the goal of revolution, rather than simply the means for realizing a radical notion of freedom, including sensual happiness, which had been expounded by the pre-Marxist utopian Charles Fourier.[70] This was something quite different from his artwork essay which affirmed mass culture as the provider of present happiness, and here again Horkheimer was predisposed to agree.[71] He wrote in "Autoritärer Staat" that the purpose of the revolution was not just the socialization of the means of production, or the rationalization of the economy and unlimited control of nature, which would happen "without spontaneity in any case," but also that which "does not happen without active resistence and constantly renewed attempts of freedom: the end of exploitation."[72] Nor was freedom to be understood purely negatively, as freedom *from* oppression, but as freedom to realize that to which Horkheimer had referred since 1936 as "sensual happiness" (*sinnliches Glück*).

The *revolutionary* dialectic, wrote Horkheimer, was "not identical with development."[73] This dialectic occurred *between* consciousness and society. Without it, what appeared to be a dialectical development within objective forces alone, the technological revolution that might have ushered in true history, relapsed into a new form of oppression and repeated the vicious circle of the past. Without it, the development of rational subjectivity, instead of fulfilling its promise of demythification, relapsed itself into a new form of myth, as Adorno and Horkheimer were to argue in their collaborative study *Dialektik der Aufklärung* (1947).[74] The theoretical groundwork for this study was laid in Horkheimer's second article appearing with Benjamin's theses on history, entitled "Vernunft und Selbsterhaltung" (Reason and Self-Preservation). It sought to demonstrate how reason, originally the means of preserving the bourgeois individual from both natural and political domination, instead, because of its progressive instrumentalization, led to the destruction of the individual and the preservation of the forces of oppression. "Instrumental reason" had become the tool for a pseudo-reconciliation of subject and object, consciousness and society; it was the means for achieving goals, the value of which it could not provide the criterion to judge.[75] It led to mass society instead of classless society, conformism instead of universality, a parody of the utopian vision. The necessary, indeed the *only* possible philosophical response was to maintain a position of relentless negativity, which in no way made peace with the status quo and hence kept alive the critical independence of the subject, salvaging it from social extinction and historical oblivion. Thus the only hope of assisting in the liberation of "first nature" was "to unshackle its seeming opposite, independent thought."[76]

Horkheimer's theoretical essays reflected Adorno's thinking as well as his own, for in California during the war their work was intimately collaborative. Not only *Dialektik der Aufklärung,* but also a book-length work on the same theme in English, *Eclipse of Reason* (1947), although appearing under Horkheimer's name alone, was clearly by them both. Yet despite the mutuality of their position, there was a division of labor in their intellectual production, discernible to anyone familiar with the differences in their language and mode of representation.[77] Horkheimer provided the social-scientific and historical anchor for their production, and Adorno the aesthetic skills necessary for adequate philosophical representation. It proved to be a fruitful way of collaborating, their approaches providing a dynamic balance between the poles of science and art. They worked together in a way Adorno never could have with Benjamin whose artistic proclivities were perhaps too close to his own not to clash.

Adorno commented that while he had convinced Horkheimer of the importance of "representation" and "strengthened" his antipositivism, the latter in turn had "protected" him from "aestheticism."[78] Awareness of his own weakness and of the limits of art as a model for philosophical cognition might help explain his rather puzzling choice of themes for his contribution to the commemorative issue of the journal containing Benjamin's theses on history. It was an essay on the correspondence between the poets Stefan George and Hugo von Hofmannsthal.[79] Adorno had not treated the subject before (although in his Husserl study he had described parallels between this philosopher and Hofmannsthal).[80] The present essay made no mention of his own correspondence with Benjamin, yet clearly there were parallels, as George, like Benjamin, had been significantly older than Hofmannsthal, his brilliant protégé,[81] and the years of their correspondence (1891–1906) were not unmarred by disputes between them. But here the similarities stop. George and Hofmannsthal were apolitical at best, racist or chauvinist at worst. Adorno criticized the lack of theoretical substance in their correspondence, in which poetic discussions were limited to questions of formal technique,[82] and disagreements centered on personal slights, power, prestige, and, ultimately, "intellectual property."[83]

Despite the esotericism of Benjamin's language (which Adorno adopted in the early thirties and never abandoned), the atmosphere of their circle in Berlin was far from the neoromantic cultism of the George circle. Both in intended and unintentional effect, the work of the two groups can hardly be compared. Yet as Adorno described the fundamental weakness of George's approach, implied was his criticism of Benjamin, unmistakable now that part of their own correspondence has been published. Adorno interpreted George's poetic attitude toward sensory objects in the same critical terms he had used against Benjamin's (and also Husserl's) philosophical one, claiming that the objects remained "opaque" because they were experienced in their given form as "still life" by a "blind intuition without concept."[84] The problem — as with Benjamin — was that George eliminated the role of the critical subject, allowing himself to become "the mouthpiece of things," seeking to "save himself by throwing himself away":[85] "The poet of modernity lets himself be overwhelmed by the power of things like an outsider by a cartel."[86]

Later Adorno wrote that Benjamin "was more indebted to the George School than those who were taught by him let themselves notice. . . ."[87] In fact not only had Benjamin corresponded with Hofmannsthal,[88] but also the original inspiration for Benjamin's "dialectical images" was the poetic images, or Denkbilder, of George, in which seemingly subjective and accidental experiences were granted objective meaning.[89] Yet if Adorno's 1942 essay connected George with Benjamin, implied was a self-criticism as well, a warning against his own aestheticism and against his own preoccupation with "culture," which, as Benjamin cautioned in the theses[90] and Adorno echoed here,[91] was always tainted with barbarism.

Adorno's description of George and particularly Hofmannsthal as personalities was hardly flattering. Yet he would have been the last to challenge the validity of their work on psychological grounds, judging its truth value instead in terms of its adequacy as a reflection of social objectivity. Stubbornly, Adorno held onto his basic tenet that neither the artist's intent nor his character or political beliefs could be the criterion for criticizing his production. He interpreted Hofmannsthal's snobbism and George's self-induced ostracism positively, claiming they were correct at least in impulse, even if that impulse fell short due to their blindness to theoretical understanding.[92] Moreover, claimed Adorno, truth appeared through the ideological veil of their poetry precisely where it seemed to fail, foundering on the wreckage of language. Hofmannsthal's famous letter to Lord Chandos admitting he could no longer write because he doubted the very possibility of communication through words[93] was, claimed Adorno, not mere theatrics, but based on

> . . . an extremely real insight: that language no longer allows anything to be said as it is expressed. Language is either the reified and banal, the sign of commodities, falsifying thought from the start; or it installs itself, ceremonious without ceremony, as the mighty without power, ensconced by its own force — in short, of the type that Hofmannsthal attacked in the George School.[94]

Although "to renounce communication is better than to adjust,"[95] Adorno maintained that the more courageous choice than Hofmannsthal's was to keep trying:

> The passionate attempt to express oneself in language which shuns banality like a taboo, is the attempt, however hopeless, to distance experience from its most deadly enemy, one which grows stronger in late bourgeois society: oblivion.[96]

"What survives," concluded Adorno with Hegel's term, "is determinate negation":[97] If language could no longer presume to rectify reality, it should not abandon its more modest power, the critical power to call reality by its right name, making manifest the truth within appearance.

SOCIAL PHYSIOGNOMICS

When Adorno first came to the United States, his (largely unappreciated) work at the Princeton Radio Research Project was a quite literal translation of the Königstein program from philosophical to sociological analysis. Its terminology was familiar as was its project, analyzing the alteration of aural sense experience decipherable within the radio transmission of music. Building on his 1938 article for the Institute's journal on the fetish character of music,[98] Adorno wrote a series of essays which he later tried, unsuccessfully, to publish in book form under the title *Current of Music*.[99] In Adorno's philosophical works, texts were read as reality and concepts translated into matter (for example, Kierkegaard's texts were read as images of the bourgeois *intérieur*); in his sociological writings, matter was read as a text, translated from nonverbal signs into words. Adorno referred to his sociological method as "physiognomics," noting that this term had been used by the psychoanalysts Sandor Ferenczi and Siegfried Bernfeld.[100] Yet clearly Adorno's own familiarity with physiognomy was through Benjamin, who in turn had absorbed it from literary-aesthetic rather than scientific channels. Just as Benjamin had attempted to analyze the surrealist "face" of metropolitan Paris to reveal its impact on subjective experience,[101] so Adorno analyzed the "face" or, more properly, the "voice" of radio[102] in order to understand its impact on listeners.[103] "Social physiognomics" in fact employed Adorno's old method of "constructing constellations," or, to use his more current Hegelian vocabulary, the procedure of "determinate negation." Its distinguishing characteristic, and where it differed from the method of pure phenomenological description which Adorno had criticized in his Husserl study,[104] was that instead of accepting the given appearance of the phenomena without further analysis, "physiognomics" interpreted the phenomena critically as unintentional expressions of truth about a faulty social totality.[105] The structure of this totality appeared within the illusory appearance of the radio voice, but not without the active intervention of the interpreting subject, who unlocked the "rebus"[106] of surface details, adhering to them with "exactitude,"[107] yet at the same time going beyond them through the mediation of theory to demonstrate that "the unity of the radio phenomenon in itself, as far as it really has the structure of a unity, is simply the unity of society which determines all the individual and apparently accidental features"[108] — features like radio's penetration as a public voice into the private sphere of the bourgeois *intérieur*,[109] its standardizing tendencies despite "pseudo-individuation," the resulting atomization of radio's mass audience, who passively consumed "canned" music and whose freedom was limited to switching the station.[110] An analysis of these elements of the radio voice so that the structure of the social totality appeared within it "in microcosm"[111] made radio "less an instrument of influence than of social revelation."[112] In line with his earlier work, Adorno's point was not to reduce the cultural phenomenon of radio to the socioeconomic structure, but to reveal how radio, as well as being produced by that structure, continuously *re*produced it by reproducing its characteristics as psychological traits in those subjects who alone might have changed it. At the same time, the article intervened in that process, aiming at breaking the spell of its circular repetition. Physiognomics showed how the superstructure details contained the substructure totality in monadological abbreviation, so that the particular, once interpreted, became a historical, a dialectical image of the whole. Although "the intermediary links are missing,"[113] the analysis made palpable for the reader the mediated relationship between the detail and the whole which "for itself is so hard to deduce causally."[114]

THE AUTHORITARIAN PERSONALITY

It would be difficult to imagine a method more against the American grain of acceptable research methods than Adorno's social physiognomics. Sociology in the United States at that time was quantitative rather than qualitative, using relatively sophisticated statistical methods to discover averages and aggregate norms, while Adorno's method focused on singular, seemingly insignificant phenomena on the extreme fringes of society rather than at its center.[115] The notion that one could "measure culture" was for him a contradiction in terms.[116] "All love from us both," he and his wife wrote to Benjamin; "We are looking out on the Hudson and observe with amazement the ice floes being driven up-river."[117] Typically, his gaze caught the exception rather than the rule. Totally alien to him as well was the antitheoretical bias of the Princeton Radio Research Project, with its questionnaires which simply asked radio listeners to register their "likes" and "dislikes" in programming, presuming that the options offered to them allowed for meaningful choice. The consequently tautological recommendation that the radio industry give the people "what they want" excluded the possibility of questioning the social source of these wants and hence their ultimate validity. Adorno believed that needs were not static; they only appeared that way in a static society. The actual fulfillment of needs, even the false ones of capitalist society, would in itself change the nature of needs:[118]

> The idea, for example, that movies are necessary along with food and shelter for the reproduction of labor power is "true" only in a world which shapes human beings for the reproduction of labor power and forces their needs into harmony with the employer's interests in profit and control.[119]

Adorno speculated that his idea of philosophical experience as the way to discovery of truth might be inalterably opposed to the bourgeois conception of scientific experimentation:

> Perhaps from very early on in the bourgeois era the experiment became a surrogate for authentic experience. . . . The cruelty, shrinking back from nothing, not even cruelty against oneself, is intimately connected with it — seeing how a person handles himself under such and such conditions, for example, when he is castrated or murdered, or how one himself reacts. The new anthropological type has become internally what earlier was true only of the method: the subject of natural science — of course also the object.[120]

His difficulties at the Princeton Radio Research Project had made painfully clear that the task of translating his reflections into research terms "was equivalent to squaring the circle":[121]

... I immersed myself in observations of American musical life, especially the radio system, and set down theories and hypotheses about it; but I could not construct questionnaires and interview-schemes that would get to the heart of the matter. Of course, I was somewhat isolated in my endeavors. The unfamiliarity of the things that concerned me had the effect of inducing skepticism rather than cooperation from my colleagues. Interestingly enough, the so-called secretarial workers were immediately attracted to my ideas. . . . But the higher up in the scientific hierarchy the more unpleasant the situation became.[122]

In California, Adorno once again found himself involved in a sociological research project and with the problem of "squaring the circle." This time, however, conditions were more auspicious. In 1944 Horkheimer managed to get sizable funding for a multivolume series of *Studies in Prejudice.* The money came from the American Jewish Committee, which placed him at the head of its new Department of Scientific Research.[123] Adorno became codirector of a central part of the project, a five-year study on anti-Semitism which was published in 1950 as *The Authoritarian Personality,*[124] now considered a classic in the literature of social psychology.[125] His collaborators were R. Nevitt Sanford, Daniel Levinson, and Else Frenkel-Brunswik, a group of social psychologists who called themselves the Berkeley Public Opinion Study Group. Adorno recalled with pleasure the "'perfect team work' without any hierarchical restrictions" which characterized their collaboration.[126] The group was bound by a "common theoretical orientation toward Freud" which was neither revisionist nor rigidly dogmatic.[127] The fact that through their help Adorno was indeed able to translate his unique cognitive methodology into a plan for empirical research was all the more remarkable as the plan incorporated principles of Freudian clinical practice never before used in this way. Surely the imagination and theoretical openness of his colleagues was indispensable for its success, although the originality of the project's conceptual design was primarily indebted to Adorno. *The Authoritarian Personality* was perhaps less a sublation than a sublimation of his Benjaminian epistemological method, allowing qualitative, philosophical speculation to get past the quantitative, positivistic censorship of the social science establishment.

Adorno's writings had dealt with anti-Semitism several times before, most notably his study of Richard Wagner in the thirties[128] and more recently, several short memoranda for the Institute[129] which contained ideas developed in the concluding chapter of *Dialektik der Aufklärung.*[130] The latter, a strictly theoretical essay entitled "Elements of Anti-Semitism," reflected Adorno at his most speculative and demonstrated the skill with which he was able to reconcile the antagonistic theories of Marx and Freud without falling into a revisionist, safe middle position regarding either. Marx had argued that the Jewish question was essentially an economic problem, not one of religion or politics.[131] Adorno agreed and extended the argument: "Bourgeois anti-Semitism has a specific economic reason: the concealment of domination in production."[132] With the aid of Freud yet fully in the spirit of Marx, he explained the psychological dynamics of the problem. The "ultimate target" of domination in the production process was the worker,[133] but due to his "half-education" (*Halbbildung*),[134] his immediate awareness of his plight was not raised to the level of critical self-consciousness which would reveal the true source of domination. Real experience of his condition was blocked by the necessity of conforming to the given social system in order to survive. The result was suppressed aggression: "the hatred felt by the led, who can never be satisfied economically or sexually, knows no bounds."[135] The deflection of this aggression onto the Jews was the psychological dynamics which fascism used to its advantage, "in that it seeks to make the rebellion of suppressed nature against domination directly useful to domination."[136] Instead of criticizing society, the workers mimicked its reification and authoritarianism, masochistically consenting to be led, while falsely projecting upon the Jews as "outsiders" their own socially unacceptable (hence potentially revolutionary) traits and desires.[137] The correct "countermovement" to this false projection would be the realization of man as a "species being,"[138] that is, as he could and should be, through "individual and social emancipation from domination."[139]

Adorno had not written on Freud directly since his first *Habilitationsschrift* of 1927 which, it will be recalled,[140] defended Freud from an idealist, Kantian position and then switched in the concluding pages to a Marxist, materialist analysis of the ideological reasons for the lack of acceptance of Freud. But his subsequent writings gave evidence that he had absorbed the social-psychological work of Horkheimer's Institute during the 1930s, most especially that of Erich Fromm, with whom he differed,[141] but who as the Institute's only practicing analyst at the same time taught him much. Now, in 1942, Adorno wrote a series of notes toward a new anthropology ("Notizen zur neuen Anthropologie") which, unpublished and in rough-draft form, worked out implications of the mediated relationship between Marxian and Freudian theory. He began with an immanent criticism of Freud, demonstrating, predictably, that the language Freud used to describe a supposedly *biological* theory, in particular the "exchange schema" governing the "economy of instincts," unintentionally illuminated the *social* origins of that theory and of the psychological structures which it described.[142] This meant, from a materialist perspective, that what appeared as shortcomings in Freud's theory when judged from the criteria of absolute and universal truth, were seen as precisely the grounds for its validity.

But that validity was limited to a particular historical stage of bourgeois society which, so Adorno argued, no longer existed. The "subject" of Freud's times had been replaced by a new anthropological type. Characteristic of its psychological formation was not repression, but the immediate substitute gratification provided by mass culture, not anal possessiveness, but the consumer-readiness to treat all objects as fungible and disposable.[143] Against Fromm's thesis that the authoritarian character had its source in the bourgeois individual's escape from freedom into sadomasochistic dependence,[144] Adorno claimed that social pressures to conform prevented the formation of a self-contained ego which could properly be called an individual in the first place.[145] Whereas Freud had conceived of nature (the id instincts) in rebellion against society, nature was now seen by mass man no differently than society, as a superior power to which one must submit as to blind fate, and in this context, the neurotic's deviance had a positive moment, as a rebellion against adapting to the given.

These theoretical speculations preceded Adorno's work with the Berkeley Study Group, which was launched in 1944. That same year he began a book of aphorisms and fragments, *Minima Moralia*,[146] which presented his theoretical ideas by approaching details of twentieth-century existence as Benjamin had those of the nineteenth century: phenomena were deciphered as images, gestures as codes, figures as a stage for social reality. Adorno wrote on fear of the non-identical:

> German words of foreign derivation are the Jews of language.[147]

On racism:

> The familiar argument of tolerance, that all people and all races are equal, is a boomerang. . . . Abstract utopia is all too compatible with the most insidious tendencies of society. That all men are alike is exactly what society would like to hear. It considers actual or imagined differences as stigmas indicating that not enough has yet been done; that something has still been left outside its machinery, not quite determined by its totality. The technique of the concentration camp is to make the prisoners like their guards, the murdered, murderers. . . . An emancipated society, on the other hand, would not be a unitary state, but the realization of universality in the reconciliation of differences.[148]

On mass culture and alienating labor:

> . . . one could no more imagine Nietzsche in an office, with a secretary minding the telephone in an anteroom, at his desk until five o'clock, than playing golf after the day's work was done. Only a cunning intertwining of pleasure and work leaves real experience still open, under the pressure of society. Such experience is less and less tolerated. Even the so-called intellectual professions are being deprived, through their growing resemblance to business, of all joy. . . . No fulfilment may be attached to work, which would otherwise lose its functional modesty in the totality of purposes, no spark of reflection is allowed to fall into leisure time, since it might otherwise leap across to the workaday world and set it on fire. While in their structure work and amusement are becoming increasingly alike, they are at the same time being divided ever more rigorously by invisible demarcation lines. Joy and mind have been expelled from both.[149]

On reading the totality within the particular:

> Beauty of the American landscape: that even the smallest of its segments is inscribed, as its expression, with the immensity of the whole country.[150]

On the liquidation of the ego:

> In many people it is already an impertinence to say "I."[151]

On the disintegration of experience:

> Technology is making gestures precise and brutal, and with them men. . . .
> [W]hich driver is not tempted, merely by the power of his engine, to wipe
> out the vermin of the street, pedestrians, children and cyclists? The move-
> ments machines demand of their users already have the violent, hard-hitting,
> unresting jerkiness of Fascist maltreatment. Not the least to blame for the
> withering of experience is the fact that things, under the law of pure func-
> tionality, assume a form that limits contact with them to mere operation,
> and tolerates no surplus, either in freedom of conduct or in autonomy of
> things, which would survive as the core of experience, because it is not con-
> sumed by the moment of action.[152]

Minima Moralia was dedicated to Horkheimer, who, however, contributed
to it more by his absence than his presence, as Adorno composed it during the
time he spent waiting for his friend, and Horkheimer, notoriously late, provided
him with frequent opportunities.[153] Subtitled *Reflections from Damaged Life*, it
included much that was autobiographical, but, like Benjamin's *Berliner Kindheit*
and *Einbahnstrasse*,[154] it illuminated less about the author than about the objective conditions of society. Indeed, in both style and themes, the book was
strongly reminiscent of Benjamin's work.

The mode of *Minima Moralia* was aesthetic. *The Authoritarian Personality*
treated the same themes "scientifically." Thus the works turned on different
centers but converged in their truth content.[155] How to make the transposition
from the aesthetic to the scientific mode was Adorno's central methodological
problem in his work with the Berkeley Study Group. His resolution was itself
dialectical, a bipolar research program combining quantitative and qualitative
analysis. The theory expounded in *Dialektik der Aufklärung* provided the interpretive frame for both poles (and was at the same time verified by them):
elements of anti-Semitism were not seen as limited to isolated, overt manifestations of bigotry. Instead they were shown to form a psychological configuration
which reflected the entire constellation of factors which Adorno and Horkheimer
claimed characterized the fascist tendencies of the present social structure — conformism, sexual repression, false projection, authoritarian submission which
alternated with aggressive domination, a lack of critical reflection, and the stere-
otypy that resulted from an incapacity for experiencing the nonidentical or the
new.[156] The innovative quantitative method of *The Authoritarian Personality*
consisted in developing a set of questionnaire items (the famous F scale) which,
instead of treating opinions as isolated data,[157] recorded a "cluster" of opinions
identifying the presence of each of these elements. When the elements existed
in correlation, they were considered to form a latent structural pattern of the
potentially fascist personality. The fixity of this personality type was due precisely to its unmediated reflection of the fixed social structure,[158] whereas the
antifascist type, as a critical, nonconforming individual, had, predictably, more
diverse characteristics.[159] Whether or not the authoritarian personality types
actualized their fascist potential depended

. . . primarily upon the situation of the most powerful economic interests, upon whether they, by conscious design or not, make use of this device for maintaining their dominant status. This is a matter about which the great majority of people would have little to say.[160]

Hence without denying the primacy of objective economic factors, *The Authoritarian Personality* developed a quantitative method for revealing those psychological factors which, in opposition to the rational self-interest of the masses, were an indispensable component in fascism's success.

The idea that a cluster of elements which on the surface appeared to be unrelated and irrational (in this case, responses to an opinion questionnaire) could be rearranged in various trial combinations (the final F scale was the product of many such arrangements) until they fell into a configuration with an inner logic which could be read as meaningful (here the structure of the authoritarian personality) fully paralleled the method of constructing constellations which Adorno had outlined in his 1931 inaugural address, and hence his and Benjamin's Königstein position.[161] The fact that the tests were administered not to a "random sample," but to groups representing "extremes" (from middle-class students to inmates of a prison and a psychiatric institution) also reflected Benjamin's approach, just as the distinction between the latent and manifest meaning of the questionnaire items paralleled Benjamin's distinction between intention and "unintentional truth." Indeed, *The Authoritarian Personality* could be described as a (socio-psychological) representation of the "idea" of fascism. At the same time, the empirical method of *The Authoritarian Personality* avoided what Adorno had considered the defect of Benjamin's later work (and reflected Horkheimer's influence) in that all the elements of the constellation were related to a general theory of anti-Semitism and their interpretation was in every case mediated by that theory.

Traces of Benjamin were more directly visible in the qualitative pole of the study. As a corrective and enrichment of the questionnaire responses,[162] certain subjects, particularly high- and low-scoring "extremes," were chosen for in-depth interviews, and the task of interpreting the significance of the interview material was not surprisingly assumed by Adorno.[163] As a sociological method, such "content analysis" was considered new and innovative among American sociologists, although it was a procedure with which Adorno was already very much at home. Not only was it basic to his method of philosophical interpretation. He had employed it as a specifically sociopsychological procedure in 1943, in an analysis of the speeches of a West Coast radio demagogue, Martin Luther Thomas,[164] which, Adorno later commented, "supplied me with a good deal of stimulation for items that were useful in *The Authoritarian Personality*. The study must have been one of the first critical and qualitative content analyses to be carried out in the United States."[165]

According to Adorno, the aim of the qualitative research in *The Authoritarian Personality* was to develop through a close textual analysis of the interview material a "phenomenology" which both verified the theory of anti-Semitism and refined it,[166] and here Adorno was clearly in his element. He noted the advantages of the procedure, the "concreteness" it achieved by concentration on seemingly insignificant textual details.[167] The chance to consider "unique" and "extreme" statements rather than the more typical, quantifiable responses gave his interpretive fantasy free reign at the same time that the consistency of the theoretical frame provided for exactness, "a safeguard against arbitrariness."[168] Adorno predictably focused on the contradictions and logical gaps in the interview responses, and his interpretations of these gaps, as well as the language imagery and even the body gestures of those interviewed, were elaborated with characteristic dialectical complexity. His conclusions based on concrete evidence from the in-depth interviews verified his previous theoretical assumption:

> The extremely prejudiced person tends toward "psychological totalitarianism," something which seems to be almost a microcosmic image of the totalitarian state at which he aims. Nothing can be left untouched, as it were; everything must be made "equal" to the ego-ideal of a rigidly conceived and hypostatized ingroup.[169]

Adorno interpreted his interviews with people who had low scores on the F scale in a way that substantiated his notion of the manner in which the philosophical subject should approach reality. Low scorers' attitude toward Jews was characterized by "empathic rationality" which had a "double aspect": they identified anti-Semitism as "the problem of the anti-Semite, not of the Jew," and they viewed issues of race and minority not as second nature, but "with historical and sociological perspective and thus . . . open to rational insight and change. . . ."[170]

The tyrannical refusal of the high scorers to tolerate the nonidentity of Jews as "outsiders" was seen as a "means for pseudo-orientation in an estranged world, and for 'mastering' this world by being able completely to pigeonhole its negative aspects."[171] At the same time, Adorno explicitly and repeatedly insisted that authoritarian needs had their origin in objective conditions,[172] that the prevalence of authoritarian responses "must be because we are living in potentially fascist times."[173] The "ignorance and confusion" among high scorers with regard to politics and economics was connected with "the 'reification' of a social reality which is determined by property relations in which the human beings themselves are, as it were, mere appendages."[174]

> The ultimate reason for this ignorance might well be the opaqueness of the social, economic, and political situation to all those who are not in full command of all the resources of stored knowledge and theoretical thinking. In its present phase, our social system tends objectively and automatically to produce "curtains" which make it impossible for the naive person to see what it is all about.[175]

The populist, anti-intellectualism of the protofascist type Adorno, predictably, considered "ominous,"[176] but he claimed the source of such sentiments was objective, "enhanced by powerful economic and social forces which, purposely or automatically, keep the people ignorant."[177] Ultimately the problem was "capitalism," which in an "era of transition" was on the defensive, reflecting "the transformation of our social system from something dynamic into something conservative, a *status quo*, struggling for its perpetuation. . . ."[178]

Chapter 12. Epilogue:
The Method of Negative Dialectics

There is something false about speaking of Adorno's "theories." In fact he had none, just as he had no "concept" of history.[1] And just as he typically defined concepts by their polar opposites ("history" by "nature," "individual" by "society"), so now he constructed whole theories out of opposing and contradictory tenets. His theory of fascism was based simultaneously on the premise of bureaucratic rationalization with its "instrumental reason" and the notion of the irrational, charismatic leader, two conceptions which Max Weber had developed to describe *mutually exclusive* realities. Adorno never gave up his characterization of society as fragmented, discontinuous (*brüchig*), and in a state of disintegration (*Zerfall*); he simply added to it the opposite idea, that it formed a closed, air-tight system, that "the total organization of society through big business and its omnipresent technology has . . . taken unbroken [*lückenlos*] possession of the world and imagination. . . ."[2] If Horkheimer's thinking described a dialectical pattern, Adorno's thinking *was* that pattern. He understood Hegel's "self-movement of the concept" not as a "theory of development,"[3] but as a movement of thought in which "all categories are themselves and not themselves,"[4] in which a concept was "observed so closely that it was maintained and transformed at the same time."[5]

In 1942 Adorno wrote three short pieces similar in format to Benjamin's theses on history.[6] But whereas Benjamin juxtaposed opposites in a visual sense, using theological images (the angel of history, the Messiah, the chess-playing dwarf) to express historical materialism, its polar opposite, Adorno's pieces "developed" dynamically from one pole to another. He used dialectical argument to construct "models" of thought which, no matter where they began, always moved in the opposite direction. Hence an analysis of the authoritarian personality pointed to the character of the society which had produced it; but in any discussion of social structure, Adorno moved to a consideration of the psychology which *re*produced it: In "Reflexionen zur Klassentheorie" (Reflections on Class Theory), his analysis of class society hinged on an analysis

185

of mass psychology which prevented the experience of class,[7] while in "Thesen über Bedürfnis" (Theses on Needs), his analysis of psychological needs turned in fact on an analysis of social constraints: "the idea that a revolutionary society would cry out for the bad performances of Hedy Lamar or bad soup from Campbell's is absurd. The better the soup, the more gladly they will do without Lamar."[8]

When he interpreted the history of class struggle, it was in terms of a theory of history as the ever-identical;[9] but he addressed the ontological issues of anthropology in terms of historical change.[10] He defined social atomization by social conformism, alienation by collectivization.[11] The suffering of the masses was identified as the inability to experience suffering;[12] sexual license was seen as an expression of bourgeois asceticism.[13] On the philosophical level, Adorno criticized not only the dualism between alienated subject and reified object but simultaneously the identity between subject and object. This identity in turn took several forms: subjectivity was a box which entrapped the subject on the one hand; on the other, the subject alternately dominated the object and yielded to it to the point of its own extinction.

Adorno's originality lay not in the material substance of his theoretical arguments, but in the way he put them together. His work on anti-Semitism, for example, relied heavily on psychological concepts developed by Erich Fromm. But Fromm, who was just as insistent regarding the mutual mediation of psychological character and social structure and just as aware of the "double character"—in Freudian language, the ambivalence—of psychological phenomena, still wanted to construct a positive description of modern man. For him the goal of knowledge was to have something—a new and lasting theory—at the end, whereas Adorno, whose concern was a new social reality, saw in the desire to possess even a theory the risk of reproducing the commodity structure within consciousness. His was a negative anthropology, and its goal as knowledge was to keep criticism alive.[14]

The purpose of what in Adorno's case could be called "antitheories" was to avoid such conformism at all costs. This lends to negative dialectics the quality of quicksilver: just when you think you have grasped the point, by turning into its opposite it slips through your fingers and escapes.

But even though Adorno appeared to be arguing opposite positions simultaneously, what gave his models logical coherence was his identification of the point of convergence between opposites: in every case it was the structure of domination. That structure, which in turn converged with the structure of commodities, emerged whenever one side of a polarity gained the upper hand, thereby duplicating the social structure and enabling that structure to continue: If in thinking about reality the (reified) object was allowed to dominate the subject, the result was the reification of consciousness and the passive acceptance of the status quo; if the subject dominated the object, the result was domination of nature and the ideological justification of the status quo.

Only by keeping the argument circling in perpetual motion could thought escape compromising with its revolutionary goal.

There was no waning of Adorno's commitment to revolution as both necessary and desirable. The problem was "not the possibility of barbarism after the revolution, but the hindering of revolution throughout the whole society."[15] Even within the liberal-democratic language of *The Authoritarian Personality* one can find revolutionary statements, such as Adorno's comment "The argument that first the people should be changed before the world can be changed belongs to the old anti-utopian armory. It leads to a vicious circle. . . ."[16] Nor did he retreat from a Marxist position regarding the class nature of the revolutionary struggle:

> It is true, of course, as a matter of economic and social fact, that the crucial role in the struggle against increasing concentration of economic power will have to be played by the working people. . . .[17]

And he never gave up hope for social transformation, although he believed that hope could no longer express itself positively. Even that stultifier of consciousness, mass culture, when reflected upon critically, might foster revolutionary awareness, if only because the very ideology of equality and identity which it perpetrated illuminated the actuality of class differences as nothing more than "naked usurpation."[18]

Adorno's position had changed, however, in that his faith in the autonomy of culture, his belief that intellectual practice could successfully revolutionize its own material or "means of production," had been shaken. In recognition of the preeminent power of socioeconomic forces, his position had become actually more "Marxist" rather than less. He wrote with some candor:

> In America I was liberated from a certain naïve belief in culture and attained the capacity to see culture from the outside. To clarify the point: in spite of all social criticism and all consciousness of the primacy of economic factors, the fundamental importance of the mind – "Geist" – was quasi a dogma self-evident to me from the very beginning. The fact that this was not a foregone conclusion, I learned in America, where no reverential silence in the presence of everything intellectual prevailed, . . . and the absence of this respect inclined the intellect toward critical self-scrutiny. This particularly affected the European presuppositions of musical cultivation in which I was immersed.[19]

The theme of *Dialektik der Aufklärung* was a criticism of "progress" in reason, which, failing a revolution in the socioeconomic structure, began to duplicate the characteristics of that structure and fell back into myth. In an essay on Schönberg which Adorno wrote just prior to this collaborative study (1940–1941), he made the same argument, as an act of self-criticism, regarding "progress" in music. The essay circulated among German immigrant intellectuals during the forties as an unpublished manuscript.[20] Thomas Mann, who had

begun work on the novel *Doktor Faustus*, read it in 1943 with "a feeling of
. . . strange familiarity,"[21] and he subsequently collaborated closely with Adorno
on the musical theory on which the novel was based,[22] referring to him as the
"Privy Councillor" of the work.[23]

The Schönberg essay and the introduction which accompanied its first
publication in 1949 make it clear that Adorno had not altered his position as
to the essentially dialectical structure of Schönberg's composing, and his description of the process was replete with the characteristic Benjaminian phrase-
ology. He had not capitulated regarding his fundamental tenent that the validity
of art rested on the artist's relation to his material rather than to the working
class.[24] But whereas he had been formerly optimistic as to the progressive
possibilities of intellectual practice, now he saw the danger that "non-conform-
ing music," preserving its truth through "indifference to the public," allowed
its "truth to wither":[25] "In the process of pursuing its own inner logic, music
is transformed more and more from something significant into something
obscure — even to itself."[26]

Adorno's new argument was essentially this: Schönberg's atonal revolution
had indeed succeeded in freeing the musical material from the tyrannical "second nature" laws of the bourgeois tonal system, but as a revolution within the
superstructure alone, its liberating impulse could not be maintained. Atonality
led to twelve-tone composition, the principles of which became a new musical
dogma.[27] Schönberg used the term "model" to describe thematic material in
his music, the identity of which remained throughout a series of variations.
The material was

> . . . all "the same thing." But the meaning of this identity reveals itself
> as nonidentity. The thematic material is of such a nature that to attempt
> to secure it is tantamount to varying it.[28]

This description demonstrates that Schönberg's "models" were still prototypical
of Adorno's own. But was Adorno not also aware that his philosophy was
threatened with the same pitfalls as well?

In describing atonality's lapse into a new system, which he now interpreted
as revolutionary failure, Adorno pointed to the principles of variation in the
twelve-tone system — retrograde, or reversal of the tone row, inversion, and
retrograde inversion — whereby, he claimed, the dynamic principle of variation
turned static by falling back into a predictable and closed structure.[29] I have
already suggested[30] that the same compositional techniques governed the
structure of Adorno's essays: the principle of reversal found its counterpart
in his arguments demonstrating that polar extremes were both true, that opposites converged; the principle of inversion coincided with his showing that
what appeared to be subjective was objective, or vice versa: immanent criticism
of texts revealed that theory was an image of social reality, while social physiognomics interpreted social reality as an image of theory. In the tone row, no one
note had more significance than the others, and Adorno treated social phenom-

ena similarly, so that, for example, "automobile junk yards . . . drowned cats, all these apocryphal realms on the edges of civilization move suddenly into the center."[31]

The real issue is whether Adorno's attempt at a revolution within philosophy, modeled self-consciously after Schönberg, in fact succumbed to the same fate, whether his principle of antisystem itself became a system. The whole point of his relentless insistence on negativity was to resist repeating in thought the structures of domination and reification that existed in society, so that instead of reproducing reality, consciousness could be critical, so that reason would recognize its own nonidentity with social reality, on the one hand, and material nature's nonidentity with the categorizing consciousness that passed for rationality, on the other. While the first of these (reason's nonidentity with reality) was the essence of Horkheimer's Critical Theory, the second (the object's nonidentity with the concept) was indebted to Benjamin:

> Benjamin's concept of experience refers to the particular, and almost the entire effort of his philosophy can be defined as an attempt to rescue the particular. The disgrace in America consists of the fact that precisely here, where the particular is totally destroyed by the general, where in place of experience there exists the repetition of the ever-identical, the attempt is made to represent the particular as if it survived.[32]

It cannot be disputed that despite its dialectical complexity, Adorno's position had an immanent consistency – indeed, he was philosophically the most stringent of all the Frankfurt "School." But at the boundaries of his thinking loomed a paradox which even dialectics couldn't dissolve. According to Adorno, "nonparticipation" (*nicht-mitmachen*) was absolutely necessary in order to keep alive the capacity for experience of the nonidentical:

> . . . being consumed, swallowed up, is indeed just what I understand as "participation" [*Mitmachen*] which is so totally characteristic for the new anthropological [type] – the lack of curiosity. No longer wanting to know anything new, above all anything that is open and unguarded. The guardedness as well of the revolution. . . .[33]

But at the same time, in order to prevent identifying with the given, thought could never experience the new as new: "Only he who recognizes the most modern as the ever-identical serves that which would be different."[34]

Hence, in the name of revolution, thought could never acknowledge a revolutionary situation; in the name of utopia, it could never work for utopia's realization. Adorno ensured perhaps too successfully that reason did not become "instrumental." For instrumental reason preserved a moment of "use value" which negative dialectics had to abandon. The result was that as opposites, they too converged: instrumental reason lost sight of rational goals, ceased to be a means, and became an end in itself; but negative dialectics abrogated political utility, and thus became an end in itself as well. The name of the constellation in which they converged was fetishism, and once again, twelve-tone music provides the model.[35] Adorno recognized that twelve-tone composing, in an attempt to avoid the domination of tonality, adhered to rules more constraining than before: "It enchains music by liberating it."[36] But did he see that the logical structure of his own essays became increasingly predictable, so that, just as in twelve-tone composing,

> Structure as such is to be correct rather than meaningful. The question which twelve-tone music asks of the composer is not how musical meaning is to be organized, but rather, how organization is to become meaningful.[37]

In *Negative Dialektik*, Adorno warned that thinking must avoid making the dialectic itself a first principle – *"prima dialectica."*[38] But he was driven toward this in spite of himself, perhaps indeed by the "objective demands" of the material. When the principle of twelve-tone technique became "total," the dynamics of the new music was "brought to a standstill."[39] But when the method of negative dialectics became total, philosophy threatened to come to a standstill as well, and the New Left of the 1960s not unjustly criticized Adorno for taking Critical Theory into a dead end. The staticness, the quality of incantation, that he so criticized in Benjamin's work was not lacking in his own. Did the perpetual motion of Adorno's arguments go anywhere? Did they lead out of the bourgeois *intérieur* or simply hang suspended within it like the new art form of mobiles?

In his criticism of Husserl, Adorno praised this bourgeois thinker for taking idealism to its limits, claiming he had only to "step through the open door to the world of things"[40] in order to transcend idealism and escape the confines of subjectivity. But it is debatable whether Adorno himself made that step, which perhaps would have necessitated breaking the taboo against positivity. What he criticized in Husserl was ultimately true of himself: "the philosophical creator, who once planned a better social contract, is once again only the creator of philosophy."[41]

An acquaintance of Adorno once commented:

> Adorno, as far as I can see, never took a trip out of the simple desire to see. Europe sufficed for him entirely. No India or China, no Third World, not the people's democracies and not the workers' movements.[42]

This personal characteristic is perhaps not insignificant. The material of the philosopher in the bourgeois era is the written text, and no matter how much he "enters into it," he remains within a private sphere:

> In his text, the writer sets up house. Just as he trundles papers, books, pencils, documents untidily from room to room, he creates the same disorder in his thoughts. They become pieces of furniture that he sinks into, content or irritable. He strokes them affectionately, wears them out, mixes them up, re-arranges, ruins them. For a man who no longer has a homeland, writing becomes a place to live.[43]

Notes

CHAPTER 1

1. Jay reports that Adorno was asked by Friedrich Pollock to drop the Wiesengrund from his name when he came to join the exiled *Institut für Sozialforschung* in New York in 1938 "because there were too many Jewish-sounding names on the Institute's roster." (Martin Jay, *The Dialectical Imagination: A History of the Frankfurt School and the Institute of Social Research, 1923-1950* [Boston: Little, Brown, 1973], p. 34.) Already, however, in the twenties, he had taken to signing his published articles Wiesengrund-Adorno, not out of expediency, but perhaps for aesthetic reasons (he began to use the hyphenated name when he was studying composition with Berg in Vienna) or for personal ones (he identified more closely with his mother's side of the family).

2. She was seventy-three in 1939, according to a letter from Adorno to Benjamin, February 1, 1939 (Frankfurt am Main, Adorno Estate).

3. Horkheimer wrote that Agathe "played a decisive role in bringing him up. Adorno spoke warmly of Agathe as a second mother." (Max Horkheimer, "Über Theodor W. Adorno: Ein Gespräch am 8. August 1969, aufgezeichnet von Bernhard Landau," in Hermann Schweppenhäuser, ed., *Theodor W. Adorno zum Gedächtnis: Eine Sammlung* [Frankfurt am Main: Suhrkamp Verlag, 1971], p. 20.) Agathe's death in the summer of 1935 was a great blow to Adorno (letter, Adorno to Benjamin, July 1935, Frankfurt am Main, Adorno Estate).

4. When he traveled to Italy, Adorno discovered (not without pleasure) that his Italian ancestors had held a title of nobility.

5. Jay, *The Dialectical Imagination*, p. 22.

6. Theodor W. Adorno, "Vierhändig, noch einmal" (1933), *Impromptus: Zweite Folge neu gedruckter musikalischer Aufsätze* (Frankfurt am Main: edition Suhrkamp, 1969), p. 142.

7. *Ibid.*

8. *Ibid.*

9. Walter Benjamin, "The Work of Art in the Age of Mechanical Reproduction" (1936), *Illuminations*, ed. and introd. Hannah Arendt, trans. Harry Zohn (New York: Schocken Books, 1969), pp. 217-251.

10. Adorno, "Vierhändig, noch einmal" (1933), *Impromptus*, p. 143.

11. While studying in Vienna with Berg (himself Catholic), Adorno flirted with conversion to Catholicism (which the Jewish-born Schönberg had also done) but decided against it because of the religious metaphysics he would have had to accept. This is documented in Adorno's correspondence to Ernst Krenek in 1934: "If I am not mistaken, you have recently taken on strongly Catholic standards. They are very, very familiar to me. I myself once thought it would be possible through the Catholic *ordo* to reconstruct the world come apart at the seams, and at that time, ten years ago, I stood just short of conversion, which lay close enough to me as the son of a very Catholic mother. I wasn't able to do it. The integration of the *philosophia perennis* appeared to me irredeemably romantic and in contradiction to every feature of our existence; and in Schönberg I was not able to discover a trace." (Letter, Adorno to Krenek, October 7, 1934, *Theodor W. Adorno und Ernst Krenek: Briefwechsel*, ed. Wolfgang Rogge [Frankfurt am Main: Suhrkamp Verlag, 1974], p. 46.)

12. In the 1960s Max Horkheimer's discourse took on a religious tone; this was not true of Adorno.

13. Cf. Peter Gay's chapter on "The Revolt of the Son," *Weimar Culture: The Outsider as Insider* (New York: Harper Torchbooks, 1968), pp. 102-118.

14. Jews in Frankfurt numbered about 29,000 in 1925, the second largest Jewish community in Germany. The first was Berlin with six times that number (173,000). Cf. Otto Friedrich, *Before the Deluge: A Portrait of Berlin in the 1920's* (New York: Harper & Row, 1972), p. 110.

15. Theodor W. Adorno, "Der wunderliche Realist: Über Siegfried Kracauer" (1964), *Noten zur Literatur*, vol. 3 (Frankfurt am Main: Suhrkamp Verlag, 1965), p. 85.

16. *Ibid.*, p. 83.

17. Cf. Fritz K. Ringer, *The Decline of the German Mandarins: The German Academic Community, 1890-1933* (Cambridge, Mass.: Harvard University Press, 1969).

18. Adorno, "Der wunderliche Realist" (1964), *Noten zur Literatur*, vol. 3, pp. 83-84. On the friendship between Adorno and Kracauer, see Martin Jay, "The Extraterritorial Life of Siegfried Kracauer," *Salmagundi* 31/32 (Fall 1975-Winter 1976): 49-106.

19. "The Frankfurt University was at that time one of the youngest in Germany. At the same time it belonged to the old ones, at least indirectly. In its present form it was established through the forced move of the German part of the University of Strassburg to Frankfurt towards the end of the first World War." (Ernst Erich Noth, "In der vermeintlichen Hochburg des Liberalismus: Wie man im Frankfurt der dreissiger Jahre studierte," *Frankfurter Rundschau*, no. 269, Saturday, November 20, 1971, feuilleton, p. v.)

20. Signed T. Wiesengrund, "Expressionismus und künstlerische Wahrhaftigkeit: Zur Kritik neuer Dichtung," *Die Neue Schaubühne* [Dresden], 2, 9 (1920): 233–236.

21. Theodor Wiesengrund, " 'Die Hochzeit des Faun': Grundsätzliche Bemerkungen zu Bernhard Sekles' neuer Oper," *Neue Blätter für Kunst und Literatur* [Frankfurt am Main] 4 (1921–1922): 61–62; and 5 (1921–1922): 68–70.

22. So Adorno described himself (*tierisch ernst*) as he was in the mid-1920s. (Theodor W. Adorno, *Berg: Der Meister des kleinsten Übergangs* [1968], *Gesammelte Schriften*, vol. 13: *Die Musikalischen Monographien*, ed. Gretel Adorno and Rolf Tiedemann [Frankfurt am Main: Suhrkamp Verlag, 1971], p. 361.) In subsequent notes, Adorno's *Gesammelte Schriften* will be abbreviated to *GS*.

23. This development, which both Adorno and Benjamin were to consider so significant, had been observed before the war by Werner Sombart and articulated in his influential essay "Technik und Kultur," *Archiv für Sozialwissenschaft und Sozialpolitik* [Tübingen] 33 (1911): 305–347.

24. Wiesengrund, "Expressionismus und künstlerische Wahrhaftigkeit" (1920), p. 235.

25. In 1962, Adorno cautioned against a recent tendency to idealize the era of the twenties, but he admitted: "In spite of this the image of the twenties as the world in which, as it says in Brecht's 'Mahagonny,' everything is allowed, as a utopia, has an element of truth." (Theodor W. Adorno, "Jene zwanziger Jahre" [1962], *Eingriffe: Neun kritische Modelle* [Frankfurt am Main: edition Suhrkamp, 1963].) He expressed the same thought, with no little nostalgia, in a radio conversation with Lotte Lenya in the late 1950s (tape recording, Frankfurt am Main, Adorno Estate).

26. Ernst Bloch, *Geist der Utopie* (Munich: Duncker & Humblot, 1918). 2nd ed., rev. (Berlin: Paul Cassirer, 1923) trans. as *Man on His Own* by E. B. Ashton (New York: Herder and Herder, 1972). Earlier that year he had read Georg Lukács's *Die Theorie des Romans,* which also had a lasting influence on him (discussed below in Chapter 3). Bloch and Lukács, at the time close friends, struck Adorno as similar thinkers. (Theodor W. Adorno, "Henkel, Krug und frühe Erfahrung," *Ernst Bloch zu Ehren: Beiträge zu seinem Werk,* ed. Siegfried Unseld [Frankfurt am Main: Suhrkamp Verlag, 1965], p. 10.)

27. T. W. Adorno, "Für Ernst Bloch," *Aufbau-Reconstruktion* [New York] 8, 48 (November 27, 1942), p. 15.

28. Adorno, "Henkel, Krug und frühe Erfahrung," *Ernst Bloch zu Ehren,* p. 10.

29. Adorno, "Für Ernst Bloch" (1942), p. 15.

30. Bloch was Jewish, but his religiosity was pansectarian.

31. Ernst Bloch, *Thomas Münzer als Theologe der Revolution* (Munich: Duncker & Humblot, 1921). Lukács criticized Bloch's argument, not because it stressed utopian themes, but because it failed to see the element of transcendence already contained within (a proper interpretation of) Marxism: "When Ernst Bloch claims that this union of religion with socio-economic

revolution points the way to a deepening of the 'merely economic' outlook of historical materialism, he fails to notice that his deepening simply by-passes the real depth of historical materialism." (Georg Lukács, *History and Class Consciousness*, trans. Rodney Livingstone [Cambridge, Mass.: The M.I.T. Press, 1968], p. 193.)

32. See George L. Mosse, "Left-Wing Intellectuals in the Weimar Republic," *Germans and Jews: The Right, the Left and the Search for a "Third Force" in Pre-Nazi Germany* (New York: Howard Fertig, 1970), pp. 171–225.

33. Gershom Scholem, "On the 1930 Edition of Rozenzweig's Star of Redemption," *The Messianic Idea in Judaism* (New York: Schocken Books, 1971).

34. Franz Rosenzweig, *The Star of Redemption*, trans. (from 2nd ed. of 1930) William W. Hallo (New York: Holt, Rinehart and Winston, 1970), p. 188.

35. *Ibid.*, p. 52.

36. *Ibid.*, p. 13.

37. ". . . art, then, is the language of what is otherwise still unpronounceable. . . . Art remains piecework so that life might be and become whole." (*Ibid.*, p. 191.)

38. *Ibid.*, p. 238.

39. *Ibid.*, p. 45. These individually existing phenomena "had been the stumbling block of idealism, and thus of philosophy as a whole from Parmenides to Hegel." (*Ibid.*, p. 47.)

40. *Ibid.*, pp. 186–187.

41. *Ibid.*, p. 186.

42. They were first introduced by Hermann Edler Grab von Hermannswörth, sociologist, musician, and friend of Adorno (cf. editors' note, Walter Benjamin, *Briefe,* 2 vols., ed. Gershom Scholem and Theodor W. Adorno [Frankfurt am Main: Suhrkamp Verlag, 1966], vol. 2, p. 559).

43. Theodor W. Adorno, "Erinnerungen" (1964), *Über Walter Benjamin*, ed. Rolf Tiedemann (Frankfurt am Main: Suhrkamp Verlag, 1970), p. 67. Benjamin, born in Berlin, was in Frankfurt intending to complete his *Habilitation* there. Adorno and Benjamin were also together in the sociology seminar of Gottfried Salomon-Delatour which was analyzing the newly published book on historicism by Ernst Troeltsch (*ibid*).

44. *Ibid.*, p. 70.

45. *Ibid.*

46. Walter Benjamin, "Über das Programm der kommenden Philosophie" (1918), *Zur Kritik der Gewalt und andere Aufsätze*, afterword by Herbert Marcuse (Frankfurt am Main: edition Suhrkamp, 1971), p. 27.

47. Gustav Wyneken was the director. Benjamin worked on the journal of this circle in 1913–14. (Adorno, "A l'écart de tous les courants" [1969], *Über Walter Benjamin*, p. 97.)

48. In that year Scholem left for Palestine. Their friendship continued by means of a voluminous correspondence, and they spent time together in Paris in 1927 and 1938. (Gershom Scholem, "Erinnerungen" [1966], in Theodor

W. Adorno et al., *Über Walter Benjamin* [Frankfurt am Main: Suhrkamp Verlag, 1968], pp. 30–31.)

49. Scholem has written in retrospect: "I think one can say without disrespect that hardly ever had there been a Jewish theology of such vacuity and insignificance as existed in the decades before World War I. . . . [O]rthodox theology has suffered from what one might call 'Kabbalah-phobia.'" (Scholem, *The Messianic Idea in Judaism*, p. 321.)

50. Cf. Walter Benjamin, *Der Begriff der Kunstkritik in der deutschen Romantik* (1920); *Goethes Wahlverwandtschaften* (1924); *Ursprung des deutschen Trauerspiels* (1928); all republished in Walter Benjamin, *Gesammelte Schriften*, 6 vols., ed. Rolf Tiedemann and Hermann Schweppenhäuser, vol. I:1: *Abhandlungen* (Frankfurt am Main: Suhrkamp Verlag, 1974).

51. Adorno used both these words to describe what he referred to as "our theology" in a letter to Benjamin, December 17, 1934. (Adorno, *Über Walter Benjamin*, pp. 103–104.) Discussed below, Chapter 8.

52. Gershom Scholem, *Walter Benjamin: Die Geschichte einer Freundschaft* (Frankfurt am Main: Suhrkamp Verlag, 1975), p. 76.

53. After Scholem moved to Palestine in 1923, however, Benjamin talked repeatedly of joining him, although these plans never materialized. (*Ibid.*, p. 173 and *passim.*)

54. Kracauer's involvement had terminated by 1926, when he wrote a strongly critical review of the Buber-Rosenzweig translation of the Bible (See Martin Jay, "The Extraterritorial Life of Siegfried Kracauer," 51.) On Rabbi Nobel's group, see Nahum N. Glatzner, "The Frankfurt Lehrhaus," *Year Book I,* Leo Baeck Institute (London, 1956). (London, 1956).

55. Cf. above, note 11.

56. Cornelius (1863–1947) came to Frankfurt from Munich in 1910. He was "a passionate teacher . . . in many ways the opposite of the current image of a German university professor, and in strong opposition to most of his colleagues." (Friedrich Pollock, cited in Jay, *The Dialectical Imagination,* p. 45.)

57. This was Adorno's description in the preface to his first *Habilitationsschrift*, which was based on Cornelius's theory. (Theodor W. Adorno, "Der Begriff des Unbewussten in der transzendentalen Seelenlehre" [1927], *GS*, vol. 1: *Frühe philosophische Schriften,* ed. Rolf Tiedemann [Frankfurt am Main: Suhrkamp Verlag, 1973], p. 81.)

58. Cornelius came from a famous Munich family of painters and composers. A lover of Italian culture, he led the life of an artist, flaunted convention, and married a woman many years his senior. He was gifted in both painting and music. He had taught painting in Munich during the war, and gave Horkheimer private instruction in composition theory. (Helmut Gumnior and Rudolf Ringguth, *Max Horkheimer in Selbstzeugnissen und Bilddokumenten*, Rowohlts Monographien, no. 208, ed. Kurt Kusenberg [Hamburg: Rowohlt Taschenbuch Verlag, 1973], p. 22.)

59. Hans Cornelius, *Grundlagen der Erkenntnistheorie: Transcendentale Systematik* (1916), 2nd ed. (Munich: Verlag von Ernst Reinhard, 1926), p. 261.

60. Quoted in letter, Friedrich Pollock to Martin Jay, March 24, 1970, cited in the ms. of Jay's book *The Dialectical Imagination* (p. 8) but omitted in the published version.

61. Hans Cornelius, "Leben und Lehre" (1923), cited in (and trans. by) Jay, *The Dialectical Imagination*, p. 45.

62. Lenin's book was translated and published in German in 1922. Hanns Eisler recalled: "We were already waiting for the book. Lenin was still alive then. It was a real sensation." (Hans Bunge, *Fragen Sie mehr über Brecht: Hanns Eisler im Gespräch*, afterword by Stephen Hermlin [Munich: Rogner & Bernhard, 1970], p. 156.)

63. Cornelius, *Einleitung in die Philosophie* (1903), cited in W. I. Lenin, *Werke*, vol. 14: *Materialismus und Empiriokritizismus* (Berlin: Dietz Verlag, 1968), pp. 216-217.

64. *Ibid.*, p. 216.

65. Recalled by Theodor W. Adorno, *Philosophische Terminologie: Zur Einleitung*, 2 vols., ed. Rudolf zur Lippe (Frankfurt am Main: Suhrkamp Verlag, 1973), vol. 1, pp. 121-122. Despite what he said, there were limits to Cornelius's encouragement of individualistic thinking among his students. One gets the feeling from reading the young Adorno's work that they could criticize every philosophy except Cornelius's. Adorno went to great pains in his doctoral dissertation to identify his own method with Cornelius's. This was true as well for his first *Habilitationsschrift*, which, however, Cornelius did not accept (see below). Horkheimer testified to the limits of Cornelius's tolerance when he wrote in 1921: "Yesterday I had a talk with a young philosopher about the task of philosophy. He was very enthusiastic. Unfortunately, I discovered only today that Cornelius had been in the next room, and must have heard my exposition, which was totally directed against him." (Cited in Gumnior and Ringguth, *Max Horkheimer*, p. 23.)

66. Friedrich Pollock, cited in Jay, *The Dialectical Imagination*, p. 44.

67. Max Horkheimer, *Aus der Pubertät: Novellen und Tagebuchblätter*, ed. Alfred Schmidt (Munich: Kosel-Verlag, 1974), pp. 149-159.

68. *Ibid.*, pp. 150-151.

69. *Ibid.*, p. 151.

70. Cf. Alfred Schmidt, "Frühe Dokumente der Kritischen Theorie," editorial afterword, *ibid.*, p. 362. He fell in love with the private secretary of his father, Rose Christine Riekher (whom he called Maidon), eight years older than he was, and a Christian. He persisted in the relationship and married her in 1926.

71. *Ibid.*, pp. 158-159.

72. *Ibid.*, p. 153.

73. Schmidt in *ibid.*, p. 362.

74. Cf., e.g., Jay, *The Dialectical Imagination*, p. 258. Horkheimer's writings in

puberty documenting this early influence of Schopenhauer remained unpublished until 1974.

75. Theodor W. Adorno, "Offener Brief an Max Horkheimer," *Die Zeit,* February 12, 1965, p. 32.

76. Horkheimer, *Aus der Pubertät,* p. 154.

77. Gumnior and Ringguth, *Max Horkheimer,* p. 22. Horkheimer also met Martin Heidegger, then Husserl's assistant, and wrote to Maidon in 1921: "I am aware today that Heidegger was one of the most important personalities who has spoken to me. Whether I agree with him? – How can I say, as I know just one thing about him for certain, that for him the motive of philosophizing emerges not from intellectual ambition and a prefabricated theory, but every day anew, out of his own experiences." (Cited in *ibid.,* p. 24.)

78. Horkheimer's dissertation, for which he received his degree *summa cum laude,* was on Kant's third critique: "Zur Antinomie der teleologischen Urteilskraft" (unpublished, 1922).

79. Adorno, "Offener Brief an Max Horkheimer" (1965), p. 32.

80. *Ibid.*

81. For a history of the Institute's early years, see Chapter 1 of Jay, *The Dialectical Imagination,* pp. 3–40.

82. The fact that their academic writings were fully apolitical does not rule out an early interest in radical politics. Horkheimer, at least, seems to have had the conscience of a socialist since puberty, and socialist thinking was certainly in the air. But no connection with radical politics, socialism, or Marxism can be documented in Adorno's case until the late 1920s.

83. Theodor W. Adorno, "Die Transzendenz des Dinglichen und Noematischen in Husserl's Phänomenologie" (1924), *GS* 1, pp. 7–77.

84. Theodor W. Adorno, Husserl ms., "Zur Philosphie Husserls" 1934–1937, Frankfurt am Main, Adorno Estate.

85. This version was substantially the same as the 1930s manuscript. The new introduction reflected the Frankfurt Institute's analysis of fascism, which maintained that domination, rather than the Marxian categories of reification and exchange, was the key structural principle of society. (See Jay, "The *Institut*'s Analysis of Naziism," *The Dialectical Imagination,* pp. 143–172.)

86. Scherchen (b. Berlin, 1891) had collaborated with Schönberg in the first production of "Pierrot lunaire" in 1911. He succeeded Furtwängler as conductor in Frankfurt am Main in 1923.

87. Theodor W. Adorno, "Erinnerungen," newly written in 1968 from the essay "Erinnerungen an den Lebenden," published (1936) in the music journal *23* under the pseud. Hektor Rottweiler, in Adorno, *Berg, GS* 13, p. 340.

88. In 1922 Adorno had written a favorable article on Hindemith (reprinted as Adorno, "Paul Hindemith," *Impromptus,* pp. 53–57). After his experience

in Vienna he wrote critically of Hindemith's composing because of the anachronism of his neoclassicist musical means. (Adorno, "Kammermusik von Paul Hindemith" [1926], *ibid., pp. 58–62.)

89. Adorno, "Erinnerungen" (1936), *GS* 13, p. 340.

90. Cited in Henry Schnitzler, "Gay Vienna: Myth and Reality," *Journal of the History of Ideas* 15, 1 (January 1954): 100.

91. Ernst Mach and Franz Brentano taught there before World War I. Mach influenced the Vienna Circle, including Ludwig Wittgenstein; Brentano was Husserl's teacher (and also Freud's). The neo-Kantian philosophical climate was not limited to the university: "In Wittgenstein's Vienna, everyone in the educated world discussed philosophy and regarded the central issues in post-Kantian thought as bearing directly on his own interests, whether artistic or scientific, legal or political." (Allan Janik and Stephen Toulmin, *Wittgenstein's Vienna* [New York: Simon and Schuster, 1973], p. 26.)

92. Ernst Krenek, biographical essay, in Bruno Walter, *Gustav Mahler* (New York: The Greystone Press, 1941), p. 197.

93. Theodor W. Adorno, conversation with Lotte von Tobisch, tape recording, Frankfurt am Main, Adorno Estate.

94. Carl E. Schorske, "Politics and the Psyche in *fin-de-siècle* Vienna: Schnitzler and Hofmannsthal," *American Historical Review* 66, 4 (July 1961): 935.

95. Cited in *ibid.,* 944.

96. Cf. Harry Zohn, *Karl Kraus,* Twayne's World Author Series, no. 116 (New York: Twayne Publishers, 1971), p. 26.

97. *Ibid.,* p. 42. This was the theme of his book *Sittlichkeit und Kriminalität,* which Adorno (and also Benjamin) admired highly. (Cf. Theodor W. Adorno, "Sittlichkeit und Kriminalität" [1964], *Noten zur Literatur,* vol. 3 [Frankfurt am Main: Suhrkamp Verlag, 1969], pp. 57–82.) Adorno, like Kraus, defended the individual's private sphere, maintaining that it should be free from society's incursions. (Cf. Theodor Wiesengrund-Adorno, "Opernprobleme: Glossiert nach Frankfurter Aufführungen," *Musikblätter des Anbruch* 8, 5 [1926]: 205–208.) This position was central to the critical theory of "culture industry" developed by the Institute after Adorno officially joined in 1938.

98. His goal was an analysis of language "which, by presenting horrors of syntax, would aim at getting closer to the possibilities, and thus the mysteries, of the most profound language, whose obscene use has led to the horrors of blood." (Kraus, cited in Zohn, *Karl Kraus,* p. 23.) Kraus's indifference to politics ended in what Benjamin described as *Die Fackel's* "capitulation to Austrian fascism" in 1934. (Benjamin, *Briefe,* vol. 2, p. 623.)

99. *Ibid.,* p. 27.

100. "The main feature of Kraus' incomparable work is plainly a certain conservatism: he perceives a God-given harmony of mind and nature which he realizes in language, the first home of man, and sees localised historically in past literary ages crystallising round the mighty figure of this or that poetic genius – and he is anxious to protect this harmony from the onslaught of ruin and decay, disguised as technical progress." (Ernst Krenek,

"Karl Kraus and Arnold Schönberg" [1934], *Exploring Music,* trans. Margaret Shenfield and Geoffrey Skelton [New York: October House, 1966], p. 83.)

101. "Far from originating in Wittgenstein's *Tractatus* . . . the idea of regarding language, symbolisms and media of expression of all kinds as giving us 'representations' (*Darstellungen*) or 'pictures' (*Bilder*) had by 1910 become a commonplace in all fields of Viennese cultural debate. Among scientists, this notion had been in circulation at least since the time of Hertz, who had characterized physical theories as providing just such a *Bild* or *Darstellung* of natural phenomena. At the other extreme, it was equally familiar among artists and musicians. Arnold Schönberg, for instance, wrote an essay on musical thought, with the title, *Der musikalische Gedanke und die Logik, Technik, und Kunst seiner Darstellung.*" (Janik and Toulmin, *Wittgenstein's Vienna,* p. 31.) The notion surfaces in Adorno's writings as well (discussed below, Chapters 6 and 7), and it is likely that he absorbed it from the Viennese intellectual climate. The importance of *Darstellung* and the equation of *Bild* with truth were motifs in Benjamin's writings also by 1926 (see below, Chapter 6), yet they were absent from those of Horkheimer and the other Institute members.

102. Cited in *ibid.,* p. 102.

103. Adorno, *Berg* (1968), *GS* 13, p. 357.

104. On the similarities between Kraus and Schönberg, see Krenek, "Karl Kraus and Arnold Schönberg" (1934), *Exploring Music,* pp. 83–86; also Janik and Toulmin, *Wittgenstein's Vienna,* p. 102 and *passim.*

105. However, Schopenhauer's statements on music included some very un-Wagnerian theses: music was nonconceptual "form moving in sounds"; program music was thus inferior, and music formed a "closed world" pursuing its own laws. That this view in fact anticipated the anti-Wagnerian position of Eduard Hanslick has been recently observed by Alan Walker in his *TLS* commentary, "Schopenhauer and Music," *Times Literary Supplement,* January 3, 1975, p. 11.

106. Hanslick's famous treatise *On the Beautiful in Music* (1854), went through nine editions. (See Janik and Toulmin, *Wittgenstein's Vienna,* pp. 103–107.)

107. Adorno noted that the following statement by Schönberg on Mahler's Ninth Symphony could well be a canon for Schönberg's own work: "In it the author scarcely speaks any longer as subject. . . . This work is no more held in the vessel of the ego. It brings, so to speak, objective, almost dispassionate substantiations, of a beauty which becomes perceptible only to those who can forego animal warmth. . . ." (Theodor W. Adorno, "Sakrales Fragment: Über Schönberg's Moses und Aron" [1963], *Quasi una Fantasia: Musikalische Schriften II* [Frankfurt am Main: Suhrkamp Verlag, 1963], p. 314.)

108. The 1922 edition (Arnold Schönberg, *Harmonielehre,* 3rd ed., rev. and enl. [Vienna: Universal-Edition, 1922]), has been used here: it was the one with which Adorno was familiar. The English translation by Robert D. W. Adams (New York: Philosophical Library, 1948) omits "much

philosophical, polemic material" (translator's preface, p. xi), precisely those parts which are of greatest interest in this study.

109. Schönberg, *Harmonielehre*, p. 4.

110. *Ibid.*, p. 3.

111. *Ibid.*

112. *Ibid.*, p. 6. In 1899 Schönberg wrote a symphonic poem, *Verklärte Nacht*, which used the ninth chord (a favorite of the romantics when used in its root position) in an inverted form with the ninth as the base note of the chord. He later told how a concert society refused to perform the piece because "It is self-evident; there is no such thing as the inversion of a ninth chord; therefore, there is no such thing as the performance of it; for one really cannot perform something that does not exist. So I had to wait several years." (Cited in René Leibowitz, *Schoenberg and His School: The Contemporary State of the Language of Music*, trans. Dika Newlin [New York: Philosophical Library, 1949], p. 48.)

113. "And I would be proud if I . . . could say: 'I have taken from composition students a bad aesthetics, but given them in its place a good theory of handicraft.'" (Schönberg, *Harmonielehre*, p. 7.)

114. *Ibid.*, p. 2.

115. Adorno, *Berg* (1968), *GS* 13, p. 359.

116. Paul Collaer, *A History of Modern Music*, trans. Sally Abeles (New York: The World Publishing Company, 1961), pp. 68–69.

117. "It is not that Schönberg, the rebel, sacrificed the forms, in order to give himself more freedom: Rebellion and freedom became his duty, because the forms were decayed." (Theodor Wiesengrund-Adorno, "Die Serenade: Zur Aufführung von Schönbergs Serenade in Venedig," *Pult und Taktstock* 2, 7 [September 1925]: 115–118.)

118. Hanns Eisler (1898–1962) had studied with Schönberg in 1917–1918. Although he was in Berlin in 1925–1926, the music circles of Vienna and Berlin were closely connected, and Adorno met him in 1925 (see Adorno's afterword to Theodor W. Adorno and Hanns Eisler, *Komposition für den Film* [1944] [Munich: Rogner & Bernhard, 1969], p. 213). Adorno favorably reviewed one of Eisler's compositions in 1926 (Theodor Wiesengrund-Adorno, "Hanns Eisler, Duo für Violine und Violoncell, op. 7, Nr. 1," *Musikblätter des Anbruch* 7, Sonderheft Italien [1925]: 422–423). In the late 1920s Eisler began to write music for Bertolt Brecht's proletarian poems and dramas, and remained a close friend of Brecht throughout his life. Eisler dropped Schönberg's cerebral approach to composition for a more popular style suited to Brecht's political messages and effects. Yet he retained a tremendous respect for Schönberg, who had taught him gratis when Eisler was unable to pay. (See Bunge, *Fragen Sie mehr über Brecht*, pp. 167–178.)

119. Adorno's understanding of the dialectic at this time was probably close to that of Georg Lukács in *Die Theorie des Romans*, which impressed Adorno greatly when he read it in 1921 (see Adorno, "Henkel, Krug und frühe Erfahrung," *Ernst Bloch zu Ehren*, p. 10). This pre-Marxist, Dilthey-

influenced study and its importance for Adorno are discussed in detail in Chapter 3, below.

120. Berg's *Wozzeck* was considered the epitome of expressionist opera. Adorno argued that its significance was objective and historical, accomplishing, as had Schönberg's works, a dialectical reversal of tradition. (Theodor Wiesengrund-Adorno, "Alban Berg: Zur Uraufführung des 'Wozzeck,'" *Musikblätter des Anbruch* 7, 10 [December 1925]: 531–537.)

121. Theodor Wiesengrund-Adorno, "Anton Webern: Zur Aufführung der fünf Orchesterstücke in Zürich," *Musikblätter des Anbruch* 8, 6 (June–July 1926): 280.

122. *Ibid.*

123. *Ibid.*, 281.

124. Theodor W. Adorno, "Der dialektische Komponist" (1934), *Impromptus*, pp. 39–44, discussed in Chapter 8, pages 129–131.

125. Adorno, Husserl ms. (1934–1937), revised and published in 1956 as *Zur Metakritik der Erkenntnistheorie.*

126. Adorno, *Berg* (1968), *GS* 13, p. 360.

127. *Ibid.*, p. 362. Kolisch (b. 1896) was a violinist who had studied with Schönberg and formed his own string quartet in 1922. The Kolisch Quartet, which premiered works by Schönberg, Berg, and Webern, was in existence until 1939. Adorno's meeting with Kolisch led to plans to collaborate on a theory of musical reproduction (Adorno's first article on this theme was published in 1925) which was to center on the problem of how past works of music ought to be performed in the present. Throughout his life Adorno kept notebooks on this topic (*Reproduktionstheorie*, 3 vols., unpublished, Frankfurt am Main, Adorno Estate, n.d.), and he remained friends with Kolisch, but the planned collaborative study never materialized.

128. The one letter to Adorno in Schönberg's published correspondence (December 6, 1930) asked in rather formal terms whether Adorno would be interested in working on an encyclopedia of new music. (Arnold Schönberg, *Letters*, ed. Erwin Stein, trans. Eithne Wilkins and Ernst Kaiser [New York: St. Martin's Press, 1965], p. 145–146.) Although Adorno later did contribute to the American *Encyclopedia of the Arts* (1946), in which his friend Ernst Krenek was involved (the contribution was an article on jazz), he clearly envisioned his intellectual work in grander, more original terms. Schönberg seems to have had little patience for Adorno's interest in grounding the new music in an aesthetic theory. Adorno cited a letter from Schönberg to Kolisch, July 27, 1932, warning against emphasizing "what I have always fought against: the knowledge of how [the music] is *composed*: while I have always aided knowledge as to what it *is*! I have already repeatedly tried to make that intelligible to Wiesengrund, and also Berg and Webern. But they don't believe what I say." (Theodor W. Adorno, introduction to *Moments Musicaux: Neugedruckte Aufsätze, 1928* bis *1962* [Frankfurt am Main: edition Suhrkamp, 1964], p. 10.) Adorno wrote a monograph on Schönberg in the 1940s in California (later pub-

lished in *Philosophie der neuen Musik*) which inspired Thomas Mann in
in his conception of the novel *Doktor Faustus*. Schönberg was angry
with Mann for the indirect, uncredited utilization of him and his work as a
model for the novel's central character, the composer Adrian Leverkühn.

129. Berg once related to Adorno that "even long after they were adults, he
and Webern conversed with him [Schönberg] only in the form of questions." (Adorno, *Berg* [1968], *GS* 13, pp. 346–347.)

130. "If intellectuals should not be fathers, then Berg was the most unfatherly
that one could hope for; his authority was that of a perfect absence of
authoritarian nature. He succeeded in not growing up, without remaining
infantile." (*Ibid.*, p. 367.)

131. "A lesson with Berg would generally run as follows: he would take the
pupil's exercises and tentative compositions in the most friendly manner
and lay them on the piano. Then he would let his eye run over them from
the top, emitting plenty of exclamations of agreement and encouragement
of a general sort, such as 'not bad,' 'a good idea,' 'not bad at all,' 'good,
good.' Then he would invite the pupil — who was naturally highly pleased
with this praise — to sit next to him at the piano, and go through his work
bar for bar, and note for note, with the following result: after his correc-
tions had been carried out — the pages usually looked like desolated
battlefields — a completely different composition emerged, with little in
common with what the pupil had brought along. But he would never
write a single note in the manuscript unless the pupil was genuinely convinced, and sanctioned it completely — not submitting merely to the
authority of the brilliant teacher. The sharpest criticism he was ever
heard to utter was 'You haven't quite heard that out yet!'" (Willi Reich,
Alban Berg, trans. Cornelius Cardew [New York: Harcourt, Brace &
World, 1963], p. 72. Adorno contributed to the original German edition
of Reich's book on Berg [Vienna: Verlag Herbert Reichner, 1937], but
his essays, analyses of specific compositions by Berg, are not in this English
edition. They are reprinted in Adorno, *Berg* [1968], *GS* 13.)

132. Adorno, *Berg* (1968), *GS* 13, p. 365.

133. *Ibid.*, p. 355. Once he remarked to Berg that he would have liked a way
of eliminating men's beards altogether to save the time of daily shaving,
but Berg said "that the smoothly shaven face pleasing to women could
not be separated from the fact that they feel the sprouting beard underneath. In these sorts of nuances he discovered the dialectic for himself."
(*Ibid.*)

134. *Ibid.*, p. 342. Benjamin was "utterly taken" with Berg's *Wozzeck* (*ibid.*).

135. "Berg's recollection is lethal. Only because it brings back the past as
irretrievable does it grant it to the present." (*Ibid.*, p. 350.)

136. *Ibid.*, pp. 329–330, 346.

137. *Ibid.*, p. 353.

138. *Ibid.*, p. 352.

139. *Ibid.*, pp. 339–340.

140. Eduard Steuermann (b. 1892 in Poland) was a pianist who had cham-

pioned Schönberg's music since 1912. (Cf. Theodor W. Adorno, "Nachruf auf einen Pianisten: Zum Tode von Eduard Steuermann" [1964], *Impromptus*, pp. 150–156.)

141. "After the Berlin premiere of *Wozzeck* and the dinner at Töpfer's where it was celebrated and he, embarrassed like a young boy, was scarcely able to respond, I was with him until deep into the night, in order literally to console him over its success." (Adorno, *Berg* [1968], *GS* 13, p. 336.)

142. Eisler was also friends with Steuermann and Kolisch. (Bunge, *Fragen Sie mehr über Brecht*, p. 167.)

143. Ernst Krenek (b. 1900 in Vienna) followed his teacher Franz Schreker to Berlin (1920–1923), was exposed to neoclassicism in Paris (1924), and assisted Paul Bekker, general manager, at Cassel and then Wiesbaden, of the state opera (1925–1927) where he wrote the immensely successful opera *Jonny spielt auf*, about a Negro jazz musician. In 1928 he returned to Vienna and studied Schönberg's twelve-tone technique. Adorno's friendship with Krenek began in the late twenties, and it continued, despite their differences on issues of musical theory, throughout Adorno's life. Their correspondence has been published: *Theodor W. Adorno und Ernst Krenek: Briefwechsel.*

144. Adorno was a member of the editorial board of *Anbruch* from 1929 to 1931.

145. Adorno, *Berg* (1968), *GS* 13, p. 344.

146. *Ibid.*

147. The compositions in Adorno's estate include several cycles of songs, a women's chorus, and some short orchestral pieces. In the 1930s he worked on an opera for the text of Mark Twain's *Tom Sawyer*. Only one of his partiturs was published, and this not until late in his life.

148. His very successful friend Krenek helped to premiere one of Adorno's song cycles in Vienna in March 1935 (cf. letter, Krenek to Adorno, March 27, 1935, *Adorno und Krenek: Briefwechsel*, p. 74).

149. Adorno, *Berg* (1968), *GS* 13, p. 361. "To be sure, I was at that time brutally earnest, and that could get on the nerves of a mature artist. Out of blatant deference, I strove never to say anything except what I considered to be particularly deep. . . ." (*Ibid.*) Cf. the description of Adorno by Arthur Koestler, who roomed in the same boarding house as Adorno, the Pension Glaser in the Alsergrund district of Vienna: "Dr. Theodore (*sic*) Wiesengrund-Adorno" was one of "the first highbrow intellectuals I had come across. . . . He was a shy, distraught and esoteric young man with a subtle charm which I was too callow to discern. . . . He shared a small table in the dining-room with a blond and equally withdrawn woman: the actress Anny Mewes, who had been a friend of Rainer Maria Rilke. . . . Adorno and Anny Mewes occasionally spoke a few friendly words to me from their remote intellectual heights." (Arthur Koestler, *Arrow in the Blue: An Autobiography*, 2 vols. [New York: The Macmillan Company, 1952], vol. 1, p. 131.)

150. Cf. Theodor Wiesengrund-Adorno, "Orchesterstücke op. 16," *Pult und*

Taktstock 4, Schönberg Sonderheft (1927): 36-43, and *Idem*, "Schönbergs Bläserquartet" (1928) in *Moments Musicaux*. In 1929 Adorno called the twelve-tone system "the rational fulfillment of a historical force in which progressive consciousness undertakes to purify its material from the decomposition of organic decay. . . ." (Theodor Wiesengrund-Adorno, "Zur Zwölftontechnique," *Anbruch* 11 [1929]: 290-294.)

151. By the late 1940s Adorno was explicitly critical: "The total rationality of music is its total organization. By means of organization, liberated music seeks to reconstitute the lost totality – the lost power and the responsibly binding force of Beethoven. Music succeeds in so doing only at the price of its freedom, and thereby it fails." (Theodor W. Adorno, *Philosophy of Modern Music*, trans. Anne G. Mitchell and Wesley V. Blomster [New York: The Seabury Press, 1973], p. 69.)

152. Adorno's own compositions were atonal. He never accepted the twelve-tone schema as the *only* valid form of composition, even in the twenties. Its validity, he claimed, had been always as a *negation* of tonality, not as a new system detachable from the historical development of music. There was, he felt, no reason why a tone row couldn't contain eleven instead of twelve tones. (Letter, Adorno to Krenek, April 9, 1929, *Adorno und Krenek: Briefwechsel*, pp. 11-18.) By 1934 Adorno's reservations regarding the twelve-tone system had increased. (*Ibid.*, pp. 48-56.)

153. There was in philosophy a Kierkegaard renaissance and a popularity of *Lebensphilosophie* in general. In art, certain aspects of the *neue Sachlichkeit* (new objectivity) were the opposite of objective; in music, primitivism and modernity converged with the impact of jazz.

154. Schönberg and Berg were not alone in their interest in astrology and the occult. Horoscopes were widely read, and mediums did a great business in Frankfurt (see Madlen Lorei and Richard Kirn, *Frankfurt und die goldenen zwanziger Jahren* [Frankfurt am Main: Verlag Frankfurter Bücher, 1966], pp. 123-124). On irrationalism as a theme of the new motion pictures, see Siegfried Kracauer, *From Caligari to Hitler: A Psychological History of the German Film* (Princeton, N.J.: Princeton University Press, 1947).

155. "Der Begriff des Unbewussten in der transcendentalen Seelenlehre" (1927), published posthumously in Adorno, *GS* 1, pp. 81-322.

156. Adorno noted that in the Parallelogism section of the *Critique of Pure Reason* Kant's argument ruled out an ontological psychology of the unconscious; however, the possibility of a rational psychology was not challenged. (*Ibid.*, p. 105.)

157. Adorno argued that the weakness in Kant's theory which had provided irrationalist philosophies of the unconscious with a ground for legitimation was connected with the thing-in-itself doctrine that left the way open for a return of metaphysical dogmatism. (*Ibid.*, p. 95.)

158. By demonstrating that these philosophers of the unconscious were internally contradictory, that they were actually dependent on the Kantianism they purported to transcend, Adorno justified returning to a Kantian approach to the problem. (*Ibid.*, p. 103.)

159. In Adorno's own time vitalist and organicist theories were most prevalent in the field of psychology. The "dominant streams" in psychology, including Gestaltist theory, "operate with the concept of the *organic* as central, and believe to have in this concept an effective means for fighting against every 'rationalism,'" and to this end, they "make use of the concept of the unconscious." (*Ibid.*, p. 316.)

160. A Freudian Institute was founded in Berlin in the twenties, and Adorno may have had his interest sparked through friends there. Ernst Bloch (whom he did not, however, befriend until 1928) wrote a very *avant-garde* early article, "Beitrag zu den Träumen nach Coitus interruptus," *Zentralblatt für Psycho-Analyse* 2 (1911-1912), and Freud is mentioned in Bloch's *Geist der Utopie* (which Adorno read in 1921).

161. Adorno wrote later to Benjamin that he read Freud while on the Italian Riviera: "I know San Remo from 1927; first I was there for a while with Gretel [Karplus, later Adorno's wife], then for several months alone; it was the period during which I was busy with Freud." (Letter, Adorno to Benjamin, December 5, 1934, Frankfurt am Main, Adorno Estate.) It is possible that Gretel, who studied biology and medicine in Berlin, first interested Adorno in Freud.

162. Freud wrote the "Vorlesungen zur Einführung in die Psychoanalyse" before he posited the death instinct as an ontological source of aggression, and before his interpretation of history in the metaphysical terms of a "battle of giants" between Eros and Thanatos. Adorno noted that even in these early lectures, there were ontological tendencies which "one could not avoid recognizing" (he included the Oedipal theory) (*ibid.*, pp. 288–289); but he claimed that Freud's theory "divorces itself much further from metaphysical arbitrariness than, for example, the theories of Jung and Adler. . . ." (*Ibid.*, p. 240.)

163. Shortly before his death, Adorno commented that the "major mistake" of his Kant-Freud study was "that it relates Freud onesidedly to the cognitive theory of, e.g., Mach and Avenarius, and that it neglects the materialist moment which is present in Freud from the very beginning, which is signified by him through the fundamental concept of genital desire [*Organlust*]." (Adorno, cited in the editorial afterword, *ibid.*, pp. 381-382.)

164. *Ibid.*, p. 236.

165. *Ibid.*, p. 231.

166. Early support for Freud had come from the aesthetic *avant-garde*, especially the surrealists, as Adorno was well aware.

167. *Ibid.*, p. 317.

168. *Ibid.*, p. 318.

169. *Ibid.*

170. *Ibid.*

171. *Ibid.*, p. 319.

172. *Ibid.*

173. *Ibid.*

174. *Ibid.*

175. *Ibid.*, p. 321.

176. *Ibid.* Adorno cited, however, Freud's statement "The motive of human society is in the last analysis an economic one. . . ." (*Ibid.*, p. 322.)

177. ". . . with the knowledge of unconscious contents alone nothing is achieved, so long as the situation of social reality remains unchanged." (*Ibid.*, p. 321.)

178. *Ibid.*

179. *Ibid.*, p. 316.

180. *Ibid.*, p. 322.

181. Horkheimer's *Habilitationsschrift*, also written for Cornelius, was entitled, "Kants Kritik der Urteilskraft als Bindeglied zwischen theoretischer und praktischer Philosophie." Horkheimer argued that the Kantian duality between practical and pure reason could and must be reconciled. (Jay, *The Dialectical Imagination*, p. 77.)

182. In regard to Freudian theory, whether Horkheimer prompted Adorno's interest or vice versa cannot be discerned. But in 1928 Horkheimer underwent analysis with Freud's student Karl Landauer for a brief time, allegedly concerning his difficulties in lecturing without notes. In 1929 Landauer founded the Frankfurt Psychoanalytic Institute, which soon counted Erich Fromm among its members and which worked closely with Horkheimer in the thirties on projects of the *Institut für Sozialforschung*. (*Ibid.*, pp. 27–28.) Horkheimer's reception of Freud was not identical to Adorno's. The latter was primarily impressed with psychoanalysis as a cognitive method, whereas Horkheimer, like Fromm, was interested in the application of Freudian insights to problems in social psychology. Also, Horkheimer earlier than Adorno recognized the materialism implicit in Freud's theory of sexuality.

183. See above, page 10.

184. The unimaginative nature of the Institute's Marxism in 1927 is documented in Jay, *The Dialectical Imagination*, p. 12.

185. See W. Jurinetz, "Psychoanalyse und Marxismus" (1925), in Siegfried Bernfeld et al., *Psychoanalyse und Marxismus: Dokumentation einer Kontroverse*, introd. Hans Jörg Sandkühler (Frankfurt am Main: Suhrkamp Verlag, 1971), pp. 66–136.

186. For Marx, ideology was synonymous with idealism, with its presumption that the subject, as "pure consciousness," had an *a priori*, autonomous existence.

187. He later estimated that by 1933 he had spent in sum almost four years there.

188. They married in 1938, when Adorno was in England. Adorno was not a feminist. Although his wife was university-educated, her "career" was largely as Adorno's secretary. They had no children.

189. Kracauer, who had been employed as feuilletonist for the *Frankfurter Zeitung* since 1920 and published a successful novel *Ginster* in 1928,

was promoted in 1930 to director of the *FZ*'s cultural section in Berlin. (Jay, "The Extraterritorial Life of Siegfried Kracauer," pp. 56 ff.)

190. Bloch was supporting himself as a free-lance writer, and Adorno met him through Benjamin in 1928. Bloch wrote Adorno, expressing interest in the Kant-Freud study and requesting a copy, but Adorno did not oblige the request, an indication of his own disenchantment. (Conversation with Rolf Tiedemann, Padenghe, Italy, March 1973.)

191. The year of Brecht's great success *The Three-Penny Opera*, for which Weill wrote the music and in which Lenya played the leading lady, was 1928. Karl Kraus defended Brecht in *Die Fackel* against the charge of the Berlin critic Alfred Kerr that Brecht had plagiarized Villon's songs in the opera – one example of the overlap of intellectual circles between the cities where Adorno lived. Also, Gropius, who headed the Bauhaus, with which the painter Moholy-Nagy was connected, was the third husband of Alma Mahler Werfel.

192. Radio Conversation between Adorno and Lenya, tape recording, Frankfurt am Main, Adorno Estate.

193. *Ibid.*

194. Brecht had begun reading Marx seriously in 1926, motivated by a desire to understand the machinations of capitalist economy. He became close to Erwin Piscator, whose proletarian theater was experimental in its technical aspects and in its radical leftist goal of mobilizing the masses. It was Piscator who first developed "epic drama," which became a central concept in Brecht's Marxist aesthetics.

195. Most of the Berlin group were Communist sympathizers without being Party members, although Hanns Eisler belonged to the Party.

196. Cf. Walter Benjamin, *Understanding Brecht*, trans. Anna Bostock, introd. Stanley Mitchell (London: NLB, 1973), p. 93. See also Benjamin's essays on Brecht's epic theater in *ibid.*, pp. 1–26.

197. Korsch's essay "Marxismus und Philosophie," which argued that the Hegelian dialectic was fundamental to Marxism, was published in 1923 in the journal of Carl Grünberg, director of the Frankfurt Institute from 1923 to 1927. Neither Adorno nor Benjamin was much impressed with Korsch. Benjamin wrote Adorno in 1930: "I read Korsch: *Marxismus und Philosophie*. Really weak steps – it seems to me – in a good direction." (Letter, Benjamin to Adorno, November 10, 1930, Frankfurt am Main, Adorno Estate.) During World War II Korsch lived in Boston, and was visited by Brecht. (Bunge, *Fragen Sie mehr über Brecht*, p. 92.) Brecht had known Korsch since 1928. Adorno also saw Korsch while in exile: "Karl Korsch is in Boston, and it is not uninteresting to be together with this intelligent and eccentric man once in a while, who is really so far left, that he practically comes out again on the right." (Letter, Adorno to Krenek, October 20, 1938, *Adorno und Krenek: Briefwechsel*, p. 131.)

198. "Discussion of the theoretical and practical issues raised by *Geschichte und Klassenbewusstsein* and *Marxismus und Philosophie* in the years following the immediate uproar of the 1923–1926 period was more

extensive than published sources indicate. This was particularly true of the discussion of Lukács's book. Hans Mayer, for example, has noted that during the middle and late 1920s the 'indirect, underground impact' of *Geschichte und Klassenbewusstsein* was 'amazing.' Many intellectuals and professors studied it, Mayer recalls, and he adds that 'around 1930 it was stylish to speak of "reification" and to apply Lukács' interpretation of the Marxian concept of "commodity fetishism" to the problems of culture.'" (Paul Breines, "Praxis and Its Theorists: The Impact of Lukács and Korsch in the 1920's," *Telos* 11 [Spring 1972] : 95.)

199. Georg Lukács, *History and Class Consciousness*, trans. Rodney Livingstone (Cambridge: The M.I.T. Press, 1971), p. 1.

200. Cf. Paul Honigsheim, "Der Max-Weber-Kreis in Heidelberg," *Kölner Vierteljahreshefte für Soziologie* 5 (1926): 270–287. Honigsheim wrote that despite their ongoing theoretical disputes, Bloch and Lukács were intellectually two sides of the same coin, and often found themselves in accord when arguing against Max Weber. He noted that Heidelberg was then a center for foreign radicals and thus "it is no accident that so many revolutionaries and Bolsheviks" at that time often came to tea at Weber's home. (*Ibid.*, p. 272.)

201. Before this time, Adorno was not influenced by this book, but by an earlier, pre-Marxist study by Lukács, *Die Theorie des Romans*, which he read in 1921. This influence, too, was lasting, and will be discussed in detail in Chapter 3 below.

202. Ernst Erich Noth, "In der vermeintlichen Hochburg des Liberalismus: Wie man im Frankfurt der dreissiger Jahre studierte," *Frankfurter Rundschau*, no. 269 November 20, 1971, feuilleton, p. v.

203. This was the program for the Institute which Horkheimer outlined in his inaugural lecture as director. (See Max Horkheimer, "Die gegenwärtige Lage der Sozialphilosophie und die Aufgaben eines Instituts für Sozialforschung" [1931], *Sozialphilosophische Studien: Aufsätze, Reden und Vorträge, 1930-1972*, ed. Werner Brede [Frankfurt am Main: Athenäum Fischer Taschenbuch Verlag, 1972], pp. 33–46.)

204. Of course, a Marxist analysis of art could not be separated from social analysis, and Adorno had close ties to the Institute when Horkheimer became director. Some of Adorno's most original work was in establishing a sociology of music, and this was the topic of the two articles he contributed to the Institute's journal, the *Zeitschrift für Sozialforschung*, before becoming an official member of the Institute in 1938: "Zur gesellschaftlichen Lage der Musik" (1932), discussed in Chapter 2, and "Über Jazz" (1936), discussed in Chapter 6.

205. Benjamin referred to the importance of these "Frankfurt discussions" in a later letter to Adorno, May 31, 1935 (Benjamin, *Briefe*, vol. 2, p. 663.)

206. It was first evident in Theodor W. Adorno, "Schubert" (1928), *Moments Musicaux*, pp. 18–36.

207. See above, page 13.

208. See above, page 6. Benjamin's interest in Scholem's theological research was still (and would remain) strong, particularly his work in the mystical tradition of the Kabbalah. (Benjamin, *Briefe*, vol. 2, p. 489 and *passim*.)

209. Asja Lacis (b. 1891) studied acting, directing, and film in Moscow during the war. In the early twenties she came to Germany and assisted Brecht as director, later also Piscator. A Communist, she was connected with the Soviet embassy in Berlin. She has published her (not totally reliable) memoirs: Asja Lacis, *Revolutionär im Beruf: Berichte über proletarisches Theater, über Meyerhold, Brecht, Benjamin und Piscator*, ed. Hildegaard Brenner (Munich: Rogner & Bernhard, 1971).

210. Bloch visited them there. (Bloch, "Erinnerungen," Adorno et al., *Über Walter Benjamin*, p. 16.) Benjamin wrote Scholem that although the trip to Capri hurt his work, it was "to the great benefit of an existential liberation and an intensive insight into the actuality of a radical communism. I made the acquaintance of a Russian revolutionary from Riga [Lacis], one of the most splendid women that I have ever met." (Cited by the editors in Walter Benjamin, *Gesammelte Schriften*, 6 vols., ed. Rolf Tiedemann and Hermann Schweppenhäuser, vol. I:3: *Abhandlungen* [Frankfurt am Main: Suhrkamp Verlag, 1974], p. 878.)

211. Lacis proclaimed: "I can safely say that the fact that Walter Benjamin did not go to Palestine was my doing." (Lacis, *Revolutionär im Beruf*, p. 45.) She was certainly instrumental in Benjamin's repeated postponement of his trip to Palestine (see his letter to Scholem September 18, 1929, in Benjamin, *Briefe*, vol. 2, p. 501), yet up until his death in 1940 he never totally dismissed the possibility of resettling there.

212. Benjamin, *Gesammelte Schriften* I:3: *Abhandlungen*, pp. 878–879.

213. Lacis, *Revolutionär im Beruf*, pp. 43–45. Benjamin had already begun to concern himself with the problem of a materialist aesthetics, and was reading Lukács's *Geschichte und Klassenbewusstsein* in that connection. But although he mentioned Lukács in the *Trauerspiel* book, it "does not exhibit the slightest trace of his concern with Marxism." (Editor's comment, Benjamin, *Gesammelte Schriften* I:3: *Abhandlungen*, p. 879.)

214. Cf. above, page 6.

215. Walter Benjamin, *Der Begriff der Kunstkritik in der deutschen Romantik* (first published Bern: Francke Verlag, 1920), in Benjamin, *Gesammelte Schriften* I:1: *Abhandlungen*, pp. 7–122.

216. Cornelius claimed he couldn't understand a word of it. The story of Benjamin's great struggle to habilitate and thereby enter an academic career is documented in Benjamin, *Gesammelte Schriften* I:3: *Abhandlungen*, pp. 869–884.

217. He visited Moscow with Asja Lacis in the winter of 1926–1927, and then lived and wrote in Berlin, where Lacis introduced him to Brecht. Benjamin's friendship with him dates from May 1929 (see Scholem, *Walter Benjamin: Die Geschichte einer Freundschaft*, p. 198).

218. See above, page 20.

219. Letter, Adorno to Benjamin, November 10, 1938, Adorno, *Über Walter Benjamin*, p. 136.

220. Letter, Benjamin to Adorno, May 31, 1935, Benjamin, *Briefe*, vol. 2, p. 663.

221. Adorno, "Erinnerungen" (1966), *Über Walter Benjamin*, p. 69. Precisely which excerpts Benjamin read to Adorno, cannot be determined, as the *Passagenarbeit*, which was never finished, is composed of a largely undated collection of essays, notes and drafts written during the thirteen years from 1927 until Benjamin's death.

222. Letter, Benjamin to Max Rychner, March 7, 1931, Benjamin, *Briefe*, vol. 2, p. 523.

223. Benjamin's statement that knowledge of the Kabbalah was necessary for understanding his *Trauerspiel* study mystified Scholem, who didn't at all consider it a Kabbalist text (Scholem, *Walter Benjamin: Die Geschichte einer Freundschaft*, p. 158). But the similarity was one of cognitive structure rather than content. The method of Kabbalist exegesis was to decipher both texts and natural phenomena as hieroglyphs in which even the smallest details could be made to reveal truth unintended by the words of the texts or the every-day meaning of the phenomena. The method was through a logic of correspondences across the boundaries of conceptual schema; the goal was the revelation of truth which took on meaning within a constellation with the present, and this often meant a total overturning of traditional, rabbinical interpretations (*idem, Major Trends in Jewish Mysticism* [New York: Schocken Books, 1967]). All of these were characteristics of Benjamin's and Adorno's "dialectical," "materialist" method as well, as will be demonstrated.

224. Benjamin, "Über das Programm der kommenden Philosophie" (1918), *Zur Kritik der Gewalt und andere Aufsätze;* see above, page 6.

225. Already in 1924, while working on the non-Marxist *Trauerspiel* study, Benjamin was struck with the fact that "Lukács, starting from political reflections, comes at least partially, and perhaps not quite so fully as I first thought, to statements in cognitive theory which are very familiar to me or faithful [to my own thinking]." (Benjamin, *Gesammelte Schriften* I:3: *Abhandlungen*, pp. 878–879.)

226. Benjamin wrote to Adorno that it was necessary "not to 'apply' Marxism to the letter, but to work with him and that means, for us all, to struggle with him." (Letter, Benjamin to Adorno, July 17, 1931, Frankfurt am Main, Adorno Estate.)

227. Letter, Benjamin to Adorno, May 31, 1935, Benjamin, *Briefe*, vol. 2, p. 663.

228. As was noted (see note 206), Adorno's 1928 article, "Schubert" used Benjamin's vocabulary. But there was nothing Marxist about it, and moreover, it spoke affirmatively of "ontology," which their Königstein program explicitly opposed. Significantly, Adorno deleted all references to ontology when he republished the Schubert essay in *Moments Musicaux* in 1964.

The foreword to this edition noted that he had made changes only when "too embarrassed" by the original.

229. It had indeed the quality of a conversion, even if Adorno clearly influenced Benjamin at this meeting as well as vice versa. The theoretical task begun by Benjamin was henceforth one that they shared.

230. Cf., however, Adorno's article, "Nachtmusik" (1929), reprinted in *Moments Musicaux*, which appeared in the first months of that year, and which referred to the ideological function of joy in contemporary music and its relationship to the class structure of society, but did not make use of Benjamin's vocabulary. The 1928 Schubert essay had the *Trauerspiel* language but not the Marxist critique; "Nachtmusik" had the Marxist critique and not the *Trauerspiel* language. But from the fall of 1929 on they were always there in combination.

231. ". . . the suffering of every individual has entered into the class struggle and turned itself against the continuance of the bourgeois order." (Theodor Wiesengrund-Adorno, "Die Oper Wozzeck" [1929], *Der Scheinwerfer: Blätter der Städtischen Bühnen Essen* 3, 4 [1929-1930], p. 5.)

232. The roughness of the article lay in the fact that this convergence was simply postulated, affirmed on the basis of analogy, rather than analytically demonstrated, as it would be in his later articles. Cf., e.g., the statement: "Still, just as the suffering of oppressed people even today has not been removed by the class struggle [a critique of the USSR?], so little, too, has art disappeared which has this suffering as its object. Out of such contradictions the music of *Wozzeck* emerges." (*Ibid.*, p. 5.)

233. *Ibid.*, pp. 7-8.

234. These included the concepts of tragic drama, mythic images (*Bilder*), disintegration, and "the smallest particles."

235. The more muted radicalism of the Kierkegaard study (and other writings by Adorno in the thirties) compared with the 1929 article on *Wozzeck* can be explained by historical events (world depression brought the Nazis, not the leftist revolutionaries, into power) as well as by the fact that Marxist theory was not popular in academic circles.

236. Adorno's Kierkegaard study, written in 1929-1931, revised and first published in 1933, is discussed in some detail in Chapter 7.

237. Tillich's intellectual position was quite different, and he cannot be said to have influenced Adorno. Their relationship was a personal one. (Tillich was friends with Horkheimer as well.) Tillich's widow has recently written that "the immensely talented Teddy Adorno" was included in their group of friends in Frankfurt: "Our friend Teddy played the Threepenny [Opera] melodies on ecstatic evenings — after a good dinner and many good wines in the good city of Frankfurt.

"Marlene Dietrich's 'Falling in Love Again' and Lotte Lenya's songs from *The Threepenny Opera* were the songs of the day. When Teddy sat down at the great piano and let go, we all listened." (Hannah Tillich, *From Time to Time* [New York: Stein and Day, 1973], pp. 142-143.)

CHAPTER 2

1. This 1931 speech, which contained in embryonic form the theoretical position of his 1966 philosophical testament, *Negative Dialektik,* was not published in Adorno's lifetime. It first appeared in 1973, in Theodor W. Adorno, *Gesammelte Schriften,* vol. 1: *Frühe philosophische Schriften,* ed. Rolf Tiedemann (Frankfurt am Main: Suhrkamp Verlag, 1973), pp. 325-344.

2. Cf., e.g., Martin Jay, *The Dialectical Imagination: A History of the Frankfurt School and the Institute of Social Research, 1923-1950* (Boston: Little, Brown, 1973), pp. 56 and 262.

3. Theodor W. Adorno, *Negative Dialectics,* trans. E. B. Ashton (New York: The Seabury Press, 1973), p. 3; cf. pp. 143, 205-206, 244-245.

4. Jay, *The Dialectical Imagination,* pp. 43-44. It should be noted, however, that Horkheimer also never outlined a program for revolutionary praxis in his writings. And although the Institute under his direction compiled a major research project on proletariat consciousness (see *Studien über Autorität und Familie,* ed. Max Horkheimer [Paris: Felix Alcan, 1936]), this work was not combined with direct political engagement.

5. Adorno did specifically mention the proletariat in several of his early music articles, and on at least one occasion he made positive reference (if indirect) to revolutionary violence of an anarchist nature. Speaking of the gallery, the cheapest seats in the theater (folding chairs, out of which to build the barricades), he envisioned the simultaneous freeing of both art and its occupants: "Not until the shot let loose from the gallery goes through the heart of the player of the main villain like a shooting-range figure does the gallery rescue itself and the stage at the same time." (Theodor W. Adorno, "Galerie" (1931), *Quasi una Fantasia: Musikalische Schriften II* [Frankfurt am Main: Suhrkamp Verlag, 1963], p. 99.)

6. Cf. Theodor W. Adorno, "Marginalien zu Theorie und Praxis" (n.d.), *Stichworte: Kritische Modelle 2* (Frankfurt am Main: edition Suhrkamp, 1969), pp. 169-191.

7. Georg Lukács, *History and Class Consciousness,* trans. Rodney Livingstone (Cambridge, Mass.: The M.I.T. Press, 1971), p. 170.

8. *Ibid.,* p. 34.

9. *Ibid.,* p. 170.

10. It should be noted that Lukács was strongly indebted not only to his former teacher Max Weber, but to the neo-Hegelian Wilhelm Dilthey, for the idea that a common structure was manifested in all societal aspects of a given historical era. Lukács himself acknowledged his debt to Dilthey. (*Ibid.,* p. 153.) But there was a significant difference. Dilthey's concept of structures was merely descriptive, whereas Lukács' commodity structure was an analytical tool which was supposed to reveal the true nature of society and of its historical development.

11. *Ibid.,* p. 83.

12. *Ibid.,* p. 54.

13. *Ibid.*

14. Alfred Schmidt, "Die *Zeitschrift für Sozialforschung*: Geschichte und gegenwärtige Bedeutung," introduction to *Zeitschrift für Sozialforschung,* 2nd ed. (Munich: Kösel-Verlag, 1970), vol. 1, p. 34.

15. Cf. Adorno's first article for the *Zeitschrift für Sozialforschung,* journal of Horkheimer's Frankfurt Institute, "Zur gesellschaftlichen Lage der Musik" (1932), discussed below.

16. Theodor W. Adorno, *Negative Dialektik* (1966), *Gesammelte Schriften,* vol. 6, ed. Rolf Tiedemann (Frankfurt am Main: Suhrkamp Verlag, 1973), p. 191.

17. Lukács, *History and Class Consciousness,* p. 83. Adorno was criticizing his own earlier position when he wrote in 1966: "Thought easily flatters and consoles itself with the belief that in the solution of reification and commodity structure it possesses the philosopher's stone." (Adorno, *Negative Dialektik,* p. 189).

18. Adorno, "Die Aktualität der Philosophie" (1931), *GS* 1, p. 337.

19. See Chapter 1.

20. For a discussion of their stress on cognitive "truth" in comparison with Horkheimer's orientation toward ethical praxis, see Chapter 4, pages 65–69. In 1923 Benjamin expressly rejected the evaluation of art in terms of its effects: "No poem is intended for the reader, no picture for the beholder, no symphony for the listener." (Walter Benjamin, "The Task of the Translator" [1923], *Illuminations,* ed. and introd. Hannah Arendt, trans. Harry Zohn [New York: Schocken Books, 1969], p. 69.)

21. Letter, Benjamin to Max Rychner, March 7, 1931, in Walter Benjamin, *Briefe,* 2 vols., ed. Gershom Scholem and Theodor W. Adorno (Frankfurt am Main: Suhrkamp Verlag, 1966), vol. 2, p. 524. Later in the thirties, when Benjamin, under Brecht's influence, wrote essays affirming the consciousness of the proletariat in its present state, Adorno reprimanded him for forsaking his own earlier position. (See Chapter 9 below, page 148.)

22. Lukács, *History and Class Consciousness,* p. 149.

23. Kettler has argued that despair over the cultural crisis was the reason Lukács himself embraced Marxism, and that he identified the revolution with a cultural renewal (*Kulturerneuerung*). See David Kettler, *Marxismus und Kultur* (Neuwied: Luchterhand Verlag, 1967).

24. At the time Lukács noted: "Among intellectuals it has gradually become fashionable to greet any profession of Marxism with ironical disdain." (Lukács, *History and Class Consciousness,* p. 1.)

25. Jones has argued that Lukács introduced the concept as a *deus ex machina* to provide the missing link in a geometrical proof. (See Gareth Stedman Jones, "The Marxism of the Early Lukács: An Evaluation," *New Left Review* 70 [November–December 1971]: 46.) Lukács himself, in his 1967 preface to the book, questioned: "Can a genuinely identical subject-object be created by self knowledge . . . ?" He admitted that the concept was "no

materialist consummation that overcomes the constructions of idealism. It
is rather an attempt to out-Hegel Hegel. . . ." (Lukács, *History and Class
Consciousness*, p. xxiii.)

26. Whether Lukács's concept of history was metaphysical is a disputed point.
For an argument against this interpretation, see Maurice Merleau-Ponty,
"'Western' Marxism," *Adventures of the Dialectic*, trans. Joseph Bien
(Evanston, Ill.: Northwestern University Press, 1973), pp. 30–58. Jürgen
Habermas argues the other side in *Theorie und Praxis: Sozialphilosophische
Studien* (Frankfurt am Main: Suhrkamp Verlag, 1971), p. 444 and *passim*.

27. Lukács, *History and Class Consciousness*, p. 321.

28. *Ibid.*, p. 320.

29. *Ibid.*, p. 325.

30. *Ibid.*, p. 41.

31. *Ibid.*, p. xiii.

32. *Ibid.*, p. xxviii.

33. *Ibid.*, p. 198.

34. Erich Eyck, *A History of the Weimar Republic*, 2 vols., trans. Harlan P.
Hanson and Robert G. L. Waite (New York: John Wiley & Sons, 1967),
vol. 2, pp. 279–280, 300.

35. Adorno seems to have been as naive as the Communist Party in underestimating Hitler's strength. Almost until the outbreak of World War II,
he thought Nazism would be short lived (see page 138).

36. Lukács, *History and Class Consciousness*, p. 334.

37. *Ibid.*, p. 327.

38. *Ibid.*, p. 319 (italics Lukács's).

39. Cited in *ibid.*, p. 290.

40. *Ibid.*, p. 292.

41. Cited in Paul Breines, "Praxis and Its Theorists: The Impact of Lukács
and Korsch in the 1920's," *Telos* 11 (Spring 1972): 87.

42. Cited in *ibid.*, p. 89.

43. George Lichtheim, *Georg Lukács* (New York: The Viking Press, 1970),
p. 87.

44. Georg Lukács, "Die Bedeutung von 'Materialismus und Empiriokritizismus'
für die Bolschewisierung der kommunistischen Parteien," trans. Gisela Braun
from *Pod Znamenem Marksizma*, 4 (1934), in Furio Cerutti, et al., eds.,
Geschichte und Klassenbewusstsein Heute: Diskussion und Dokumentation,
Schwarze Reihe, no. 12, (Amsterdam: Verlag de Munter, 1971), p. 260. Of
course, there were in fact idealist elements in Lukács's early theory. His
acceptance of Party criticism was not mere servility.

45. Letter, Adorno to Benjamin, March 18, 1936, Theodor W. Adorno, *Über
Walter Benjamin* (Frankfurt am Main: Suhrkamp Verlag, 1970), p. 132.

46. Adorno (pseud. Hecktor Rottweiler), "Musikpädagogische Musik: Brief an
Ernst Krenek" (1936), *Theodor W. Adorno und Ernst Krenek: Briefwechsel*,
ed. Wolfgang Rogge (Frankfurt am Main: Suhrkamp Verlag, 1974), p. 220.

47. Lukács, *History and Class Consciousness*, p. 103.

48. Breines, "Praxis and Its Theorists," p. 17.

49. It may be worth noting, however, that regarding his support of the independent status of philosophy and his rejection of historical determinism, Adorno was in accord with the official Soviet interpretation of 1931. I am indebted to Gary Ulmen for this observation. Assuming such a correlation was more than accidental, it presents no necessary contradiction to Adorno's stance of "non-participation." For he never claimed that what the Party said was necessarily untrue; only the reverse, that the Party did not necessarily speak the truth. For an excellent account of the Soviet position on Marxist philosophy at this time, see Russell Jacoby, "Towards a Critique of Automatic Marxism: The Politics of Philosophy from Lukács to the Frankfurt School," *Telos* 10 (Winter 1971): 134–137.

50. What Adorno then knew of Hegel was probably through Horkheimer. He did not study Hegel in depth until the late thirties and the forties. Benjamin was quite ignorant of Hegelian philosophy, and the resulting undialectical tendencies in his materialism were repeatedly criticized by Adorno, as their correspondence indicates. (Cf. Adorno, "Aus Briefen an Walter Benjamin," *Über Walter Benjamin*, pp. 103–161.)

51. Lukács read Marx's 1844 *Manuscripts* for the first time in 1930, and reported their "overwhelming effect" upon him, especially Marx's critical distinction in the dialectical process of labor between alienation (*Entfremdung*) and realization (*Entäusserung*). (Lukács, *History and Class Consciousness*, p. xxxvi.)

The Frankfurt Institute received photostated copies of Marx's early manuscripts in the late 1920s from David Ryazanov, director of the Marx-Engels Institute in Moscow, who was then compiling them for the *Marx-Engels Historisch-Kritische Gesamtausgabe (MEGA)*, of which he was editor. Ryazanov had spent some time in Frankfurt in the early thirties, was a friend of the early *Institut für Sozialforschung*, and published an article in the Institute's journal in 1930. He lost his directorship in the thirties, a victim of Stalin's purges. (Jay, *The Dialectical Imagination*, pp. 13, 19.)

Marcuse wrote an article on Marx's 1844 *Manuscripts* in 1932: "Neue Quellen zur Grundlegung des Historischen Materialismus," reprinted and translated as "The Foundation of Historical Materialism" in Herbert Marcuse, *Studies in Critical Philosophy*, trans. Joris de Bres (Boston: Beacon Press, 1973), pp. 1–48.

52. *Writings of the Young Marx on Philosophy and Society*, trans. and ed. Loyd D. Easton and Kurt H. Guddat (Garden City, N.Y.: Doubleday, Anchor Books, 1967), p. 321.

53. *Ibid.*, p. 322.

54. The original German word *wissenschaftlich* refers to the humanistic as well as the natural sciences; note the more specific meaning of the English translation "scientifically."

55. *Writings of the Young Marx on Philosophy and Society*, p. 306.

56. I have seen no reference to the 1844 *Manuscripts* in Adorno's early writings,

published or unpublished. This is not surprising, as Adorno very rarely referred to Marx directly. However, in a 1956 essay on Hegel, Adorno explicitly acknowledged Marx as the first to see social labor as the essence of Hegel's dialectic of spirit, and cited the 1844 mss. as documentation. See Theodor W. Adorno, "Aspekte," *Drei Studien zu Hegel* (Frankfurt am Main: Suhrkamp Verlag, 1963), p. 30.

57. "Der Autor als Produzent" (1934), in Walter Benjamin, *Understanding Brecht,* trans. Anna Bostock, introd. Stanley Mitchell (London: NLB, 1973) pp. 84–103.

58. Renato Poggioli, *The Theory of the Avant-Garde,* trans. Gerald Fitzgerald (Cambridge, Mass.: Belknap–Harvard University Press, 1968), pp. 9 ff.

59. *Ibid.,* pp. 135–136.

60. See above, Chapter 1, page 20. In this sense Brecht's concept of *Kopfarbeiter* was not the same as the Council of Mental Workers (*Rat der Geistigen Arbeiter*) which Kurt Hiller founded in Berlin during the 1918 revolution. Although the latter was also composed of *avant-garde* artists free from Party dictates, it saw itself, like the Party, as an elitist group providing leadership and education for the masses, rather than as a group of workers themselves involved in the revolutionary seizure of the means of their own production. Not surprisingly (like Franz Pfemfert's contemporary journal *Die Aktion*) the Berlin Council quickly drifted to a more orthodox Communist position, although Kurt Hiller protested the move. (See George L. Mosse, *Germans and Jews* [New York: Howard Fertig, 1970], pp. 189–190.)

61. Ernst Bloch, "Bemerkungen zur 'Erbschaft dieser Zeit," *Vom Hasard zur Katastrophe: Politische Aufsätze, 1934–1939,* afterword by Oskar Negt (Frankfurt am Main: Suhrkamp Verlag, 1972), p. 64. In 1937 a debate over materialist aesthetics between Lukács and Brecht's Berlin circle began in the journal *Das Wort,* and it centered around an evaluation of expressionism. Lukács held expressionism was bourgeois decadence, and could only be interpreted critically, as ideology; he supported novelists like Balzac and Thomas Mann for their "social realism," and condemned experimental novelists such as Joyce, Proust, Kafka, and Dos Passos. Brecht, Bloch, and others defended these novelists' techniques – inner monologue, montage, distancing – claiming they could indeed be "refunctioned" into tools of critical enlightenment and used to produce "social realist" art, as they understood it. (Cf. Werner Mittenzwei, "Marxismus und Materialismus: Die Brecht-Lukács Debatte," *Das Argument 46* 10, 1/2 [March 1968]: 12–43.)

62. See Adorno, "Musikpädagogische Musik," *Adorno und Krenek: Briefwechsel,* p. 217.

63. Max Horkheimer, "Notes on Science and the Crisis" (1932), *Critical Theory: Selected Essays,* trans. Matthew J. O'Connell and others (New York: Herder and Herder, 1972), p. 4. Horkheimer claimed this position was Marx's own: "In the Marxist theory of society science is regarded as one of man's productive powers." (*Ibid.,* p. 3.) In fact this was the early Marx's contention in the passage from the 1844 mss. cited above. But the early

Marx was talking ontologically about man's essence, his "species-being" (and Horkheimer, as well as Adorno, was critical of ontology). Once Marx dropped this Feuerbachian orientation, once he discovered the proletariat as the historical subject, all of "man's" productive powers needed to be analyzed concretely, as they existed within the capitalist socioeconomic structure, and that meant an *economic* analysis of, e.g., science as a sector of capitalist production (the financing of research, the economic uses of science, etc.). Neither Adorno nor Horkheimer nor Benjamin had any interest in (or knowledge of) economics, that "dismal science" which Marx considered essential.

64. Max Horkheimer, "Traditional and Critical Theory" (1937), *ibid.*, p. 205.

65. See above, footnote 61.

66. Bertolt Brecht, *Über Politik und Kunst,* ed. Werner Hecht (Frankfurt am Main: Suhrkamp Verlag, 1971), p. 18. In the mid-twenties Brecht had felt differently: "In my view it is certain that Socialism, and indeed the revolutionary kind, will change the face of our country inside of our lifetime. . . . As far as the artists are concerned, I consider it best for them to do what they want to do without worrying: Otherwise they can't produce good works." (*Ibid.*, p. 11.)

67. Letter, Adorno to Krenek, October 8, 1930, *Adorno und Krenek: Briefwechsel,* p. 20. The following notice appeared in the January, 1931 issue: "Dr. Theodor Wiesengrund-Adorno has parted on friendly terms from the editorial staff of *Anbruch,* to which he belonged for two years. He will continue to make his valuable contributions available to *Anbruch.*" (*Anbruch,* 13, 1 [January 1931]: 18.) In fact only one article by Adorno appeared in 1931, and three in 1932. The same January issue praised Brecht's play *The Measures Taken,* particularly the proletarian choruses of Hanns Eisler, which Adorno attacked in 1932 (see below, pages 40–41).

68. It took several years, but by the mid-1930s their differences had reached the point of hostility, largely because Adorno considered Brecht's influence on Benjamin harmful (see Chapter 8).

69. Benjamin, "The Author as Producer" (1934), *Understanding Brecht,* p. 86.

70. *Ibid.,* p. 102.

71. *Ibid.,* p. 93.

72. *Ibid.,* p. 94.

73. *Ibid.,* p. 101.

74. Benjamin probably knew as much. This essay was written for presentation (April 27, 1934), at the Paris Institute for the Study of Fascism, a Communist front organization, and the speech's open sympathies toward the Soviet Union (*ibid.,* pp. 88, 102) may have been opportunistically motivated. At any rate, his own writings did not consistently follow the view he expressed here. He knew better than to send the essay to Adorno, as it praised Eisler's proletarian music which Adorno had criticized (see below page 40), and he neglected out of embarrassment to send it to Scholem, who other-

wise routinely received copies of Benjamin's work (see Gershom Scholem, *Walter Benjamin: Die Geschichte einer Freundschaft* [Frankfurt am Main: Suhrkamp Verlag, 1975], p. 250).

75. Adorno, *Über Walter Benjamin*, pp. 116, 128, 131-132, 141-142.

76. Hans Bunge, *Fragen Sie mehr über Brecht: Hanns Eisler im Gespräch* (Munich: Rogner & Bernhard, 1970), pp. 29-31.

77. *Ibid.*, p. 43.

78. Theodor W. Adorno, "Der dialektische Komponist" (1934), *Impromptus: Zweite Folge neu gedruckter musikalischer Aufsätze* (Frankfurt am Main: edition Suhrkamp, 1969), pp. 39-44. The article is discussed in detail in Chapter 8.

79. Theodor Wiesengrund-Adorno, "Exkurse zu einem Exkurs," *Der Scheinwerfer: Blätter der Städtischen Bühnen Essen* 5, 10 (1932): 17. Cf. his statement in 1930 that the fact that the public didn't like Ravel as much as Strauss or Stravinsky "proves nothing against Ravel, but only in every case something against society. . . ." (Theodor W. Adorno, "Ravel" [1930], *Moments Musicaux: Neugedruckte Aufsätze, 1928 bis 1962* [Frankfurt am Main: edition Suhrkamp, 1964], p. 68.)

80. Theodor Wiesengrund-Adorno, "Zur gesellschaftlichen Lage der Musik," part I, *Zeitschrift für Sozialforschung*, 1, 1/2 (1932): 105.

81. Adorno, "Musikpädagogische Musik" (1936), *Adorno und Krenek: Briefwechsel*, pp. 215-216.

82. Adorno, "Die Aktualität der Philosophie" (1931), *GS* 1, pp. 339-340 (italics mine). The difference between such philosophy and the new music was that musical language was nonconceptual and thus could not be read directly in terms of its revolutionary *social* function. Adorno saw this as the ,task of the critic. Here he was indebted to Benjamin's work on Novalis's and Schlegel's concept of aesthetic criticism: the "truth" expressed by the artwork was not revealed until the critic brought it to speech. Cf. Walter Benjamin, *Der Begriff der Kunstkritik in der deutschen Romantik* [first published, 1920], ed. Hermann Schweppenhäuser (Frankfurt am Main: Suhrkamp Verlag, 1973).

83. Adorno, "Der dialektische Komponist" (1934), *Impromptus*, p. 40.

84. Adorno, "Zur gesellschaftlichen Lage der Musik," part I (1932), p. 104.

85. Adorno, "Die Aktualität der Philosophie" (1931), *GS* 1, p. 338.

86. Adorno, "Musikpädagogische Musik" (1936), *Adorno und Krenek: Briefwechsel*, p. 220.

87. Letter, Adorno to Krenek, September 30, 1932, *ibid.*, p. 37.

88. *Ibid.*

89. The article was printed in two parts, the first of which was the more significant. It is considered one of Adorno's most important theoretical essays, although he later had reservations about its republication because it argued by analogy rather than dialectically: "it simply equates the concept of musical production with the priority of the economic sphere of production, without consideration of how greatly that which is called musical

production already presupposes the social production and is just as much dependent upon it, as separate from it. That alone prompted the author not to republish this essay, the draft for a complete sociology of music." (Theodor W. Adorno, *Gesammelte Schriften,* vol. 14: *Dissonanzen; Einleitung in die Musiksoziologie,* ed. Rolf Tiedemann [Frankfurt am Main: Suhrkamp Verlag, 1973], p. 425.)

90. Adorno, "Zur gesellschaftlichen Lage der Musik," part I (1932), p. 103.

91. In a letter to Krenek Adorno explained: "The commodity character of music is not determined by the mere fact that it is exchanged, but by the fact that it is *abstractly* exchanged, as Marx explained the commodity structure; that, therefore, there exists no immediate, but instead a 'reified' exchange relationship." (Letter, Adorno to Krenek, September 30, 1932, *Adorno und Krenek: Briefwechsel,* p. 36.)

92. Adorno, "Zur gesellschaftlichen Lage der Musik," part I (1932), p. 103.

93. In another article he explained this was no fault of the composer: "If fulfilling the material demands [of music] does not make it possible to induce a social bond, then the reason lies . . . therein . . . that the present power relations in society simply do not allow art a social bond, and especially art with essential truth [*Wahrheitsgehalt*]." (Ernst Krenek and Theodor Wiesengrund-Adorno, "Arbeitsprobleme des Komponisten: Gespräch über Musik und soziale Situation" [1930], *Adorno und Krenek: Briefwechsel,* p. 192.)

94. Adorno, "Zur gesellschaftlichen Lage der Musik," part I (1932), p. 104.

95. *Ibid.,* p. 106.

96. *Ibid.,* p. 105.

97. *Ibid.*

98. *Ibid.,* p. 106.

99. *Ibid.,* pp. 106–107.

100. Here were the roots of Adorno's rejection of the 1960s counterculture. Adorno was well aware of the impotence of such protests against fascism. He wrote in 1936: "The musicians [of *Gemeinschaftsmusik*] conserve on an island the offensive noise of the *Wandervögel* which has long been drowned out on the political mainland." (Adorno, "Musikpädagogische Musik" [1936], *Adorno und Krenek: Briefwechsel,* p. 220.) For a discussion of the origins of the *Gemeinschaft* movement and its contribution to the rise of fascism, see Karl Dietrich Bracher, *Die Auflösung der Weimarer Republik,* 3rd ed., rev. and enl., *Schriften des Instituts für politische Wissenschaft,* vol. 4 (Villingen-Schwarzwald: Ring Verlag, 1960), pp. 128–148.

101. There was a crucial distinction between "dropping out" of society and Adorno's stance of "non-participation." The former was an attempt to forget society; the latter was an attempt to *know* it through critical reflection.

102. Adorno, "Zur gesellschaftlichen Lage der Musik," part I (1932), p. 123.

103. *Ibid.*

104. *Ibid.*

105. *Ibid.,* p. 116.

106. *Ibid.,* p. 117.

107. *Ibid.,* p. 120.

108. *Ibid.,* p. 111.

109. *Ibid.*

110. Cf. Theodor W. Adorno, *Philosophy of Modern Music,* trans. Anne G. Mitchell and Wesley V. Blomster (New York: The Seabury Press, 1973).

111. Adorno, "Zur gesellschaftlichen Lage der Musik," part I (1932), p. 112. Adorno's rejection of harmonious, closed aesthetic forms because they obscured the fragmentary, antagonistic nature of reality was a position which Brecht shared, against Lukács (see footnote 61).

112. *Ibid.,* p. 122.

113. *Ibid.*

114. *Ibid.*

115. *Ibid.,* p. 123.

116. *Ibid.,* p. 124.

117. *Ibid.*

118. *Ibid.*

119. Cf. Benjamin, "The Author as Producer" (1934), *Understanding Brecht,* p. 86, cited above. In this essay Benjamin in fact quoted Eisler with approval: " 'Music without words acquired its great importance and its full development only under capitalism.' This suggests that the task of transforming concert music requires help from the word. Only such help can, as Eisler puts it, transform a concert into a political meeting. The fact that such a transformation may really represent a peak achievement of both musical and literary technique – this Brecht and Eisler have proved with their didactic play *The Measures Taken.*" (*Ibid.,* p. 96.)

120. Theodor Wiesengrund-Adorno, "Anton von Webern" (1932), *Impromptus,* pp. 49–50.

121. Adorno, "Musikpädagogische Musik" (1936), *Adorno und Krenek: Briefwechsel,* p. 219.

122. Bunge, *Fragen Sie mehr über Brecht,* p. 30.

123. Letter, Benjamin to Adorno, February 7, 1936, cited in Walter Benjamin, *Gesammelte Schriften,* 6 vols., ed. Rolf Tiedemann and Hermann Schweppenhäuser, vol. I:3: *Abhandlungen* (Frankfurt am Main: Suhrkamp Verlag, 1974), p. 987.

CHAPTER 3

1. Theodor W. Adorno, "Stravinsky: Ein dialektisches Bild" (1962), *Quasi una Fantasia: Musikalische Schriften II* (Frankfurt am Main: Suhrkamp Verlag, 1963), p. 208.

2. Theodor W. Adorno, notebooks on *Reproduktionstheorie*, 3 vols., unpublished, Frankfurt am Main, Adorno Estate, n. d., vol. 1, p. 51.

3. See Theodor W. Adorno, "Henkel, Krug und frühe Erfahrung," *Ernst Bloch zu Ehren: Beiträge zu seinem Werk*, ed. Siegfried Unseld (Frankfurt am Main: Suhrkamp Verlag, 1965), p. 9.

4. Georg Lukács, *Die Theorie des Romans* (first published 1920) (Neuwied: Luchterhand, 1971). In the preface to the 1962 edition Lukács spoke of the influence the book had on Adorno and others in the twenties to the detriment of their politics. He commented: "A considerable portion of the leading bourgeois intelligentsia in Germany, among them also Adorno, have taken up camp in the 'Grand Hotel Abyss,' a – as I once wrote *a propos* of a critique of Schopenhauer – 'beautiful hotel, furnished with all the luxuries, at the edge of the abyss, of nothing, of meaninglessness. And the daily view of the abyss, between comfortably enjoyed meals or artistic productions, can only increase the pleasure of these refined comforts.'" (*Ibid.*, p. 16.)

5. *Ibid.*, p. 47.

6. Cf. above, Chapter 2, page 35.

7. Cf. Theodor Wiesengrund-Adorno, "Zum Problem der Reproduktion: Fragmente," *Pult und Taktstock* 2 (1925): 51–55. In the 1930s Adorno made plans to work with Rudolph Kolisch (violinist, brother-in-law of Schönberg) in developing a theory of musical reproduction. He kept notebooks for this study during the rest of his life. These will appear as one of the appended volumes of the *Gesammelte Schriften* under the title *Reproduktionstheorie*.

8. Wiesengrund-Adorno, "Zum Problem der Reproduktion," 55.

9. Theodor Wiesengrund-Adorno, "Drei Dirigenten," *Musikblätter des Anbruch*, 8(1926): 314–315.

10. Concerning Schönberg's theory of composition, Leibowitz has written: "just as every sound-form considered by itself has a tradition *behind* it and *in* it, even so all the sound-forms of a given historical moment *imply* all the sound-forms of the past. . . . It is this total continuity which embraces tradition *as a whole* . . . that has passed to the living present, which in its turn is asserting itself as a tradition, that is to say as a new point of departure for the same tradition. . . . [T]he perfect assimilation of the laws of the musical syntax of the past brings the would-be master to this syntax of today – the only one in which the mastery may be expressed." (René Leibowitz, *Schoenberg and His School*, trans. D. Newlin [New York: Philosophical Library, 1949], pp. 263, 265.)

11. Arnold Schönberg, *Harmonielehre* (Vienna: Universal-Edition, 1922), pp. 3–4.

12. Georg Lukács, *Die Theorie des Romans*, pp. 53–54. The concept of "second nature" is discussed below.

13. Theodor Wiesengrund-Adorno, "Opernprobleme: Glossiert nach Frankfurter Aufführung," *Musikblätter des Anbruch* 8 (1926): 205–208.

14. Theodor Wiesengrund-Adorno, "Die Serenade: Zur Aufführung von Schönbergs Serenade in Venedig," *Pult und Taktstock* 2 (September 1925): 115.

15. Theodor W. Adorno, "Nachtmusik" (1929), *Moments Musicaux: Neugedruckte Aufsätze, 1928 bis 1962* (Frankfurt am Main: edition Suhrkamp, 1964), p. 62.

16. Georg Lukács, *History and Class Consciousness*, trans. Rodney Livingstone (Cambridge, Mass.: The M.I.T. Press, 1971), p. 67 (italics Lukács's).

17. Theodor W. Adorno, "Die Aktualität der Philosophie" (1931), *Gesammelte Schriften*, vol. 1: *Frühe philosophische Schriften*, ed. Rolf Tiedemann (Frankfurt am Main: Suhrkamp Verlag, 1973), p. 325. (Cf. Lukács, *Die Theorie des Romans*, pp. 25-26.)

18. Theodor W. Adorno, Husserl ms., "Zur Philosophie Husserls," 1934-1937, Frankfurt am Main, Adorno Estate, p. 141, repeated p. 423.

19. Theodor Wiesengrund-Adorno, "Die Idee der Naturgeschichte" (1932), *GS* 1, p. 357.

20. Lukács, *History and Class Consciousness*, p. 181.

21. *Ibid.*, p. 71.

22. *Ibid.*, p. 76.

23. Lukács had not intended to slip into a metaphysics of history. Indeed, he expressly denounced as myth Hegel's claim that absolute spirit in itself had the power to bring reason into existence, arguing that such a view was as deterministic as the economism of vulgar Marxists (*ibid.*, pp. 146-147). He attempted to make a distinction between historical necessity and historical inevitability (*ibid.*, pp. 197-198). Nonetheless, the distinction tended to blur in these essays.

24. Jones has capsulized Lukács's argument: "all truth is relative to the standpoint of individual classes; the proletariat is by its essence a universal class; its subjectivity is universal; but a universal subjectivity can only be objective." (Gareth Stedman Jones, "The Marxism of the Early Lukács: An Evaluation," *New Left Review* 70 [November-December 1971]: 47.)

25. Karl Mannheim argued just this in *Ideologie und Utopie* (Bonn: F. Cohen, 1929), as Adorno was well aware.

26. Adorno, "Die Idee der Naturgeschichte" (1932), *GS* 1, p. 362.

27. *Ibid.*

28. Adorno, Husserl ms., 1934-1937, p. 423.

29. Adorno, "Die Aktualität der Philosophie" (1931), *GS* 1, p. 325.

30. Max Horkheimer, *Anfänge der bürgerlichen Geschichtsphilosophie* (Stuttgart: Kohlhammer, 1930), p. 46.

31. Cf. Chapter 1.

32. It was Horkheimer who in 1932 wrote the most explicit attack against Hegel's metaphysics of history. He criticized the Hegelian system because "all joy and suffering of individual human beings, poverty and wealth, indeed, absolutely all contradictions of the empirical world receive the reconciliatory sign of the 'merely' mortal." (Max Horkheimer, "Hegel

und das Problem der Metaphysik," *Festschrift für Carl Grünberg: Zum 70. Geburtstag* [Leipzig: Verlag von C. L. Hirschfeld, 1932], p. 188.)

33. Lukács, *History and Class Consciousness*, p. 234.

34. *Ibid.*, p. 319.

35. Friedrich Nietzsche, *The Will to Power*, trans. Walter Kaufmann and R. J. Hollingdale (New York: Random House, 1967), p. 223.

36. Horkheimer, *Anfänge der bürgerlichen Geschichtsphilosophie*, p. 44.

37. The year was 1940. For a period in the mid-thirties, under Brecht's influence, Benjamin wrote affirmatively of the course of history in a way that evoked strong criticism from Adorno (see Chapter 9).

38. Walter Benjamin, *Über den Begriff der Geschichte. Gesammelte Schriften*, 6 vols., ed. Rolf Tiedemann and Hermann Schweppenhäuser, vol. I:2: *Abhandlungen* (Frankfurt am Main: Suhrkamp Verlag, 1974), p. 696.

39. *Ibid.*, pp. 696–697.

40. See below, Chapter 11, pages 168–172.

41. See Theodor W. Adorno, "Spengler Today," *Studies in Philosophy and Social Science* 9 (1941): 305–325.

42. See especially Walter Benjamin, "Über die Sprache überhaupt und über die Sprache des Menschen" (1916), *Schriften*, 2 vols., ed. Theodor W. Adorno and Gretel Adorno (Frankfurt am Main: Suhrkamp Verlag, 1955), vol. 2, pp. 417–418.

43. Theodor W. Adorno, "Reaktion und Fortschritt" (1930), *Moments Musicaux*, p. 160.

44. Cf. Horkheimer's 1932 critique of Hegel: "There exists no essentiality or uniform power which could bear the name of 'history.' . . . All these totalities [history, being, etc.] through which the grand totality of subject-object is determined are highly meaningless abstractions, and in no way something like the mind of the real, as Hegel believed. In critical philosophy, they can be made comprehensible as 'tasks.' But Hegel postulated them as already existing." (Horkheimer, "Hegel und das Problem der Metaphysik," p. 192.)

45. I am indebted to Martin Jay for pointing out this similarity. Cf. also Grenz's discussion in Hegelian language of Adorno's conception of appearance as the locus of truth: "On three levels one can take false appearance seriously: one can take it seriously and consider it true, thus coming to rest on its falseness; one can take it seriously and recognize it as false, thus negating it; one can also, however — and only now does one in Adorno's sense really take it seriously — recognize it as false and nonetheless as a regulative idea. Only then has one made it true. This figure is that of the specific negation [*bestimmte Negation*], correctly recognizing the nullity of the false and nonetheless preserving the claim which it makes, because only in the false, the ideological, can the idea of correct life arise." (Friedemann Grenz, *Adornos Philosophie in Grundbegriffen: Auflösungen einiger Deutungsprobleme* [Frankfurt am Main: Suhrkamp Verlag, 1974], p. 74.)

46. The testing of reality by the concept was of course Hegel's phenomenological method. It was the basic methodological procedure of the
Frankfurt Institute's Critical Theory.

47. Adorno, "Reaktion und Fortschritt" (1930), *Moments Musicaux*, p. 159.

48. See Chapter 2, page 32.

49. For example, on the interpretation of past musical works, Adorno wrote:
"the truth of the interpretation does not lie in history as something
alien . . . but history lies in the truth of the interpretation, as something
which unfolds according to its immanent laws." (Adorno, notebooks on
Reproduktionstheorie, vol. 1, p. 5.)

50. Adorno, "Reaktion und Fortschritt" (1930), *Moments Musicaux*, pp.
153-154.

51. Frenzel's comment speaks precisely to this point: "Marx could launch
Hegel's idealism only because he, like Hegel, was convinced that history is
reasonable. That is to say that the principle on which history progresses
is an analogy of human reason. Only by virtue of this principle are revolutions legitimate." (Ivo Frenzel, "Utopia and Apocalypse in German Literature," *Social Research* 39 [Summer 1972]: 315.) In contrast, Adorno's
position had undeniable affinities to Nietzsche, who wrote: "Profound
aversion to reposing once and for all in any one total view of the world.
Fascination with the opposing point of view: refusal to be deprived of the
stimulus of the enigmatic." (Nietzsche, *The Will to Power*, p. 262.)

52. See above, page 45.

53. Adorno, "Reaktion und Fortschritt" (1930), *Moments Musicaux*, p.
153.

54. Adorno, "Neue Tempi" (1930), *ibid.* p. 74.

55. Adorno, "Reaktion und Fortschritt" (1930), *ibid.* p. 154.

56. When, after 1950, Adorno taught Kant and Hegel in his seminars, his
interpretations were mediated by present sociohistorical reality.

57. He wrote to Krenek: "If I regard atonality as the only possible kind of
composing today, then not because I would consider it ahistorically
'better,' something like a handier reference system than tonality. But
instead I believe that tonality has *disintegrated*, that every tonal chord
has a meaning which we can no longer comprehend, that once we have
grown away from the 'natural givenness' of tonal material, we can no
more return to that material than we can produce economically on the
level of use value. . . ." (Letter, April 9, 1929, *Theodor W. Adorno und
Ernst Krenek: Briefwechsel*, ed. Wolfgang Rogge [Frankfurt am Main:
Suhrkamp Verlag, 1974], p. 12.)

58. Adorno, "Nachtmusik" (1930), *Moments Musicaux*, p. 62.

59. Adorno, "Mahogonny" (1930), *ibid.*, p. 131.

60. Theodor W. Adorno, "Über Mannheims Wissenssoziologie," 1947(?),
unpublished essay, Frankfurt am Main, Adorno Estate, p. 6. Horkheimer
had made the same point in an earlier critique of Mannheim: the problem
of relativism made sense "only from the biased assumption of a static

ontology." (Max Horkheimer, "Ein neuer Ideologiebegriff?" [1930], *Sozialphilosophische Studien: Aufsätze, Reden und Vorträge, 1930-1972*, ed. Werner Brede [Frankfurt am Main: Athenäum Fischer Taschenbuch Verlag, 1972], p. 23.) This conception of the historical process was dialectical in a Hegelian sense (minus, of course, Hegel's identification of that process with the realization of Reason). Adorno wrote: "Instead of succumbing to the relativization of truth, here [in the Hegelian dialectic] movement becomes the very substance of truth, and truth determines itself solely by the power of this movement. Even the standpoint of relativism and skepticism, which takes the false, static absolute to be the only absolute, is then recognized as a specific historical relationship between subject and object, and at the same time, its function in reality is seen as the resignation of the mind before overpowering relationships of which it no longer can, or will, be master. The dialectic does not overcome the so-called problem of relativism by denying it, but rather, by the process of specific negation it transforms the concrete relativizing of isolated truth into an instrument of truth itself." (Adorno, "Über Mannheims Wissenssoziologie," p. 4.)

61. Adorno's methodological stress on "inner history" (which had affinities to Husserl's notion of "sedimented meaning" as well as to Benjamin's thinking) does not seem to have been shared by Horkheimer. A comparison of the analytical procedure of their early essays demonstrates this point: Whereas Horkheimer would trace the historical development of a philosophical concept (e.g., history, truth, materialism), demonstrating its relation to "outer" history (that is, its ideological functions), Adorno's approach was to analyze that concept in its most current form in a way which released past history which had become sedimented within it.

62. "The concept of life is given its due only if everything that has a history of its own, and is not merely the setting for history, is credited with life." (Benjamin, "The Task of the Translator" [1923], *Illuminations*, ed. and introd. Hannah Arendt, trans. Harry Zohn [New York: Schocken Books, 1969], p. 71.)

63. Adorno, "Reaktion und Fortschritt" (1930), *Moments Musicaux*, p. 159.

64. Adorno, "Die Aktualität der Philosophie" (1931), *GS* 1, p. 334.

65. Benjamin, ms. for the *Passagenarbeit*, cited in Rolf Tiedemann, *Studien zur Philosophie Walter Benjamins*, introd. Theodor W. Adorno (vol. 16 of Institut für Sozialforschung, *Frankfurter Beiträge zur Soziologie*, ed. Theodor W. Adorno and Walter Dirks) (Frankfurt am Main: Europäische Verlagsanstalt, 1965), p. 125.

66. See Max Horkheimer, "Zum Problem der Wahrheit" (1935), *Kritische Theorie: Eine Dokumentation*, 2 vols., ed. Alfred Schmidt (Frankfurt am Main: S. Fischer Verlag, 1968), vol. I. The idea of the *Parteilichkeit* (partisanship, "partyness") of theoretical work was originally Lenin's; in Soviet Russia it came to stand for work subordinated to the practical needs of the Party, rather than, as Horkheimer used it, for *critical* theory.

67. This was essentially Horkheimer's argument in his critique of Mannheim's *Ideologie und Utopie*, "Ein neuer Ideologiebegriff?" (1930).

68. The speech was published for the first time posthumously in Adorno, *GS* 1, pp. 345–365.

69. See the chapter "Weltgeist und Naturgeschichte," Theodor W. Adorno, *Negative Dialektik, Gesammelte Schriften*, vol. 6, ed. Rolf Tiedemann (Frankfurt am Main: Suhrkamp Verlag, 1973), esp. pp. 343–353.

70. Theodor W. Adorno, "Erinnerungen" (1964), *Über Walter Benjamin* (Frankfurt am Main: Suhrkamp Verlag, 1970), p. 67. The seminar was given by the sociologist Gottfried Salomon-Delatour. The book was Ernst Troeltsch, *Der Historisismus und seine Probleme*.

71. Siegfried Kracauer, *History: The Last Things before the Last* (New York: Oxford University Press, 1969), p. 196.

72. See Karl Mannheim, "Historisismus," *Archiv für Sozialwissenschaft und Sozialpolitik*, 52, 1 (1924): 1–60.

73. Gershom Scholem, *Walter Benjamin: Die Geschichte einer Freundschaft* (Frankfurt am Main: Suhrkamp Verlag, 1975), p. 150.

74. Hence, for example, he accepted Freud's tenant that "all human experiences have a meaning," but this did not answer the ontological question of *the* meaning of human existence (see above, pages 17 ff).

75. Adorno, unpublished Mannheim article, 1947(?), p. 4. Adorno also knew him in London, where Mannheim lived in emigration after 1933. He recalled: "what we had in common with each other was the conviction that truth lay solely in the unflinching and illusion-free consequence of knowledge. The question was only what was to be concretely understood under such consequences." (*Ibid.*)

76. The unpublished Mannheim article in the Adorno Estate is dated in pencil 1937, but it refers to Mannheim's death, which was in 1947. This article, minus the first few pages of personal comments cited here, is in content essentially the same as the version which appeared in 1953 in *Prismen*, with the significant exception that certain Marxist terms (e.g., "Marxist theory of ideology," "materialist dialectic") are deleted. Adorno referred to an earlier critique of Mannheim in a 1934 letter to Benjamin: "I have written a more lengthy critique of Mannheimian bourgeois sociologism, the most strongly Marxist work that I have undertaken as yet; but he asked that I postpone finishing up this essay until after the appearance of his book, and out of loyalty I couldn't refuse him." (Letter, Adorno to Benjamin, November 6, 1934, Frankfurt am Main, Adorno Estate.) In the 1947 essay on Mannheim (p. 1), Adorno wrote: "In order to prevent a heated controversy in the German intellectual emigration in the years just before the war, the publication of a piece I wrote on Mannheim's sociology of knowledge did not take place. Yet he was familiar with it, and it offended him due to the sharpness of the formulation." Any drafts of the critique written in the 1930s appear to have been lost.

77. Adorno, unpublished Mannheim article, 1947 (?), p. 2. Again, Adorno's conviction seems to have been based on aesthetic experience. In his notes

on the reproduction of music he wrote that in musical experience the difference between true and false could be known: "Formal-logically it could be done otherwise, but in experience it *cannot,* because every step deeper into the matter is at the same time one into necessity in regard to its presentation." (Adorno, notebooks on *Reproduktionstheorie*, vol. 2, p. 31.)

78. See particularly Adorno's 1928 article, "Schubert," reprinted in 1964 in *Moments Musicaux,* which notes in the foreword: "The author has changed only those places where he was too much ashamed of his old shortcomings." In the case of the essay on Schubert, the most significant change was Adorno's deletion of the word "ontological," which appears recurrently, in the original, published in *Die Musik* 21,1 (1928): 1–12.

79. See Chapter 1, page 22.

80. Adorno's position on this point played a part in his intellectual estrangement from Siegfried Kracauer during the thirties. Kracauer's position at that time must have anticipated his much later statement "– Adorno's unfettered dialectics . . . eliminates ontology altogether. His rejection of any ontological stipulation in favor of an infinite dialectics which penetrates all concrete things and entities seems inseparable from a certain arbitrariness, an absence of content and direction. . . . The concept of Utopia is then necessarily used by him in a purely formal way, as a borderline concept which at the end invariably emerges like a *deus ex machina.* But Utopian thought makes sense only if it assumes the form of a vision or intuition with a definite content of a sort." (Kracauer, *History,* p. 201.)

81. He argued that the gap between existence and meaning was an objective, real problem, not one which it was in the power of philosophy to resolve. (See Adorno, "Die Idee der Naturgeschichte" [1932], *GS* 1, p. 347.) Marcuse argued in an article published the same year (on Marx's 1844 *Manuscripts*) that Marxism *was* compatible with a materialist ontology. (Herbert Marcuse, "The Foundation of Historical Materialism" [1932], *Studies in Critical Philosophy,* trans. Joris de Bres [Boston: Beacon Press, 1973].) He had earlier argued the same Heidegger-influenced position in "Contributions to a Phenomenology of Historical Materialism" (1928), *Telos* 4 (Fall 1969): 3–32. Adorno's mixed review of Marcuse's 1932 book *Hegels Ontologie* reflected their differences, which remained especially acute during the thirties before Adorno joined the *Institut für Sozialforschung.* (See Russell Jacoby, "Towards a Critique of Automatic Marxism: The Politics of Philosophy from Lukács to the Frankfurt School," *Telos* 10 [Winter 1971]: 137–140.)

82. Adorno, "Die Idee der Naturgeschichte" (1932), *GS* 1, p. 346.

83. *Ibid.*

84. *Ibid.*

85. This aspect was not defined directly in the 1932 speech. It was, however, implied, as it was in his 1930 statement "[It is not true that] social relations have become 'better,' even if the [Marx's] prognosis of increasing misery has not been confirmed." (Adorno, "Reaktion und Fortschritt" [1930], *Moments Musicaux,* p. 153.) The static side of history as the

"ever-identical" (*Immergleiche*) became Adorno's primary emphasis after 1940 (see Chapter 11).

86. Adorno criticized Heidegger in his speech because the latter's abstract, anthropological concept of "historicity" as "an all-encompassing structure of being" was "synonymous . . . with its own ontology." He noted that this position was reflected in Heidegger's recent move in the direction of Hegel. (Adorno, "Die Idee der Naturgeschichte" [1932], *GS* 1, pp. 350–351, 354.)

87. *Ibid.*, pp. 354–355 (italics Adorno's).

88. *Ibid.*, p. 355.

89. *Ibid.*, p. 357.

90. *Ibid.*, p. 364.

91. *Ibid.*, p. 354.

92. *Ibid.*, p. 365.

93. *Ibid.*, p. 356.

94. Horkheimer later noted that the origins of the term date back to Democritus. (See Max Horkheimer, "Bemerkungen zur philosophischen Anthropologie," *Kritische Theorie* I, p. 220.)

95. Indeed, Adorno referred in his speech to Lukács's description of the alienated world as the "world of commodities," even though Lukács did not discuss "second nature" in the context of commodities until *History and Class Consciousness*. (See Adorno, "Die Idee der Naturgeschichte" [1932], *GS* 1, p. 355.)

96. This was a term which Benjamin had discovered in Baudelaire.

97. Cf.: "People are themselves dominated by nature: by that hollow and questionable concept of nature. . . . The immediacy [of music], now lost, is misinterpreted as nature, and it is actually no more than a potpourri of past conventions." (Theodor W. Adorno, "Musikpädagogische Musik: Brief an Enrst Krenek" [1936], *Adorno und Krenek: Briefwechsel*, p. 219.)

98. Adorno, "Die Idee der Naturgeschichte" (1932), *GS* 1, p. 358.

99. *Ibid.*, p. 361.

100. *Ibid.*, p. 357.

101. *Ibid.*, p. 358.

102. Benjamin, cited in *ibid.*, p. 357.

103. Benjamin, cited in *ibid.*, p. 359.

104. Walter Benjamin, *Ursprung des deutschen Trauerspiels* (Frankfurt am Main: Suhrkamp Verlag, 1972), p. 195.

105. *Ibid.*

106. Adorno, "Die Idee der Naturgeschichte" (1932), *GS* 1, p. 359.

107. Benjamin, *Ursprung des deutschen Trauerspiels*, p. 42. In *Die Theorie des Romans* Lukács argued that the decay of the sense of wholeness had gone so far that even the attempt to create a *subjective* totality by means of the literary form of the novel had become problematic, that for art to develop further, reality needed to change, and that "art can never be the agent of

such a transformation" (p. 152). Later he found the necessary agent in the proletariat class and began to advocate the politization of art and defend socialist realism against late capitalist artistic "decadence" (epitomized by expressionism). Adorno and Benjamin were suggesting that what made expressionist art valid was that instead of the novelist's idealist, ideological attempt to create a false, subjective totality, it expressed (like allegory before it) the *truth* about reality, its disintegration, its contradictions, and its human suffering. This was and remained Adorno's criterion for the validity of present-day philosophy as well as art.

108. Adorno, "Die Idee der Naturgeschichte" (1932), *GS* 1, pp. 357–358.

109. *Ibid.*, p. 362.

110. *Ibid.*

111. *Ibid.*, p. 359.

112. *Ibid.*

113. *Ibid.*, p. 345.

114. *Ibid.*, p. 359. The notion of historical time as "discontinuous" was also Simmel's, and Adorno probably inherited it through his early mentor, Siegfried Kracauer.

115. Theodor W. Adorno, *Kierkegaard: Konstruktion des Aesthetischen* [1933]: *Mit zwei Beilagen,* 3rd ed., enl. (Frankfurt am Main: Suhrkamp Verlag, 1966), p. 62.

116. Horkheimer, cited in Tiedemann, *Studien zur Philosophie Walter Benjamins,* p. 117.

117. *One-Way Street (Einbahnstrasse)* was the name of Benjamin's 1928 book of fragmentary recollections.

118. Walter Benjamin, "Goethes Wahlverwandtschaften" (1924), *Schriften,* 2 vols., ed. Theodor W. Adorno and Gretel Adorno (Frankfurt am Main: Suhrkamp Verlag, 1955), vol. 1, p. 140.

119. Theodor W. Adorno, "Portrait of Walter Benjamin," *Prisms,* trans. Samuel and Sherry Weber (London: Neville Spearman, 1967), p. 233. Benjamin's own theory of history ran into problems when in the 1930s he allowed cognitive concepts to be transformed from the critical negation to the positive affirmation of past and present, that is, when he attempted to "rescue" the phenomena in the sense of a theological redemption, and when he affirmed the actual course of historical development, including the empirical consciousness of the proletariat class. For a discussion of this ambivalence in Benjamin's writings, see Jürgen Habermas, "Bewusstmachende oder rettende Kritik: Die Aktualität Walter Benjamins" (1972), *Kultur und Kritik: Verstreute Aufsätze* (Frankfurt am Main: Suhrkamp Taschenbuch, 1973), pp. 302–344.

120. Adorno referred only briefly to the relationship between historical dynamics and archaic images in "Die Idee der Naturgeschichte," (*GS* 1, pp. 362–364). But see the discussion of historical images in Chapter 6 below.

121. See above, Chapter 2.

122. Hence, if Adorno stressed the fragmentary nature of social reality in the 1930s and in the 1940s began to call society a "closed system" (*lücken-*

loses System), he was not being inconsistent. Although the weight given to each pole varied given the particular constellation of each essay, Adorno continued to consider both integration and disintegration characteristic of late bourgeois society. Indeed, he planned to publish a collection of his sociological essays under the title *Integration-Disintegration* and to write an introductory essay on this theme. (See "Editorische Nachbemerkung," Theodor W. Adorno, *Gesammelte Schriften*, vol. 9: *Soziologische Schriften II*, ed. Susan Buck-Morss and Rolf Tiedemann, 2 vols. [Frankfurt am Main: Suhrkamp Verlag, 1975].)

123. See below, Chapter 11. Completed in 1944 and first published in Amsterdam in 1947, the book was practically unknown until its republication in 1969 when its impact on the German New Left was considerable. It has since been translated into a number of different languages, including the following English edition: Max Horkheimer and Theodor W. Adorno, *Dialectic of Enlightenment*, trans. John Cumming (New York: Herder and Herder, 1972).

124. Martin Jay, *The Dialectical Imagination: A History of the Frankfurt School and the Institute of Social Research, 1923-1950* (Boston: Little, Brown, 1973), p. 256.

125. See below, Chapter 11.

126. Horkheimer and Adorno, *Dialectic of Enlightenment*, p. 43.

127. The Institute received a copy in 1941 and published it under the title *Über den Begriff der Geschichte* in a special Institute edition, *Walter Benjamin zum Gedächtnis*, in 1942. See ed. note, (Walter Benjamin, *Gesammelte Schriften*, vol. I:3, *Abhandlungen*, ed. Rolf Tiedemann and Hermann Schweppenhäuser [Frankfurt am Main: Suhrkamp Verlag, 1974], p. 1223.)

128. The importance of the theses, as well as their esotericism, has occasioned a book of interpretive essays: *Materialien zu Benjamins Thesen "Über den Begriff der Geschichte": Beiträge und Interpretationen*, ed. Peter Bultkaup (Frankfurt am Main: Suhrkamp Verlag, 1975).

129. In the mid-thirties, under Brecht's influence, he had written affirmatively about the course of history in a much more orthodox Marxist sense. (See especially Benjamin, "Das Kunstwerk im Zeitalter seiner technischen Reproduzierbarkeit" [1936], *Gesammelte Schriften* I:2.)

130. "Historicism presents the 'eternal' image of the past; historical materialism presents a unique experience with the past." (Benjamin, *Über den Begriff der Geschichte* [1940], *Gesammelte Schriften* I:2, p. 702.)

131. *Ibid.*, p. 704.

132. *Ibid.*, p. 695.

133. Horkheimer and Adorno, *Dialectic of Enlightenment*, p. 54. *Urgeschichte* is translated here as "prehistory."

134. Even after *Dialektik der Aufklärung* Adorno defended Marx's historical periodization, "the dialectical schema [of feudal, bourgeois, and classless] epochs," against Mannheim's translation of this schema into "the fluid, changing modes of behavior of socialized man in general, in which the determinant oppositions disappear." Adorno, "The Sociology of Knowl-

edge and Its Consciousness" (1953), *Prisms*, p. 42. The phrase bracketed here appears in Adorno's typescript of this essay but not in the published form.

135. So Benjamin wrote Scholem in 1940 (see Benjamin, *Gesammelte Schriften* I:3, p. 1228).

136. See the close textual analysis of Benjamin's theses by Rolf Tiedemann in his article "Historischer Materialismus oder politischer Messianismus?" *Materialien zu Benjamins Thesen "Über den Begriff der Geschichte,"* pp. 77–121.

137. Benjamin, *Über den Begriff der Geschichte* (1940), *Gesammelte Schriften* I:2, p. 698.

138. Benjamin, *Gesammelte Schriften* I:3, p. 1232.

139. The theoretical implications of the Institute's empirical work had been developed by Horkheimer in an essay, "Autoritärer Staat" which, significantly, was included in the special Institute publication in memory of Walter Benjamin, in which the latter's theses on history appeared.

140. Horkheimer and Adorno, *Dialectic of Enlightenment*, p. 26.

141. *Ibid.*, p. 6.

142. Adorno, "Portrait of Walter Benjamin," *Prisms*, p. 236.

143. The epic age of Greece was the era of holistic cosmology which Lukács had praised in *Die Theorie des Romans*. For the influence of ancient Greece over modern German thought, see E. M. Butler, *The Tyranny of Greece over Germany* (Boston: Beacon Press, 1935).

144. Jay, *The Dialectical Imagination*, p. 256.

145. On this issue see Jacoby, "Towards a Critique of Automatic Marxism," pp. 140–146. If Jay errs by equating the Frankfurt "School" with the position of Horkheimer, Jacoby in his account of the Frankfurt Institute's understanding of nature and history errs by equating it with the position of Adorno.

146. Adorno, "Die Idee der Naturgeschichte" (1932), *GS* 1, p. 27.

147. See above, pages 31–32. Although Adorno did not cite the 1844 *Manuscripts* directly in his 1932 speech, he later drew upon writings of both the early and late Marx to illustrate his concept of natural history (see Adorno, *Negative Dialektik, GS* 6, pp. 347–351).

148. [Karl Marx,] *Writings of the Young Marx on Philosophy and Society*, ed. and trans. Loyd D. Easton and Kurt H. Guddat (Garden City, N.Y.: Doubleday, Anchor Books, 1967), p. 312.

149. *Ibid.*, pp. 314–337, esp. pp. 333–337.

150. *Ibid.*, pp. 301–314, esp. pp. 308–310.

151. *Ibid.* p. 306. The utopian themes of sensual pleasure in these early writings had appeared earlier in Horkheimer's essays, in particular "Egoismus und Freiheitsbewegung" (1936).

152. Jay notes that Marcuse's 1932 article on the 1844 *Manuscripts* spoke of Marx's desire for the unity of man and nature, but he claims that this was "the very goal which Adorno and Horkheimer were later to emphasize in

opposition to Marx." (Jay, *The Dialectical Imagination*, p. 144.) He has noted that the question of interpretation here is whether the young Marx's goal was the total *identity* of *Geist* and *Natur* (which Adorno and Horkheimer did not support) or merely their mutual mediation (i.e., "reconciliation"). (Letter, Martin Jay to me, September 21, 1973.)

153. In 1966 Adorno wrote that despite Marx's materialist reversal of Hegel's dialectic of history, both Engels *and* Marx tended to deify history, and their faith in economic forces encouraged them to endorse the bourgeois program of domination of nature. (Adorno, *Negative Dialektik*, GS 6, pp. 242, 315.) Still, even when the late Marx in the introduction to *Kapital* spoke of the evolution of capitalist society as a "process of natural history" which moved "with iron necessity towards inevitable results," Adorno argued (against Engels) that this needed to be interpreted in the critical spirit which he had made his own, i.e., that Marx's use of the term "nature" was meant to criticize capitalist development as not truly historical, as "pre-history" (*vor-Geschichte*), as Marx elsewhere defined all previous history. (*Ibid.*, pp. 347–349.)

For a critique of the interpretation that Marx had a teleology of history, see Alfred Schmidt, *Der Begriff der Natur in der Lehre von Marx*, rev. and enl. (Frankfurt am Main: Europäische Verlagsanstalt, 1971), pp. 29–30. Schmidt states that "the materialist dialectic is non-teleological. . . . He who has grasped human history up until the present has in no way thereby grasped a direction of the world." (*Ibid.*, p. 29.)

154. Of course Adorno had always maintained this position (see Chapter 2, pages 35–36), but there is no doubt that in the early thirties he believed the revolution in art and the disintegration of bourgeois cognitive forms in some way heralded a progressive social revolution, and hence was himself not fully free of the bourgeois myth of progress. If *Dialektik der Aufklärung* is a more sober estimate of the revolutionary powers of reason, his important critique of Schönberg written during the same period was based on a parallel argument: Schönberg's dialectical break from bourgeois tonality, which liberated music from the domination of tonal laws, had fallen back into a new form of domination, the closed system and set rules of twelve-tone composition. (See Theodor W. Adorno, *Philosophy of Modern Music*, trans. Anne G. Mitchell and Wesley V. Blomster (New York: The Seabury Press, 1973.)

155. Horkheimer and Adorno maintained the position that the triumph of the bourgeois class, and also of the Soviet dictatorship of the proletariat, had transformed the economic base while leaving the structure of domination intact.

CHAPTER 4

1. Adorno's advocacy of a principle of nonidentity may have been prompted as a critical response to Heidegger's focus on identity as the central theme, not only of bourgeois idealism, but of all Western philosophy since Par-

menides. Of course, rejection of the Hegelian identity of subject and object (i.e., belief that the real is rational, and the rational is real) was an early notion, dating back to Adorno's first acceptance of Marxism. It was actually Horkheimer who first articulated the case against this idealist premise. (See especially Max Horkheimer, *Anfänge der bürgerlichen Geschichtsphilosophie* [Stuttgart: Kohlhammer, 1930], pp. 185-197; *idem*, "Hegel und das Problem der Metaphysik," *Festschrift für Carl Grünberg: Zum 70. Geburtstag* [Leipzig: Verlag von C. L. Hirschfeld, 1932], pp. 185-197.) The implications of this rejection of identity for Adorno's theory of history have been discussed in Chapter 3. However, rejection of Hegel's subject-object identity comprised only one aspect of Adorno's "principle of non-identity." Other levels were far more indebted to Benjamin than to either Hegel or Horkheimer, as will be demonstrated.

2. He first used this term in his Hegel seminars during the 1950s, but his philosophy was not officially christened "negative dialectics" until 1966, with the appearance of the book by the same name. As late as the 1963 foreword to his three essays on Hegel, Adorno referred only generally to his efforts as formulations of "an altered concept of the dialectic." (Theodor W. Adorno, *Drei Studien zu Hegel* [Frankfurt am Main: Suhrkamp Verlag, 1969], p. 8.)

3. In a note to the German edition of *Negative Dialektik* (which has been omitted in the English translation) Adorno wrote: "The idea of a logic of disintegration is the oldest of his [the author's] philosophical conceptions, going back to his student years." (Theodor W. Adorno, *Negative Dialektik*, *Gesammelte Schriften*, vol. 6, ed. Rolf Tiedemann [Frankfurt am Main: Suhrkamp Verlag, 1973], p. 409.) That its intention was compatible with Adorno's later theory is clear from the following statement: "Its [negative dialectic's] notion does not tend to the identity in the difference between each object and its concept; instead it is suspicious of all identity. Its logic is one of disintegration. . . ." (Theodor W. Adorno, *Negative Dialectics*, trans. E. B. Ashton [New York: The Seabury Press, 1973], p. 145.)

4. See Chapter 3.

5. Walter Benjamin, "Paris: — The Capital of the Nineteenth Century" (1935), trans. Quintin Hoare, in *Charles Baudelaire: A Lyric Poet in the Era of High Capitalism*, trans. Harry Zohn (London, NLB, 1973), p. 176.

6. See above, Chapter 2.

7. The word in German is more dialectical than this English translation: the prefix *um* implies the reversal, not just a reshaping, of the categories. However, the translation in the passage below seems overintellectualized and abstract: "Brecht has coined the phrase 'functional transformation' [*Umfunktionierung*] to describe the transformation of forms and instruments of production by a progressive intelligentsia — an intelligentsia interested in liberating the means of production and hence active in the class struggle." (Walter Benjamin, "The Author as Producer," *Understanding Brecht*, trans. Anna Bostock [London: NLB, 1973], p. 93.)

8. For Hegel (and for Adorno) philosophical method was not a formal set of rules to be learned, but an activity to be experienced and articulated.

9. As Adorno noted, the term "Critical Theory" was "Horkheimer's phrasing" (Adorno, *Negative Dialectics*, p. 197); it was Horkheimer who first outlined its distinguishing characteristics in his 1937 article in the *Zeitschrift für Sozialforschung* "Traditionelle und kritische Theorie." (See Max Horkheimer, "Traditional and Critical Theory," *Critical Theory*, trans. Matthew J. O'Connell et al. [New York: Herder and Herder, 1972], pp. 188-243.)

10. As he later recalled in comparing himself to Horkheimer: "I, however, by background and early development, was an artist, a musician, yet animated by an impulse to account for art and its possibility in the present, where something objective desired expression as well, a suspicion of the insufficiency of naive aesthetic procedure in view of the tendencies of society." (Theodor W. Adorno, "Offener Brief an Max Horkheimer," *Die Zeit*, February 12, 1965, p. 32.)

11. A study of Mannheim went through two revisions (1934 and 1937) yet never appeared in the journal — a third revision was finally published elsewhere (Theodor W. Adorno, "Über Mannheims Wissenssoziologie" [1953] reprinted in *Prismen* [Frankfurt am Main: Suhrkamp Verlag, 1955]). A 1937 article on Husserl, revised by Adorno in 1938, was never published. Copies of both drafts are in the Adorno Estate.

12. In the 1932 article (which was discussed in detail in Chapter 2) and the more than forty short pieces on music which he published in a variety of journals and newspapers during the thirties, Adorno laid the groundwork for an aesthetic philosophy whose formulation occupied him until his death. (A lengthy, unfinished book ms., *Aesthetische Theorie*, was published posthumously in 1970 as vol. 7 of the *Gesammelte Schriften*.) I am not suggesting that the early music essays in the *Zeitschrift für Sozialforschung*, which contained elements of an aesthetic theory as well as a critical theory of mass culture, were insignificant compared with his book-length philosophical studies; my point is simply that, whereas the Institute was more interested in a (philosophical) *sociology* of art, Adorno's primary concern was in (sociological) *philosophy* — of aesthetics as well as of epistemological cognition.

13. As he stated in 1932, the idealist premise, the identity of subject and object, "has long since collapsed, and with it, the edifice of Hegelian philosophy. . . . 'Absolute' philosophy . . . is a thing of the past." (Horkheimer, "Hegel und das Problem der Metaphysik," p. 192.)

14. Horkheimer's faith that the social sciences could answer the traditional questions of philosophy through empirical research was not something Adorno shared. Against this tendency, Adorno, as he later recalled, tried to "strengthen the antipositivistic, speculative bent" of Horkheimer. (Theodor W. Adorno, "Offener Brief an Max Horkheimer," p. 32.)

15. These two theories, he felt, provided "a formulation of the old [philosophical] questions more appropriate to the state of our present knowledge. . . ." (Max Horkheimer, "Die gegenwärtige Lage der Sozialphilosophie und die Aufgaben eines Instituts für Sozialforschung" [1931], *Sozialphilosophische Studien: Aufsätze, Reden und Vorträge, 1930-1972*, ed. Werner Brede [Frankfurt am Main: Athenäum Fischer Taschenbuch Verlag, 1972], p. 43.)

16. He advocated "a continuous dialectical penetration and development between philosophical theory and the practice of the single scientific disciplines. . . ." (*Ibid.*, p. 40.)

17. As he wrote in his inaugural speech: "Only an essentially undialectical philosophy, one which aims at ahistorical truth, could maintain that the old problems could simply be removed by forgetting them and starting fresh from the beginning." (Theodor W. Adorno, "Die Aktualität der Philosophie" [1931], *Gesammelte Schriften*, vol. 1: *Frühe philosophische Schriften*, ed. Rolf Tiedemann [Frankfurt am Main: Suhrkamp Verlag, 1973], p. 339.)

18. In a letter to Benjamin, March 18, 1936, Adorno wrote: "I might perhaps first adhere to our old method of immanent criticism." (Theodor W. Adorno, *Über Walter Benjamin* [Frankfurt am Main: Suhrkamp Verlag, 1970], p. 127.)

19. For an English summary of Horkheimer's writings of the early thirties see Martin Jay, *The Dialectical Imagination: A History of the Frankfurt School and the Institute of Social Research, 1923-1950* (Boston: Little, Brown, 1973), pp. 44-65.

20. Horkheimer's prime concern was *Ideologiekritik*, i.e., how it was that (bourgeois) "views valid in themselves and theoretical and aesthetic works of undeniably high quality can in certain circumstances operate ideologically. . . ." (Horkheimer, "Notes on Science and the Crisis" [1932], *Critical Theory*, p. 7.) Adorno, convinced as he was that the *social* invalidity of bourgeois thought was manifested *immanently*, would not have held that such thought could be "valid in itself"; at the same time he believed that ideology, correctly interpreted, was the source of truth.

21. The distinction can be illustrated by comparing Adorno's critical analysis of the concept of history with two early essays by Horkheimer. Adorno's approach, outlined in his 1932 speech to the *Kantgesellschaft* in Frankfurt, was to juxtapose the antithetical concepts of nature and history in such a way that neither was posited as the foundation of an affirmative philosophy of history. His argument was dialectical and polemical rather than descriptive. In contrast, in a 1930 essay, *Anfänge der bürgerlichen Geschichtsphilosophie*, Horkheimer's approach was to outline the historical development of the bourgeois concept of history from Machiavelli to Vico and Hegel, identifying both progressive and regressive elements in it, in view of those elements' ideological function. His program for a present theory of history, which he outlined in a speech delivered to the same *Kantgesellschaft* mentioned above, suggested that the problem, formerly the concern of the metaphysician, could now best be dealt with by Marx's "scientific" theory and (Freudian) psychology. (See "Geschichte und Psychologie" [1932], reprinted in Max Horkheimer, *Kritische Theorie: Eine Dokumentation*, 2 vols. ed. Alfred Schmidt [Frankfurt am Main: S. Fischer Verlag, 1968], vol. I, pp. 9-30.)

22. His aim was "to point out the common structural characteristics of well known developments in modern history." (Max Horkheimer, "Egoismus und Freiheitsbewegung," *Kritische Theorie* II, p. 106.) For a discussion

of Horkheimer's evaluation of Dilthey, his criticisms as well as the points of agreement, see Jay, *The Dialectical Imagination*, pp. 48–53.

23. Ricoeur's description of the interpretive methods of Marx, Freud, and Neitzsche as an "exercise in suspicion," a "hermeneutics of demystification," applies as well to Adorno. (Paul Ricoeur, *Freud and Philosophy: An Essay on Interpretation*, trans. Denis Savage [New Haven, Conn.: Yale University Press, 1970], p. 33.)

24. When, for example, Horkheimer criticized the acceptance of what had historically evolved as "second nature," he was concerned not only that as "a suprahistorical eternal category" it was in fact incorrect, but that, in regard to moral will, it was "a sign of contemptible weakness." (Horkheimer, "Traditional and Critical Theory" [1937], *Critical Theory*, p. 210.)

25. *Ibid.*, p. 215 (italics mine). Cf. "The chasm between the moral standards which the Europeans have acknowledged since the advent of Christianity, and those which these Europeans in fact practice, is immeasurable." (Max Horkheimer [pseud. Heinrich Regius], *Dämmerung: Notizen in Deutschland* [Zurich: Verlag Oprecht und Helbling, 1934], p. 193.)

26. Adorno, "Offener Brief an Max Horkheimer," p. 32.

27. *Ibid.*

28. Adorno was still struggling with the question of the possibility of metaphysics in the final chapter of *Negative Dialektik*. Cf. Horkheimer's statement in 1934: "I do not know how far metaphysicians are correct; perhaps there exists somewhere an especially compelling metaphysical system or fragment. But I do know that metaphysicians are usually only minimally impressed by that which torments and afflicts human beings." (Max Horkheimer, *Dämmerung*, p. 86.) Horkheimer's moral concern for physical suffering (of animals as well as human beings) as opposed to Adorno's more cerebral orientation is illustrated by Adorno's recollection "Once you [Horkheimer] said to me that I perceived animals as human whereas you saw humans as animals. There is something to that." (Adorno, "Offener Brief an Max Horkheimer," p. 32.)

29. As Adorno wrote: "Nonetheless, the tension between the poles from whence we came did not disappear, and grew to be fruitful for us." (*Ibid.*)

30. Here, as elsewhere, Horkheimer was closer to the early Lukács of *History and Class Consciousness*. He viewed the intellectual's role as the articulater of imputed class consciousness, although, like Adorno, he refused to sanction Party control of the intellectual's theoretical work. (See Horkheimer, "Traditional and Critical Theory" [1937], *Critical Theory*, pp. 221–224.)

31. In his inaugural address as director he wrote: "the discussion concerning society crystalizes gradually and with increasing clarity around one question, namely the question of the connection between the economic life of society, the psychic development of the individuals, and transformations in the cultural realm. . . ." (Horkheimer, "Die gegenwärtige Lage der Sozialphilosophie und die Aufgaben eines Instituts für Sozialforschung" [1931], *Sozialphilosophische Studien*, p. 43.) The problem led Horkheimer, as it did Wilhelm Reich (see his *Massenpsychologie des Faschismus* [Copen-

hagen: Verlag für Sexualpolitik, 1933]), to merge Marxist social theory with Freudian psychology: "What needs to be examined is how the psychological mechanism evolves whereby it is possible for the tensions between social classes to remain latent, tensions which, due to the economic situation, press toward conflict." (Horkheimer, "Geschichte und Psychologie" [1932], *Kritische Theorie"* I, p. 21.)

32. See above, Chapter 2. Although neither saw theory as subservient to political praxis, for Adorno the relationship between the two was more highly mediated, and developments in theory remained more self-contained.

33. In *The Dialectical Imagination,* Martin Jay has stressed the similarities between Adorno and Horkheimer. The difference between our interpretations may be less one of substance than of focus. As Jay expressed it: "From your more pointillist perspective, the differences between Adorno and his colleagues seem clearer than they did from mine. . . ." (Letter, Martin Jay to me, September 21, 1973.)

34. In his 1931 speech Adorno noted that philosophy would "have to take its specific disciplinary material preponderantly from sociology. . . ." (Adorno, "Die Aktualität der Philosophie" [1931], *GS* 1, p. 340.)

35. See above, Chapter 3.

36. In a 1932 essay Horkheimer, referring to the tasks philosophy had still to do, reflected the same spirit of philosophy which Adorno had articulated in his inaugural address the year before: "It is also fully possible to present the results of empirical research in such a way that the life of the objects comes to expression on all sides." (Horkheimer, "Hegel und das Problem der Metaphysik," p. 195.)

37. Letter, Adorno to Benjamin, June 8, 1938 (Frankfurt am Main, Adorno Estate).

38. *Ibid.* See below, Chapter 11.

39. *Dialektik der Aufklärung* was in a sense a preliminary study for *Negative Dialektik,* as a comprehensive analysis of the history of the Enlightenment and how it had run amok: one had to know what had gone wrong with reason in order to redeem it.

40. ". . . owing to the fact that the concept is to be formed under the aspect of the historical totality to which it pertains, sociology should be able to develop this changing [social] pattern from the very content of the concept instead of adding specific contents from without." (Max Horkheimer, "Notes on Institute Activities," *Studies in Social Science* 9, 1 [1941]: 123.)

41. The method was described as "inductive," not in the traditional sense of collecting individual experiences until they attained the weight of universal laws," but in the sense of seeking "the universal within the particular, not above or beyond it," because "society is a 'system' in the material sense that every single social field or relation contains and reflects in various ways the whole itself." (*Ibid.*) Adorno claimed Benjamin's method had "redeemed induction" (see below, page 94).

42. It should be noted that the mature Adorno was not without criticism of

his own early efforts. In a note to the 1966 reprinting of his Kierkegaard study he said he now found the book too affirmative, too hopeful; in reprinting his early music essays he sometimes altered sections which seemed "inexcusably idealistic." But it is still remarkable that Adorno could publish so many of his early essays alongside his mature works with little or no revision.

43. [Institut für Sozialforschung,] *Studien über Autorität und Familie*, ed. Max Horkheimer (Paris: Felix Alcan, 1936). We may note, however, that criticism of the domination of nature was already explicit in Adorno's Kierkegaard study (written 1928–1933), and that it played a role in his critique of Wagner, also written before Adorno joined the Institute; whereas, in the year Adorno published his Kierkegaard book Horkheimer could still write: "For true human freedom is not to be equated either with indeterminateness or with mere arbitrariness; instead, it is identical with the domination of nature within and without us through rational decision." (Max Horkheimer, "Zum Problem der Voraussage in den Sozialwissenschaften" [1933], reprinted in Horkheimer, *Kritische Theorie* I, p. 117.)

44. See below, Chapter 11.

45. Adorno, *Negative Dialectics*, p. xx.

46. Written 1934–1937, and revised and published in 1956.

47. In an editor's note to the first (posthumous) publication of the address, Tiedemann commented that this and several other early essays, "unusually programmatic for Adorno's thinking," introduced motifs and ideas which "anticipate something like a companion piece to *Negative Dialektik.*" (Rolf Tiedemann, "Editorische Nachbemerkung," in Adorno, *GS* 1, p. 383.)

48. I have already noted (see note 1 for this chapter) that nonidentity took on many levels of meaning in Adorno's theory, only one of which was the rejection of Hegel's subject-object synthesis, and that his use of the expression may have been motivated as a critical response to Heidegger's fascination with the problem. In a 1957 essay, "Identität und Differenz," Heidegger reviewed the history of identity theory in Western philosophy, noting that in its evolution it took on several distinct forms. These included, on the level of cognition, that concept and thing are the same (or the thing is a case of its concept): the ontological form, that a thing remains identical with itself (the problem of essence and appearance); the logical form A=A (the identity of a concept with itself; contradiction seen as error); and the metaphysical level (God is identical with the world; reason is one with reality). Adorno reversed all these assumptions, and as we will see, these reversals were already implicit in his 1931 program for philosophy.

49. The speech was to have been dedicated to Benjamin in published form, but the planned publication never occurred. (See Tiedemann, "Editorische Nachbemerkung," in Adorno, *GS* 1, p. 383.)

50. In most cases, the 1973 English translation *Negative Dialectics* has been used, but I have when I considered it necessary made my own translations from the German original.

51. Adorno, *Negative Dialektik*, pp. 19–20. The same sentiment was expressed

in almost identical wording in Adorno's Husserl ms. (1934-1937), p. 423. The word *faul* in German (here translated "foul") means not only decayed or rotten, but idle, lazy, worthless.

52. Adorno, "Die Aktualität der Philosophie" (1931), *GS* 1, p. 331.

53. *Ibid.* p. 339.

54. *Ibid.*, p. 331. Cf. "Its [philosophy's] task would be to inquire whether and how there can still be a philosophy at all, now that Hegel's has fallen. . . ." (Adorno, *Negative Dialectics*, p. 4.)

55. Cf. Chapter 3. In *Negative Dialektik*, Adorno expressed the same notion of the historical obsolescence of philosophical phenomena, but his metaphor was mediated by a new social present: "The introverted thought architect dwells behind the moon that is taken over by extroverted technicians. The conceptual shells that were to house the whole, according to philosophical custom, have in view of the immense expansion of society and of the strides made by positive natural science come to seem like relics of a simple barter economy amidst the late stage of industrial capitalism." (Adorno, *Negative Dialectics*, p. 3.)

56. Adorno's inaugural address can be interpreted as a counter-program to that of Heidegger, whose *Sein und Zeit*, published in 1927, was extremely influential within faculty circles at Frankfurt University. Adorno referred to setting Heidegger "on his feet" in a letter to Benjamin, December 17, 1934. (Adorno, *Über Walter Benjamin*, p. 106.) Indeed, the entire corpus of Adorno's writings can be read fruitfully as a critical response to Heidegger, all the more effective the more unspoken his intent and indirect his attack. (Hence Adorno's book expressly devoted to attacking Heidegger, *Jargon der Eigentlichkeit* [1964], is one of his least satisfying compared, for example, to his study of Kierkegaard [1933], which challenges Heidegger indirectly by challenging his existentialist heritage.) A detailed comparison of Adorno and Heidegger awaits a competent scholar. We can here only suggest points at which their thought converged (although in nonidentical configurations). Like Adorno, Heidegger was convinced that present philosophers had to radically rethink the fundamentals of their discipline. But to Heidegger this meant establishing a new ontology of man's existence, whereas Adorno, criticizing the ideological affirmation of the social status quo inherent in all ontology, saw "radical" philosophy in terms of the critical negation of the existing idealism. Against the ontological categories of "being," "thrownness," and "historicity," Adorno insisted on the historical specificity of men's (not "man's") condition. Both were strongly influenced by Husserl, both agreed that subject and object were necessarily related (Husserl had argued that thought was always thought of something, and Adorno agreed, while Heidegger spoke in terms of man's being [*Dasein*] as always being in the world); but Heidegger simply posited this relation as immediately given in experience, while Adorno revealed their mediated relationship through the experience of dialectical argumentation. Both wanted to establish a concrete, "materialist" analysis of phenomena, a phenomenological hermeneutics of the profane world, but to Heidegger this meant unveiling a general, "essential" truth out of the particulars of man's lived existence, whereas Adorno

wanted to expose within the particular the general structure of a historically developed society. "Materialist" to Heidegger meant relating particulars to the ontological categories of being; to Adorno it meant relating them to Marxian categories of society. Heidegger internalized the Hegelian dialectic of being and nonbeing, conceiving it in terms of man's being-to-death, while Adorno saw it in terms of the relationship between subject and object. Both men were critics of mass culture and technological society. But Heidegger saw the *Angst* which men suffered as an existential, ontological condition, demanding that man transform himself; Adorno insisted in the transformation of society. As the latter wrote Benjamin, "The goal of the revolution is the elimination of anxiety [*Angst*]" (letter, Adorno to Benjamin, March 18, 1936, in Adorno, *Über Walter Benjamin*, p. 132). Indeed, the fact that Heidegger could endorse the young Marx's treatment of alienation in his "Letter on Humanism" (1947) was reason enough for Adorno's suspicion of Marxist humanism.

57. Adorno, "Die Aktualität der Philosophie" (1931), *GS* 1, p. 325.

58. *Ibid.*

59. *Ibid.*, p. 326.

60. Horkheimer, "Materialism and Metaphysics" (1933), *Critical Theory*, p. 12.

61. The phrase was first used by Otto Liebmann in 1865.

62. Lukács had already brought this idea into connection with the theme of decay in *History and Class Consciousness.* He wrote with reference to the "crisis in culture": "This ideological crisis is an unfailing sign of decay. The bourgeoisie has already been thrown on the defensive; however aggressive its *weapons* may be, it is fighting for self-preservation. Its power to dominate has vanished beyond recall." (Georg Lukács, *History and Class Consciousness,* trans. Rodney Livingstone [Cambridge, Mass.: The M.I.T. Press, 1971], p. 67.)

63. ". . . for the truth content of a problem is in principle different from the historical and psychological conditions out of which it grows." (Adorno, "Die Aktualität der Philosophie" [1931], *GS* 1, p. 337.) Hence *Ideologiekritik* was only the impetus of philosophical criticism, not its culmination.

64. *Ibid.*, p. 326.

65. *Ibid.*

66. As Adorno described it in *Negative Dialektik,* paraphrasing the English adage, Husserl "wanted to eat the cake and have it too." (Adorno, *Negative Dialektik,* p. 77.)

67. Cf. Adorno, "Die Aktualität der Philosophie" (1931), *GS* 1, p. 327.

68. Cf. Adorno, "Die Transzendenz des Dinglichen und Noematischen in Husserls Phänomenologie" (1924), *GS* 1, pp. 45–49.

69. *Ibid.*, p. 49 (italics Adorno's).

70. It is perhaps significant that at the beginning of the bourgeois era what Kant had called the "scandal" instigated by Hume's attack on reason did not evoke the same *Angst* as did the threat to reason in the early twentieth century, the time of the bourgeois cultural decline.

71. Ellipsis Sartre's.

72. Jean-Paul Sartre, *Nausea*, trans. Lloyd Alexander (New York: New Directions Publishing, 1964), pp. 126–128.

73. "[Sartre's] plays disavow the philosophy with whose theses they deal." (Adorno, *Negative Dialectics*, p. 50.)

74. "The word absurdity is coming to life under my pen. . . . And without formulating anything clearly, I understood that I had found the key to Existence, the key to my Nauseas, to my own life. In fact, all that I could grasp beyond that returns to this fundamental absurdity. . . . [T]he world of explanations and reasons is not the world of existence. A circle is not absurd, it is clearly explained by the rotation of a straight segment around one of its extremities. But neither does a circle exist. This root, on the other hand, existed in such a way that I could not explain it." (Sartre, *Nausea*, p. 129.)

75. Adorno, "Die Aktualität der Philosophie" (1931), *GS* 1, p. 336.

76. Theodor W. Adorno, *Kierkegaard: Konstruktion des Aesthetischen* (1933): *Mit zwei Beilagen*, 3rd ed., enl. (Frankfurt am Main: Suhrkamp Verlag, 1962), p. 142.

77. "For Hegel, the totality was the totality of reason, a closed ontological system, finally identical with the rational system of history. Hegel's dialectical process was thus a universal ontological one in which history was patterned on the metaphysical process of being. Marx, on the other hand, detached dialectic from this ontological base. . . . The totality that the Marxian dialectic gets to is the totality of class society, and the negativity that underlies its contradictions and shapes its every content is the negativity of class relations." (Herbert Marcuse, *Reason and Revolution: Hegel and the Rise of Social Theory* 2nd ed., enl. [New York: The Humanities Press, 1954], p. 314.)

78. Adorno, *Kierkegaard* (1933), p. 142.

79. Heidegger's phenomenological approach was to simply ignore the fetish character of objects as commodities. He spoke of things as if their use value were still intact, rather than, as Marx (and Adorno) insisted, having been superseded by the abstract exchange value characteristic of bourgeois commodities. (See Martin Heidegger, *Sein und Zeit* [1927], 9th ed., unchanged [Tübingen: Niemeyer Verlag, 1960], pp. 68–69.)

80. See above, Chapter 3.

81. Adorno, "Die Aktualität der Philosophie" (1931), *GS* 1, p. 336. Cf.: "The objective worth of those themes [of Western metaphysics] is indeed inescapable in philosophy, but neither can we rely on our ability to cope with the great topics. We must be so wary of the beaten tracks of philosophical reflection that our emphatic interest will seek refuge in ephemeral objects not yet overdetermined by intentions." (Adorno, *Negative Dialectics*, p. 17.)

82. Cornelius had argued that the phenomena could never be entirely known but remained "always partly alien to us." (Hans Cornelius, *Grundlagen der Erkenntnistheorie: Transcendentale Systematik*, 2nd ed. [Munich: Ernst Reinhardt, 1926], p. 261. Cf. "No object is wholly known. . . ." [Adorno,

Negative Dialectics, p. 14].) Ernst Simmel, comparing philosophy to Einstein's new physics, observed: "The totality of truth is perhaps as little true as the totality of matter is heavy." ("Aussprüche" of Simmel, collected by Ernst Bloch, *Buch des Dankes an Georg Simmel*, ed. Kurt Gassen and Michael Landmann [Berlin: Duncker & Humblot, 1958], p. 251; cf. "The totality is the untrue." [Theodor W. Adorno, *Minima Moralia* (Frankfurt am Main: Suhrkamp Verlag, 1969), p. 57].) Arnold Schönberg, arguing against theoretical systems of composition, wrote: "laws of nature know no exceptions: theories of art are founded above all on exceptions." (Arnold Schönberg, *Harmonielehre* [Vienna: Universal-Edition, 1922], p. 6.) Horkheimer's rejection of Hegel's identity of history and truth because of the suffering of *particular individuals* has already been discussed in Chapter 3.

83. When Lukács analysed the structure of bourgeois theory and found within it the commodity structure of the social totality, he provided the model for Adorno's own efforts to find the general within the particular; but the difference lay precisely here, in Lukács's impatience with details and his unmistakable preference for totalistic visions. Cf., e.g., his statement "The greater the distance from pure immediacy[,] the larger the net encompassing the 'relations,' and the more complete the integration of the 'objects' within the system of relations, the sooner change will cease to be impenetrable and catastrophic, the sooner it will become comprehensible." (Lukács, *History and Class Consciousness*, p. 154.)

84. Ernst Bloch, "Erinnerung," in Theodor W. Adorno et al., *Über Walter Benjamin* (Frankfurt am Main: Suhrkamp Verlag, 1968), p. 17. Bloch recalled: "He was capable of asking something like this – it was the first question he posed to my then-fiancée – we saw him wistful, so to say, on the Kurfürstendamm [in Berlin] – wandering with lowered head – and she, the then-fiancée Karola, who was seeing him for the first time, and had heard through me so much about him, she asked him what he was thinking about and he answered: 'My dear, has the sickly appearance of Marzipan figures ever occurred to you?' " (*Ibid.*, p. 18.)

85. Cf. "We are not to philosophize about concrete things; we are to philosophize, rather, out of these things." (Adorno, *Negative Dialectics*, p. 33.)

86. Adorno, "Die Aktualität der Philosophie" (1931), *GS* 1, p. 326.

87. Ernst Bloch knew Simmel personally and provided a sympathetic channel through which Adorno was exposed to his thought. Adorno recognized his debt to Simmel in a lecture delivered in New York April 19, 1940. (Theodor W. Adorno, "Über das Problem der individuellen Kausalität bei Simmel," Frankfurt am Main, Adorno Estate.) See also *idem, Negative Dialectics*, p. 13; also the quotation in the following note.

88. "Georg Simmel . . . was surely the first, despite all his psychological idealism, to accomplish that return to concrete objects. . . . If at one time our reaction against Simmel was especially strong, then only because that with which he enticed us with the one hand, he held back from us with the other." (Theodor W. Adorno, "Henkel, Krug und frühe Erfahrung," *Ernst Bloch zu Ehren: Beiträge zu seinem Werk*, ed. S. Unseld [Frankfurt am

Main: Suhrkamp Verlag, 1966], pp. 11–12. On another occasion Adorno noted that Benjamin's efforts were related to Simmel's: "to lead philosophy out of the 'ice-deserts of abstraction' and to bring thoughts into concrete historical images." (Adorno, *Über Walter Benjamin*, p. 38.)

89. Georg Lukács, "Georg Simmel," originally published in *Pester Lloyd*, October 2, 1918, reprinted in *Buch des Dankes an Georg Simmel*, p. 172. In Lukács's pre-Marxist book of essays *Die Seelen und die Formen* (Berlin: Egon Fleischel & Co., 1911), some of this same concern for particularity was evident, but later, under the influence of Hegel, Lukács's thinking took on a holistic orientation. In other ways, however, Lukács remained indebted to Simmel. For example, it was Simmel who deplored the ossified cultural forms and saw them as the source of modern man's alienation, the same position which underlay Lukács's concept of "second nature."

90. Georg Simmel, "Soziologie der Mahlzeit," *Brücke und Tür* (Stuttgart: K. F. Koehler Verlag, 1957), p. 243.

91. *Ibid.*, pp. 245–250.

92. Walter Benjamin, *Einbahnstrasse* (1928), *Gesammelte Schriften*, 6 vols., ed. Rolf Tiedemann and Hermann Schweppenhäuser, vol. IV: *Kleine Prosa*, 2 vols., ed. Tillman Rexroth (Frankfurt am Main: Suhrkamp Verlag, 1972), vol. IV:1, p. 125.

93. Adorno later called such "Simmelia" as the "frame of mind, when one drinks a cup of tea, that the entire depth of being is immediately contained" in this moment an example of what Lukács "at a time when he was still really an autonomous thinker" called "making thought shallow by making it deep [*Verflachung durch Tiefe*]." (Theodor W. Adorno, *Philosophische Terminologie: Zur Einleitung*, 2 vols., ed. Rudolf zur Lippe [Frankfurt am Main: Suhrkamp Taschenbuch Verlag, 1973], vol. 1, p. 139.)

94. Theodor W. Adorno, "Einleitung zu Benjamins *Schriften*" (1955), *Über Walter Benjamin*, ed. Rolf Tiedemann (Frankfurt: Suhrkamp Verlag, 1970), p. 42.

95. Adorno, "Die Aktualität der Philosophie" (1931), *GS* 1, p. 336.

96. The theme of the dinner party invites a comparison with Horkheimer as well. In 1934 he published a book of aphorisms which also interpreted the social significance of everyday phenomena. One aphorism criticized the pseudo-fraternal spirit of New Year's Eve parties at hotels or nightclubs, which made it appear that "the differences between people, above all between poor and rich, are harmless." But that spirit was exposed as ideology by the gesture of a working girl who spilled wine on her dress: "While her face beamed with enthusiasm, reflecting the general gaiety, her hands proceeded with unconscious haste to remove the stain. This isolated hand betrayed the whole festive communality." (Max Horkheimer, *Dämmerung* [1934], p. 15.) Horkheimer's concern with the way a specific act reflected the particular class structure of society separated him too from Simmel. But despite important similarities with Benjamin, Horkheimer's approach was not identical: whereas he used gestures and details of behavior symbolically to illustrate social injustice by concrete example, Benjamin approached

the detail as a mystery containing the general in a way that had to be deciphered: natural objects needed to be "brought to speech" inductively, by means of critical interpretation. Adorno referred to "a certain broadness of interpretation" in Horkheimer's *Dämmerung* which at first "annoyed me in certain aphorisms"; but when he read the finished book he could "almost completely identify with it — so completely that it is difficult for me to point to differences." (Letter, Adorno to Lowenthal, July 6, 1934, cited in Jay, *The Dialectical Imagination,* p. 66.)

97. Walter Benjamin, *Der Begriff der Kunstkritik in der deutschen Romantik* (first published 1920), ed. Hermann Schweppenhäuser (Frankfurt am Main: Suhrkamp Verlag, 1973).

98. See above, Chapter 1.

99. Cf. "It is not up to philosophy to exhaust things according to scientific usage, to reduce the phenomena to a minimum of propositions. . . . Instead, in philosophy we literally seek to immerse ourselves in things that are heterogeneous . . . without placing those things in prefabricated categories." (Adorno, *Negative Dialectics,* p. 13.) That the particular could not even be adequately comprehended as a case of the concept has been illustrated in Chapter 3: a natural object was not only natural but historical; a historical phenomenon was not merely history but material nature. (Cf. "objects do not go into their concepts without leaving a remainder. . . ." *[Ibid.,* p. 5.]*)

100. One is reminded of Marx's comment "A Negro is a Negro. He only becomes a slave in certain relations." (Karl Marx, "Wage Labour and Capital," *Karl Marx and Frederick Engels: Selected Works* (New York: International Publishers, 1972), p. 81.

101. Leibniz challenged the principle of identity as it applied to the issue of universals and the problem of the identity of indiscernibles. In his *Monadology* he wrote: "It is necessary, indeed, that each monad be different from every other. For there are never in nature two beings which are exactly alike and in which it is not possible to find an internal difference. . . ." (Gottfried Wilhelm Leibniz, *"Die Monadologie," Hauptschriften zur Grundlegung der Philosophie,* ed. Ernst Cassirer [Leipzig, 1906], vol. 2, pp. 436–437.)

102. "The idea is a monad. That means in brief, every idea contains an image of the world." (Walter Benjamin, *Ursprung des deutschen Trauerspiels,* ed. Rolf Tiedemann [Frankfurt am Main: Suhrkamp Taschenbuch Verlag, 1972], p. 32.)

103. Cf. "What dissolves the fetish [i.e., the "given" object] is the insight that things are not simply so and not otherwise, that they have come to be under certain conditions." (Adorno, *Negative Dialectics,* p. 52.)

104. See above, Chapter 3.

105. "While he [Bloch] pursued the historico-philosophical character of utopia materialistically in the illusionless struggle for the fundamental necessities of life, he searched for the 'traces' of utopia, of finite redemption shining into [the present], in the smallest features of . . . reality. . . ." (T. W. Adorno, "Für Ernst Bloch," *Aufbau-Reconstruction* 8, 48 [November 27, 1942], p. 17.)

106. Bloch introduced this term in *Geist der Utopie* (1923).

107. Bloch had published a book in 1930 which described these "traces" in aphoristic fragments. (See Ernst Bloch, *Spuren*, new ed., enl. [Frankfurt am Main: Suhrkamp Verlag, 1969].)

108. Adorno, "Die Aktualität der Philosophie" (1931), *GS* 1, p. 325.

109. Theodor W. Adorno, "Schubert" (1928), *Moments Musicaux: Neugedruckte Aufsätze, 1928 bis 1962* (Frankfurt am Main: edition Suhrkamp, 1964), p. 26.

110. Adorno, "Die Aktualität der Philosophie" (1931), *GS* 1, p. 325.

111. Cf., e.g., Horkheimer, "Hegel und das Problem der Metaphysik" (1932); Herbert Marcuse, "The Concept of Essence" (1936), *Negations: Essays in Critical Theory*, trans. Jeremy J. Shapiro (Boston: Beacon Press, 1968), pp. 43-87.

112. Cf. "the concept of ideology makes sense only in relation to the truth or untruth of what it refers to." (Adorno, *Negative Dialectics*, p. 197.)

113. A summary of the *Trauerspiel* theory is given below, pp. 91-92.

114. Benjamin, *Ursprung des deutschen Trauerspiels* (1927), p. 17.

115. Brentano (1838-1917) was a neo-Kantian philosopher who taught in Vienna.

116. It was the meaning of what Adorno later called the "*Vorrang des Objects*" ("preponderence of the object"). (See Adorno, *Negative Dialectics*, pp. 182-186.)

117. Cf. Adorno, *Metakritik der Erkenntnistheorie*, *GS* 5, pp. 7-245.

118. This was, of course, just the point on which Adorno's early mentor, Hans Cornelius, had "fallen behind Kant." (See above, Chapter 1.)

119. "The idea of life and afterlife in a work of art should be regarded with an entirely unmetaphorical objectivity. Even in times of narrowly prejudiced thought there was an inkling that life was not limited to organic corporeality." (Walter Benjamin, "The Task of the Translator" [1923], *Illuminations*, ed. and introd. Hannah Arendt, trans. Harry Zohn [New York: Schocken Books, 1969], p. 71.)

120. In *Dialektik der Aufklärung* (first published in 1947) Adorno wrote that the archaic origin of "aura" was the "mana" of natural objects whereby primitive men acknowledged the objects' otherness. Mana was the source of both terror and sacredness. "When the tree is no longer approached merely as tree, but as evidence for an Other, as the location of *mana*, language expresses the contradiction that something is itself and at the same time something other than itself, identical and not identical." That Adorno's conception of the object had more in common with this view of the tree than with Husserl's of his apple tree is clear. (Max Horkheimer and Theodor W. Adorno, *Dialectic of Enlightenment*, trans. John Cumming [New York: Herder and Herder, 1972], p. 15.)

121. One of Husserl's motives for attempting to establish phenomenology as a "pure" and "scientific" method was to fight the kind of relativism which, as he was well aware, had caused such trouble for Dilthey because he had acknowledged historical particularity. (Nonetheless, Husserl late in life be-

gan to see validity in Dilthey's concept of *Leben*, and worked with it in his own theoretical writings.)

122. Adorno, "Die Aktualität der Philosophie" (1931), *GS* 1, p. 334.

123. Dilthey's stress on intentional meaning led his theory into an irreconcilable paradox: If the goal of interpreting historical texts was reliving through empathetic understanding the psychological experiences of past eras, then implied was the assumption of an ahistorical similarity of subjects, a universal core of human nature which cancelled out the very historical particularity which had been the *raison d'être* of a *geisteswissenschaftliche* method in the first place. The Diltheyan interpreter reexperienced himself; he could understand only his own likeness, and hence his knowledge could disclose nothing new. As Rolf Tiedemann has written: "thus the Diltheyan historian acknowledges in history only what extends into the present, which is an 'expression' of his own 'life,' and thereby accessible to his 'understanding.' " (Tiedemann, *Studien zur Philosophie Walter Benjamins*, p. 115.) Dilthey became caught in a circle of psychological subjectivism, while historical relativism threatened all judgments concerning reality external to the subject. But when the nonidentity between written word and subjective intent was recognized, and when the former rather than the latter became the focus of interpretation, as historical phenomena with no eternal meaning but instead a life and death of their own, then the whole Diltheyan difficulty was avoided (cf. Chapter 3).

124. Adorno, "Die Aktualität der Philosophie" (1931), *GS* 1, p. 336.

125. Cf. Walter Benjamin, "Goethes Wahlverwandtschaften" (1924), reprinted in Johann Wolfgang Goethe, *Die Wahlverwandtschaften* (Frankfurt am Main: Insel Verlag, 1972), p. 273.

126. "Wanting to make the *Wahlverwandtschaften* accessible to understanding by means of the author's own words is a misplaced effort. They are precisely suited for barring criticism from access. . . . [The reason lies] in the tendency to leave unnoticed all that which the author's own explanation disavows." (*Ibid.*, p. 275.)

127. For Benjamin, the truth content of an artwork was not identical to its substantive content: "For, in separating within the work, they [*Wahrheitsgehalt* and *Sachgehalt*] decide the question of its immortality. In this sense, the history of the works prepares their critique, the power of which is thus increased by historical distance." (*Ibid.*, pp. 255–256.)

128. Cf. above, Chapter 3.

129. Theodor W. Adorno, "Sakrales Fragment: Über Schönberg's Moses und Aron," lecture in Berlin (April 1963), in *Quasi una Fantasia: Musikalische Schriften II* (Frankfurt am Main: Suhrkamp Verlag, 1963), p. 308.

130. Walter Benjamin, *Passagenarbeit* ms., cited in Tiedemann, *Studien zur Philosophie Walter Benjamins*, p. 106.

131. [Adorno] , "Kunst und Musiksoziologie," *Soziologische Exkurse*, p. 93.

132. A comparison with Lukács on this point is illuminating. Lukács condemned late bourgeois philosophy almost *in toto* as ideology (see Georg Lukács, *Die Zerstörung der Vernunft: Der Weg des Irrationalismus von Schelling zu*

Hitler [Berlin: Aufbau Verlag, 1953]). Yet he considered art another matter. With his preference for classical aesthetics, he continued to praise writers like Shakespeare, Balzac, and Thomas Mann, claiming their objectivity enabled them to capture social truth in their works despite their lack of radical political consciousness. What allowed him to make an exception of certain bourgeois artists was far less his Marxist theory than a residual romantic concept of the artist as capable of immediate intuitions of truth. In contrast, Adorno's opposition, whether or not it was more "Marxist," was at least more consistent.

133. Lukács, *History and Class Consciousness,* p. 122.

134. However, the theme of ruptures and breaks occurs in Benjamin's early writings as well: first, in the sense that reality is *"brüchig"* and forms no harmonious totality; second in his notion of the rupture between the truth (*Wahrheitsgehalt*) and substance (*Sachgehalt*) of a work of art occurring with the historical passage of time (Benjamin, "Goethes Wahlverwandtschaften," pp. 255–256).

135. Theodor W. Adorno, "Der wunderliche Realist: Über Siegfried Kracauer," *Noten zur Literatur,* vol. 3 (Frankfurt am Main: Suhrkamp Verlag, 1965), p. 84.

136. Adorno, "Die Aktualität der Philosophie" (1931), *GS* 1, p. 334.

137. *Ibid.,* p. 336.

138. Cited in Benjamin, *Der Begriff der Kunstkritik in der deutschen Romantik,* p. 54.

139. Positivism and existentialism converged in their passive acceptance of the object as given. Hence, for example, Heidegger's "materialist" assertion that there was no realm of essences behind the phenomena could be interpreted as a positivistic element in his existentialist phenomenology.

140. Adorno, "Die Aktualität der Philosophie" (1931), *GS* 1, p. 334.

141. Cf. "In sharp contrast to the usual ideal of science, the objectivity of dialectical cognition needs not less subjectivity but more. Philosophical experience withers otherwise. But our positivistic *Zeitgeist* is allergic to this need." (Adorno, *Negative Dialectics,* p. 40.)

CHAPTER 5

1. See Chapter 2.

2. *"Das Einzelne ist nichts, das Volk alles."*

3. In *Negative Dialektik* Adorno called this line "as false as any bromide ever. A dissenter's exact imagination [*exakte Fantasie* — discussed below] can see more than a thousand eyes peering through the same pink spectacles, confusing what they see with universal truth, and regressing. Against this stands the individuation of knowledge." (Adorno, *Negative Dialectics,* trans. E. B. Ashton [New York: The Seabury Press, 1973], pp. 46–47.)

4. Georg Lukács, *History and Class Consciousness,* trans. Rodney Livingstone (Cambridge Mass.: The M.I.T. Press, 1971), p. 193.

5. Cf. "For Lukács the counter-concept to reification was that of class consciousness. For Adorno it is the concept of experience. . . ." Friedemann Grenz, *Adornos Philosophie in Grundschriften: Auflösung einiger Deutungsprobleme* (Frankfurt am Main: Suhrkamp Verlag, 1974), p. 44.

6. Cf. "The individual consciousness is almost always the unhappy one, and with good reason. In his aversion to it, Hegel refuses to face the very fact he underscores where it suits him: how much universality is inherent in that individuality." (Adorno, *Negative Dialectics*, p. 45.)

7. It is a mistake to interpret Adorno's stress on the individual as fundamentally Left Hegelian. He was not reducing reality to the ego, not placing the "I" at the center of thought, nor was he holding that a change in consciousness was sufficient for changing reality. Instead he was saying that cognitive experience was always particular and individual, and that the nature of the social whole was revealed to the individual through the specific configuration of empirical matter.

8. Ernst Bloch, *Geist der Utopie*, 2nd ed., rev. (Berlin: Paul Cassirer, 1923), p. 226.

9. Adorno, *Negative Dialectics*, p. xx.

10. Adorno, "Die Aktualität der Philosophie (1931), *Gesammelte Schriften*, vol. 1: *Frühe philosophische Schriften*, ed. Rolf Tiedemann (Frankfurt am Main: Suhrkamp Verlag, 1973), p. 333.

11. Max Horkheimer, "Hegel und das Problem der Metaphysik," *Festschrift für Carl Grünberg: Zum 70. Geburtstag* (Leipzig: Verlag von C. L. Hirschfeld, 1932), p. 191.

12. In positing the priority of matter, Adorno was opposing the whole thrust of idealism which, because it viewed objective reality as first constituted by the subject, could not consider that reality as a prerequisite for subjectivity, and thus was led to develop the theory of the transcendental subject.

13. The important document in this connection is Max Horkheimer's 1936 article in the *Zeitschrift für Sozialforschung*, "Egoism und Freiheitsbewegung," which influenced Adorno considerably.

14. This orientation separates Adorno's concept of *Erfahrung* from the *Erlebnis*, or "lived experience," of *Lebensphilosophie*. For the latter, lived experience came first, and philosophical reflection followed (the existence-precedes-essence postulate of all existentialism); but for Adorno reflection was itself lived experience, dialectical social praxis that was somatic as well as cerebral.

15. Adorno, "Charakteristik Walter Benjamins" (1950), *Über Walter Benjamin* (Frankfurt am Main: Suhrkamp Verlag, 1970), p. 11. (The English translation in *Prisms* [p. 240] has not been used here because it is incorrect.)

16. Horkheimer, "Traditional and Critical Theory" (1937), *Critical Theory: Selected Essays*, trans. Matthew J. O'Connell et al. (New York: Herder and Herder, 1972), p. 211.

17. Cf. [Institut für Sozialforschung,] *Studien über Autorität und Familie*, ed. Max Horkheimer (Paris: Felix Alcan, 1936).

18. While Horkheimer *described* the individual as dialectically related to the totality of class society, Adorno dialectically *juxtaposed* "individual" and "society" so that each provided a criticism of the other (see above, Chapter 3).

19. Cf. Theodor W. Adorno, "Über Mannheims Wissenssoziologie," 1947(?), Frankfurt am Main, Adorno Estate, p. 5.

20. Adorno, unpublished Mannheim article, 1937, p. 5. Cf. also the introduction to *Negative Dialektik*, where a rare acknowledgment of the role of class appears almost parenthetically in an argument which first defends the "privileged" character of philosophical experience: "Elitist pride would be the last thing to befit the philosophic experience. He who has it must admit to himself how much, according to his possibilities in existence, his experience has been contaminated by existence, and ultimately by the class relationship." (Adorno, *Negative Dialectics*, p. 42).

21. Adorno, "Über Mannheims Wissenssoziologie," 1947(?), p. 4.

22. See above, Chapter 3.

23. On the dialectical nature of this interrelationship, see a later essay (unsigned but surely by Adorno): "The [bourgeois] individual misconstrues the world, upon which the very core of him depends, mistaking it for his own." (Institut für Sozialforschung, "Individuum," *Soziologische Exkurse* [vol. 4 of *Frankfurter Beiträge zur Soziologie*, eds. Theodor W. Adorno and Walter Dirks] [Frankfurt am Main: Europäische Verlagsanstalt, 1956], p. 49.)

24. The corollary, of course, was its definition of false consciousness as "conformism" (*Anpassung*), a concept central to Adorno's critique of mass culture.

25. That such heroes abounded in Adorno's generation, and that precisely these "outsiders" formed the intellectual "insiders" of Weimar Germany, has been argued by Peter Gay in *Weimar Culture: The Outsider as Insider* (New York: Harper Torchbooks, 1968). Just what the socioeconomic conditions were which enabled this generation of outsiders to flourish and remain at least solvent economically during the twenties is a question Adorno never addressed, any more than he dealt with the role of class or social relations of production in the work of the intellectual.

26. This failure is documented in the history of Franz Pfemfert's journal *Die Aktion*, which began in 1911 as a platform for expressionist literature and radical politics. The inability to merge aesthetic and political radicalism led Pfemfert to abandon the former and turn *Die Aktion* into a purely political (Communist-revolutionary) organ. (Cf. *Ich schneide die Zeit aus: Expressionismus und Politik in Franz Pfemfert's 'Die Aktion,' 1911–1918*, ed. Paul Raabe [Munich: Deutscher Taschenbuch Verlag, 1964].)

27. It should be pointed out that when Adorno rejected the bourgeois conception of the subject as a transcendental universal, he also challenged its democratic implications (the universality of human rational faculties, the principle of government by consensus, the axiomatic "one man, one vote" which affirmed the identity and exchangeability of subjects). Yet

Adorno was nothing if not a democrat. Some of his most exciting thoughts involve the implications of the principle of nonidentity for a new conception of political democracy, one based on the acknowledgment of individual uniqueness where "discrimination" loses its pejorative, racist connotation and becomes the ability to discern what makes for social justice in qualitative as well as quantitative terms. (See, e.g., Adorno, *Negative Dialectics*, pp. 43–44 and *passim*.)

28. Fritz K. Ringer, *The Decline of the German Mandarins: The German Academic Community, 1890–1933* (Cambridge, Mass.: Harvard University Press, 1969).

29. "Granted, philosophical experiences are indeed not equally accessible to everyone. . . . [T]he virtually subjectless rationality of a scientific idea . . . regards all men as interchangeable. . . . While the argument pretends to be democratic, it ignores what the administered world makes of its compulsory members. Only a mind which it has not entirely molded can withstand it. Criticizing privilege becomes a privilege — the world's course is as dialectical as that." (Adorno, *Negative Dialectics*, p. 41.)

30. See above, Chapter 2.

31. The attempt of, e.g., Martin Buber to transform the subject-object dialectic of Hegel into an intersubjective I-thou relationship left Adorno singularly unimpressed, as did Dilthey's notion of knowledge as "understanding" (*Verstehen*) through "empathy" (*Einfühlung*). Benjamin once commented to Adorno: "I am interested not in men, but only in things."

32. Adorno, *Negative Dialectics*, p. 41.

33. But the dimension of intersubjectivity was fundamental to the *social* (as opposed to purely cognitive) nature of the dialectic, both in its Hegelian form (the master-slave dialectic) and the Marxian form of class struggle. It was in fact the hinge between cognition and the real transformation of society. Habermas's recent theory of social interaction and his conception of utopia in terms of a truly democratic consensus achieved through "undistorted communication" can be seen as an attempt to remedy this gap in Adorno's theory. At the same time, like Adorno, Habermas holds on to the individuality of the subject — consensus is to be reached by a dialogue between equals, not by the dictates of ruling class or Communist Party. (See Jürgen Habermas, "Können komplexe Gesellschaften eine vernünftige Identität ausbilden?" in *idem* and Dieter Henrich, *Zwei Reden: Aus Anlass des Hegel-Preises* [Frankfurt am Main: Suhrkamp Verlag, 1974].)

34. Adorno, *Negative Dialectics*, p. 25.

35. Letter, Benjamin to Adorno, December 1, 1932, cited by the editor in Walter Benjamin, *Gesammelte Schriften*, 6 vols., ed. Rolf Tiedemann and Hermann Schweppenhäuser, vol. III: *Kritiken und Rezensionen*, ed. Hella Tiedemann-Bartels (Frankfurt am Main: Suhrkamp Verlag, 1972), p. 661.

36. Letter, Adorno to Benjamin, August 7, 1935, in Adorno, *Über Walter Benjamin*, p. 112.

37. Benjamin, *Ursprung des deutschen Trauerspiels*, ed. Rolf Tiedemann (Frankfurt am Main: Suhrkamp Verlag, 1972), p. 17.

38. Adorno, *Negative Dialectics*, p. 28.

39. "to those objects, philosophy would truly give itself rather than use them as a mirror in which to reread itself, mistaking its own image for concretion." (*Ibid.*, p. 13.)

40. Adorno, "Die Aktualität der Philosophie" (1931), *GS* 1, pp. 341–342.

41. *Ibid.*, p. 342. The term "fantasy" had recently been revived in philosophical parlance by Husserl, whose phenomenological method granted "fantasy" objects (the mermaids and unicorns) the same philosophical dignity as empirical phenomena. Adorno's meaning was quite different. Indeed, he claimed even fiction could not bracket out empirical reality. In his critique of Husserl he wrote: "The material of every fantasy is bound to experience; hence . . . the shabby, illusory character of fantasy as fiction. . . . There is no pure fantasy; it is itself a fiction and indeed a false one, that is, one which fails to recognize the fundamental reference of thought to the factual." (Theodor W. Adorno, Husserl ms., 1934–1937, Frankfurt am Main, Adorno Estate, p. 122.)

42. Benjamin's tendency to allow the philosophical subject to sink so totally into the object that it disappeared became a central issue in his intellectual quarrel with Adorno during the thirties. (See Chapters 9 and 10.)

43. Adorno, "Die Aktualität der Philosophie" (1931), *GS* 1, p. 341. One year prior to this Benjamin had written a book review in which he juxtaposed the concepts of "exactness" and "fantasy." (See Benjamin, "Ein Jakobiner von heute" [1930], *Gesammelte Schriften* III, p. 260.) The term *exakte Fantasie* (translated as exact imagination) also appears in *Negative Dialectics*, p. 46 and *passim*.

44. Cf. Dilthey, who described the subject's role as one necessitating "imagination" (*Vorstellen*) in order to interpret cultural phenomena by reliving the human experience which they recorded. In contrast to Adorno's idea of the interpretive experience (*Erfahrung*) as a mimetic transformation of the nonidentical object, Dilthey's "lived" experience (*Erlebnis*) was based on the premise of intersubjective identity, i.e., the ability to put oneself in another's shoes.

45. Cf. one of the few passages in Horkheimer's writings where the word "fantasy" appears and has a very different meaning: "One thing which this way of thinking [Critical Theory] has in common with fantasy is that an image of the future which springs indeed from a deep understanding of the present determines men's thoughts and actions even in periods when the course of events seems to be leading far away from such a future and seems to justify every reaction except belief in fulfillment. It is not the arbitrariness and supposed independence of fantasy that is the common bind here, but its obstinacy." Fantasy here was the stubbornness of the moralist, his critical power to protest the given and imagine that things could and should be different. (Max Horkheimer, "Traditional and Critical Theory" (1937), *Critical Theory*, p. 220.)

46. Adorno, "Die Aktualität der Philosophie" (1931), *GS* 1, p. 342.

47. *Ibid.*, p. 334.

48. Benjamin, *Ursprung des deutschen Trauerspiels*, p. 10.

49. Cf. Walter Benjamin, "The Task of the Translator" (1923), *Illuminations*, ed. and introd. Hannah Arendt, trans. Harry Zohn (New York: Schocken Books, 1969), pp. 69-82. Adorno noted that he read this essay, which introduced Benjamin's Baudelaire translation, even before it was published, and it no doubt influenced his thinking in regard to musical reproduction. (Adorno, *Über Walter Benjamin*, p. 68.)

50. Cf. Theodor W. Adorno, notebooks on *Reproduktionstheorie*, 3 vols., unpublished, Frankfurt am Main, Adorno Estate, n.d., pp. 54 ff.

51. In 1936 Benjamin wrote that in the present era, the technological reproduction of artworks (by film, recording, etc.) had robbed art of its "aura" and transformed it into a political weapon. Adorno rightly considered Benjamin's affirmation of this development a betrayal of their earlier common position. (See Benjamin, "The Work of Art in the Age of Technical Reproduction," *Illuminations*, pp. 217-251; cf. letter, Adorno to Benjamin, March 18, 1936, *Über Walter Benjamin*, pp. 126-134.)

52. Rolf Tiedemann, *Studien zur Philosophie Walter Benjamins*, introd. Theodor W. Adorno (vol. 16 of Institut für Sozialforschung, *Frankfurter Beiträge zur Soziologie*, ed. Theodor W. Adorno and Walter Dirks) (Frankfurt am Main: Europäische Verlagsanstalt, 1965), p. 32.

53. Martin Jay, *The Dialectical Imagination: A History of the Frankfurt School and the Institute of Social Research, 1923-1950* (Boston: Little, Brown, 1973), p. 269.

54. *Ibid.* Jay mentions specifically its use by Tarde, LeBon, and Freud.

55. Max Horkheimer and Theodor W. Adorno, *Dialectic of Enlightenment*, trans. John Cumming (New York: Herder and Herder, 1972), p. 9.

56. *Ibid.*, pp. 18-19. Hence, because of its "aura": "The work of art still has something in common with enchantment" (p. 19).

57. Walter Benjamin, "Über das mimetische Vermögen" (n.d.), *Schriften*, 2 vols., ed. Theodor W. Adorno and Gretel Adorno (Frankfurt am Main: Suhrkamp Verlag, 1955) vol. 1, p. 507.

58. *Ibid.*

59. Tiedemann, *Studien zur Philosophie Walter Benjamins*, p. 125.

60. Cf. below, pages 101 ff.

61. Adorno, "Einleitung zu Benjamins 'Schriften'" (1955), *Über Walter Benjamin*, p. 34; also p. 71.

62. Theodor W. Adorno, "Thesen über die Sprache des Philosophen" (n.d., but clearly written in the early thirties), *GS* 1, p. 369.

63. Adorno wrote: "with his philosophy of language oriented on the cabbala, Benjamin saw subjective unity as scribbling of the name. That links his materialistic period with his theological one." (Adorno, "A Portrait of Walter Benjamin" [1950], *Prisms*, trans. Samuel and Shierry Weber [London: Neville Spearman, 1967], p. 236.)

64. Benjamin, "Über Sprache überhaupt und über die Sprache des Menschen" (1916), *Schriften*, vol. 2, p. 410.

65. Benjamin, *Ursprung des deutschen Trauerspiels*, p. 19.

66. Cf. *ibid.*, p. 18.

67. *Ibid.* Cf. "There is a gap between words and the thing they conjure up. . . ." (Adorno, *Negative Dialectics*, p. 53.)

68. Benjamin, "Über Sprache überhaupt . . ." (1916), *Schriften*, vol. 2, p. 417. "The crux of Benjamin's theory of language springs from its opposition to the traditional procedure of either making the phenomena dependent on the subject, in that arbitrary signs are affixed to them, or making it necessary for the speakers to mimetically identify themselves with the objects. Just as 'all great works' of literature contain 'between the lines their virtual translation' [Benjamin, "The Task of the Translator"] into other languages, so the names of the phenomena are virtually contained within them. Thus . . . [is Benjamin's theory of language] a theory of translation." (Tiedemann, *Studien zur Philosophie Walter Benjamins*, p. 32.)

69. Max Horkheimer, *Eclipse of Reason* (New York: Oxford University Press, 1947), p. 179. The language and the idea of this passage are more characteristic of Adorno than of Horkheimer.

70. Adorno, *Negative Dialectics*, pp. 17–18.

71. In a similar vein, Ernst Bloch had written in *Geist der Utopie* (1923): "Millions of proletariat have not yet spoken their word." (Bloch, *Geist der Utopie*, p. 318.)

72. Adorno, "Thesen über die Sprache des Philosophen," *GS* 1, p. 367.

73. Karl Marx, *Capital: A Critique of Political Economy*, 3 vols., ed. Frederick Engels and trans. Samuel Moore and Edward Aveling from 3rd German ed. (New York: International Publishers, 1967), vol. 1, p. 71. Cf. also Ernst Bloch: "Marx finally calls private interest by name as the strongest of all drives. . . ." (Bloch, *Geist der Utopie*, p. 322.)

74. Theodor W. Adorno, "Mahagonny" (1930), *Moments Musicaux* (Frankfurt am Main: edition Suhrkamp, 1964), pp. 132–133.

75. Rolf Tiedemann, "Nachwort," in Walter Benjamin, *Charles Baudelaire: Ein Lyriker im Zeitalter des Hochkapitalismus*, ed. Rolf Tiedemann (Frankfurt am Main: Suhrkamp Verlag, 1969), p. 169.

76. Adorno, "A Portrait of Walter Benjamin" (1950), *Prisms*, p. 231.

77. Benjamin was himself aware of the incompatibilities. Writing Adorno concerning the latter's *Versuch über Wagner*, he noted that this study's basic conception was polemical, but the concept of redeeming Wagner through criticism was problematic: "Redemption is a cyclical form, the polemic is a progressive one." (Letter, Benjamin to Adorno, June 19, 1938, Frankfurt am Main, Adorno Estate.)

78. An interesting early attempt by Adorno to translate the notion of the name from a theological to a Marxist context is his short piece "Notiz über Namen," which appeared in the *Frankfurter Zeitung*, August 7, 1930. Adorno pointed here to the class distinction which governed the relation-

ship of the individual to his name, and the social conditions which came to expression within the names themselves. (Frankfurt am Main, Adorno Estate.)

79. Cf. in *Eclipse of Reason*, a passage which again (cf. note 69) sounds more like Adorno than Horkheimer: "The transformation of this [the mimetic] impulse into the universal medium of language rather than into destructive action means that potentially nihilistic energies [the polemical side of "naming things"?] work for reconciliation." (Horkheimer, *Eclipse of Reason*, p. 179.)

80. Cf. Adorno and Horkheimer, *Dialectic of Enlightenment*, pp. 11 ff. In *Negative Dialektik*, Adorno summarized this notion: "The idea of discrimination, of the nuance . . . has never been quite forgotten. . . . Its postulate of a capacity to experience the object — and discrimination is the experience of the object turned into a form of subjective reaction — provides a haven for the mimetic element of knowledge, for the element of elective affinity between the knower and the known.

"In the total process of enlightenment this element gradually crumbles. But it cannot vanish completely if the process is not to annul itself. Even in the conception of rational knowledge, devoid of all affinity, there survives a groping for that concordance which the magical delusion used to place beyond doubt. If this moment were extinguished altogether, it would be flatly incomprehensible that a subject can know an object; the unleashed rationality would be irrational. In being secularized, however, the mimetic element in turn blends with the rational one. The word for this process is discrimination." (Adorno, *Negative Dialectics*, pp. 44–45.)

81. Cf. "The language of philosophy approaches that name by denying it. The claim of immediate truth for which it chides the words is almost always the ideology of a positive, existent identity of word and thing." (Adorno, *Negative Dialectics*, p. 53.) This statement was an explicit criticism of Benjamin, whom Adorno felt came to depend too much on the cognitive power of the "name."

82. *Ibid.*

83. *Ibid.*

84. In his speech Adorno manifested certain misgivings about the term, suggesting also "a less astrological and scientifically more current expression: . . . trial combinations [*Versuchsanordnungen*]. . . ." The term was actually from Brecht's theory of epic theater. (Adorno, "Die Aktualität der Philosophie" [1931], *GS* 1, p. 335.) Yet the word *Konstellation* keeps appearing in his writings, including his major late works (cf. *Negative Dialectics*, pp. 162–164 and *passim*), and this despite his own critical study of horoscopes and astrology as a "culture industry" (cf. Theodor W. Adorno, "The Stars Down to Earth" [1952–1953], *Gesammelte Schriften*, vol. 9: *Soziologische Schriften II*, vol. 2, ed. Susan Buck-Morss and Rolf Tiedemann [Frankfurt am Main: Suhrkamp Verlag, 1975]).

85. Benjamin, "Über das mimetische Vermögen" (n.d.), *Schriften*, vol. 1, p. 508.

86. Walter Benjamin, "Über das Programm der kommenden Philosophie" (1918), *Zur Kritik der Gewalt und andere Aufsätze*, afterword by Herbert Marcuse (Frankfurt am Main: edition Suhrkamp, 1965), p. 10.

87. The word "constellation" occurs occasionally in Horkheimer's essays (e.g., *Critical Theory*, p. 237), but it refers to clusters of elements in reality rather than the structure of their interpretation.

88. Benjamin, "Über das Programm der kommenden Philosophie," p. 10.

89. *Ibid.*, p. 23.

90. There were also statements the ambivalence of which became the source of controversy between them in the thirties.

91. Steiner has written regarding Benjamin's *Trauerspiel* chapter: "The preliminary '*Erkenntniskritische Vorrede*' (an almost untranslatable rubric) is notorious as being one of the most opaque, charged texts in the entirety of European thought." (George Steiner, "The Uncommon Reader," *Times Literary Supplement*, October 25, 1974, p. 1198.)

92. Benjamin had written a critical study of Goethe's novel, *Elective Affinities*, in 1924 (cf. Walter Benjamin, "Goethes Wahlverwandtschaften," *Schriften*, vol. 1, pp. 55–140).

93. Cf. above, page 87.

94. Benjamin, *Ursprung des deutschen Trauerspiels*, p. 11.

95. *Ibid.*, p. 10.

96. *Ibid.*, p. 15.

97. In Benjamin's *Trauerspiel* theory, knowledge and truth, like concept and idea, although not identical, were not totally separate either. As Tiedemann notes: "truth retains a logical character; it is comprehensible only as 'knowledge.' . . ." (Tiedemann, *Studien zur Philosophie Walter Benjamins*, p. 22.)

98. Cf. Benjamin, *Ursprung des deutschen Trauerspiels*, p. 15.

99. The *Trauerspiel* chapter appears to be ambiguous as to the role of the subject. On the one hand, it maintains that the idea is "a pre-given" (*ein Vorgegebenes*) which presents itself to the contemplative gaze, a Husserlian (and also a mystical) notion, implying that the subject is less the constructor of the ideas than their discoverer. (Such manifestations of an undialectical positivist tendency in Benjamin's theory were a point of dispute between him and Adorno in the 1930s.) On the other hand, he made it quite clear that the pregiven ideas were not identical to the phenomena in their empirical form — "The ideas are not given in the world of phenomena" (p. 17) — and that conceptualizing which broke the phenomena apart into their elements was necessary before they became represented as ideas. The ambiguity in Benjamin's meaning is lessened by keeping in mind that for him the "concept" was virtually synonymous with the "name"; that is, it didn't generalize, but articulated the object's concrete particularity, and *transformed* the object at the same time by translating it into words. As Tiedemann has pointed out, the existence of the ideas was dependent upon their philosophical, verbal representation by the subject: "Truth only comes to be in its construction." (Tiedemann,

Studien zur Philosophie Walter Benjamins, p. 22.) Further, as nonidentical to the "given," the ideas were antipositivistic and indeed, socially critical: "Their existence [*Sein*] falls together with the negation of the specific historical products; it is a criticism of the merely existing reality [*des bloss Seienden*]." (*Ibid.*, p. 33.)

100. Benjamin, *Ursprung des deutschen Trauerspiels*, p. 16.

101. Adorno, "Portrait of Walter Benjamin," *Prisms*, p. 231.

102. Cf.: Tiedemann, *Studien zur Philosophie Walter Benjamins*, p. 23.

103. "The ideas are eternal constellations and in grasping the elements in such constellations, the phenomena are divided up [via concepts] and redeemed at the same time." (Benjamin, *Ursprung des deutschen Trauerspiels*, p. 16.)

104. *Ibid.*, p. 17.

105. Cf. "The interpretative eye which sees more in a phenomenon than it is — and solely because of what it is — secularizes metaphysics." (Adorno, *Negative Dialectics*, p. 28.)

106. See above, Chapter 1.

107. Benjamin, *Ursprung des deutschen Trauerspiels*, p. 13.

108. "The program of Benjamin's philosophy from the time of the *Trauerspiel* book is the anti-idealistic construction of the intelligible world" [that noumenal realm which Kant had sundered from the world of empirical experience]. (Tiedemann, *Studien zur Philosophie Walter Benjamins*, p. 23.)

109. In the case of Benjamin, precise documentation of this development is difficult, because his most significant work, the *Passagenarbeit*, which was begun in the late twenties and remained unfinished in manuscript form at the time of his death in 1940, is largely undated.

110. Adorno, "Die Aktualität der Philosophie" (1931), *GS* 1, p. 336.

111. Benjamin, *Ursprung des deutschen Trauerspiels*, p. 19.

112. "Only an essentially undialectical philosophy directed toward ahistorical truth could suppose that the old problems would be laid aside by forgetting them and starting again from scratch." (Adorno, "Die Aktualität der Philosophie" [1931], *GS* 1, p. 339.)

113. Adorno, "Thesen über die Sprache des Philosophen" (n.d.), *GS* 1, p. 368.

114. The theme of redemption in Adorno's inaugural lecture lacked such a theological connotation. Borrowing an image from Heidegger (yet reversing its context), Adorno compared the philosopher to a cat burglar stealing what he can use from the decaying edifice of bourgeois culture: "For this house, this big house, has long since decayed in its foundations, and threatens not only to destroy all inside it, but to cause all things to vanish which are stored within it, and of which much is irreplaceable. If the cat burglar steals these things, singular, often half-forgotten things, he does a good deed, provided that they are only rescued; he will scarcely hold onto them for long, since they are for him of only scant worth." (Adorno, "Die Aktualität der Philosophie" [1931], *GS* 1, p. 340.)

115. Letter, Adorno to Benjamin, December 5, 1934 (Frankfurt am Main, Adorno Estate).

116. Benjamin, *Ursprung des deutschen Trauerspiels*, p. 30.

117. *Ibid.*, pp. 32–33. Cf. "Only a philosophy in the form of fragments would give to the monads, which idealism illusorily proposed, their proper place." (Theodor W. Adorno, *Negative Dialektik, Gesammelte Schriften*, vol. 6, ed. Rolf Tiedemann [Frankfurt am Main: Suhrkamp Verlag, 1973], p. 39.)

118. Benjamin, *Ursprung des deutschen Trauerspiels*, p. 20.

119. "Every idea is a sun and relates to its own kind just as suns relate to each other." (*Ibid.*, p. 19.) The image is suggestive of the mystic-influenced tradition of neo-Platonism.

120. *Ibid.*

121. *Ibid.*, pp. 8, 29.

122. *Ibid.*, p. 26.

123. Cf. Adorno, "Die Aktualität der Philosophie" (1931), *GS* 1, pp. 343–344.

124. *Ibid.*, p. 334.

125. *Ibid.*, p. 335.

126. Theodor W. Adorno, "Soziologie und empirische Forschung" (1957), *Gesammelte Schriften*, vol. 8: *Soziologische Schriften I* (Frankfurt am Main: Suhrkamp Verlag, 1972), p. 196.

CHAPTER 6

1. ". . . the function which the traditional philosophical question expected of supra-historical, symbolically meaningful ideas is accomplished by inner-historically constituted, non-symbolic ones." (Theodor W. Adorno, "Die Aktualität der Philosophie" [1931], *Gesammelte Schriften*, vol. 1: *Frühe philosophische Schriften*, ed. Rolf Tiedemann [Frankfurt am Main: Suhrkamp Verlag, 1973], p. 337.)

2. Karl Marx, *Capital: A Critique of Political Economy*, 3 vols., ed. Frederick Engels, trans. Samuel Moore and Edward Aveling from 3rd German ed. (New York: International Publishers, 1967), vol. 1, p. 72.

3. Adorno, "Die Aktualität der Philosophie" (1931), *GS* 1, p. 342. Again, the prefix *um* implies a dialectical reversal.

4. ". . . because precisely as a program, as general and complete, this program does not allow itself to be worked out. . . ." (*Ibid.*, p. 339.)

5. *Ibid.*, p. 334.

6. *Ibid.* and *passim*.

7. *Ibid.*, p. 340.

8. "The old idealism chose too large. . . . [Its ontological categories, such as "man"] don't even come close to fitting the keyhole; pure philosophical sociologism chooses too small [e.g., "social groups"]; granted, the key

goes in, but the door doesn't open." (*Ibid.*) In 1966 Adorno stressed the necessity of more than one key: "As a constellation, theoretical thought circles the concept it would like to unseal, hoping that it may fly open like the lock of a well-guarded safe-deposit box: in response, not to a single key or a single number, but to a combination of numbers." Theodor W. Adorno, *Negative Dialectics,* trans. E. B. Ashton [New York: The Seabury Press, 1973], p. 163.)

9. Adorno, "Die Aktualität der Philosophie" (1931), *GS* 1, p. 336.

10. Marx's critical concepts related the particular to the social totality rather than abstracting it from its sociohistorical context by classifying it as a case of the general. Mannheim's deradicalization of Marx's concept of ideology in *Ideologie und Utopie* (1929) was an example of the latter.

11. It has been argued in this study that the concept of the proletariat played no substantial role in Adorno's theory (see Chapter 2) and that he rejected the idea that class struggle could provide history with meaning in the sense of teleological progress (Chapter 3). Only in the sense described above, as a sociological category which could be used as an interpretive tool, did Adorno incorporate the concept of class into this theory (and even here, it was the bourgeois class, not the proletariat, which was the focus of his analysis). In the 1940s he questioned the adequacy of Marx's concept of class as well, and considered its reformulation necessary. (See Adorno, "Reflexionen zur Klassentheorie" [1942], *Gesammelte Schriften,* vol. 8: *Soziologische Schriften I,* ed. Rolf Tiedemann [Frankfurt am Main: Suhrkamp Verlag, 1972], pp. 373-391.)

12. Here Adorno drew on the sociopsychoanalytic research of the *Institut für Sozialforschung* (especially Erich Fromm's work) on problems of authoritarianism and the family. In fact, Adorno's understanding of the relationship between interpretive philosophy and knowledge as research paralleled his own relationship with the Institute.

13. Theodor W. Adorno, "Musikalische Warenanalysen" (written 1934-1940, first published 1955), *Quasi una Fantasia: Musikalische Schriften II* (Frankfurt am Main: Suhrkamp Verlag, 1963), p. 60.

14. *Ibid.* The combination of "daring" and "security" in this description is an example of the juxtaposition of extremes, discussed below.

15. *Ibid.,* p. 61.

16. *Ibid.*

17. *Ibid.*

18. Theodor W. Adorno, *Versuch über Wagner* (written 1937-1938) (Frankfurt am Main: Suhrkamp Verlag, 1952), p. 34.

19. *Ibid.*

20. Adorno preferred the word "image" (*Bild*) to "symbol," because the latter had too subjective a connotation, referring to the mental mediation of reality whereby a sensory object acquires *intentional* meaning. "Images," on the other hand, were pictures of objective representations; they were *unintentional* truth.

21. See below, pages 101-103.

22. Marx, *Capital,* vol. 1, pp. 35-83.

23. In differentiation, mimesis and conceptualization converged. Cf. "In being secularized, however, the mimetic element in turn blends with the rational one. The word for this process is discrimination. It contains the faculty of mimetic reaction as well as the logical organ for the relation of genus, species, and *differentia specifica*." (Adorno, *Negative Dialectics*, p. 45.)

24. Theodor W. Adorno, "Ravel" (1930), *Moments Musicaux: Neugedruckte Aufsätze, 1928 bis 1962* (Frankfurt am Main: Suhrkamp Verlag, 1964), p. 69.

25. *Ibid.*, p. 70.

26. Adorno not infrequently affirmed aristocratic consciousness over that of the bourgeoisie. Yet if the superfluous social function of the nobility made possible a certain clarity of vision, it was a limited one, stopping short of revolutionary implications. On Ravel: "His sorrow chooses the image of child-likeness because the image congeals into nature, and, concretely as music, into the [second-] nature material of tonality and the harmonic row." (*Ibid.*)

27. Cf. above, Chapter 3.

28. "*Das Leben lebt nicht.*" (Actually a quotation from Ferdinand Kürnberger which Adorno used as a motto for part I of his *Minima Moralia* [Frankfurt am Main: Suhrkamp Verlag, 1969], p. 13.)

29. "The new phase of musical consciousness of the masses is defined by hostility to gratification within gratification [*Genussfeindschaft in Genuss*]." (Theodor W. Adorno, "Über den Fetischcharakter in der Musik und die Regression des Hörens" [1938], *Dissonanzen: Musik in der verwalteten Welt*, 4th ed. [Göttingen: Vandenhoeck & Ruprecht, 1969], p. 14.) Cf. "Aldous Huxley raised the question in an essay: who in an amusement house still actually amuses himself? With equal right it may be asked: whom does entertainment music still entertain?" (*Ibid.*, p. 10.)

30. Walter Benjamin, *Ursprung des deutschen Trauerspiels*, ed. Rolf Tiedemann (Frankfurt am Main: Suhrkamp Verlag, 1972), p. 16.

31. See above, Chapter 3.

32. Adorno (pseud. Hektor Rottweiler), "Über Jazz" (1936), reprinted in Adorno, *Moments Musicaux*, p. 86.

33. *Ibid.*, p. 89.

34. When Adorno referred to the "origin" (*Ursprung*) of a phenomenon, he meant it in a historical but not a historian's sense. He was less concerned with the possibility of actually documenting a connection between an earlier and a later phenomenon (although he did this when possible), more concerned with historical archetypes, prototypes for the structure of present phenomena. "Origin" really meant the appearance of something in history in a particular social constellation through which its present meaning could be deciphered. Again, Benjamin's influence was evident. (The latter's definition of "origin" in the *Trauerspiel* study is translated below, in note 84 for this chapter.)

35. Adorno, "Über Jazz" (1936), *Moments Musicaux*, p. 105.

36. Adorno, *Versuch über Wagner*, p. 16.

37. *Ibid.*, p. 12.

38. *Ibid.*, p. 23.

39. Discussed in Chapter 3. Cf. "Regression is not origin, but origin is the ideology of regression." (Theodor W. Adorno, *Prisms*, trans. Samuel and Shierry Weber [London: Neville Spearman, 1967], p. 127.) Also: "as joy became unreal in society, the unreal joy began serving society ideologically. . . ." (Adorno, "Nachtmusik" [1929], *Moments Musicaux*, pp. 59–60.) One of Adorno's most often-cited statements (from *Minima Moralia*), "*das Ganze ist das Unwahre*" ("the whole is the untruth"), was a reversal of Hegel's sentence from the preface to the *Phenomenology of Mind* "*das Wahre ist das Ganze*" ("the truth is the whole").

40. Adorno, "Über Jazz" (1936), *Moments Musicaux*, pp. 85–105.

41. Adorno, "Musikalische Warenanalysen" (1934–1940), *Quasi una Fantasia*, pp. 66–68.

42. *Ibid.*, pp. 67–68.

43. *Ibid.*, p. 68.

44. *Ibid.*

45. *Ibid.*

46. Adorno, "Die Aktualität der Philosophie" (1931), *GS* 1, p. 334.

47. *Ibid.*, p. 335.

48. Adorno wrote of Benjamin: "The rebus becomes the model of his philosophy." (Adorno, *Über Walter Benjamin*, p. 12.)

49. Horkheimer's 1934 book *Dämmerung* was a collection of aphorisms, not "images." They symbolized a general concept, were daily-life *examples* of theory, and functioned as moral-political proverbs. As for his critical essays, their language was singularly nonpictorial, with few exceptions, e.g., "One can regard as symbols [*Sinnbilder*] of this epoch of unbridled self-interest those Renaissance paintings in which the patrons with relentless and cunning faces kneel as humble saints beneath the cross." This rare example of a pictorial image *illustrates* a point rather than being the point, as with Adorno. (Max Horkheimer, "Egoismus und Freiheitsbewegung" [1936], *Traditionelle und kritische Theorie: Vier Aufsätze* [Frankfurt am Main: Fischer Bucherei, 1970], p. 106.)

50. Benjamin, *Ursprung des deutschen Trauerspiels*, p. 90; cf. Rolf Tiedemann, *Studien zur Philosophie Walter Benjamins*, introd. Theodor W. Adorno (vol. 16 of Institut für Sozialforschung, *Frankfurter Beiträge zur Soziologie*, ed. Theodor W. Adorno and Walter Dirks (Frankfurt am Main: Europäische Verlagsanstalt, 1965), pp. 44–47.

51. ". . . according to my conception, history would no more be the place from which ideas arise, stand out independently and disappear again; instead the historical images would at the same time themselves be ideas, whose configuration constituted unintentional truth. . . ." (Adorno, "Die Aktualität der Philosophie" [1931], *GS* 1, pp. 337–338.)

52. *Ibid.*, p. 341.

53. Discussed below, Chapter 9. Adorno criticized Benjamin's method in 1938

as not "dialectical" enough. In "Das Paris des Second Empire bei Baude-laire" Benjamin had merely enumerated factual data without theoretical interpretation. For a summary of the issues of the dispute, see Rolf Tiede-mann's editorial "Nachwort," in Walter Benjamin, *Charles Baudelaire: Ein Lyriker des Hochkapitalismus* (Frankfurt am Main: Suhrkamp Verlag, 1969), pp. 167–191.

54. The title page described these fragments as "Vexierbilder und Miniaturen." Cf. Adorno, "A Portrait of Walter Benjamin," *Prisms,* p. 241.

55. Adorno, "Musikalische Warenanalysen" (1934–1940), *Quasi una Fantasia,* p. 62.

56. *Ibid.,* pp. 63–64.

57. Cf. above, pages 87–88. Translation not only from one language to another but from one mode to another was to be understood as no mere analogy. Thus Adorno's comment on the parallels between Ravel's music and im-pressionist painting: "He is called an impressionist. If the word is to mean something more rigorous than a mere analogy to the preceding movement in painting, then it names music which, by the strength of the infinitely small unity of the transition, totally breaks apart its natural material and nonetheless remains tonal." (Adorno, "Ravel" [1930], *Moments Musicaux,* p. 67.)

58. Adorno, "Über Jazz" (1936), *Moments Musicaux,* p. 102.

59. "Which popular tune will be a success and which will not – that allows prediction with apodictic certainty as little as the fate of a security." (*Ibid.,* p. 92.)

60. *Schief* also means crooked, distorted, false.

61. Adorno, "Naturgeschichte des Theaters" (1931–1933), *Quasi una Fantasia,* pp. 99–100. (French terms have been used in the translation to connote the bourgeois revolutionary slogans, as Adorno intended.)

62. *Ibid.,* p. 102.

63. *Ibid.,* p. 97. The politics of this early essay came close to surrealism (see below, Chapter 8).

64. The republished version contained some minor revisions of language which are not significant to this discussion.

65. The essay made it clear that precisely this aspect of his analysis, marking its nonidentity to the Institute's method, was the one he considered crucial: "If theory desires to penetrate . . . into the core of jazz's social function, or considered psychologically, into its latent dream content, namely the concrete, historically determined constellation of social identification and sexual instinct-energy, whose stage [*Schauplatz*] it is, then it must pose the problem of contingency with regard to the 'hot music' [i.e., the im-provisational "breaks" of the jazz subject] . . . ; out of it, if at all, the idea of jazz must be constructed." (Adorno, "Über Jazz" (1936), *Moments Musicaux,* p. 109.)

66. *Ibid.,* pp. 110–111.

67. I noted earlier (note 34 for this chapter) that Adorno, following Benjamin,

used the term "origin" to denote historical source, but not in the sense that historians use the word. His jazz interpretation is a good illustration: he acknowledged the fact (which would be of prime interest to traditional historians) that jazz developed out of American Negro culture and ultimately was derived from African music, but considered it irrelevant to the present social function of jazz and its musical elements (thus challenging the thesis that its "primitivism" could rejuvenate a dying Western culture). (*Ibid.*, p. 95.) He instead discovered the relevant historical source *within* the phenomenon: structural and functional similarities pointed to the nineteenth-century figure of the eccentric as the prototype of the jazz subject. Adorno then called on historical research to demonstrate an external connection which would correspond to this internal one: "the historical question of the degree to which the first step-dances [connected with the eccentric] came out of Variety [a mass-culture forerunner of jazz] would thus be factually of utmost importance to a fully developed theory of jazz." (*Ibid.*, p. 111.)

68. *Ibid.*, p. 111.

69. *Ibid.*, p. 112.

70. *Ibid.*

71. The ability to achieve such an interpretation was what Adorno considered the real significance of the 1936 jazz essay: "it sets artistic-technical and social reflections into one." (*Ibid.*, p. 9.)

72. *Ibid.*, pp. 112–113. The fact that Hitler's party had condemned jazz was, claimed Adorno, irrelevant to its essential totalitarianism. (*Ibid.*, p. 105.)

73. Adorno, "A Portrait of Walter Benjamin" (1950), *Prisms*, p. 238.

74. Adorno explained that this phrase, coined in Holland and used by the poet Stefan George, was meant to replace philosophy's time-worn term "ideas." It implied a criticism of the neo-Kantian notion of ideas as subjective categories and was a return to the Platonic conception "according to which the idea is no mere imagined conception, but a thing existing in itself, which then, if only mentally, allows itself to be seen." (Adorno, "Benjamins Einbahnstrasse" [1955], *Über Walter Benjamin*, p. 52.)

75. "With [Stefan] George's [thought-images] Benjamin's have only this in common, that exactly those experiences which to superficial inspection are judged as merely subjective and accidental are granted objectively, indeed, that the subjective is conceived solely as a manifestation of something objective. . . ." (*Ibid.*)

76. Benjamin, "Ein Jakobiner von heute" (1930), *Gesammelte Schriften* III, p. 265.

77. Adorno, "Einleitung zu Benjamins Schriften" (1955), *Über Walter Benjamin*, p. 43.

78. Tiedemann, *Studien zur Philosophie Walter Benjamins*, p. 130.

79. Discussed in Chapters 8 and 9.

80. Adorno, "Charakteristik Walter Benjamins" (1950), *Über Walter Benjamin*, p. 23. (The English translation [*Prisms*, p. 237] has not been used because its imprecision distorts the meaning of the original.)

81. The prefix "ur" means "archaic," "original."

82. Tiedemann suggests: "The terminological change seems to indicate that the conception of the Baroque book [*Trauerspiel*], that only fragmentary moments of the archaic extended into later epochs, is given up." (Tiedemann, *Studien zur Philosophie Walter Benjamins,* p. 123.) In its place was the more radically critical notion of the modern itself as primitive.

83. Adorno, "Die Idee der Naturgeschichte" (1932), *GS* 1, pp. 345–365, discussed in detail in Chapter 3 above.

84. As, according to Tiedemann (cf. note 82), Benjamin had earlier attempted in the *Trauerspiel* study. Yet even here Benjamin's understanding was not that of the traditional historian. In such Benjaminian terms as *Ursprung, Urgeschichte,* and *Urbild* the notion of origin referred not to a single historical event as source, but to an archetypal constellation, the construction of which was mediated by the historical present, the reference point of all knowledge (cf. Chapter 3). The notion is one of Benjamin's most difficult, and his position did not lack internal equivocation. Here is a translation of Benjamin's *Trauerspiel* definition of origin (*Ursprung*); interpreting its meaning must be left up to the reader: "With origin is meant no becoming of what has arisen; much more, that which arises out of becoming and disappearing. The origin stands in the stream of becoming as a whirlpool, and in its rhythm it snatches the origin-material up into it. The originating does not present itself to knowledge in naked, open, factual existence, and its rhythm stands open only to a double insight. It wants to be known as restoration, as reinstatement on the one hand, and precisely therefore as incomplete, unclosed, on the other. In every origin-phenomenon is determined the figure within which an idea continuously opposes itself to the historical world, until it lies there complete in the totality of its history. Hence origin arises not out of the actual conditions, but instead it concerns their previous and future history. The guiding principles of philosophical observation are drawn in the dialectic which is inherent within the origin. Out of it, one-time-ness and repetition, as mutually determining, show themselves in all characteristics. The category of origin is, therefore, not as [the neo-Kantian] Cohen meant, purely logical; it is historical." (Benjamin, *Ursprung des deutschen Trauerspiels,* pp. 29–30.)

85. Adorno, "Charakteristik Walter Benjamins" (1950), *Über Walter Benjamin,* pp. 23–24. Again, I have made my own translation, as the *Prisms* translation (p. 237) is not precise.

86. Adorno reported that at the time of the second plan for the *Passagenarbeit* (1935), Benjamin "happened to come across a forgotten work, written in prison by Auguste Blanqui, *L'éternité par les astres,* which, in accents of absolute despair, anticipates Nietzsche's theory of the eternal return." (Adorno, *Prisms,* p. 238.)

87. Adorno, "Einleitung zu Benjamins Schriften" (1953), *Über Walter Benjamin,* p. 43. Adorno claimed that, unlike Jung's archetypes, Benjamin's idea of redemption applied only to the transitory phenomena, not to the dialectical images: "That which is eternal in them is only the transitory." (*Ibid.,* pp. 42–43.) Yet there *was* some equivocacy in Benjamin's position

which Adorno was not acknowledging here, but which did emerge as a part of his disagreement with Benjamin in the thirties.

88. Adorno, "Die Idee der Naturgeschichte" (1932), *GS* 1, p. 364.

89. His French contemporary, Lévi-Strauss was trying something similar, yet drawing from it antithetical conclusions. Adorno's purpose was to criticize the present (reified) structure of consciousness; Lévi-Strauss wanted to establish the present structure as a universal, ontological first principle.

90. These pieces were first published together in 1958, and are reprinted under the title "Naturgeschichte des Theaters" in Adorno, *Quasi una Fantasia*, pp. 94–112.

91. This theme of the individual's passivity and consequent impotence, which remained so crucial to Adorno's critique of mass culture, is expressed in another fragment of his series in terms of the Odysseus myth (which appears again, without the humor and deadly serious, in *Dialektik der Aufklärung*). It is in his interpretation of the orchestra seats as the stage for bourgeois reality (cf. above): "In the well ordered, rationally arranged orchestra, which allots to each his exact seat, adventure no longer exists. Only the eye is still allowed to have one [it can shut itself]. . . . Or it may make an odyssey over the sea of human heads and, anonymous like they, set out on its daring journey to the stage. First it frees itself from the captivity of Calypso, a fat woman whose hair-do bars the way out of the grotto. It winds between Scylla and Charybdis, who bow together and separate, dashing to pieces everything between them. It touches on the island of the Sirens, on the slender neck of a maiden, in the midday sun of her blond hair. The Phaecian in the first row with the bald head is already no longer a danger to it. Blissful, Odysseus the Eye lands on the knees of the coloratura-soubrette as on the coast of his Ithica. (Adorno, "Parkett," in "Zur Naturgeschichte des Theaters," *Quasi una Fantasia*, pp. 100–101.)

92. Adorno, "Applaus" (1931), *Die Musik*, reprinted in "Zur Naturgeschichte des Theaters," *Quasi una fantasia*, pp. 94–96. Later in this set of critiques Adorno sees the theater's orchestra as an arena in an image presaging Hitler's religious persecutions: "Evil dreams which again introduce animal sports into our customary theaters allow, through these passageways, Bengalese king tigers to rush triumphantly from out of cloakroom cages." (*Ibid.*, p. 102.)

93. To solve the "riddle" of jazz, to interpret its technical function "as a cipher of its social one" (Adorno, "Über Jazz" [1936], *Moments Musicaux*, p. 86), Adorno performs a double-level critique, similar to his approach in interpreting "natural history" (Chapter 3): against the affirmative argument that jazz's primitivism will regenerate Europe's current musical "decadence," Adorno counters that its alleged primitivism is modern, the result of bourgeois society's commodity structure (*ibid.*, pp. 94–95); but against the argument that jazz's modern elements are progressive, Adorno claims that precisely these elements are the archaic ones (*ibid.*, p. 84).

94. *Ibid.*, p. 88.

95. *Ibid.*, p. 95.
96. *Ibid.*, pp. 95–96.
97. *Ibid.*, p. 106. Again, this dialectical reversal from demythification, through secularization into a new myth, anticipates *Dialektik der Aufklärung*.
98. *Ibid.*, p. 108.
99. *Ibid.*, p. 110.
100. *Ibid.*, p. 113.
101. Along with Adorno's "Über den Fetischcharackter in der Musik und die Regression des Hörens" (1938), which argued similarly that music had become a commodity, a fetish, and music's reified relation to the public resulted in psychological regression.
102. While Adorno's critique of jazz was an "idea" or "constellation," "culture industry" was indeed a *theory*. As the presentation of an "idea," his jazz essay used a dialectical method of immanent criticism to interpret the sociohistorical truth of the phenomenon which Adorno later called "social physiognomics." In contrast, the *theory* of culture industry laid bare a structural frame for such ideas. The distinction is discussed in Chapter 11.
103. Edward Shils, "Daydreams and Nightmares: Reflections on the Criticism of Mass Culture," *Sewanee Review* 65, 4 (Autumn 1957), pp. 587–608. Shils's article was a book review of Bernard Rosenberg and David Manning White, eds. *Mass Culture* (New York: Free Press, 1957), in which Adorno's article "On Popular Music" appeared. The review also referred to articles in the Institute's journal, and Marcuse's *Eros and Civilization*.
104. ". . . the effect of jazz is as little bound to the dominant class as their consciousness sharply separates itself from that of the dominated: the mechanism of psychic mutilation, the continuance of which is indebted to present conditions, also has power over the mutilators themselves, and if in their instinct-structure they are similar enough to those whom they sacrifice, then the sacrificed are in turn compensated, in that they are allowed just such a portion of the goods of the rulers as are aimed at a mutilated instinct-structure." (Adorno, "Über Jazz" [1936], *Moments Musicaux*, pp. 89–90.)
105. No object, be it jazz, an artwork, or a philosophy, was in itself "truth"; instead, truth appeared, emerging within the phenomena under the scrutiny of critical interpretation. The only phenomena which were totally ideological (and hence totally "irredeemable," in Adorno's sense of the term) were those in which all antagonisms, all contradictions were denied, and which, hence, were totally conciliatory to the status quo. But jazz, as a configuration of opposites, of salon-music individualism on one hand and military-march collectivism on the other, caught hold of a real social contradiction, out of which truth could be interpreted. Should these two poles of jazz break apart, Adorno wrote, becoming two separate jazz genres, each without internal contradiction, then "jazz can no longer be redeemed." (*Ibid.*, p. 115.)
106. *Ibid.*, p. 113.

107. *Ibid.*, p. 90.
108. *Ibid.*, p. 86.
109. Adorno, "Oxforder Nachträge" (1937) appended to *ibid.*, p. 120.

CHAPTER 7

1. The historical relativity of the interpreter's own position did limit the validity of its application to phenomena of the bourgeois era – the archaic, magic, and myth could be interpreted only when mediated by the present in whose context alone they acquired meaning.

2. Although Adorno's theory adhered to no rigid distinction between these branches of philosophy, his writings do tend to focus on the specific problems which one or the other of them raised. On ontology, see especially his study of *Kierkegaard* (1933), of Heidegger, *Jargon der Eigentlichkeit* (1964), and part I of *Negative Dialektik* (1966). On epistemology, see *Zur Metakritik der Erkenntnistheorie* (1956); on metaphysics, *Drei Studien zu Hegel* (1963) and "Meditationen zur Metaphysik" in *Negative Dialektik* (1966). On aesthetics, see *Philosophie der neuen Musik* (1949), "Der Essay als Form" in *Noten zur Literatur*, vol. 1 (1958), and *Aesthetische Theorie* (*Gesammelte Schriften*, vol. 7, 1970). A critique of bourgeois ethics was really Horkheimer's terrain, although the critique of Kant's practical reason, Exkurse II in *Dialektik der Aufklärung*, while actually written by Horkheimer, reflected Adorno's thinking as well. Adorno's aphorism collection *Minima Moralia* (1951) is a book about ethics, but the method is through a critique of phenomena of contemporary life, rather than criticizing the ethical philosophies of idealism directly. But see his later critique of Kant's practical reason, "Freiheit," in *Negative Dialektik* (1966). Adorno had plans for a book on ethics when he died (which, together with *Negative Dialektik* and *Aesthetische Theorie*, would correspond to Kant's division of philosophy into three critiques: metaphysics, ethics, aesthetics).

3. Cf. Horkheimer, who, with his moralist orientation, was more concerned with proving that *society* was absolutely wrong: "The critical acceptance of the [commodity] categories which rule social life contains simultaneously their condemnation. This dialectical character of the self-interpretation of contemporary man is what, in the last analysis, also caused the obscurity of the Kantian critique of reason. Reason cannot become transparent to itself as long as men act as members of an organism which lacks reason." (Max Horkheimer, "Traditional and Critical Theory" [1937], *Critical Theory: Selected Essays*, trans. Matthew J. O'Connell et al. [New York: Herder and Herder, 1972], p. 208.)

4. This systematic ordering of objects external to, and dominated by, the subject was the characteristic which Adorno together with Horkheimer interpreted in the 1940s as the key to the structure of totalitarianism (cf. Exkurse II in *Dialektik der Aufklärung*). Adorno's critique of the structure of domination centered, as could be expected, on its manifesta-

tions within bourgeois logic and cognitive experience. This was the topic of his 1956 introduction to the Husserl critique written in the thirties (but first published in 1956) *Zur Metakritik der Erkenntnistheorie.*

5. Cf. Theodor W. Adorno, "A Portrait of Walter Benjamin" (1950), *Prisms,* trans. Samuel and Shierry Weber (London: Neville Spearman, 1967), p. 233.

6. Theodor W. Adorno, "Die Aktualität der Philosophie" (1931), *Gesammelte Schriften,* vol. 1: *Frühe philosophische Schriften,* ed. Rolf Tiedemann (Frankfurt am Main: Suhrkamp Verlag, 1973), p. 337.

7. *Ibid.,* p. 335.

8. *Ibid.,* p. 339. In Vienna the logical positivists around Carnap (and at Cambridge Bertrand Russell's circle) were also "liquidating" the traditional questions of philosophy, but not *dialectically.* They were ignoring tradition, simply dismissing problems of metaphysics and morals as meaningless. Adorno *demonstrated* the meaninglessness of philosophical problems instead by taking them seriously, and in his negation of idealism the tradition of idealism remained sublated (*aufgehoben*). As Adorno wrote in 1966, one question should not be missing from philosophy, "and that is the question how a thinking obliged to relinquish tradition might preserve and transform tradition. For this and nothing else is the mental experience." (Theodor W. Adorno, *Negative Dialectics,* trans. E. B. Ashton [New York: The Seabury Press, 1973], pp. 54–55.)

9. *Ibid.,* p. 3.

10. *Ibid.,* p. 17.

11. Adorno, "Die Aktualität der Philosophie" (1931), *GS* 1, p. 335.

12. The association between Platonism and Benjamin's theory of ideas, and hence the elements of an inverted Platonism in Adorno's own writings, were discussed in Chapter 4 above.

13. This was the indirect influence of the Kabbalah, via Scholem, through Benjamin, on Adorno.

14. Light imagery was used by the German romantic poets (Novalis, Schlegel, Goethe) who influenced the young Benjamin. (See Walter Benjamin, *Der Begriff der Kunstkritik in der deutschen Romantik* [1920], ed. Hermann Schweppenhäuser [Frankfurt am Main: Suhrkamp Verlag, 1973].) In his 1931 speech Adorno referred to Goethe in defending the validity of his own method on the basis of its "fruitfulness." (Adorno, *GS* 1, p. 342.) Cf. Goethe's description of the intuitional "feeling of truth" which "'leads with lightning-like speed to a fruitful knowledge.'" (Cited in Rolf Tiedemann, *Studien zur Philosophie Walter Benjamins,* introd. Theodor W. Adorno [vol. 16 of Institut für Sozialforschung, *Frankfurter Beiträge zur Soziologie,* ed. Theodor W. Adorno and Walter Dirks] [Frankfurt am Main: Europäische Verlagsanstalt, 1965], p. 43.)

15. The element of shock was what tied it (via Benjamin) to Brecht and to surrealism.

16. Adorno's pieces in the thirties spoke frequently of "exploding" (*sprengen*) the "spell" (*Bann*) of idealism. Cf. also the closing statement of his in-

augural lecture: "it may be possible to penetrate the detail, to explode in miniature the mass of merely existing reality." (Adorno, "Die Aktualität der Philosophie" [1931], GS 1, p. 344.)

17. Adorno later used the image of a camera flashing critically in interpreting Husserl's categorical intuition (cf. Theodor W. Adorno, Husserl ms., 1934–1937, Frankfurt am Main, Adorno Estate, p. 64).

18. Adorno, "Die Aktualität der Philosophie" (1931), GS 1, p. 341.

19. Letter, Adorno to Benjamin, November 10, 1938, in Theodor W. Adorno, Über Walter Benjamin (Frankfurt am Main: Suhrkamp Verlag, 1970), pp. 138–139. Adorno was referring to the 1938 article "Das Paris des Second Empire bei Baudelaire," which Benjamin had hoped to publish in the Institute's Zeitschrift für Sozialforschung (see Chapter 10).

20. "Philosophical thinking is the same as thinking in models; negative dialectics is an ensemble of analyses of models." (Adorno, Negative Dialectics, p. 28.) The terms "model" and "constellation" were used as synonyms in both the 1931 inaugural speech and Negative Dialektik (1966), as well as in Benjamin's Ursprung des deutschen Trauerspiels (1927).

21. In Negative Dialektik, Adorno spoke of thought models in terms not so much of exploding problems as circling the object in perpetual motion, while the source of light was the unnamed utopia: "thought is [utopia's] servant," and philosophy "the prism in which its colors are caught." (Adorno, Negative Dialectics, p. 57.)

22. His first Habilitationsschrift, the study on Kant and Freud, had been rejected by Cornelius in 1927 (cf. Chapter 1). By the time of Adorno's second attempt, Cornelius had left Frankfurt, emigrating to Finland (from choice, rather than political necessity). The first reader of Adorno's Kierkegaard study was Paul Tillich, who accepted it less for its affinities with his own position (Adorno cannot be said to have been influenced by Tillich) than for his personal acquaintance with both Adorno and Horkheimer. Tillich wrote a short but favorable review of the book while at the Union Theological Seminary, which appeared in the American Journal of Philosophy (Paul Tillich, "Theodor Wiesengrund-Adorno: Kierkegaard: Konstruktion des Aesthetischen," Journal of Philosophy 31 [November 8, 1934]: 640). The book was also reviewed by Benjamin (see below) and by Karl Löweth in the Deutsche Literatur-Zeitung 5, 3F, 5 (1934).

23. Adorno wrote Ernst Krenek in September that he was under great pressure to meet a November 1 publishers' deadline; that although he had intended only to edit the original version, he was revising it "radically": "to be sure, all the building blocks have been retained, but none remains on top of the other; every sentence is newly formulated; the whole thing is only now really fully constructed (the first version presents only a conception when compared to the present one), and much, and indeed central passages, have been totally rethought." (Letter, Adorno to Krenek, September 30, 1932, Frankfurt am Main, Adorno Estate.) I have not seen a copy of the earlier version, but a comparison would document the development of Adorno's thinking during a crucially formative period, and answer just what stage of this development is reflected in the inaugural lecture. We

can assume, however, that the later version was even more intensely influenced by Benjamin: Adorno had meanwhile taught a seminar on the *Trauerspiel* theory; he completed revising the Kierkegaard study in Berlin, where Benjamin was also. When Benjamin read the revised version, he responded enthusiastically: "There is indeed, then, something like collaboration after all, and sentences which make it possible for one person to stand up for the other." (Letter, Benjamin to Adorno, December 1, 1932, cited in editorial notes, Walter Benjamin, *Gesammelte Schriften*, 6 vols., ed. Rolf Tiedemann and Hermann Schweppenhäuser, vol. III: *Kritiken und Rezensionen*, ed. Hella Tiedemann-Bartels [Frankfurt am Main: Suhrkamp Verlag, 1972], p. 661.)

24. In a note to the third edition (1966), Adorno stated there was "much which after thirty years no longer pleases the author," that he now understood both Kierkegaard and Hegel better, and that "he would no longer demonstrate metaphysical intentions so affirmatively, and the tone strikes him frequently as more ceremonial, more idealistic than justified." (Adorno, "Notiz," *Kierkegaard: Konstruktion des Aesthetischen* [1933]: *Mit Zwei Beilagen*, 3rd ed., enl. [Frankfurt am Main: Suhrkamp Verlag, 1966], p. 321.) At the same time, he made it clear that the study's obsolescence was objective rather than simply the result of his own personal development; that the truth content of Kierkegaard was not absolute, but changed with changing conditions.

25. The Kierkegaard revival of the twenties moved from theological circles (cf. Karl Barth) to philosophy, when Karl Jaspers and Martin Heidegger "emancipated" his existentialism from its religious context and "turned it into an anthropological ontology." (Theodor W. Adorno, "Kierkegaard einmal" [1963], in *ibid.*, p. 299.)

26. Heidegger's program for philosophy was also to establish a "materialist" metaphysics, and like Adorno he felt the most promising direction lay in fusing Husserl's phenomenology with the Hegelian tradition, but as it was passed down by Kierkegaard rather than Marx.

27. Because Kierkegaard did not attempt a positive ontology, Adorno considered Kierkegaard's position superior to Heidegger's: "The question of the 'meaning' of existence [*Dasein*] is for him [Kierkegaard] not what existence is authentically [*eigentlich*], but rather: what would give meaning to existence, in itself meaningless." (Adorno, *Kierkegaard*, p. 128.) Kierkegaard's was a negative ontology in that the uncertainty of meaning was itself the meaning. (*Ibid.*, p. 129.)

28. Kierkegaard placed aesthetics on the lowest rung of modes of experience, below ethics and religion; Hegel did too, below religion and philosophy. Adorno reversed the hierarchical principle, valuing spirituality negatively in comparison with art because it was further from sociohistorical reality, and hence further from truth.

29. Paul Tillich's review called Adorno's style "heavy and peculiar" (Tillich, "Theodor Wiesengrund-Adorno's *Kierkegaard*," p. 640); Jay referred to the book's "unapologetically abstruse style and demandingly complex analysis. . . ." (Martin Jay, *The Dialectical Imagination: A History of*

the Frankfurt School and the Institute of Social Research, 1923–1950 [Boston: Little, Brown, 1973], p. 66.) Adorno seemed to be following the advice of his teacher Alban Berg, whose maxim was, To make the piece better, make it more complex!

30. "Where his philosophy . . . encounters 'aesthetic' determinations it comes closest to the truth: that of its own situation of objectless inwardness just as well as that of the alien objects which confront it. Nowhere is social reality seen by Kierkegaard in sharper contours as in the 'aesthetic' Diapsalm. . . ." (Adorno, *Kierkegaard*, pp. 122–123.)

31. *Ibid.*, p. 73.

32. *Ibid.*

33. *Ibid.*, p. 74.

34. *Ibid.*, p. 60.

35. Here was the point at which, despite his rejection of Hegel's identity theory, Kierkegaard himself affirmed an identity principle, one which fell behind Hegel because *present* reality was granted the status of absolute truth.

36. "For Kierkegaard, situation is not, as for Hegel, objective history which can be grasped through its construction in the concept, but [it is grasped] solely through the spontaneous decision of the autonomous human being. In it [situation] Kierkegaard discovers, idealistically speaking, the indifference between subject and object." (*Ibid.*, p. 70.)

37. *Ibid.*, p. 55.

38. *Ibid.*

39. *Ibid.*, p. 59.

40. *Ibid.*, p. 156.

41. *Ibid.*, p. 55.

42. *Ibid.*, p. 63.

43. Benjamin, "Kierkegaard: Das Ende des philosophischen Idealismus" (April 2, 1933), *Gesammelte Schriften* III, p. 381.

44. Adorno, "Die Aktualität der Philosophie" (1931), *GS* 1, p. 337.

45. Again, it was Benjamin who first focused on the bourgeois *intérieur* as an expression of bourgeois decay. In *Einbahnstrasse* (1928) he wrote: "The bourgeois *intérieur* of the 1860s to the 1890s, with its gigantic buffets overflowing with wood-carving, the sunless corners where the palms stand, the landing fortified by banisters, and the long corridors with their singing gas flames, is adequate alone for housing a corpse. On this sofa the aunt can only be murdered." (Benjamin, *Einbahnstrasse, Schriften*, 2 vols., ed. Theodor W. Adorno and Gretel Adorno [Frankfurt am Main: Suhrkamp Verlag, 1955], vol. 1, p. 519.)

46. Adorno, *Kierkegaard*, p. 76.

47. *Ibid.*

48. *Ibid.*, p. 77.

49. The *flâneur*, the man of leisure "who goes botanizing on the asphalt," strolling the city streets to observe the panoramic surface of the crowd and

the marketplace, was a key figure in Benjamin's *Passagenarbeit*, functioning as a stage for making visible the historical reality of Paris in the early nineteenth century. The *flâneur* was at home in the shopping arcade, itself "a cross between a street and an *intérieur*"; he made of the outside world his own interior: "the street becomes a dwelling for the *flâneur*; he is as much at home among the facades of houses as a citizen is in his four walls." (Walter Benjamin, "The Paris of the Second Empire in Baudelaire" [1938], *Charles Baudelaire: A Lyric Poet in the Era of High Capitalism*, pp. 36–37.)

50. Adorno, *Kierkegaard*, p. 78.
51. *Ibid.*, p. 77.
52. "... spy ... in the service of the idea" (cited in *ibid.*, p. 78).
53. *Ibid.*
54. *Ibid.*
55. *Ibid.*, p. 80.
56. *Ibid.*, p. 81.
57. *Ibid.*
58. *Ibid.*
59. *Ibid.*
60. *Ibid.*, p. 83.
61. *Ibid.*, p. 82.
62. *Ibid.*
63. *Ibid.*, p. 79.
64. What Kierkegaard himself calls the "sickness of the times" is interpreted as an inner condition (cf. *ibid.*, pp. 109–114).
65. *Ibid.*, p. 79.
66. *Ibid.*, pp. 84–85.
67. *Ibid.*, p. 84.
68. *Ibid.*, p. 86.
69. *Ibid.*
70. *Ibid.*, pp. 93–94.
71. *Ibid.*, pp. 95–96.
72. *Ibid.*, pp. 105, 142–155. This theme, that the attempt to transcend mythical nature paradoxically falls back into myth, became the central argument in Adorno's and Horkheimer's *Dialektik der Aufklärung* (1947). Cf. also a later article on Kierkegaard by Adorno published in English in the Institute's journal: "He sets out to expel nature with a pitchfork, only to become Nature's prey himself." (Theodor W. Adorno, "On Kierkegaard's Doctrine of Love," *Studies in Philosophy and Social Science* 8 [1939–1940]: 417.)
73. Adorno, *Kierkegaard*, pp. 156–163.
74. *Ibid.*, pp. 107 ff.
75. *Ibid.*, p. 148.
76. *Ibid.*, p. 181.

77. *Ibid.*, p. 79.

78. *Ibid.*, p. 135.

79. *Ibid.*, p. 168.

80. Martin Heidegger, *Being and Time*, trans. John Macquarrie and Edward Robinson (London: SCM Press, 1962), pp. 97–98.

81. See above, Chapter 4.

82. Adorno, "On Kierkegaard's Doctrine of Love" (1939), 423.

CHAPTER 8

1. This was something he explicitly and repeatedly rejected (see below, page 133).

2. See James A. Leith, *The Idea of Art as Propaganda in France, 1750–1799: A Study in the History of Ideas* (Toronto: University of Toronto Press, 1965). For the propaganda uses of music in particular, see Alexander L. Ringer, "J. J. Barthelemy and Musical Utopia in Revolutionary France," *Journal of the History of Ideas*, 30, 3 (July–September 1961): 355–368.

3. For a discussion of their different conceptions of "socialist realism," see Werner Mittenzwei, "Marxismus und Realismus: Die Brecht-Lukács Debatte," *Das Argument* 10, 46 (March 1968): 12–43.

4. Theodor W. Adorno, "The Problem of Experimentation in Music Psychology," March 7, 1939 (Frankfurt am Main, Adorno Estate), p. 2.

5. See Martin Jay, *The Dialectical Imagination: A History of the Frankfurt School and the Institute of Social Research, 1923–1950* (Boston: Little, Brown, 1973), pp. 44–46.

6. Introduction to Arnold Schönberg, *Harmonielehre* (1911), 3rd ed., rev. and enl. (Vienna: Universal-Edition, 1922), pp. 3 ff.

7. Werner Heisenberg, *Philosophic Problems of Nuclear Science*, trans. F. C. Hayes (New York: Pantheon, 1952), p. 119. It is perhaps not accidental that certain formulations used by Heisenberg during the early thirties to describe the new scientific paradigm were identical to the philosophical notions of Adorno and Benjamin, for example, the idea of transcending the old physics "from within," and of "riddle-solving" as the liquidation of questions which proved to be "meaningless." (*Ibid.*, pp. 14, 17, and *passim.*)

8. See above, Chapter 2, page 31.

9. Simmel identified this kind of aestheticism with socialism: based on ideals of uniformity, symmetry and the harmonious integration of parts, the socialist goal was to make society an artwork, an aesthetic whole, by means of its rational reorganization. (Georg Simmel, "Soziologische Aesthetik," *Brücke und Tür* [Stuttgart: K. F. Koehler Verlag, 1957], p. 203.)

10. Now in Walter Benjamin, *Gesammelte Schriften*, 6 vols., ed. Rolf Tiedemann and Hermann Schweppenhäuser, vol. I: 1: *Abhandlungen* (Frankfurt am Main: Suhrkamp Verlag, 1974), pp. 7–122.

11. *Ibid.*, p. 69.

12. *Ibid.*, p. 91.

13. Benjamin, *Gesammelte Schriften* I: 3, p. 801.

14. Steven C. Schaber, "Novalis' Theory of the Work of Art as Hieroglyph," *The Germanic Review*, 48, 1 (January 1973): 43.

15. Letter, Benjamin to Adorno, May 31, 1935, Walter Benjamin, *Briefe*, 2 vols. ed. Gershom Scholem and Theodor W. Adorno (Frankfurt am Main: Suhrkamp Verlag, 1966), vol. 2, pp. 662-663.

16. Surrealism was not a strong movement in Germany. Bloch wrote in 1937: "Surrealism (into which, in France and Czechoslovakia, much of the essence of expressionism has fled) found little response in Germany. The world around us torn to pieces and the phosphorescing on the edges − all this uncanny reality found no official expression. Or the expression, when it half-way appeared, as for example in the 'Three Penny Opera,' was comfortably misunderstood, [or] in other cases ridiculed." (Ernst Bloch, "Der Expressionismus" [November, 1937], *Vom Hasard zur Katastrophe: Politische Aufsätze aus den Jahren 1934-1939*, afterword by Oskar Negt [Frankfurt am Main: Suhrkamp Verlag, 1972], pp. 273-274.)

17. Walter Benjamin, "Der Sürrealismus: Die letzte Momentaufnahme der europäischen Intelligenz" (1929), *Angelus Novus: Ausgewählte Schriften* (Frankfurt am Main: Suhrkamp Verlag, 1966), p. 213.

18. Surrealism was of course incompatible with the socialist realism that became the Party line, and the support was not reciprocated. Some surrealists followed Louis Aragon, who broke with Breton and joined the Communist Party in 1932. Breton was laughed out of a Moscow congress on culture in 1935. He declared himself a Trotskyite and in 1936 purged his movement of Stalinist communism.

19. Breton (1935), cited in J. H. Matthews, *An Introduction to Surrealism* (University Park: The Pennsylvania State University Press, 1965), p. 45.

20. André Breton, "Speech to the Congress of Writers" (Paris, 1935), *Manifestoes of Surrealism*, trans. Richard Seaver and Helen R. Lane (Ann Arbor: The University of Michigan Press, 1969), p. 241.

21. *Ibid.*, p. 14.

22. Karl Marx (1843) cited in Georg Lukács, *History and Class Consciousness*, trans. Rodney Livingstone (Cambridge, Mass.: The M.I.T. Press, 1971), p. 2.

23. The rejection of identity, fundamental to Adorno, was also the surrealist project. Cf. Breton: "Who knows if, thus, we are not preparing ourselves to escape some day the principle of identity." (Cited in Matthews, *An Introduction to Surrealism*, pp. 105-106.)

24. Breton, "Manifesto of Surrealism" (1924), *Manifestoes of Surrealism*, p. 37.

25. André Breton, *Les Vases communicants* (Paris: Gallimard, 1955), p. 129.

26. The first surrealist films were by Luis Buñuel and Salvador Dali: *Un Chien andalou* (1929) and *L'Age d'or* (1930). Surrealists self-consciously transposed the techniques of film to painting and literary media.

27. Benjamin, "Der Sürrealismus" (1929), *Angelus Novus*, p. 206.

28. Adorno, "Charakteristik Walter Benjamins" (1950), *Über Walter Benjamin* (Frankfurt am Main: Suhrkamp Verlag, 1970), p. 23.

29. See particularly Walter Benjamin, *Einbahnstrasse* (1928), *Gesammelte Schriften*, 6 vols., ed. Rolf Tiedemann and Hermann Schweppenhäuser, vol. IV:1: *Kleine Prosa*, ed. Tillman Rexroth (Frankfurt am Main: Suhrkamp Verlag, 1972), pp. 83–148. Cf. Rolf Tiedemann, *Studien zur Philosophie Walter Benjamins*, introd. Theodor W. Adorno (vol. 16 of Institut für Sozialforschung, *Frankfurter Beiträge zur Soziologie*, ed. Theodor W. Adorno and Walter Dirks) (Frankfurt am Main: Europäische Verlagsanstalt, 1965), pp. 48–49.

It can be noted here that although Adorno expressed concern over this aspect of the surrealist model (*Über Walter Benjamin*, p. 112–113), he paid attention to his own dreams and left in his estate a file of *Traumprotokolle* (records of dreams). He published several of these during the emigration years: Theodor W. Adorno, "Träume in Amerika: Drei Protokolle," *Aufbau-Rekonstruktion* [New York] 8, 40 (October 2, 1942): 17.

30. Walter Benjamin, *Über Haschisch: Novellistisches, Berichte, Materialien*, ed. Tillman Rexroth, introd. Hermann Schweppenhäuser (Frankfurt am Main: Suhrkamp Verlag, 1972), p. 95. Benjamin corresponded with Hesse, sending him in 1934 the manuscript of *Berliner Kindheit um Neunzehnhundert*, a collection of childhood memory fragments which he had written two years earlier and tried repeatedly but unsuccessfully to publish. Hesse's response was favorable, and Benjamin hoped he would help to find a publisher, but this didn't happen. (Letters, Benjamin to Adorno, March 18, 1934, and April 9, 1934, Frankfurt am Main, Adorno Estate.)

31. In several of the sessions Ernst Bloch participated, also a woman referred to by Benjamin as "G.," not Gretel Karplus Adorno, but, according to Scholem, "a girlfriend who later committed suicide." (Gershom Scholem, *Walter Benjamin: Die Geschichte einer Freundschaft* [Frankfurt am Main: Suhrkamp Verlag, 1975], p. 221.) Also present were two medical doctors, Ernst Joël and Fritz Fränkel, who were friends of Benjamin and whose reports of the sessions are included in the published volume *Über Haschisch*. There is no evidence that Adorno participated in these or any other drug experiments.

32. Benjamin, "Der Sürrealismus" (1929), *Angelus Novus*, p. 212.

33. Benjamin, *Über Haschisch*, p. 202.

34. *Ibid.*, p. 213.

35. *Ibid.*, p. 202.

36. In his notes Benjamin referred to these as "trial combinations" (*Versuchsanordnungen*) (*ibid.*, p. 73 and *passim*), the same term Adorno used to describe his own philosophical constellations in his 1931 inaugural speech (cf. above, page 102). The term was part of the vocabulary of Brecht's theory of epic theater.

37. Benjamin, *Über Haschish*, p. 73.

38. Cf. Chapter 4, above, page 78. During a hashish session in March 1930

Benjamin developed this theory with friends, distinguishing it from the then popular theosophical (i.e., Buddhist, Brahmanic, pantheistic) views: "First, authentic aura appears in all things, not only in particular ones, as the people [theosophists] imagine. Second, the aura changes thoroughly and fundamentally with every movement which the thing makes, and of which it is the aura. Third, authentic aura can in no way be thought of as the clean and tidy spiritual beam of magic, as the vulgar mystical books portray and describe it. The ornament is much more the distinguishing characteristic of authentic aura, an ornamental envelopment in which the thing or essence lies secure as if sunken in a case." (Benjamin, *Über Haschisch*, p. 107.)

39. *Ibid.,* p. 108.

40. *Ibid.,* p. 107.

41. Walter Benjamin, "Paris: The Capital of the Nineteenth Century" (1935), trans. Quintin Hoare, *Charles Baudelaire: A Lyric Poet in the Era of High Capitalism,* trans. Harry Zohn (London: NLB, 1973), p. 171: "Ambiguity is the figurative appearance of the dialectic, the law of the dialectic at a standstill. This standstill is utopia. . . ."

42. Adorno, "Einleitung zu Benjamins Schriften" (1955), *Über Walter Benjamin,* p. 45.

43. Their disagreements are discussed in detail in Chapters 9 and 10, below.

44. Theodor W. Adorno, "Mahagonny" (1930), *Moments Musicaux: Neugedruckte Aufsätze, 1928 bis 1962* (Frankfurt am Main: edition Suhrkamp, 1964), p. 137.

45. *Ibid.,* p. 136.

46. *Ibid.* Cf. "Fortschritt und Reaktion" (1930), in *ibid.,* pp. 157–158.

47. Adorno, "Mahagonny" (1930), *ibid.,* p. 132. Cf. his evaluation of Berg's "almost montage-like" style as a reflection of the true nature of reality, "a world which allows continuity and totality only as farce. . . ." (Theodor W. Adorno, "Berg: Erinnerung" [1937], *Gesammelte Schriften,* vol. 13: *Die Musikalischen Monographien,* ed. Gretel Adorno and Rolf Tiedemann [Frankfrut am Main: Suhrkamp Verlag, 1971], p. 349.)

48. Letter, Benjamin to Adorno, December 1, 1932 (Frankfurt am Main, Adorno Estate).

49. Cited in Matthews, *An Introduction to Surrealism,* p. 82.

50. Breton, "Manifesto of Surrealism" (1924), *Manifestoes of Surrealism,* pp. 29–30.

51. Theodor W. Adorno, "Der Sürrealismus" (1956),*Noten zur Literatur,* vol. 1 (Frankfurt am Main: Suhrkamp Verlag, 1958), p. 157.

52. *Ibid.,* p. 161.

53. *Ibid.,* p. 157.

54. Breton, "Surrealist Situation of the Object" (1935), *Manifestoes of Surrealism,* p. 259.

55. Breton, "Manifesto of Surrealism" (1924), *ibid.,* p. 21.

56. *Ibid.,* pp. 27–28.

57. Bertolt Brecht, "Neue Technik der Schauspiel Kunst" (1935-1941), *Gesammelte Werke*, vol. 15: *Schriften zum Theater 1* (Frankfurt am Main: Suhrkamp Verlag, 1967), p. 364.

58. See Chapter 2, above.

59. Letter, Adorno to Benjamin, November 6, 1934 (Frankfurt am Main, Adorno Estate).

60. "Der dialektische Komponist," first published in *Arnold Schönberg zum 60. Geburtstag* (Vienna, September 13, 1934), republished in Theodor W. Adorno, *Impromptus: Zweite Folge neu gedruckter musikalischer Aufsätze* (Frankfurt am Main: Suhrkamp Verlag, 1969), pp. 39-44.

61. *Ibid.*, p. 41. The necessarily active role of the composer and also the musician as subject, precisely when they yielded to the demands of the material, was for Adorno the crucial issue. As he wrote: "The sinking of contemplative subjectivity into the *oeuvre*, and the subject's participation in the constitution of its objectivity are one and the same." (Theodor W. Adorno, notebooks on *Reproduktionstheorie*, 3 vols., unpublished, Frankfurt am Main, Adorno Estate, n.d., vol. 1, p. 76.)

62. Adorno, "Der dialektische Komponist," *Impromptus*, p. 43.

63. This statement is from a 1935 article, Theodor Wiesengrund-Adorno, "Eine Geschichte der Musikästhetik," *Der Auftakt*, 15, 1-2: 18.

64. Adorno, "Der dialektische Komponist," *Impromptus*, p. 41.

65. *Ibid.*, p. 42.

66. *Ibid.*, p. 45.

67. See Chapter 1, page 15.

68. ". . . the utmost stringency, namely the consistency of technique, in the last resort reveals itself as in fact utmost freedom, namely, as putting at man's disposal his music which began in myth and softened in reconciliation, as the structure of that which stood opposed to him and in the end belonged to him by the power of a procedural method which takes possession of that structure insofar as it belongs to it fully." (Adorno, "Der dialektische Komponist," *Impromptus*, p. 44.)

69. See above, Chapter 2, pages 33-35.

70. In his letter to Benjamin of March 18, 1936, he referred to this article as one "with which you are not familiar." (Adorno, *Über Walter Benjamin*, p. 127.)

71. The Husserl study was first published in revised form in 1956 as *Zur Metakritik der Erkenntnistheorie* (now in Adorno, *GS*, vol. 5). I have consulted the original typed draft, written 1934-1937 at Oxford. The full passage is "(NB one might compare H[usserl']s concept of the object as actually somewhat like the merely chromatic functionality of Reger, compared to the step-like dialectical [functionality] of Schönberg. It is perhaps generally allowable at this point to allude to the model-character of musical logic, in which the matter's validity reveals [itself] as immanent within the material, with the subject as simply the executing organ." (Theodor W. Adorno, Husserl ms., 1934-1937, Frankfurt am Main, Adorno Estate, p. 58. Cf. p. 122.)

72. Actually, it was with *Jugendstil,* the aesthetic contemporary of Husserlian phenomenology, that Adorno made explicit comparison in the manuscript. (*Ibid.,* pp. 294 ff.)

73. *Ibid.,* p. 58.

74. See above, Chapter 2, page 35.

75. Letter, Adorno to Krenek, October 7, 1934, *Theodor W. Adorno und Ernst Krenek: Briefwechsel,* ed. Wolfgang Rogge (Frankfurt am Main: Suhrkamp Verlag, 1974), p. 46.

76. Adorno, "Reaktion und Fortschritt" (1930), *Moments Musicaux, ibid.,* p. 180.

77. Letter, Adorno to Krenek, October 7, 1934, *Adorno und Krenek: Briefwechsel,* p. 46.

78. With the overthrow of tonality, "the material has become clearer and more free, rescued from the mythic confines of number which dominate harmonic rows and tonal harmony." (Adorno, "Reaktion und Fortschritt" (1930), *Moments Musicaux,* p. 180.)

79. In 1935 Adorno suggested to Benjamin a return to the latter's earlier term "model," as the "immanent structure of the dialectical image," rather than an effort to interpret the nonstructural surface features as themselves a "dialectical image." (Letter, Adorno to Benjamin, August 2, 1935, *Über Walter Benjamin,* p. 114.)

80. In the 1940s Adorno began to argue that twelve-tone composing had become a formalized, closed "system," lapsing back into ideology: "To be sure, among the rules of twelve-tone techniques there is not one which does not proceed necessarily out of compositional experience – out of the progressive illumination of the natural material of music. But this experience had assumed a defensive character. . . . What once found a highly perceptive ear has been distorted to a concocted system wherein musical correctness supposedly can be gauged in the abstract." (Theodor W. Adorno, *Philosophy of Modern Music,* trans. Anne G. Mitchell and Wesley V. Blomster [New York: The Seabury Press, 1973], pp. 68–69.)

81. Adorno, "Der dialektische Komponist" (1934), *Impromptus,* p. 39.

82. *Ibid.,* p. 42.

83. Letter, Adorno to Krenek, September 30, 1932, *Adorno und Krenek: Briefwechsel,* p. 38.

84. Adorno, Husserl ms., 1934–1937, p. 7.

85. Cf. Schönberg: "In Counterpoint, it is not so much a matter of the combination itself (that is, it is not an end in itself) as of such a many-sided presentation of the idea. The theme is so constructed that it already contains within itself these many figures, through which the many-sided presentation [*Darstellung*] of the idea is made possible." (Arnold Schönberg, cited in Allan Janik and Stephen Toulmin, *Wittgenstein's Vienna* [New York: Simon and Schuster, 1973], p. 108.)

86. Theodor Wiesengrund-Adorno, "Zur gesellschaftlichen Lage der Musik," part I, *Zeitschrift für Sozialforschung* 1, 1/2 (1932): 109–110. The structural relationship between Freud's *psycho*analysis and Adorno's *socio*-

analysis was clear, although the latter, looking at external reality rather than the inner realm of psychic phenomena, faced in the opposite direction. Both focused on the smallest, seemingly insignificant details, which Adorno, following Freud's formulation, referred to as the "refuse of the world of appearance" (*Abhub der Erscheinungswelt*). Both looked to the ruptures, the logical gaps in appearances as the place where truth appeared in *unintentional* configurations. Both solved the riddles of these configurations by reconstructing the inner logic governing their paradoxical appearance. Reification and ideology distorted the outer world, as repression and rationalization distorted the inner one. In both cases, knowledge as a process of discovery was itself an act of liberation, and in both cases the model for that process was a dialectical experience, rather than logical ordering on the one hand or mere reflection of the "given" on the other.

87. Adorno, "Einleitung zu Benjamins 'Schriften'" (1955), *Über Walter Benjamin*, p. 46. Yet although this limited comparison had validity, the fact of the matter is that the mode of Benjamin's thinking had very little in common with that of music, whose structural principles he scarcely understood. If he appreciated anything Schönbergian, it (predictably) was Berg's *Wozzeck*, the music of which had a static quality, and which had been heralded as the first "surrealist" opera. (Cf. Theodor W. Adorno, "Berg: Erinnerungen" [1937], *GS* 13, p. 342.)

88. *Gematria* was a gnostic method which established equivalences between nonideational systems: letters could be transformed into numbers and, conversely, numbers into words. Unlike traditional Aristotelian logic, this procedure made it possible to demonstrate identities between phenomena without eliminating their particularity and difference. (Cf. Gershom Scholem, *Major Trends in Jewish Mysticism* [New York: Schocken Books, 1967], p. 223.)

89. Max Horkheimer and Theodor W. Adorno, *Dialektik der Aufklärung* (Amsterdam: Querido Verlag, 1947).

90. "The musical sense is the NEW — something which cannot be traced back and subsumed but springs out of the configuration of the known, if the listener comes to its aid. This new is not something material — no thing — but the functional interrelationship of given musical elements." (Theodor W. Adorno, "Listening Habits: An Analysis of Likes and Dislikes in Light Popular Music," in "Current of Music: Elements of a Radio Theory," unpublished ms. 1939, Frankfurt am Main, Adorno Estate, p. 52.

91. Theodor W. Adorno, *Gesammelte Schriften*, vol. 7: *Aesthetische Theorie*, ed. Gretel Adorno and Rolf Tiedemann (Frankfurt am Main: Suhrkamp Verlag, 1970).

92. Theodor W. Adorno, *Negative Dialektik, Gesammelte Schriften*, vol. 6, ed. Rolf Tiedemann (Frankfurt am Main: Suhrkamp Verlag, 1973).

93. The study will be published as vol. 21 of the *Gesammelte Schriften*.

94. Theodor W. Adorno, "Die Aktualität der Philosophie" (1931), *Gesammelte Schriften*, vol. 1: *Frühe philosophische Schriften*, ed. Rolf Tiedemann (Frankfurt am Main. Suhrkamp Verlag, 1973), p. 332.

95. Theodor W. Adorno, *Kierkegaard: Konstruktion des Aesthetischen: Mit zwei Beilagen,* 3rd ed., enl. (Frankfurt am Main: Suhrkamp Verlag, 1966), pp. 27–28.

96. Adorno, *Negative Dialektik, GS* 6, p. 26.

97. Letter, Adorno to Krenek, May 26, 1935, *Adorno und Krenek: Briefwechsel,* pp. 85–86.

98. *Ibid.,* p. 85.

99. *Ibid.:* "The transcendental aesthetic of Kant's *Critique of Pure Reason* is more art than all the aesthetic things subjectively presented by Schopenhauer, Kierkegaard or Nietzsche, which exactly by redeeming the subjective moment fall back into reified philosophizing."

100. Theodor W. Adorno, "Charakteristik Walter Benjamins" (1950), *Über Walter Benjamin,* p. 14.

101. Letter, Adorno to Krenek, May 26, 1935, *Adorno und Krenek: Briefwechsel,* p. 86.

102. Adorno, "Thesen über die Sprache des Philosophen" (n.d.), *GS* 1, p. 369.

103. *Ibid.,* pp. 366–367.

104. Adorno, "Charakteristik Walter Benjamins" (1950), *Über Walter Benjamin,* p. 25.

105. In the 1960s Adorno delivered a lecture on the relationship between music and painting which argued in predictable fashion that precisely and only in their distinctiveness and difference did these two aesthetic modes converge. (Theodor W. Adorno, "Über einige Relationen zwischen Musik und Malerei," *Anmerkungen zur Zeit,* vol. 12: *Die Kunst und die Künste* [Berlin: Akademie der Künste, 1967], pp. 5–23.)

106. Of course, vertical harmonies provided a moment of simulteneity in music, but their meanings were dialectically dependent on the horizontal development of thematic material.

107. "The musical texts cannot be read adequately without interpretation." (Theodor W. Adorno, notebooks on *Reproduktionstheorie,* vol. 1, p. 2.

108. Thus he worked on a theory of musical reproduction throughout his life because he considered the problems faced in interpreting and performing music of central importance to philosophy as well. (See *ibid.*)

109. Adorno, "Thesen über die Sprache des Philosophen" (n.d.), *GS* 1, p. 369.

110. Theodor W. Adorno, "Fragment über Musik und Sprache" (1956–1957), *Quasi una Fantasia: Musikalische Schriften II* (Frankfurt am Main: Suhrkamp Verlag, 1963), p. 9.

111. *Ibid.,* p. 12.

112. *Ibid.* Elsewhere Adorno wrote that even if music lacked concepts, its interpretation necessitated analysis as well as mimesis, which meant that its affinity to philosophy was even greater. (Adorno, notebooks on *Reproduktionstheorie,* vol. 2, pp. 49 ff.)

113. Adorno, *Negative Dialektik, GS* 6, p. 23.

CHAPTER 9

1. Walter Benjamin, *Gesammelte Schriften*, 6 vols., ed. Rolf Tiedemann and Hermann Schweppenhäuser, vol. III: *Kritiken und Rezensionen*, ed. Hella Tiedemann-Bartels (Frankfurt am Main: Suhrkamp Verlag, 1972), p. 383.

2. Martin Jay, *The Dialectical Imagination: A History of the Frankfurt School and the Institute of Social Research, 1923-1950* (Boston: Little, Brown, 1973), p. 29.

3. In his note to the 1966 edition of the Kierkegaard study, Adorno wrote that despite the critical intent of the book it was not censored by the Nazis and continued to sell after the author had emigrated: "It estimated, perhaps, the stupidity of the censors. Particularly the criticism of existential ontology which it practiced may have already then reached the intellectual opposition in Germany." (Theodor W. Adorno, *Kierkegaard: Konstruktion des Aesthetischen* [1933]: *Mit zwei Beilagen*, 3rd ed., enl. [Frankfurt am Main: Suhrkamp Verlag, 1966], p. 321.) Yet the book was no revolutionary tract. Specifically, Adorno made no attempt to criticize Kierkegaard's focus on the individual, nor favored in contrast a concept of the subject that was collective and revolutionary. Adorno in fact retained Kierkegaard's stress on the individual, although he sharply criticized the latter for not acknowledging the dialectical relationship between individual and society.

4. That is, his paternal name, Wiesengrund, which he used (Wiesengrund-Adorno) until he came to the United States in 1938.

5. Friedrich T. Gubler, earlier *feuilleton* editor of the *Frankfurter Zeitung*, transferred to the *Vossische Zeitung* in 1933.

6. The *Vossische Zeitung* was the oldest and most prestigious paper in Berlin. Although owned by the conservative Ullstein concern, "Auntie Voss," as the paper was known, managed to maintain its liberal policy until it was forced to shut down in 1934.

7. Letter, Adorno to Krenek, October 7, 1934, *Theodor W. Adorno und Ernst Krenek: Briefwechsel*, ed. Wolfgang Rogge (Frankfurt am Main: Suhrkamp Verlag, 1974), p. 43.

8. *Ibid.*, p. 44.

9. Jay, *The Dialectical Imagination*, pp. 29-30.

10. Benjamin wrote Gretel Karplus in Berlin on April 15, 1933, that he had heard from Horkheimer in Geneva, who wanted to know how Adorno's projects were developing and assured him that the Institute's journal would continue to be published. Benjamin continued: "You must tell him that Max asked about him in the above-mentioned letter with some concern." (Walter Benjamin, *Briefe*, 2 vols., ed. Gershom Scholem and Theodor W. Adorno [Frankfurt am Main: Suhrkamp Verlag, 1966], vol. 2, p. 569.)

11. Benjamin, letter to Gershom Scholem, March 20, 1933, in *ibid.*, p. 567.

12. *Ibid.*, p. 562.

13. *Ibid.*, p. 566.

14. At the time he was working on an opera based on Mark Twain's *Tom Sawyer.* He wrote Krenek October 7, 1934: "I gave up the summer and fall of '33 mainly to completing the Tom Sawyer text, which is finished (also many of the compositions are already done), and to working systematically on compositional technique, as my counterpoint didn't satisfy me; strict 4-voice composition and fugue above all." (*Adorno und Krenek: Briefwechsel*, p. 43.) He sent the text to Benjamin, writing: "As you will see, the central motif is that of perjury: i.e., by means of perjury and breaking the mythic-moralistic sphere of the oath . . . Tom becomes 'free,' how indeed in a certain sense the whole thing is the execution of a dialectical demythification. But in the present version, this liberation itself still has too much of the character of a moralistic act in the name of empathy. Originally I wanted to base it solely on curiosity, which happens in the case of perjury, and thus let precisely the moralistic, in a really human sense, emerge out of psychological immorality." (Letter, Adorno to Benjamin, December 5, 1934, Frankfurt am Main, Adorno Estate.) Benjamin was critical of the project's conception, and Adorno broke off work on it. Two pieces from the libretto remain in the Adorno Estate.

15. Heinrich Gomperz, 1873–1942; professor of philosophy in Vienna, 1924–1934; emigrated to Los Angeles, 1935.

16. Letter, Adorno to Krenek, October 7, 1934, *Adorno und Krenek: Briefwechsel*, p. 44.

17. Letter, Adorno to Benjamin, April 21, 1934 (Frankfurt am Main, Adorno Estate).

18. *Ibid.*

19. Jay, *The Dialectical Imagination*, pp. 37–39.

20. "I spend a great deal of time learning English. The acquisition of a new language by an adult counts among the most peculiar experiences." (Letter, Adorno to Benjamin, March 4, 1934, Frankfurt am Main, Adorno Estate.) He later recalled that in order to learn English as quickly as possible he read "countless detective stories" without using a dictionary. (Theodor W. Adorno, *Philosophische Terminologie: Zur Einleitung*, 2 vols., ed. Rudolf zur Lippe [Frankfurt am Main: Suhrkamp Verlag, 1973], vol. 1, p. 33.)

21. The manuscript, written from 1934 to 1938, was first published (enlarged and slightly revised) as *Zur Metakritik der Erkenntnistheorie* (Frankfurt am Main: Suhrkamp Verlag, 1956).

22. Letter, Adorno to Krenek, October 7, 1934, *Adorno und Krenek: Briefwechsel*, p. 44.

23. Jay, *The Dialectical Imagination*, p. 30.

24. Hildegard Brenner, "Theodor W. Adorno als Sachwalter des Benjaminschen Werkes," *Die neue Linke nach Adorno*, ed. Wilfried F. Schoeller (Munich:

Kindler, 1969), pp. 158–175, first published in *Alternative* 59/60 (April-June, 1968). For a meticulous rebuttal of Brenner's charges see Rolf Tiedemann, "Zur 'Beschlagnahme' Walter Benjamins oder wie man mit der Philologie Schlitten fährt," *Das Argument* 46 (March 1968): 74–93.

25. The Adorno-Benjamin correspondence has not yet been published in full, although a selection of some of the most significant letters, which did not appear in the 1966 2-volume edition of Benjamin's *Briefe* (edited by Adorno and Gershom Scholem), have appeared in a collection of Adorno's writings on Benjamin published posthumously (Theodor W. Adorno, *Über Walter Benjamin*, ed. Rolf Tiedemann [Frankfurt am Main: Suhrkamp Verlag, 1970], pp. 103–161). Most of these have been translated by Harry Zohn for *New Left Review* 81 (October 1973): 55–80. An important part of Benjamin's estate remains in the *DDR Zentralarchiv* in Potsdam and is now closed to Western scholars.

26. In addition to the Adorno-Benjamin correspondence mentioned above, particularly relevant recent publications are Gershom Scholem's book of memoirs, *Walter Benjamin: Die Geschichte einer Freundschaft* (Frankfurt am Main: Suhrkamp Verlag, 1975), and the wealth of material provided by the editors of Benjamin's complete works, Rolf Tiedemann and Hermann Schweppenhäuser, in a 450-page supplement to the first volume: Benjamin, *Gesammelte Schriften,* vol. I:3: *Abhandlungen* (Frankfurt am Main: Suhrkamp Verlag, 1974).

27. See above, Chapter 1, page 22.

28. Scholem, *Walter Benjamin: Die Geschichte einer Freundschaft,* p. 256.

29. *Ibid.*, p. 198.

30. Walter Benjamin, "Karl Kraus," *Schriften*, 2 vols., ed. Theodor W. Adorno and Gretel Adorno (Frankfurt am Main: Suhrkamp Verlag, 1955), vol. 2, pp. 159–195.

31. Letter, Scholem to Benjamin, March 30, 1931, in Scholem, *Walter Benjamin: Die Geschichte einer Freundschaft,* pp. 283–287.

32. Although Horkheimer's writing developed a positive religious tone after World War II, Scholem has attested that in the thirties he and other members of the Institute outside of Adorno "didn't know where to begin" with Benjamin's theological elements (*ibid.*, p. 257).

33. See above, Chapter 8, page 125.

34. In a letter praising Benjamin's essay on Kraus (which, ironically, Scholem had found too Marxist), he encouraged his friend to ignore "the objections of that Brechtian atheism which it suits us perhaps, as inverse theology, to redeem, but in no case to accept. . . . [F]ull categorial depth must be achieved without sparing theology; but then I also believe that we help in this decisive level of Marxist theory all the more, the less we submissively appropriate [that theory] to ourselves externally; that here the 'aesthetic' will intervene into reality with incomparably more revolutionary depth than the theory of class brought in as a *deus ex machina*." (Letter, Adorno to Benjamin, November 6, 1934, Frankfurt am Main, Adorno Estate.)

35. Cited in Scholem, *Walter Benjamin: Die Geschichte einer Freundschaft*, p. 223.

36. *Ibid.*, p. 224. Cf. also letter, Benjamin to Adorno, July 17, 1931 (Frankfurt am Main, Adorno Estate).

37. He wrote a last will and testament, which is now in the Potsdam Archive in East Germany (Scholem, *Walter Benjamin: Die Geschichte einer Freundschaft*, p. 233).

38. Cited in *ibid.*

39. Benjamin addressed Scholem and, beginning in 1933, Adorno's future wife Gretel Karplus in the familiar form. He maintained the formal *"Sie"* with both Adorno and Brecht.

40. Scholem, *Walter Benjamin: Die Geschichte einer Freundschaft*, p. 224.

41. Letter, Adorno to Benjamin, November 6, 1934 (Frankfurt am Main, Adorno Estate).

42. Kracauer wrote to Scholem around 1930 that he had had a "very intense quarrel with Benjamin concerning his slavishly masochistic behavior toward Brecht. . . ." (Cited in Scholem, *Walter Benjamin: Die Geschichte einer Freundschaft*, p. 205.)

43. Benjamin was with Brecht in the latter's home in Svendborg, Denmark, from July to October 1934, and again in the summers of 1936 and 1938. In July 1935 they saw each other in Paris. Benjamin's time with Adorno was limited to a visit in Paris in October 1936 and a longer, last time with him in San Remo during January 1938. Scholem, who had gone to Palestine in 1933, saw Benjamin only once for a short time in Europe in 1938.

44. Cf. Brenner, "Theodor W. Adorno als Sachwalter des Benjaminschen Werkes," *Die neue Linke nach Adorno.*

45. A special reprint of Scholem's 100-page essay on the Kabbalah written for the *Encyclopaedia Judaica* was in Benjamin's hands by 1932 (Scholem, *Walter Benjamin: Die Geschichte einer Freundschaft*, p. 226).

46. *Ibid.*, p. 246.

47. For example: "At its most materialistic, materialism comes to agree with theology. Its great desire would be the resurrection of the flesh, a desire utterly foreign to idealism, the realm of the absolute spirit." (Theodor W. Adorno, *Negative Dialectics*, trans. E. B. Ashton [New York: The Seabury Press, 1973], p. 207.)

48. Letter, Adorno to Benjamin, March 18, 1936, Adorno, *Über Walter Benjamin*, p. 134.

49. That Adorno's appreciation of theology was limited to a "totally secular level" was clear to Scholem, who thus dismissed as "laughable" later charges that Adorno's position was theological whereas Benjamin deserted theology for materialism. (Scholem, *Walter Benjamin: Die Geschichte einer Freundschaft*, pp. 257, 269.) This was his judgment despite his "no small surprise" when he finally met and spoke with Adorno in 1938 in New York: "I had expected a Marxist, who would insist on the liquidation of this, in my opinion, most valuable continuity in Benjamin's intellectual

household. Instead I met here a mind which, even when viewed under his own dialectical perspective, related to these traits fully and openly, indeed almost positively." (*Ibid.*, p. 268.) Adorno's impression of that meeting is recorded in a letter to Benjamin: "It is not easy for me to convey my impression of Scholem. . . . My liking of him comes into play most strongly where he makes himself the advocate of the theological motif in your, and perhaps I may say also in my philosophy, and it will not have escaped you that a number of his arguments concerning the task of the theological motif, above all, that it is in truth as little eliminated in your method as in mine, converge with my San Remo discussions. . . ." (Letter, Adorno to Benjamin, May 4, 1938, Frankfurt am Main, Adorno Estate.)

50. Benjamin, *Briefe*, vol. 2, p. 624.

51. Walter Benjamin, "Franz Kafka: On the Tenth Anniversary of his Death" (1934), *Illuminations*, ed. and introd. Hannah Arendt, trans. Harry Zohn (New York: Schocken Books, 1969), p. 127.

52. *Ibid.*, p. 122.

53. *Ibid.*, p. 133.

54. *Ibid.*, p. 132.

55. *Ibid.*, pp. 128–129.

56. Scholem, *Walter Benjamin: Die Geschichte einer Freundschaft*, p. 213. Scholem continued: "Here for once the world is brought to speech in which redemption cannot be anticipated — go and make that clear to the Goyim!"

57. Cited in *ibid.*, p. 218.

58. Benjamin, *Briefe*, vol. 2, pp. 613–628.

59. Brecht's criticism was rather brutal, as Benjamin recorded in his diary during his visit in Denmark. At first, and for weeks, Brecht said nothing; then, according to Benjamin's entry of August 31: "The night before last a long and heated debate about my Kafka. Its foundation: the charge that it promotes Jewish fascism. It increases and spreads the darkness surrounding Kafka instead of dispersing it." (Walter Benjamin, *Understanding Brecht*, introd. Stanley Mitchell, trans. Anna Bostock [London: NLB, 1973], p. 110.)

60. Letter, Adorno to Benjamin, December 17, 1934, Adorno, *Über Walter Benjamin*, p. 103.

61. *Ibid.*, pp. 109–110.

62. *Ibid.*, p. 107. Adorno admitted to a similar fault: "I know well enough that the same regression, the same inadequate articulation of the concept of myth is just as attributable to me in the Kierkegaard study. . . ." (*Ibid.*, p. 106.)

63. *Ibid.*, p. 105.

64. Benjamin, "Franz Kafka" (1934), *Illuminations*, p. 122.

65. *Ibid.*

66. Letter, Adorno to Benjamin, December 17, 1934, Adorno, *Über Walter Benjamin*, pp. 105–107.

67. See above, Chapter 8, page 129.

68. Benjamin, "Zentralpark," *Schriften*, vol. 1, p. 489.

69. Adorno found the "bringing in of categories from epic theater" foreign to the material of the essay. (Letter, Adorno to Benjamin, December 17, 1934, Adorno, *Über Walter Benjamin*, p. 108.)

70. Scholem, *Walter Benjamin: Die Geschichte einer Freundschaft*, p. 250.

71. His argument was discussed in Chapter 2 above, page 35.

72. Walter Benjamin, "The Author as Producer" (1933), *Understanding Brecht*, p. 101 (italics Benjamin's). Benjamin praised the proletarian music of Hanns Eisler which, he was well aware, Adorno had criticized sharply in 1932 (see above, Chapter 2, page 40). The lecture concluded with the statement "the revolutionary struggle is not fought between capitalism and mind. It is fought between capitalism and the proletariat." (*Ibid.*, p. 103.)

73. *Ibid.*, p. 95.

74. *Ibid.*, p. 102.

75. Scholem wrote: "I never received a copy of the text, which was mentioned in his letters and discussions. When I pressured him in Paris in 1938 he said, 'I think I'd rather not give it to you to read.' Now that I know the essay, I can understand that." (Scholem, *Walter Benjamin: Die Geschichte einer Freundschaft*, p. 250.)

76. Letter, Benjamin to Adorno, May 31, 1935, Benjamin, *Briefe*, vol. 2, p. 662.

77. Letter, Benjamin to Adorno, June 10, 1935 (Frankfurt am Main, Adorno Estate).

78. It was on the basis of this memorandum that Benjamin became a member of the Institute, receiving a stipend for work on the book-length *Passagenarbeit*, as well as articles for publication in the Institute's *Zeitschrift für Sozialforschung*. (Editorial comment in Benjamin, *Gesammelte Schriften* I:3, p. 1066.)

79. The draft which Adorno received (since lost) was not quite the same, but very close to the one which was published as "Paris: Die Haupstadt des XIX. Jahrhunderts" in the two-volume edition of the Benjamin *Schriften* edited by Theodor and Gretel Adorno in 1955 (vol. 1, pp. 406–422), and translated as "Paris: The Capital of the Nineteenth Century" in Walter Benjamin, *Charles Baudelaire: A Lyric Poet in the Era of High Capitalism*, trans. Harry Zohn (London: NLB, 1973), pp. 155–176.

80. "The formulation 'the new is intermingled with the old' appears to me highly dubious. . . . There is no reversion to the old; rather, the newest, as appearance and phantasmagoria, is itself the old." (Letter, Adorno to Benjamin, August 2, 1935, Adorno, *Über Walter Benjamin*, p. 119.)

81. *Ibid.*, p. 112.

82. *Ibid.*, p. 117.

83. Letter, Benjamin to "Felizitas" (Gretel Karplus), August 16, 1935, Benjamin, *Briefe*, vol. 2, p. 686.

84. *Ibid.*, p. 687.

85. Letter, Benjamin to Scholem, May 20, 1935, *ibid.*, p. 654.

86. In the opening lines of his Hornberg letter, Adorno wrote that one of "the most important ideas" in the *exposé* was Benjamin's reference to the collector's utopian dream of a world in which things were free from the bondage of being useful. (Adorno, *Über Walter Benjamin*, p. 111; cf. Benjamin, "Paris: The Capital of the Nineteenth Century" (1935), *Charles Baudelaire*, p. 169.)

87. See above, Chapter 2.

88. Benjamin, "Paris: Die Hauptstadt des XIX. Jahrhunderts" (1935), *Schriften*, vol. 1, p. 408.

89. Letter, Adorno to Benjamin, August 2, 1935, Adorno, *Über Walter Benjamin*, p. 115.

90. *Ibid.*, pp. 114–115.

91. *Ibid.*, p. 113.

92. Parts of these essays appeared in the Institute's *Zeitschrift für Sozialforschung*, but they were first published in full in a book entitled *Versuch über Wagner* (Frankfurt am Main: Suhrkamp Verlag, 1952).

93. Letter, Benjamin to Scholem, August 9, 1935, Benjamin, *Briefe*, vol. 2, p. 685.

94. Letter, Adorno to Benjamin, August 2, 1935, Adorno, *Über Walter Benjamin*, p. 112.

95. Scholem, *Walter Benjamin: Die Geschichte einer Freundschaft*, pp. 34–35.

96. Adorno, *Über Walter Benjamin*, pp. 49, 98.

97. Letter, Benjamin to Horkheimer, October 1935, in Benjamin, *Gesammelte Schriften* I:3, p. 983.

98. There were a variety of drafts and revisions of this essay. As far as the editors of Benjamin's works have been able to establish, Horkheimer received the first definitive German draft, as did Bernhard Reich in Moscow. It is reprinted as the "Erste Fassung" in *ibid.*, I:2, pp. 431–469. Horkheimer and Benjamin decided that the article should appear in French, and the draft (somewhat revised) was soon translated for publication in the *Zeitschrift für Sozialforschung*. Adorno received a copy of the first French draft (now lost) to which he responded in his letter of March 18, 1936. The French draft was then altered considerably by people connected with the Institute *Zeitschrift* in Paris. Benjamin's strong protest to the changes led to a series of complications that delayed its publication for half a year. The changes were aimed primarily at eliminating formulations too easily taken as "a political confession" (i.e., Communist) which might provoke suspicions against the exiled Institute, causing a "serious threat" to its continued existence in the United States (*ibid.*, I:3, p. 1019). In the end Benjamin agreed to most of the changes. The draft finally published in the *Zeitschrift* in May 1936, "L'Oeuvre d'art à l'époque de sa réproduction mécanisée," is thus substantially different from the first German version. (It appears in the appendix of *ibid.*, I:2,

pp. 709–739.) Benjamin later wrote a second German version, probably in 1937–1938, which, among other changes, reinstated the more radical, more Marxist formulations. He sent it to Gretel Adorno, and it is this version which she and Theodor W. Adorno included in their 2-volume edition of Benjamin's *Schriften* published in 1955 (where it is misleadingly identified as a translation of the 1936 version printed in French in the *Zeitschrift*). From here it was translated into English as "The Work of Art in the Age of Mechanical Reproduction" in *Illuminations*, pp. 217–251. It appears as the "Zweite Fassung" in Benjamin, *Gesammelte Schriften* I:2, pp. 471–508.

99. He asked that copies not be circulated before publication, fearing his ideas would be stolen (*ibid.*, I:3, p. 983); he was pleased and flattered when André Malraux discussed the (published) essay at a London writer's congress in 1936 (*ibid.*, p. 1024).

100. Letter, Benjamin to Werner Kraft, December 27, 1935, *ibid.*, p. 986.

101. Letter, Benjamin to Adorno, February 7, 1936, *ibid.*, pp. 986–987.

102. Letter, Adorno to Benjamin, January 29, 1936, *ibid.*, p. 986.

103. He wrote to Horkheimer February 29, 1936, that this section, fundamental to the "political groundplan" of the essay, ought not to be omitted "if this work is to have informatory value for the *avantgarde* French intelligentsia" (*ibid.*, p. 992). However, censorship of clearly identifiable Marxist formulations was necessary for the Institute, given the political precariousness of its position in exile in the United States, and Benjamin's articles were treated no differently in this respect than Adorno's or others. Benjamin's final agreement to such changes was based not so much on Institute pressure and financial necessity as on sympathy for the real difficulties the Marxist formulations could have caused the Institute (*ibid.*, pp. 1018–1019).

104. Benjamin, *Das Kunstwerk im Zeitalter seiner technischen Reproduzierbarkeit* (Erste Fassung, 1935), *Gesammelte Schriften* I:2, p. 435.

105. *Ibid.*

106. See above, Chapter 2.

107. In contrast, when Adorno spoke of the dialectical process involved in the reproduction of music, he meant the subject-object relationship involved in the act of its performance. As early as 1928 he argued that the new mechanical reproduction techniques had indeed transformed that process, but its effect was negative: The family now listened to music on the gramophone instead of actively reproducing it by playing it. The result was to distance the music from the subject, whose role was reduced to passivity, indeed, subservience: The dog listening to his master's voice was the authentic trademark for the gramophone's effect. (Theodor Wiesengrund-Adorno, "Nadelkurven," *Musikblätter des Anbruch* 10, 2 [1928] : 47–50.)

108. See Chapter 8, page 127.

109. Benjamin, "L'Oeuvre d'art à l'époque de sa reproduction mécanisée" (1936), *Gesammelte Schriften* I:2, pp. 714–715.

110. *Ibid.*, p. 728.

111. *Ibid.*, p. 736.

112. Benjamin had already argued in "The Author as Producer" that this was a mark of progressive art (see above, page 000).

113. Benjamin, "L'Oeuvre d'art à lépoque de sa reproduction mécanisée" (1936), *Gesammelte Schriften* I:2, p. 724.

114. Benjamin, *Das Kunstwerk im Zeitalter seiner technischen Reproduzierbarkeit* (1935), *ibid.*, p. 369.

115. Adorno was responding to the first French draft of early 1936 (which has since been lost), an intermediary version between the first German draft of 1935 and the French draft published in the *Zeitschrift für Sozialforschung* in May 1936. For w,ant of a better solution to the philological problem, parts of both these drafts have been used here.

116. See above, Chapter 8.

117. Letter, Adorno to Benjamin, March 18, 1936, Benjamin, *Gesammelte Schriften* I:3, p. 1002.

118. *Ibid.*

119. *Ibid.*

120. ". . . politically this means nothing other than to credit the proletariat (as the subject of cinema) immediately with an achievement which, according to Lenin, it can never realize except through a theory of intellectuals as dialectical subjects, who themselves belong to the sphere of artworks which you have consigned to Hell." (*Ibid.*, p. 1003.)

121. *Ibid.*, p. 1004.

122. *Ibid.*

123. *Ibid.*, p. 1003.

124. Letter, Benjamin to Adorno, June 30, 1936, *ibid.*, p. 1022.

125. Adorno wrote Benjamin that the jazz essay "tries to express positively some of the things I have formulated negatively today. It arrives at a complete verdict on jazz, in particular by revealing its 'progressive' elements (appearance of montage, collective work, primacy of reproduction over production) as facades of something that is in truth quite reactionary." (Letter, Adorno to Benjamin, March 18, 1936, *ibid.*)

126. Letter, Benjamin to Adorno, June 30, 1936, *ibid.*, p. 1022.

127. Probably "Typescript T[1]," almost identical to the second German draft ("Zweite Fassung") of 1937-1938 in *ibid.*, vol. I:2, pp. 471-508 (see *ibid.*, vol. I:3, pp. 1032, 1060-1061).

128. Bertolt Brecht, *Arbeitsjournal*, 2 vols., ed. Werner Hecht (Frankfurt am Main: Suhrkamp Verlag, 1973), vol. 1, p. 16. (The entry is dated July 25, 1938.)

129. Scholem, *Walter Benjamin: Die Geschichte einer Freundschaft*, p. 251. He was responding to one of the French drafts which were actually less Marxist than Brecht's copy.

130. *Ibid.*

131. *Ibid.*, p. 258.

132. *Ibid.* This argument was compatible with the opening thesis of Benjamin's *Geschichtsphilosophische Thesen*, written in 1940 (see Chapter 11).
133. Benjamin, *Gesammelte Schriften* I:3, p. 985. In fact it was not published there.
134. *Ibid.*, pp. 1025–1026.
135. See above, Chapter 3.
136. Benjamin, *Gesammelte Schriften* I:3, p. 983.
137. "Several times I have seen [Hanns] Eisler [in New York]. . . . With great composure I listened to his miserable defense of the Moscow trials. . . ." (Letter, Adorno to Benjamin, May 4, 1938, Frankfurt am Main, Adorno Estate.)
138. Rolf Tiedemann, "Historischer Materialismus oder politischer Messianismus?" *Materialien zu Benjamins Thesen "Über den Begriff der Geschichte": Beiträge und Interpretationen*, ed. Peter Bulthaup (Frankfurt am Main: Suhrkamp Verlag, 1975), p. 101.
139. *Ibid.*
140. *Ibid.*, p. 102. The change which it caused in Benjamin's writings is discussed in Chapter 11.

CHAPTER 10

1. Republished in Max Horkheimer, *Kritische Theorie: Eine Dokumentation*, 2 vols., ed. Alfred Schmidt (Frankfurt am Main: S. Fischer Verlag, 1968), vol. II, pp. 1–81.
2. *Ibid.*, p. 12. Horkheimer later developed this idea with Adorno in their theory of the "culture industry."
3. See [Institut für Sozialforschung,] *Studien über Autorität und Familie*, ed. Max Horkheimer (Paris: Felix Alcan, 1936). The empirical research was carried out with German workers before the emigration. Erich Fromm, as well as Horkheimer and Herbert Marcuse, were responsible for the theoretical part of the study.
4. Horkheimer, "Egoismus und Freiheitsbewegung," *Kritische Theorie* II, p. 32.
5. *Ibid.*, pp. 50–51.
6. The relationship between Marcuse and Adorno was not close during the 1930s. Although Marcuse's frequent articles in the Institute's journal demonstrated that he shared many of Adorno's positions – on mass culture, for example, and on the centrality of dialectical argumentation – their intellectual and personal temperaments were quite far apart, and the affinities in their writing were less the result of direct influence than they were a reflection of their mutual friendship with Max Horkheimer.
7. Letter, Adorno to Benjamin, July 19, 1937 (Frankfurt am Main, Adorno Estate).
8. Cited in Martin Jay, *The Dialectical Imagination: A History of the Frank-*

furt School and the Institute of Social Research, 1923-1950 (Boston: Little, Brown, 1973), p. 188.

9. Letter, Benjamin to Horkheimer, October 13, 1936, Walter Benjamin, *Briefe,* 2 vols., ed. Gershom Scholem and Theodor W. Adorno (Frankfurt am Main: Suhrkamp Verlag, 1966), vol. 2, p. 722.

10. *Ibid.*

11. Letter, Adorno to Benjamin, November [?], 1936 (Frankfurt am Main, Adorno Estate).

12. Letter, Adorno to Benjamin, July 19, 1937 (Frankfurt am Main, Adorno Estate).

13. Letter, Horkheimer to Adorno, October 13, 1937 (Frankfurt am Main, Adorno Estate).

14. Max Horkheimer, "Traditionelle und kritische Theorie" (1937), *Zeitschrift für Sozialforschung,* trans. as "Traditional and Critical Theory," in Max Horkheimer, *Critical Theory,* trans. Matthew J. O'Connell et al. (New York: Herder and Herder, 1972), pp. 188-252.

15. Benjamin, *Briefe,* vol. 2, p. 736.

16. Scholem acknowledged the decisiveness of this support, which began in 1933: "It is impossible to imagine what would have become of him in Paris without the help that came from Friedrich Pollock and Max Horkheimer — doubtless prompted by Adorno's understanding of Benjamin's productivity and situation." (Gershom Scholem, *Walter Benjamin: Die Geschichte einer Freundschaft* [Frankfurt am Main: Suhrkamp Verlag, 1975], p. 245.)

17. *Ibid.,* p. 268.

18. *Ibid.,* p. 261.

19. *Ibid.,* pp. 247, 261, 268.

20. Letter, Adorno to Benjamin, November [?], 1937 (Frankfurt am Main, Adorno Estate).

21. See Chapter 11.

22. Benjamin was well aware of this difference: "the fundamental conception of [the] Wagner [essay] is a polemical one," and hence it mixed poorly with the concept of "rescuing" or "redemption" (*Rettung*): "Redemption is a cyclical form, the polemic is a progressive one." (Letter, Benjamin to Adorno, June 19, 1938, Frankfurt am Main, Adorno Estate.)

23. Letter, Benjamin to Horkheimer, January 6, 1938, Benjamin, *Briefe,* vol. 2, p. 741.

24. *Ibid.*

25. When Adorno began working on the Princeton Radio Research Project, he referred to his own method as "social physiognomics" (see Chapter 11, page 176).

26. Cf. above, Chapter 4.

27. Letter, Adorno to Benjamin, June 8, 1938 (Frankfurt am Main, Adorno Estate). He assured Benjamin that it would "also represent your theoretical interests in a way that will give you pleasure." (*Ibid.*)

28. Letter, Adorno to Benjamin, August 2, 1938 (Frankfurt am Main, Adorno Estate).

29. Republished in *Dissonanzen* (1956), the third edition of which is in Theodor W. Adorno, *Gesammelte Schriften*, vol. 14: *Dissonanzen; Einleitung in die Musiksoziologie,* ed. Rolf Tiedemann (Frankfurt am Main: Suhrkamp Verlag, 1973), pp. 14–50.

30. Conversation with Rolf Tiedemann, Frankfurt am Main, summer 1972.

31. Adorno, "Über den Fetischcharakter in der Musik und die Regression des Hörens" (1938), *GS* 14, p. 27.

32. *Ibid.,* p. 48.

33. *Ibid.,* p. 50.

34. He wrote to Horkheimer December 15, 1939: "Nothing in the world for me is able to replace the *Bibliothèque Nationale.*" (Benjamin, *Briefe,* vol. 2, p. 839.)

35. Letter, Benjamin to Horkheimer, April 16, 1938, Walter Benjamin, *Gesammelte Schriften,* 6 vols., ed. Rolf Tiedemann and Hermann Schweppenhäuser, vol. I:3: *Abhandlungen* (Frankfurt am Main: Suhrkamp Verlag, 1974), p. 1073. The completed essay was not published in the Institute's journal for reasons explained below. It appears as *Charles Baudelaire: Ein Lyriker im Zeitalter des Hochkapitalismus* in *ibid.,* vol. I:2, pp. 509–604, and in translation as "The Paris of the Second Empire in Baudelaire" in Walter Benjamin, *Charles Baudelaire: A Lyric Poet in the Era of High Capitalism,* trans. Harry Zohn (London: NLB, 1973), pp. 9–107.

36. Scholem, *Walter Benjamin: Die Geschichte einer Freundschaft,* p. 261.

37. *Ibid.*

38. *Ibid.,* pp. 262–263.

39. Letter, Benjamin to Kitty Marx-Steinschneider, July 20, 1938, Benjamin, *Briefe,* vol. 2, p. 767.

40. *Ibid.,* p. 768.

41. Letter, Gretel Adorno to Benjamin, August 3, 1938, Benjamin, *Gesammelte Schriften* I:3, p. 1085.

42. "Everyone proceeds from the assumption that it is absolutely necessary for your work to live in Paris. Teddie and I at least are of a different opinion. Aside from the hope that there are certain people here who could attract you, we have known you long enough in Berlin to have confidence that New York would be at least not unpleasant for you." (Letter, Gretel Adorno to Benjamin, September 12, 1938, *ibid.,* p. 1089.)

43. Letter, Adorno to Benjamin, November 10, 1938, *ibid.,* p. 1093.

44. *Ibid.,* p. 1094.

45. *Ibid.*

46. See above, page 143.

47. See above, page 156.

48. Letter, Adorno to Benjamin, November 10, 1938, Benjamin, *Gesammelte Schriften* I:3, p. 1096.

49. *Ibid.*, p. 1098. The reference is to Nikolai Bukharin and E. Preobraschensky, *Das ABC des Kommunismus* (1921).

50. "The study does not represent you as it of all your writings must represent you." (Letter, Adorno to Benjamin, November 10, 1938, Benjamin, *Gesammelte Schriften* I:3, p. 1098.)

51. *Ibid.*, pp. 1097–1098.

52. Letter, Benjamin to Adorno, December 9, 1938, *ibid.*, p. 1101.

53. *Ibid.*

54. *Ibid.*, p. 1103.

55. *Ibid.*

56. *Ibid.*, p. 1104.

57. *Ibid.*, pp. 1103–1104.

58. Hence when Adorno wrote to Benjamin that the Institute supported his position (see above, page 157), this marked a correction of his earlier evaluation. Significantly, references to the Institute in the passage from Benjamin's letter cited immediately below were deleted from its publication in the 1955 edition of Benjamin's *Briefe* (edited by Adorno and Scholem).

59. *Ibid.*, p. 1103.

60. *Ibid.*, p. 1105.

61. Benjamin admitted in a letter to Scholem (February 4, 1939): "The reservations that could be made against the manuscript are in part reasonable . . ." (*ibid.*, p. 1114). As Benjamin anticipated, Scholem's criticisms of it were very close to Adorno's (*ibid.*, p. 1118). In an addendum to the essay Benjamin's methodological comments reflected Adorno's criticism. He stated that "the matter in itself" was not "in truth"; hence it was not sufficient to "simply confront the poet Baudelaire with present-day society and answer the question as to what he has to say to this society's progressive cadres by referring to his works. . . ." (Benjamin, "Addendum to 'The Paris of the Second Empire in Baudelaire' " (n.d.), *Charles Baudelaire*, pp. 103–104.

62. Letter, Benjamin to Pollock, April 8, 1939, Benjamin, *Gesammelte Schriften* I:3, p. 1116.

63. Letter, Benjamin to Adorno, October 4, 1938, *ibid.*, p. 1092.

64. Benjamin, *Briefe*, vol. 2, p. 796.

65. Scholem, *Walter Benjamin: Die Geschichte einer Freundschaft*, p. 270.

66. Letter, Benjamin to Scholem, February 4, 1939, Benjamin, *Gesammelte Schriften* I:3, p. 1113.

67. Letter dated February 1, 1939, *ibid.*, pp. 1107–1113.

68. Letter, Gretel Adorno to Benjamin, May 5, 1939, *ibid.*, p. 1120.

69. Published in the *Zeitschrift für Sozialforschung* as "Über einige Motive bei Baudelaire," reprinted in Benjamin, *Gesammelte Schriften* I:2, pp. 605–654, and translated as "Some Motifs in Baudelaire," Benjamin, *Charles Baudelaire*, pp. 107–154.

70. Letter, Benjamin to Margarete Steffin, August 6, 1939, Benjamin, *Gesammelte Schriften* I:3, p. 1125.

71. Letter, Gretel Adorno to Benjamin, August 6, 1939, *ibid.*, p. 1125.

72. Letter, Adorno to Benjamin, n.d. (November or December 1939), *ibid.*, p. 1127.

73. Benjamin, *Gesammelte Schriften* I:2, p. 608.

74. *Ibid.*, p. 630.

75. *Ibid.*, p. 643.

76. *Ibid.*, p. 623.

77. *Ibid.*

78. *Ibid.*, p. 632.

79. *Ibid.*, p. 633.

80. Benjamin described the "aura" of objects as the power to return the viewer's gaze: "To experience the aura of an object appearing before us means to invest it with the ability to look at us in return." (*Ibid.*, pp. 646–647.) This was the theory which had appeared to Brecht the year before as "rather ghastly" mysticism (see above, page 149). Now in responding to the new essay, Adorno suggested that as "inverse" theology the idea corresponded to the Marxian concept of objects as sedimented human labor. The inability to see that human element (which would "look at us in return") would thus be synonymous with the reification of commodities. (Letter, Adorno to Benjamin, February 29, 1940, Benjamin, *Gesammelte Schriften* I:3, pp. 1131–1132.) Benjamin affirmed this interpretation, but significantly he was unwilling to totally secularize the notion of aura and argued that the "forgotten human element" of objects was not sedimented labor alone: "Tree and bush, which are invested with aura, are not made by human beings." (Letter, Benjamin to Adorno, May 7, 1940, *ibid.*, p. 1134.)

81. Benjamin, *Gesammelte Schriften* I:2, p. 618.

82. *Ibid.*, p. 631.

83. The closing section discusses the motif of the "lost halo" from a previously neglected document in Baudelaire's literary estate and juxtaposes to it a passage which anticipates Benjamin's description of Paul Klee's Angelus Novus as the angel of history (see below, page 169). The Baudelaire passage: "Lost in this mean world, jostled by the crowds, I am like a weary man whose eye sees nothing but disillusionment and bitterness looking backward into the depths of the years, and before him nothing but a tempest that contains nothing new, neither instruction nor pain." (*Ibid.*, p. 652.) The passage by Benjamin from the *Geschichtsphilosophische Thesen* (cited in full below, p. 169): "There is a painting by Klee called 'Angelus Novus.' . . . The angel of history must look like that. His face is turned toward the past. Where a chain of events appears to *us, he* sees one single catastrophe which relentlessly piles wreckage upon wreckage and hurls them before his feet. . . . [A] storm is blowing from Paradise. . . . This storm drives him irresistibly into the future . . . while the pile of debris before him grows toward the sky." (*Ibid.*, pp. 697–698.)

84. Benjamin, *Gesammelte Schriften* I:3, p. 1130.

85. This has been the conclusion of the best-qualified commentators. See par-

ticularly Rolf Tiedemann's editorial afterword in Walter Benjamin, *Charles Baudelaire: Ein Lyriker im Zeitalter des Hochkapitalismus. Zwei Fragmente* (Frankfurt am Main: Suhrkamp Verlag, 1969), pp. 167–191; also Jürgen Habermas's review of Benjamin in *Die Zeit*, September 12, 1969, p. 14.

86. Scholem, *Walter Benjamin: Die Geschichte einer Freundschaft*, pp. 274–275.

87. Letter, Benjamin to Adorno, May 7, 1940, Benjamin, *Briefe*, vol. 2, p. 848.

88. Letter, Benjamin to Horkheimer, December 15, 1939, *ibid.*, p. 839.

89. In fact the theses had a very great impact on Adorno and Horkheimer, as was evident in their study on history, *Dialektik der Aufklärung* (1947). (See above, Chapter 3, pages 59–60.)

90. So he told Hannah Arendt in Paris that winter. The Institute received two versions of the manuscript posthumously, from Arendt and Martin Domke, and published the latter in a special edition of the Institute journal dedicated to Benjamin's memory in 1942. (Scholem, *Walter Benjamin: Die Geschichte einer Freundschaft*, p. 275.)

91. Letter, Benjamin to Adorno, August 2, 1940, Benjamin, *Briefe*, vol. 2, p. 861.

92. He had mentioned intentions of suicide to Hannah Arendt in Marseilles on his way to Spain. (Scholem, *Walter Benjamin: Die Geschichte einer Freundschaft*, p. 279.)

93. Benjamin, *Gesammelte Schriften* I:2, pp. 578–579.

CHAPTER 11

1. Letter, Adorno to Benjamin, February 1, 1939 (Frankfurt am Main, Adorno Estate). Through friends in America Adorno succeeded in getting his parents a passport to Cuba; after a year's delay they emigrated and lived in Florida. (*Ibid.* and letter, Adorno to Benjamin, February 29, 1940, Frankfurt am Main, Adorno Estate.)

2. Letter, Adorno to Benjamin, February 1, 1939 (Frankfurt am Main, Adorno Estate).

3. Letter, Adorno to Krenek, July 29, 1935, *Theodor W. Adorno und Ernst Krenek: Briefwechsel*, ed. Wolfgang Rogge (Frankfurt am Main: Suhrkamp Verlag, 1974), p. 91. (The editor's note saying that Adorno was referring to the death of his mother is an error.)

4. Adorno contributed to Willi Reich's book *Alban Berg* (Vienna: Herbert Reichner Verlag, 1937), noting to Krenek (another contributor) on February 7, 1936: "Through this work I am slowly getting over Berg's death." (*Adorno und Krenek: Briefwechsel*, p. 112.)

5. *Ibid.*, pp. 112–113.

6. Documentation of Adorno's initial personal response is not available. His first published statement, an article in the American Jewish weekly *Aufbau* (October 18, 1940), said simply: "He took away a life which ever since he began to think, the world wished to deny him." (Theodor W. Adorno, *Über Walter Benjamin* [Frankfurt am Main: Suhrkamp Verlag, 1970], p. 10.)

7. "While we were still in New York [pre-1940], Horkheimer, under the impress of the gruesome things happening in Europe, got investigations under way on the problem of anti-Semitism." (Theodor W. Adorno, "Scientific Experiences of a European Scholar in America," trans. Donald Fleming, in *The Intellectual Migration: Europe and America, 1930–1960*, ed. Donald Fleming and Bernard Bailyn [Cambridge, Mass.: Belknap–Harvard University Press, 1969], p. 335.)

8. Theodor W. Adorno, "Der wunderliche Realist: Über Siegfried Kracauer" (1964), *Noten zur Literatur*, vol. 3 (Frankfurt am Main: Suhrkamp Verlag, 1965), p. 103.

9. Adorno, "Scientific Experiences of a European Scholar in America," *The Intellectual Migration*, p. 339.

10. Theodor W. Adorno, "George und Hofmannsthal: Zum Briefwechsel, 1891–1906" (1942), *Zur Dialektik des Engagements: Aufsätze zur Literatur des 20. Jahrhunderts II* (Frankfurt am Main: Suhrkamp Verlag, 1973), p. 69.

11. Adorno, "Scientific Experiences of a European Scholar in America," *The Intellectual Migration*, p. 340.

12. Cited in Martin Jay, *The Dialectical Imagination: A History of the Frankfurt School and the Institute of Social Research, 1923–1950* (Boston: Little, Brown, 1973), p. 189. It was Lazarsfeld who had offered to hire Adorno: "I was aware of . . . controversial features of Adorno's work, but was intrigued by his writings on the 'contradictory' role of music in our society [i.e., "Zur gesellschaftlichen Lage der Musik" (1932)]. I considered it a challenge to see whether I could induce Adorno to try to link his ideas with empirical research. In addition, I felt gratitude to the Frankfurt group led by Max Horkheimer, of which he was a member; they had helped support the work of the Newark Center, and I knew they wanted Adorno in this country." (Paul Lazarsfeld, "An Episode in the History of Social Research: A Memoir," *The Intellectual Migration*, pp. 322–323.)

13. Adorno, "Scientific Experiences of a European Scholar in America," *ibid.*, p. 342.

14. *Ibid.*

15. *Ibid.*, p. 343.

16. *Ibid.*

17. Lazarsfeld, "An Episode in the History of Social Research: A Memoir," *ibid.*, p. 323. The memo, dated June 1938, was entitled "Music in Radio."

18. *Ibid.* At the time Lazarsfeld sharply criticized Adorno: "You pride yourself in attacking other people because they are neurotic and fetishists, but it doesn't occur to you how open you are yourself to such attacks. . . . Don't you think that it is a perfect fetishism the way you use Latin words all through the text? . . . I implored you repeatedly to use more responsible language and you evidently were psychologically unable to follow my advice." (Cited in Jay, *The Dialectical Imagination*, p. 223.)

19. *Ibid.*, p. 324.

20. *Ibid.*

21. Jay, *The Dialectical Imagination*, p. 172.

22. *Ibid.*

23. *Ibid.*, pp. 167–168.

24. Jay, *The Dialectical Imagination*, p. 194.

25. Published as a fragment posthumously: Bertolt Brecht, *Der Tui-Roman: Fragment* (Frankfurt am Main: Suhrkamp Verlag, 1973).

26. Hans Bunge, *Fragen Sie mehr über Brecht: Hanns Eisler im Gespräch* (Munich: Rogner & Bernhard, 1970), p. 13.

27. Schönberg was also on the West Coast, but, according to Thomas Mann, Adorno "had no personal intercourse with him," although Eisler was a frequent guest at Schönberg's house. (Thomas Mann, *The Story of a Novel: The Genesis of Doctor Faustus*, trans. Richard and Clara Winston [New York: Alfred A. Knopf, 1961], p. 103.)

28. See above, Chapter 2, page 40.

29. Cited in Irving Fetscher, "Bertolt Brecht and America," *Salmagundi* 10/11, *The Legacy of the German Refugee Intellectuals* (Fall 1969-Winter 1970): 271.

30. Cited in *ibid.*

31. Bunge, *Fragen Sie mehr über Brecht: Hanns Eisler im Gespräch*, pp. 13–15.

32. Completed in September 1944, the book was first published by Oxford University Press in 1947 under Eisler's name only, as Eisler's brother Gerhard had been assailed for his radical political activities in the United States, and Adorno by his own later admission did not want to be dragged into the affair. An altered German version was published in 1949 in East Germany (where Eisler went after the war), containing politically expedient changes without Adorno's consent. Adorno authorized a second, unchanged translation which was published in West Germany in 1969. (See Adorno's note in Theodor W. Adorno and Hanns Eisler, *Komposition für den Film* [Munich: Rogner & Bernhard, 1969], pp. 213–215.)

33. A chapter on aesthetics, quite clearly by Adorno, asserted as a basic principle that music, instead of conforming to the visual image of the film, should stand in dialectical contradiction to it. Significantly, Adorno affirmed the principle of montage, claiming: "A montage correctly done is by definition also interpreting," whereas earlier he had criticized Benjamin's use of montage precisely because it excluded interpretation. (*Ibid.*, p. 107n.)

34. Theodor W. Adorno, *Minima Moralia* (Frankfurt am Main: Suhrkamp Verlag, 1969), p. 42.

35. Walter Benjamin, *Gesammelte Schriften*, 6 vols., ed. Rolf Tiedemann and Hermann Schweppenhäuser, vol. I:3: *Abhandlungen* (Frankfurt am Main: Suhrkamp Verlag, 1974), p. 1223. It is necessary to keep this in mind in order not to misinterpret the theses. Their message is that history has remained ever-identical in its oppression, barbarism, and suffering,

yet they introduce a study which tries to capture the absolutely new in human experience which emerges with industrial urbanization. Thus the two poles, the archaic and the modern, were to provide the interpretive keys to nineteenth-century Paris.

36. Of course, a reversal of Benjamin's position was already implied in the second Baudelaire essay completed in the summer of 1939. But Tiedemann has argued that the real turning point was Benjamin's disillusionment with the USSR following the Nazi-Soviet Non-Aggression Pact, which was signed several weeks later. (Rolf Tiedemann, "Historischer Materialismus oder politischer Messianismus?" *Materialien zu Benjamins Thesen "Über den Begriff der Geschichte": Beiträge und Interpretationen*, ed. Peter Bulthaup [Frankfurt am Main: Suhrkamp Verlag, 1975], p. 102.) The point is that after the pact, the right theoretical tendency and the right political tendency once more converged.

37. Benjamin, *Über den Begriff der Geschichte* (1940), *Gesammelte Schriften* I:2, p. 698. The theses were published under this title in 1940, but are better known as the *Geschichtsphilosophische Thesen*, published as such in *Illuminationen* (1955).

38. Benjamin, *Über den Begriff der Geschichte* (1940), *Gesammelte Schriften* I:2, p. 698.

39. Max Horkheimer, "Autoritärer Staat" (1942), *Gesellschaft im Übergang: Aufsätze, Reden und Vorträge 1942-1970*, ed. Werner Brede (Frankfurt am Main: Athenäum Fischer Taschenbuch Verlag, 1972), p. 25. Benjamin wrote in the theses that the revolutionary break exploded the continuum of history instead of accelerating it, and noted that this was intuitively known by the Paris workers in the July revolution when spontaneously in various parts of the city they fired at the clocks in towers. (Benjamin, *Über den Begriff der Geschichte* (1940), *Gesammelte Schriften* I:2, pp. 701-702.)

40. *Ibid.*, p. 693.

41. *Ibid.*

42. See above, Chapter 10.

43. *Ibid.*, p. 701.

44. (See Gershom Scholem, "Walter Benjamin und sein Engel," *Zur Aktualität Walter Benjamins: Aus Anlass des 80. Geburtstags von Walter Benjamin*, ed. Siegfried Unseld (Frankfurt am Main: Suhrkamp Verlag, 1972).

45. Benjamin, *Über den Begriff der Geschichte* (1940), *Gesammelte Schriften* I:2, pp. 697-698.

46. See above, Chapter 9, pages 140-146.

47. Theodor Adorno, *Minima Moralia: Reflections from Damaged Life*, trans. E. F. N. Jephcott (London: NLB, 1974), p. 247.

48. Adorno, "Zum Benjamins Gedächtnis" (1940), *Über Walter Benjamin*, p. 10.

49. He had himself already emphasized this transiency in his 1932 speech "Die Idee der Naturgeschichte" (discussed in Chapter 2).

50. Benjamin, *Über den Begriff der Geschichte* (1940), *Gesammelte Schriften* I:2, p. 695.

51. Walter Benjamin, *Schriften*, 2 vols., ed. Theodor W. Adorno and Gretel Adorno (Frankfurt am Main: Suhrkamp Verlag, 1955); *idem, Briefe*, 2 vols., ed. Gershom Scholem and Theodor W. Adorno (Frankfurt am Main: Suhrkamp Verlag, 1966).

52. See above, Chapter 10, page 154 f. This essay in turn influenced Benjamin's second Baudelaire essay (above, pages 154-155), which was on one level an act of self-criticism.

53. Cf. Theodor W. Adorno, "A Social Critique of Radio Music," *Kenyon Review*, 7, 2 (1945): 208-217; "Fernsehen als Ideologie" and "Prolog zum Fernsehen" (1953), in *idem, Eingriffe: Neun kritische Modelle* (Frankfurt am Main: Suhrkamp Verlag, 1968).

54. Theodor W. Adorno, "Einleitung zum *Positivismusstreit in der deutschen Soziologie*" (1969), *Gesammelte Schriften*, vol. 8: *Soziologische Schriften I*, ed. Rolf Tiedemann (Frankfurt am Main: Suhrkamp Verlag, 1972).

55. Theodor W. Adorno, "The Psychological Technique of Martin Luther Thomas' Radio Addresses" (1943), and "Studies in the Authoritarian Personality" (1944-1949), *Gesammelte Schriften*, vol. 9:1: *Soziologische Schriften II: Erste Hälfte*, ed. Susan Buck-Morss and Rolf Tiedemann (Frankfurt am Main: Suhrkamp Verlag, 1975).

56. Theodor W. Adorno, "The Stars Down to Earth" (1953), *Gesammelte Schriften*, vol. 9:2: *Soziologische Schriften II: Zweite Hälfte*, ed. Susan Buck-Morss and Rolf Tiedemann (Frankfurt am Main: Suhrkamp Verlag, 1975).

57. Theodor W. Adorno, "Vorrede" (1956), *Zur Metakritik der Erkenntnistheorie, Gesammelte Schriften*, vol. 5, ed. Gretel Adorno and Rolf Tiedemann (Frankfurt am Main: Suhrkamp Verlag, 1971).

58. See Jay, *The Dialectical Imagination*, pp. 143-167.

59. Institute member Franz Neumann, working on his now well-known book on Nazi Germany *Behemoth* (1944), rejected Pollock's thesis, considering the concept "state capitalism" a contradiction in terms. (*Ibid.*, pp. 162-163.)

60. *Ibid.*, pp. 152-153.

61. Horkheimer, "Autoritärer Staat" (1942), *Gesellschaft im Übergang*, pp. 13-35.

62. Benjamin, *Über den Begriff der Geschichte* (1940), *Gesammelte Schriften* I:2, p. 699.

63. Horkheimer, "Autoritärer Staat" (1942), *Gesellschaft im Übergang*, p. 33.

64. Theodor W. Adorno, "Gesellschaft," Max Horkheimer and Theodor W. Adorno, *Soziologische Exkurse* (vol. 4 of Institut für Sozialforschung, *Frankfurter Beiträge zur Soziologie*, ed. Theodor W. Adorno and Walter Dirks) (Frankfurt am Main: Europäische Verlagsanstalt, 1956), p. 30.

65. Benjamin, *Über den Begriff der Geschichte* (1940), *Gesammelte Schriften* I:2, p. 694.

66. *Ibid.*, p. 704.

67. Horkheimer, "Autoritärer Staat" (1942), *Gesellschaft im Übergang*, p. 34.

68. *Ibid.*, p. 23.

69. *Ibid.*, p. 21.

70. Benjamin, *Über den Begriff der Geschichte* (1940), *Gesammelte Schriften* I:2, p. 699.

71. Cf. Horkheimer, "Egoismus und Freiheitsbewegung" (1936), *Kritische Theorie: Eine Dokumentation*, 2 vols., ed. Alfred Schmidt (Frankfurt am Main: S. Fischer Verlag, 1968), vol. I, pp. 1–81. The article argued that sexual repression was a reflection of bourgeois asceticism, hence socially as well as biologically produced; and that sexual asceticism was not accidentally linked to Robespierre's Reign of Terror, which betrayed the revolutionary vision by the practice of totalitarian domination. (See above, pages 151–152).

72. Horkheimer, "Autoritärer Staat" (1942), *Gesellschaft im Übergang*, pp. 24–25.

73. *Ibid.*, p. 24.

74. As was suggested at the close of Chapter 3 above (pages 61–62), this book was less a falling behind Marx than it was a rereading of him in the light of the present; for Adorno, indeed, it marked a move toward Marx, because it acknowledged more rigorously than he had earlier the limitations of *geistige* praxis, the inadequacy of revolution within culture alone when what was needed was revolution within society.

75. Max Horkheimer, *Vernunft und Selbsterhaltung* (1942), (Frankfurt am Main: S. Fisher Verlag, 1970), p. 12 and *passim*.

76. Max Horkheimer, *Eclipse of Reason* (1947), (New York: The Seabury Press, 1974), p. 127.

77. Authorship of the first two chapters of *Eclipse of Reason*, for example, seems unmistakably to have been divided between them, with Horkheimer the author of pp. 3–34 and 58–72, and Adorno responsible for pp. 34–57 and 72–91.

78. Theodor W. Adorno, "Offener Brief an Max Horkheimer," *Die Zeit*, February 12, 1965, p. 32.

79. Theodor W. Adorno, "George und Hofmannsthal" (1942), *Zur Dialektik des Engagements*, pp. 45–93.

80. Theodor W. Adorno, Husserl ms., 1934–1937, Frankfurt am Main, Adorno Estate, pp. 119, 318.

81. Hofmannsthal came from a background remarkably similar to Adorno's: bourgeois (the noble *von* was awarded to his father, a successful businessman), of Italian and German heritage, Jewish in origin but Roman Catholic in upbringing.

82. "Poetry becomes the technical domination of that which does not allow itself to be mastered by consciousness." (Adorno, "George und Hofmannsthal" [1942], *Zur Dialektik des Engagements*, p. 47.)

83. *Ibid.*, p. 64. Adorno gave an objective, historical explanation for this: "Already by then friendship out of simple sympathy and taste was no longer possible, even between people of the most extraordinary productive power,

but instead only on the basis of binding common knowledge: friendship out of solidarity, which embraces theory as an element of its praxis." (*Ibid.*, pp. 63–64.)

84. *Ibid.*, p. 48. The word "intuition" (*Anschauung*) was a central concept in Husserl's philosophy.

85. *Ibid.*, p. 79.

86. *Ibid.*, p. 80.

87. Adorno, "Einleitung zu Benjamins Schriften" (1955), *Über Walter Benjamin*, p. 38.

88. See Benjamin, *Briefe*, for sixteen letters written to Hofmannsthal in the 1920s. The latter appreciated Benjamin's work and aided in its publishing. Benjamin was "very saddened" by Hofmannsthal's death in the summer of 1929 (*ibid.*, vol. 1, p. 497).

89. Adorno, "Benjamins *Einbahnstrasse*" (1955), *ibid.*, p. 52.

90. "There is never a document of culture which is not at the same time a document of barbarism." (Benjamin, *Über den Begriff der Geschichte* [1940], *Gesammelte Schriften* I:2, p. 696.)

91. "At every moment George's culture is bought at the expense of barbarism." (Adorno, "George und Hofmannsthal" [1942], *Zur Dialektik des Engagements*, p. 51.)

92. "The estrangement of art from life has a double meaning. It is not only the refusal to deal with that which exists – in contrast to the naturalists who are always tempted to affirm, just as they are, the horrors seen by them with an affectionately acute eye. George and Hofmannsthal curried favors no less from the established order; but always an order estranged from them. The staging of estrangement reveals as much about life as can be without theory, since life's essence is itself estrangement." (*Ibid.*, p. 80.)

93. "In brief, my case is this: I have completely lost the ability to think or speak coherently about anything. . . . [A]bstract words . . . disintegrated in my mouth like mouldy mushrooms." (Hofmannsthal, cited in *ibid.*, p. 88n.)

94. *Ibid.*, p. 59.

95. *Ibid.*, p. 81.

96. *Ibid.*

97. *Ibid.*, p. 82.

98. Theodor W. Adorno, "Über den Fetischcharakter in der Musik und die Regression des Hörens" (1938), *Gesammelte Schriften*, vol. 14: *Dissonanzen; Einleitung in die Musiksoziologie*, ed. Rolf Tiedemann (Frankfurt am Main: Suhrkamp Verlag, 1973), pp. 14–50, discussed above, pages 154–155.

99. A copy of Adorno's letter of inquiry to the Oxford University Press (Frankfurt am Main, Adorno Estate) described the book as consisting of eight chapters. Several were later published as articles elsewhere; copies of most of the remaining chapters exist in the Adorno Estate. The book "fragment" will be published as vol. 23 of Adorno's *Gesammelte Schriften*.

100. Theodor W. Adorno, "The Radio Voice," in Adorno, "Current of Music: Elements of a Radio Theory," 1939, Frankfurt am Main, Adorno Estate, p. 84.

101. See above, page 126.

102. "A physiognomist tries to establish typical features and expressions of the face not for their own sake but in order to use them as hints for hidden processes behind them, as well as for hints at future behavior to be expected on the basis of an analysis of the present expression. In just the same way radio physiognomics deals with the expression of the 'radio voice.'" (Theodor W. Adorno, "Radio Physiognomik" 1939, Frankfurt am Main, Adorno Estate, p. 45.)

103. "We are dwelling on the phenomenon because it is actually the phenomenon which determines the reaction of the listeners, and it is our ultimate aim to study the listener." (*Ibid.*, p. 39.)

104. Theodor W. Adorno, Husserl ms. 1934–1937.

105. ". . . the task of criticism must be not so much to search for the particular interest groups to which cultural phenomena are to be assigned, but rather to decipher the general social tendencies which are expressed in these phenomena and through which the most powerful interests realize themselves. Cultural criticism must become social physiognomy." (Theodor W. Adorno, "Cultural Criticism and Society" [1951], *Prisms*, trans. Samuel and Shierry Weber [London: Neville Spearman, 1967], p. 30.)

106. Adorno, "Radio Physiognomik," 1939, p. 46.

107. *Ibid.*, p. 43.

108. *Ibid.*, p. 53.

109. ". . . a private person in a private room is privately addressed by a public voice to which he is forced to subordinate himself." (*Ibid.*, p. 46.)

110. *Ibid.*

111. *Ibid.*, p. 44.

112. *Ibid.*, p. 45. Adorno noted explicitly that the present structure of the radio voice was not inevitable, that it was determined less by the technology itself than by the social relations of production which its present organization reflected. Characteristically, he claimed that radio programming could become most progressive by developing the possibilities of its own techniques, rather than borrowing the techniques of other media, as for example in the "pseudo-immediacy" of broadcasting live performances. (*Ibid.*, pp. 35–38, 60–63).

113. *Ibid.*, p. 44.

114. *Ibid.*, p. 46.

115. One of his major studies was a content analysis of the speeches of a West Coast radio demagogue, the remote, right-wing agitator Martin Luther Thomas, whom history books of the period ignore; another was an analysis of daily horoscope articles in the *Los Angeles Times*. (Both are reprinted in *GS* 9:1.)

116. Adorno, "Scientific Experiences of a European Scholar in America," *The Intellectual Migration*, p. 347.

117. Letter, Adorno to Benjamin, February 1, 1939 (Frankfurt am Main, Adorno Estate).

118. Theodor W. Adorno, "Thesen über Bedürfnis" (1942), *GS* 8, p. 394.

119. *Ibid.*

120. Theodor W. Adorno, "Notizen zur neuen Anthropologie," 1942, Frankfurt am Main, Adorno Estate, p. 6.

121. Adorno, "Scientific Experiences of a European Scholar in America," *The Intellectual Migration*, p. 347.

122. *Ibid.*, p. 348.

123. Jay, *The Dialectical Imagination*, pp. 220-221.

124. Theodor W. Adorno, Else Frenkel-Brunswik, Daniel J. Levinson, and R. Nevitt Sanford, *The Authoritarian Personality* (vol. 1 of *Studies in Prejudice*, ed. Max Horkheimer and Samuel H. Flowerman), Social Studies Series, publication no. III (New York: Harper & Brothers, 1950).

125. It generated not only vast numbers of similar research projects but also sufficient controversy by 1954 to produce a volume of critical essays devoted to it. See Richard Christie and Marie Jahoda, eds., *Studies in the Scope and Method of "The Authoritarian Personality"* (New York: Free Press, 1954).

126. Adorno, "Scientific Experiences of a European Scholar in America," *The Intellectual Migration*, p. 358.

127. *Ibid.*

128. Theodor W. Adorno, *Versuch über Wagner* (written 1937-1938) (Frankfurt am Main: Suhrkamp Verlag, 1952).

129. Unpublished, part of the Institute's report on prejudice to the Jewish Labor Committee in 1944, in Friedrich Pollock's papers, referred to (and cited in) Jay, *The Dialectical Imagination*, pp. 225, 229-230.

130. Max Horkheimer and Theodor W. Adorno, "Elements of Anti-Semitism: The Limits of Enlightenment," *Dialectic of Enlightenment*, trans. John Cumming (New York: Herder and Herder, 1972), pp. 168-208.

131. Karl Marx, "On the Jewish Question," *Writings of the Young Marx on Philosophy and Society*, trans. and ed. Loyd D. Easton and Kurt H. Guddat (Garden City, N.Y.: Doubleday, Anchor Books, 1967), pp. 216-248.

132. Horkheimer and Adorno, "Elements of Anti-Semitism," *Dialectic of Enlightenment*, p. 173.

133. *Ibid.*, p. 168.

134. *Ibid.*, p. 196.

135. *Ibid.*, p. 171.

136. *Ibid.*, p. 185.

137. *Ibid.*, pp. 187, 199.

138. *Ibid.*, p. 200. This was a theme in Marx's *Economic and Philosophic Manuscripts* (see *Writings of the Young Marx on Philosophy and Society*, p. 295 and *passim*).

139. Horkheimer and Adorno, "Elements of Anti-Semitism," *Dialectic of Enlightenment*, p. 200.

140. See above, Chapter 1, pages 17-20.

141. Fromm, who began to dispute Horkheimer's theoretical position and adopt a revisionist Freudian position particularly regarding its rejection of the

centrality of sexuality, left the Institute in 1939, not long after Adorno arrived. (See Jay, *The Dialectical Imagination,* pp. 227-230.)

142. Adorno, "Notizen zur neuen Anthropologie," 1942, p. 1.

143. *Ibid.,* p. 6.

144. Erich Fromm, *Escape from Freedom* (New York: Avon Books, 1969). The book was originally published in 1941.

145. Adorno, "Notizen zur neuen Anthropologie," 1942, p. 6.

146. Theodor W. Adorno, *Minima Moralia.* The book was a countereffort to Aristotle's *Magna Moralia.*

147. Theodor W. Adorno, *Minima Moralia: Reflections from Damaged Life,* p. 110.

148. *Ibid.,* pp. 102-103.

149. *Ibid.,* pp. 130-131.

150. *Ibid.,* p. 49.

151. *Ibid.,* p. 50.

152. *Ibid.,* p. 40.

153. So Adorno later recounted to his students. The book was published on the occasion of Horkheimer's fiftieth birthday. Horkheimer was the author of similar aphorisms which appeared at the end of *Dialektik der Aufklärung.*

154. Walter Benjamin, *Berliner Kindheit um Neunzehnhundert* and *Einbahnstrasse, Gesammelte Schriften,* vol. IV:1: *Kleine Prosa,* ed. Tillman Rexroth (Frankfurt am Main: Suhrkamp Verlag, 1972), pp. 235-304, 83-148.

155. Cf. Chapter 8, above, page 133.

156. Horkheimer and Adorno, "Elements of Anti-Semitism," *Dialectic of Enlightenment.* Cf. the personality variables tested for in the questionnaires, Adorno et al., *The Authoritarian Personality,* chap. VII, "The Measurement of Implicit Anti-Democratic Trends," reprinted in Adorno, "Studies in the Authoritarian Personality," *GS* 9:1, pp. 185-261, esp. pp. 194, 229-231.

157. "This approach stands in contrast to the public opinion poll: whereas the poll is interested primarily in the distribution of opinion with respect to a particular issue, the present interest was to inquire, concerning a particular opinion, with what other opinions and attitudes it was related." (*The Authoritarian Personality,* chap. I, in *GS* 9:1, p. 167.)

158. A person's susceptibility to fascist ideology depended "primarily upon his psychological needs" (*ibid.,* p. 151); but these needs in turn were not biological, but rather themselves reflections of the social structure (*ibid.,* p. 155).

159. *Ibid.,* p. 150.

160. *Ibid.,* p. 158.

161. See above, pages 22-23 and Chapter 6.

162. The F scale, despite its repeated refinements and despite its clusters of components, was after all a categorizing, hence reifying process, "not a fine enough instrument to give the true picture . . ." of the individual subject. (*Ibid.,* p. 260.)

163. *The Authoritarian Personality*, part IV, chaps. XVI–XIX, in *ibid.*, pp. 262–508.

164. Adorno, "The Psychological Technique of Martin Luther Thomas' Radio Addresses" (1943), *GS* 9:1, pp. 7–141. Jay has noted that a type of materialist "content analysis" had been developed by Adorno's long-time friend Siegfried Kracauer in the late twenties. (Martin Jay, "The Extraterritorial Life of Siegfried Kracauer," *Salmagundi* 31/32 [Fall 1975-Winter 1976]: 57.)

165. Adorno, "Scientific Experiences of a European Scholar in America," *The Intellectual Migration*, p. 365.

166. Adorno, "Introductory Remarks" to part IV, "Qualitative Studies of Ideology," *The Authoritarian Personality*, in Adorno, "Studies in the Authoritarian Personality," *GS* 9:1, p. 263.

167. *Ibid.*

168. *Ibid.*

169. Adorno, chap. XVI of *The Authoritarian Personality*, in *ibid.*, p. 302.

170. *Ibid.*, p. 318.

171. *Ibid.*, p. 289.

172. The criticism made by Hyman and Sheatsley that *The Authoritarian Personality* took "the irrationality out of the social order and impute[d] it to the respondent" is inaccurate. (See Herbert H. Hyman and Paul B. Sheatsley, "The Authoritarian Personality: A Methodological Critique," *Studies in the Scope and Method of "The Authoritarian Personality,"* p. 109.)

173. Adorno, chap. XVII of *The Authoritarian Personality*, in Adorno, "Studies in the Authoritarian Personality," *GS* 9:1, p. 335.

174. *Ibid.*, p. 348.

175. *Ibid.*, p. 342.

176. *Ibid.*, p. 338.

177. *Ibid.*, p. 342.

178. *Ibid.*

CHAPTER 12

1. See above, Chapter 3.

2. Theodor W. Adorno, "Reflexionen zur Klassentheorie" (1942), *Gesammelte Schriften*, vol. 8: *Soziologische Schriften* I, ed. Rolf Tiedemann (Frankfurt am Main: Suhrkamp Verlag, 1972), p. 376.

3. *Ibid.*, pp. 374–375.

4. Theodor W. Adorno, "Kierkegaard noch einmal" (1963), *Kierkegaard: Konstruktion des Aesthetischen* [1933]: *Mit zwei Beilagen*, 3rd ed., enl. (Frankfurt am Main: Suhrkamp Verlag, 1966), p. 306.

5. Adorno, "Reflexionen zur Klassentheorie" (1942), *GS* 8, p. 377.

6. Two of them, "Reflexionen zur Klassentheorie" and "Thesen über Bedürfnis," were first published in *GS* 8; the third, a draft entitled "Notizen zur

neuen Anthropologie" (Frankfurt am Main, Adorno Estate), will appear in a later volume.

7. Adorno, "Reflexionen zur Klassentheorie" (1942), *GS* 8, pp. 370 ff.

8. Adorno, "Thesen über Bedürfnis" (1942), *GS* 8, p. 394.

9. Adorno, "Reflexionen zur Klassentheorie" (1942), *GS* 8, p. 374.

10. Adorno, "Notizen zur neuen Anthropologie," 1942.

11. "What Benjamin calls the disintegration of aura and the destruction of experience is essentially identical with the totality principle of society." (*Ibid.*, p. 3.)

12. Adorno, "Reflexionen zur Klassentheorie" (1942), *GS* 8, pp. 377, 383 ff.

13. Adorno, "Notizen zur neuen Anthropologie," 1942, p. 4.

14. Cf.: "When a doctrine hypostatizes an isolated principle that excludes negation, it is paradoxically predisposing itself to conformism." (Max Horkheimer, *Eclipse of Reason* [1947] [New York: The Seabury Press, 1974], p. 87. In thought and expression, this statement is characteristic of Adorno. Horkheimer's own writings were far less rigorously constructed in this sense.)

15. Adorno, "Thesen über Bedürfnis" (1942), *GS* 8, p. 393.

16. Theodor W. Adorno, "Studies in the Authoritarian Personality" (1950), *Gesammelte Schriften* 9:1: *Soziologische Schriften II*, ed. Susan Buck-Morss and Rolf Tiedemann (Frankfurt am Main: Suhrkamp Verlag, 1975), p. 390.

17. *Ibid.*, p. 245.

18. Adorno, "Reflexionen zur Klassentheorie" (1942), *GS* 8, p. 391.

19. Theodor W. Adorno, "Scientific Experiences of a European Scholar in America," trans. Donald Fleming, in *The Intellectual Migration: Europe and America, 1930-1960*, ed. Donald Fleming and Bernard Bailyn (Cambridge, Mass.: Belknap–Harvard University Press, 1969), p. 367.

20. Supplemented by an essay on Stravinsky (1948) and an introduction on method, it was first published as "Schönberg und der Fortschritt" in 1949, in *Philosophie der neuen Musik*.

21. Thomas Mann, *The Story of a Novel: The Genesis of Doctor Faustus*, trans. Richard and Clara Winston (New York: Alfred A. Knopf, 1961), p. 46. "Here indeed was something important. The manuscript dealt with modern music both on an artistic and on a sociological plane. . . . [T]he whole thing had the strangest affinity to the idea of my book, to the 'composition' in which I had lived and moved and had my being. The decision was made of itself: This was my man." (*Ibid.*, p. 43.) Later Mann also read Adorno's studies of Kierkegaard and Wagner (*ibid.*, pp. 85, 94), as well as the *Trauerspiel* book by Benjamin (*ibid.*, p. 187), whom Mann erroneously remembered as Adorno's "cousin" (*ibid.*, p. 43).

22. Adorno's suggestions on the novel were totally characteristic, for example, his advice that the character of Leverkühn's works be made "open simultaneously to the criticism of bloody barbarism and to the criticism of bloodless intellectualism." (*Ibid.*, p. 156.) For an analysis of the far-reaching effect of Adorno's ideas on the novel, see the unpublished doctoral disserta-

tion by Hansjörg Dörr, "Thomas Mann und Adorno: Ihre Zusammenarbeit am Doktor Faustus an Hand der bisherigen Quellen," Marburg, 1965.

23. *Ibid.*, p. 222. Mann's report on their collaboration indicates that whatever Adorno's reservations as to the power of *Geist*, he had not compromised his own intellectualism. He was described by Mann as "uncompromising, tragically brilliant, operating on the highest level." (*Ibid.*, p. 43.) A typical conversation between them "passed from humanity as the purified chthonian element to parallels between Beethoven and Goethe, to humaneness as romantic resistance to society and convention (Rousseau) and as rebellion (the prose scene in Goethe's *Faust*)." (*Ibid.*, pp. 47–48.)

24. Theodor W. Adorno, *Philosophy of Modern Music*, trans. Anne G. Mitchell and Wesley V. Blomster (New York: The Seabury Press, 1973), pp. 130–131.

25. *Ibid.*, p. 21.

26. *Ibid.*, p. 19.

27. In articles in 1949 and 1952 in the Mexican review *Nuestra Música*, Schönberg himself was critical of the tendency to dogmatize atonality which emerged in the serial compositions produced after the war.

28. Adorno, *Philosophy of Modern Music*, pp. 55–56.

29. *Ibid.*, pp. 61–66.

30. See above, Chapter 8.

31. Adorno, "Notizen zur neuen Anthropologie," 1942, p. 4.

32. *Ibid.*, p. 3.

33. *Ibid.*, p. 12. The passage continues: "This is clearly evident with the fascists; with the Communists perhaps also for some time, precisely through the mass party. Revolution is solely the open and unguarded, and the mass party lends every act the character of a cover-up. In this sense a revolutionary mass party simply cannot exist."

34. Adorno, "Reflexionen zur Klassentheorie" (1942), *GS* 8, p. 376.

35. "The self-determined law of the row truthfully becomes a fetish at that point when the conductor relies upon it as a source of meaning." (Adorno, *Philosophy of Modern Music*, p. 111.)

36. *Ibid.*, p. 68.

37. *Ibid.*, p. 67.

38. Theodor W. Adorno, *Negative Dialectics*, trans. E. B. Ashton (New York: The Seabury Press, 1973), p. 154.

39. Adorno, *Philosophy of Modern Music*, p. 102.

40. Theodor W. Adorno, Husserl ms., 1934–1937, Frankfurt am Main, Adorno Estate, p. 34 (1937 article).

41. *Ibid.*, p. 149.

42. Hans Mayer, cited in Martin Jay, *The Dialectical Imagination: A History of the Frankfurt School and the Institute of Social Research, 1923–1950* (Boston: Little, Brown, 1973), p. 187.

43. Theodor Adorno, *Minima Moralia: Reflections from Damaged Life*, trans. E. F. N. Jephcott (London: NLB, 1974), p. 87.

Bibliography

Research for this study was carried on in several countries over a four-year period. During this time the complete works of Adorno were in the process of being compiled and published. Due to the rapid appearance of new volumes in the series (not all of which I have received), as well as other editions of Adorno's writings and those of his circle, bibliographies are almost instantly obsolete. The selected bibliography presented here is accurate at least up to January, 1975. For a more complete bibliography of Adorno's writing (but accurate only up to 1971), see the excellent work of Klaus Schultz in Hermann Schweppenhäuser, ed., *Theodor W. Adorno zum Gedächtnis: Eine Sammlung* (Frankfurt am Main: Suhrkamp Verlag, 1971), pp. 178–239.

Because this study contends that the early, pre-Institute thinking of Adorno (before 1938) is the source of his mature theory, particular attention has been given both in the notes and in the bibliography to the dates of origin of his writings (first date of publication, or date of completion of work when it is significantly earlier).

I have taken the liberty of choosing whether to use the existing English translations or to make my own, especially in the case of Adorno's writing, when I find the translations unsatisfactory.

Adorno published under the name of T. or Theodor Wiesengrund, 1920–1924; T. or Theodor Wiesengrund-Adorno, 1925–1938; and T. W. or Theodor W. Adorno, 1939–1969. In 1936 and 1937 he used the pseudonym Hektor Rottweiler.

THEODOR W. ADORNO

Complete Works

Adorno, Theodor W. *Gesammelte Schriften.* 23 vols. Edited by Rolf Tiedemann. Frankfurt am Main: Suhrkamp Verlag, 1970-. Note: The abbreviation *GS* has been used both here and in the notes.

The volumes are listed below. Those starred (*) have been consulted in this study.

*Vol. 1: *Philosophische Frühschritten.* Edited by Rolf Tiedemann. Frankfurt am Main: Suhrkamp Verlag, 1973.

Vol. 2: *Kierkegaard.* (Future.)

Vol. 3: *Dialektik der Aufklärung.* (Future.)

Vol. 4: *Minima Moralia.* (Future.)

Vol. 5: *Zur Metakritik der Erkenntnistheorie; Drei Studien zu Hegel.* Edited by Gretel Adorno and Rolf Tiedemann. Frankfurt am Main: Suhrkamp Verlag, 1971.

Vol. 6: *Negative Dialektik; Jargon der Eigentlichkeit.* Edited by Rolf Tiedemann. Frankfurt am Main: Suhrkamp Verlag, 1973.

Vol. 7: *Aesthetische Theorie.* Edited by Gretel Adorno and Rolf Tiedemann. Frankfurt am Main: Suhrkamp Verlag, 1970.

*Vol. 8: *Soziologische Schriften I.* Edited by Rolf Tiedemann. Frankfurt am Main: Suhrkamp Verlag, 1972.

*Vol. 9: *Soziologische Schriften II.* 2 vols. Edited by Susan Buck-Morss and Rolf Tiedemann. Frankfurt am Main: Suhrkamp Verlag, 1975.

Vol. 10: *Prismen; Ohne Leitbild; Kritische Modelle: Eingriffe, Stichworte.* (Future.)

Vol. 11: *Noten zur Literatur.* Edited by Rolf Tiedemann. Frankfurt am Main: Suhrkamp Verlag, 1974.

Vol. 12: *Philosophie der neuen Musik.* (Future.)

*Vol. 13: *Die musikalischen Monographien: Wagner; Mahler; Berg.* Edited by Gretel Adorno and Rolf Tiedemann. Frankfurt am Main: Suhrkamp Verlag, 1971.

*Vol. 14: *Dissonanzen; Einleitung in die Musiksoziologie.* Edited by Rolf Tiedemann. Frankfurt am Main: Suhrkamp Verlag, 1973.

Vol. 15: *Komposition für den Film; Der getreue Korrepetitor.* (Future.)

Vol. 16: *Klangfiguren; Quasi una Fantasia; Moments Musicaux; Impromptus.* (Future.)

Vols. 17–19: *Aufsätze zur Musik.* (Future.)

Vol. 20: *Miszellen.* (Future.)

Supplementary Volumes (Unfinished Fragments)

Vol. 21: *Fragmente I: Beethoven.* (Future.)

Vol. 22: *Fragmente II: Theorie der musikalischen Reproduktion.* (Future.)

Vol. 23: *Fragmente III: Current of Music.* (Future.)

Published Works Written 1920–1938:
A Chronological Listing

The following works, written before Adorno became an official member of the Frankfurt Institute, have been consulted. Original documents are in the Adorno Estate, Frankfurt am Main. Date and place of republications have been noted.

1920

"Expressionismus und künstlerische Wahrhaftigkeit: Zur Kritik neuer Dichtung." *Die Neue Schaubühne* [Dresden] 2, 9 (1920): 233–236. Republished in *GS* 11 (1974), pp. 609–611.

1921

" 'Die Hochzeit des Faun': Grundsätzliche Bemerkungen zu Bernhard Sekles' neuer Oper." *Neue Blätter für Kunst und Literatur* [Frankfurt am Main] 4 and 5 (1921–1922): 61–62 and 68–70.

1922

"Paul Hindemith." *Neue Blätter für Kunst und Literatur* 4, 7 (1921–1922): 103–106. Republished in *Impromptus* (1968), pp. 53–57.

1924

"Die Transzendenz des Dinglichen und Noematischen in Husserls Phänomenologie." Dissertation, Universität Frankfurt am Main, 1924. First published in *GS* 1 (1973), pp. 7–77.

1925

"Alban Berg: Zur Uraufführung des 'Wozzeck.' " *Musikblätter des Anbruch* [Vienna] 7, 10 (1925): 531–537.

"Hanns Eisler: Duo für Violine und Violoncell, op. 7, Nr. 1." *Musikblätter des Anbruch* 7, 7, Sonderheft Italien (1925): 422–423.

"Die Serenade: Zur Aufführung von Schönbergs Serenade in Venedig." *Pult und Taktstock* [Vienna] 2, 7 (1925): 113–118.

"Über einige Werke von Béla Bartók." *Zeitschrift für Musik* 92, 7/8 (1925): 428–430.

"Zeitgenössische Musik in Frankfurt am Main." *Zeitschrift für Musik* 92, 4 (1925): 216–218.

"Zum Problem der Reproduktion: Fragmente." *Pult und Taktstock* 2, 4 (1925): 51–55.

1926

"Drei Dirigenten." *Musikblätter des Anbruch* 8, 7 (1926): 315–319.

"Kammermusik von Paul Hindemith." *Die Musik* 19, 1 (1926–1927): 24–28. Republished in *Impromptus* (1968), pp. 58–62.

"Metronomisierung." *Pult und Taktstock* 3, 7/8 (1926): 130–134. Republished in *Impromptus* (1968), pp. 146–149.

"Opernprobleme: Glossiert nach Frankfurter Aufführungen." *Musikblätter des Anbruch* 8, 5 (1926): 205–208.

"Anton Webern: Zur Aufführung der fünf Orchesterstücke in Zürich." *Musikblätter des Anbruch* 8, 6 (1926): 280–282.

1927

"Der Begriff des Unbewussten in der transzendentalen Seelenlehre." First *Habilitationsschrift* (not accepted), Universität Frankfurt am Main, 1927. First published in *GS* 1 (1973), pp. 79–322.

"Motive" [I]. *Musikblätter des Anbruch* 9, 4 (1927): 161–162. Republished in *Quasi una Fantasia* (1963), pp. 19–21.

"Orchesterstücke op. 16." *Pult und Taktstock* 4, Sonderheft Arnold Schönberg und seine Orchesterwerke (1927): 36–43.

1928

"Hindemiths 'Cardillac'. . . ." [First words of text.] *Neue Musik-Zeitung* [Stuttgart] 49, 22 (1928): 706–707.

"Marginalien zur Sonata von Alexander Jamnitz." *Neue Musik-Zeitung* 49, 12 (1928): 387–390.

"Motive II; Motive III." *Musikblätter des Anbruch* 10, 6 and 7 (1928): 199–202 and 237–240. Republished in *Quasi una Fantasia* (1963), pp. 21–29.

"Nadelkurven." *Musikblätter des Anbruch* 10, 2 (1928): 47–50.

"Schönbergs Bläserquintett." *Pult und Taktstock* 5 (1928): 45–49. Republished in *Moments Musicaux* (1964), pp. 161–166.

"Schubert." *Die Musik* 21, 1 (1928–1929): 1–12. Republished in *Moments Musicaux* (1964), pp. 18–36.

1929

"Atonales Intermezzo?" *Anbruch* 11, 5 (1929): 187–193. Note: *Musikblätter des Anbruch* [Vienna] is called *Anbruch* beginning with volume 11 (1929).

"Hanns Eisler: Zeitungsausschnitte. Für Gesang und Klavier, op. 11." *Anbruch* 11, 5 (1929): 219–221.

"Glosse zu Richard Strauss." *Anbruch* 11, 6 (1929): 250–251. Republished in *Quasi una Fantasia* (1963), pp. 54–57.

"Motive IV: Musik von aussen." *Anbruch* 11, 9/10 (1929): 335–338. Republished in *Quasi una Fantasia* (1963), pp. 29–35.

"Nachtmusik." *Anbruch* 11, 1 (1929): 16–23. Republished in *Moments Musicaux* (1964), pp. 58–66.

"Die Oper Wozzeck." *Der Scheinwerfer: Blätter der Städtischen Bühnen Essen* 3, 4 (1929–1930): 5–11.

"Schlageranalysen." *Anbruch* 11, 3 (1929): 108–114.

"Kurt Weill: Kleine Dreigroschenmusik für Blasorchester." *Anbruch* 11, 7/8 (1929): 316–317.

"Zur Zwölftontechnik." *Anbruch* 11, 7/8 (1929): 290–294. Republished in *Theodor W. Adorno und Ernst Krenek: Briefwechsel* (1974), pp. 167–173.

1930

[With Ernst Krenek.] "Arbeitsprobleme des Komponisten: Gespräch über Musik und soziale Situation." *Frankfurter Zeitung*, December 10, 1930, pp. 1–2.

Republished in *Theodor W. Adorno und Ernst Krenek: Briefwechsel* (1974), pp. 187-193.

"Bewusstsein des Konzerthörers." *Anbruch* 12, 9/10 (1930): 274-275.

"Kierkegaard prophezeit Chaplin." *Frankfurter Zeitung*, May 22, 1930, p. 1. Republished in *Ohne Leitbild* (1967), pp. 89-90.

"Kontroverse über die Heiterkeit." *Anbruch* 12, 1 (1930): 19-21.

"Mahagonny." *Der Scheinwerfer: Blätter der Städtischen Bühnen Essen* 3, 14 (1929-1930): 12-15. Republished in *Moments Musicaux* (1964), pp. 131-140.

"Mahler heute." *Anbruch* 12, 3 (1930): 86-92.

"Motive V: Hermeneutik." *Anbruch* 12, 7/8 (1930): 235-238. Republished in *Quasi una Fantasia* (1963), pp. 35-38.

"Neue Tempi." *Pult und Taktstock* 7, 1 (1930): 1-7. Republished in *Moments Musicaux* (1964), pp. 74-83.

"Notiz über Namen." *Frankfurter Zeitung*, August 7, 1930, p. 1.

"Ravel." *Anbruch* 12, 4/5 (1930): 151-154. Republished in *Moments Musicaux* (1964), pp. 67-73.

"Reaktion und Fortschritt." *Anbruch* 12, 6 (1930): 191-195. Republished in *Moments Musicaux* (1964), pp. 153-160.

"Arnold Schönberg: Von heute auf morgen: Uraufführung in Frankfurt am Main." *Die Musik* 22, 6 (1929-1930): 445-446.

"Transatlantic." [On the opera of George Antheil.] *Modern Music* [New York] 7, 4 (1929-1930): 38-41.

1931

"Die Aktualität der Philosophie." *Antrittsvorlesung*, Universität Frankfurt am Main, 1931. First published in *GS* 1 (1973), pp. 325-344.

"Applaus; Galerie." *Die Musik* 23, 6 and 8 (1930-1931): 467 and 626. Republished in *Quasi una Fantasia* (1963), pp. 94-99.

"Berg and Webern: Schönberg's Heirs." *Modern Music* 8, 2 (1930-1931): 29-38.

"Rede über den 'Raritätenladen' von Charles Dickens." *Frankfurter Zeitung*, April 18, 1931, pp. 1-2.

1932

"Exkurse zu einem Exkurs." *Der Scheinwerfer: Blätter der Städtischen Bühnen Essen* 5, 9/10 (1931-1932): 15-18.

"Die Idee der Naturgeschichte." *Vortrag vor der Frankfurter Ortsgruppe der Kant-Gesellschaft*, July 15, 1932. First published in *GS* 1 (1973), pp. 345-365.

"Kleiner Zitatenschatz." *Die Musik* 24, 10 (1931-1932): 734-738. Republished in *Quasi una Fantasia* (1963), pp. 38-41.

"Kritik des Musikanten." *Frankfurter Zeitung*, March 12, 1932, pp. 1-2. Republished in *Impromptus* (1968), pp. 63-70.

"Anton Webern." *Schweizerische Musikzeitung und Sängerblatt* 72, 22 (1932): 679-683. Republished in *Impromptus* (1968), pp. 45-50.

"Zur Deutung Kreneks." *Anbruch* 14, 2/3 (1932): 42, 44–45. Republished in *Theodor W. Adorno und Ernst Krenek: Briefwechsel* (1974), pp. 194–198.

"Zur gesellschaftlichen Lage der Musik." *Zeitschrift für Sozialforschung.* Part I: 1 1/2 (1932): 103–124; part II: 1, 3 (1932): 356–378.

"Zur Naturgeschichte des Theaters: Fragmente." *Blätter des Hessischen Landestheaters Darmstadt* 9 and 13 (1931–1932): 101–108 and 153–156.

1933

Kierkegaard: Konstruktion des Aesthetischen. Tübingen: Verlag von J. C. B. Mohr, 1933. Republished in 1962 and 1966.

"Abschied vom Jazz." *Europäische Revue* [Berlin] 9, 5 (1933): 313–316.

"Das Foyer: Zur Naturgeschichte des Theaters." *Blätter des Hessischen Landestheaters Darmstadt* 8 (1932–1933): 98–100. Republished in *Quasi una Fantasia* (1963), 107–110.

"Vierhändig, noch einmal." *Vossische Zeitung,* December 19, 1933, pp. 5–6. Republished in *Impromptus* (1968), pp. 142–145.

1934

"Der dialektische Komponist." In *Arnold Schönberg zum 60. Geburtstag, 13 September 1934* [pamphlet]. Vienna, 1934. Pp. 18–23. Republished in *Impromptus* (1968), pp. 39–44.

1935

"Eine Geschichte der Musikästhetik." *Der Auftakt* [Prague] 15, 1/2 (1935): 16–18.

"Zur Stilgeschichte." *Der Auftakt* 15, 5/6 (1935): 65–67.

1936

[Pseud. Hektor Rottweiler.] "Erinnerung an den Lebenden." *23: Eine Wiener Musikzeitschrift* [Vienna] 24/25 (1936): 19–29. Revised in 1968 and republished in *GS* 13 (1971), pp. 335–367.

[Pseud. Hektor Rottweiler.] "Marginalien zu Mahler." *23: Eine Wiener Musikzeitschrift* 26/27 (1936): 13–19.

[Pseud. Hektor Rottweiler.] "Musikpädagogische Musik: Brief an Ernst Krenek." *23: Eine Wiener Musikzeitschrift* 28/30 (1936): 29–37. Republished in *Theodor W. Adorno und Ernst Krenek: Briefwechsel* (1974), pp. 215–223.

[Pseud. Hektor Rottweiler.] "Über Jazz." *Zeitschrift für Sozialforschung* 5, 3 (1936): 235–257. Republished in *Moments Musicaux* (1964), pp. 84–115.

[Pseud. Hektor Rottweiler.] "Zur Lulu-Symphonie." *23: Eine Wiener Musikzeit-Schrift* 24/25, Alban Berg zum Gedenken (1936): 5–11. Republished in *GS* 13 (1971), pp. 472–477.

1937

Analyses of the works of Berg. In Willi Reich. *Alban Berg: Mit Bergs eigenen Schriften und Beiträgen von Theodor Wiesengrund-Adorno und Ernst Krenek.*

Vienna: Herbert Reichner Verlag, 1937. Pp. 21–106. Republished in *GS* 13 (1971), pp. 374–401; 408–428; 451–462.

[Pseud. Hektor Rottweiler.] "Ensemble." *23: Eine Wiener Musikzeitschrift* 31/33 (1937): 15–21. Republished in *Quasi una Fantasia* (1963), pp. 44–52.

"Spätstil Beethovens." *Der Auftakt* 17, 5/6 (1937): 65–67. Republished in *Moments Musicaux* (1964), pp. 13–17.

1938

"Über den Fetischcharakter in der Musik und die Regression des Hörens." *Zeitschrift für Sozialforschung* 7, 3 (1938): 321–355. Republished in *Dissonanzen* (1956), pp. 9–45, and in *GS* 14 (1973), pp. 14–50.

Other Published Works by Adorno

The following editions have been consulted. Original publication dates, when different, are given in brackets.

Dissonanzen: Musik in der verwalteten Welt [1956]. 4th edition. Göttingen: Vandenhoeck & Ruprecht, 1969.

Drei Studien zu Hegel [1963]. Frankfurt am Main: Suhrkamp Verlag, 1969.

Eingriffe: Neun kritische Modelle. Frankfurt am Main: edition Suhrkamp, 1963.

Erziehung zur Mündigkeit: Vorträge und Gespräche mit Hellmut Becker, 1959–1969. Edited by Gerd Kadelbach. Frankfurt am Main: Suhrkamp Verlag, 1971.

"Für Ernst Bloch." *Aufbau-Reconstruction* [New York] 8, 48 (November 27, 1942): 15, 17–18.

"Gruss an Gershom G. Scholem: Zum 70. Geburtstag, 5. Dezember 1967." *Neue Züricher Zeitung,* December 2, 1967, p. 19v.

"Henkel, Krug und frühe Erfahrung." In *Ernst Bloch zu Ehren: Beiträge zu seinem Werk.* Edited by Siegfried Unseld. Frankfurt am Main: Suhrkamp Verlag, 1965. Pp. 9–20.

Impromptus: Zweite Folge neu gedruckter musikalischer Aufsätze [1968]. Frankfurt am Main: edition Suhrkamp, 1969.

Jargon der Eigentlichkeit: Zur deutschen Ideologie. Frankfurt am Main: Suhrkamp Verlag, 1964. Translated as *The Jargon of Authenticity* by Knut Tarnowski and Frederick Will. Foreword by Trent Schroyer. Evanston, Ill.: Northwestern University Press, 1973.

"Jazz." In *Encyclopedia of the Arts.* Edited by Dagobert D. Runes and Harry G. Schrickel. New York: Philosophical Library, 1946. Pp. 511–513.

Kierkegaard: Konstruktion des Aesthetischen [1933]: *Mit zwei Beilagen.* 3rd edition, enlarged. Frankfurt am Main: Suhrkamp Verlag, 1966.

Kritik: Kleine Schriften zur Gesellschaft. Edited by Rolf Tiedemann. Frankfurt am Main: edition Suhrkamp, 1971.

Minima Moralia: Reflexionen aus dem beschädigten Leben [1951]. Frankfurt am

Main: Suhrkamp Verlag, 1969. Translated as *Minima Moralia: Reflections from Damaged Life* by E. F. N. Jephcott. London: NLB, 1974.

Moments Musicaux: Neugedruckte Aufsätze, 1928 bis 1962. Frankfurt am Main: edition Suhrkamp, 1964.

Negative Dialektik. Frankfurt am Main: Suhrkamp Verlag, 1966. Translated as *Negative Dialectics* by E. B. Ashton. New York: The Seabury Press, 1973.

Noten zur Literatur. 4 vols. (Vol. 4 published posthumously, edited by Rolf Tiedemann.) Frankfurt am Main: Suhrkamp Verlag, 1958–1974.

"Offener Brief an Max Horkheimer." *Die Zeit,* February 12, 1965, p. 32.

Ohne Leitbild: Parva Aesthetica. Frankfurt am Main: edition Suhrkamp, 1967.

"On Kierkegaard's Doctrine of Love." *Studies in Philosophy and Social Science* [*Zeitschrift für Sozialforschung*] 8, 3 (1939–1940): 413–429.

"On Popular Music." In *Mass Culture.* Edited by Bernard Rosenberg and David Manning White. New York: Free Press, 1957.

Philosophie der neuen Musik [1949]. Frankfurt am Main: Verlag Ullstein, 1958. Translated as *Philosophy of Modern Music* by Anne G. Mitchell and Wesley V. Blomster. New York: The Seabury Press, 1973.

Philosophische Terminologie: Zur Einleitung. 2 vols. Edited by Rudolf zur Lippe. Frankfurt am Main: Suhrkamp Taschenbuch Verlag, 1973.

Prismen: Kulturkritik und Gesellschaft. Frankfurt am Main: Suhrkamp Verlag, 1955. Translated as *Prisms* by Samuel and Shierry Weber. London: Neville Spearman, 1967.

Quasi una Fantasia: Musikalische Schriften II. Frankfurt am Main: Suhrkamp Verlag, 1963.

Stichworte: Kritische Modelle 2. Frankfurt am Main: edition Suhrkamp, 1969.

"Scientific Experiences of a European Scholar in America." Translated by Donald Fleming. In *The Intellectual Migration: Europe and America, 1930–1960.* Edited by Donald Fleming and Bernard Bailyn. Cambridge, Mass.: Belknap–Harvard University Press, 1969.

Über Walter Benjamin. Frankfurt am Main: Suhrkamp Verlag, 1970.

Versuch über Wagner [written 1937–1938]. Frankfurt am Main: Suhrkamp Verlag, 1952.

Zur Dialektik des Engagements: Aufsätze zur Literatur des 20. Jahrhunderts II. Frankfurt am Main: Suhrkamp Verlag, 1973.

Zur Metakritik der Erkenntnistheorie: Studien über Husserl und phänomenologischen Antinomien [1956]. Frankfurt am Main: Suhrkamp Verlag, 1972.

Unpublished Materials by Adorno

The following documents, in the Adorno Estate, Frankfurt am Main, have been consulted.

Mss.

"Current of Music: Elements of a Radio Theory," 1939.

Husserl ms., "Zur Philosophie Husserls," 1934–1937. (Revised in 1956 and published as *Zur Metakritik der Erkenntnistheorie.*)

Notebooks on *Reproduktionstheorie,* 3 vols., n.d.

"Notizen zur neuen Anthropologie," 1942.

"The Problem of Experimentation in Music Psychology," March 7, 1939.

"Über Mannheims Wissenssoziologie," 1947[?].

"Über das Problem der individuellen Kausalität bei Simmel," lecture delivered in New York, April 19, 1940.

Tape Recordings

Conversation with Lotte Lenya.

Conversation with Lotte von Tobisch.

Correspondence

Letters, Adorno to Benjamin: March 4, 1934; April 21, 1934; November 6, 1934; December 5, 1934; July [?], 1935; November [?], 1936; July 19, 1937; November [?], 1937; June 8, 1938; August 2, 1938; February 1, 1939; February 29, 1940.

Letters, Benjamin to Adorno: November 10, 1930; March 18, 1934; April 9, 1934; June 19, 1938.

Collaborative Works

Adorno, T. W., Else Frenkel-Brunswik, Daniel J. Levinson, and R. Nevitt Sanford. *The Authoritarian Personality.* Vol. 1 of *Studies in Prejudice,* edited by Max Horkheimer and Samuel H. Flowerman. Social Studies Series, publication no. III. New York: Harper & Brothers, 1950.

Adorno, Theodor W., and Hanns Eisler. *Komposition für den Film* [1944]. Munich: Rogner & Bernhard, 1969.

Horkheimer, Max, and Theodor W. Adorno. *Dialektik der Aufklärung.* Amsterdam: Querido Verlag, 1947. Translated as *Dialectic of Enlightenment* by John Cumming. New York: Herder and Herder, 1972.

[Horkheimer, Max, and Theodor W. Adorno.] *Soziologische Exkurse.* Institut für Sozialforschung, *Frankfurter Beiträge zur Soziologie,* edited by Theodor W. Adorno and Walter Dirks, vol. 4. Frankfurt am Main: Europäische Verlagsanstalt, 1956.

Theodor W. Adorno und Ernst Krenek: Briefwechsel. Edited by Wolfgang Rogge. Frankfurt am Main: Suhrkamp Verlag, 1974.

WALTER BENJAMIN

A critical edition of the complete works of Benjamin is presently being compiled:

Benjamin, Walter. *Gesammelte Schriften.* 6 vols. Edited by Rolf Tiedemann and Hermann Schweppenhäuser. Frankfurt am Main: Suhrkamp Verlag, 1972–.

Vol. I: *Abhandlungen.* 3 vols. Edited by Rolf Tiedemann and Hermann Schweppenhäuser. Frankfurt am Main: Surhkamp Verlag, 1974.

Vol. I:1: *Der Begriff der Kunstkritik in der deutschen Romantik* [1920] ; *Goethes Wahlverwandtschaften* [1924] ; *Ursprung des deutschen Trauerspiels* [1928].

Vol. I:2: *Das Kunstwerk im Zeitalter seiner technischen Reproduzierbarkeit* [1935-1936] ; *Charles Baudelaire: Ein Lyriker im Zeitalter des Hochkapitalismus* [1935-1939] ; *Über den Begriff der Geschichte* [1940].

Vol. I:3: *Anmerkungen der Herausgeber.*

Vol. II: *Aufsätze, Essays, Vorträge.* (Future.)

Vol. III: *Kritiken und Rezensionen.* Edited by Hella Tiedemann-Bartels. Frankfurt am Main: Suhrkamp Verlag, 1972.

Vol. IV: *Kleine Prosa.* 2 vols. Edited by Tillman Rexroth. Frankfurt am Main: Suhrkamp Verlag, 1972.

Vol. IV:1: *Die Aufgabe des Übersetzers; Baudelaire: Tableaux Parisiens; Übertragungen; Einbahnstrasse; Deutsche Menschen; Berliner Kindheit um Neunzehnhundert; Denkbilder; Satiren, Polemiken, Glossen; Berichte.*

Vol. IV:2: *Illustrierte Aufsätze; Hörmodelle; Geschichten und Novellistisches; Miszellen; Anmerkungen des Herausgebers.*

Vol V: *Die Passagenarbeit* (Future).

Vol. VI: *Fragmente und autobiographische Schriften.* (Future.)

Other editions, texts and translations consulted are listed below.

Angelus Novus: Ausgewählte Schriften. Frankfurt am Main: Suhrkamp Verlag, 1966.

Der Begriff der Kunstkritik in der deutschen Romantik. Edited by Hermann Schweppenhäuser. Frankfurt am Main: Suhrkamp Taschenbuch Verlag, 1973.

Briefe. 2 vols. Edited by Gershom Scholem and Theodor W. Adorno. Frankfurt am Main: Suhrkamp Verlag, 1966.

Charles Baudelaire: A Lyric Poet in the Era of High Capitalism. Translated by Harry Zohn. London: NLB (New Left Books), 1973.

"Goethes Wahlverwandtschaften." In Johann Wolfgang Goethe. *Die Wahlverwandtschaften.* Frankfurt am Main: Insel Verlag, 1972. Pp. 255-333.

Illuminations. Edited and with an introduction by Hannah Arendt. Translated by Harry Zohn. New York: Schocken Books, 1969.

Schriften. 2 vols. Edited by Theodor W. Adorno and Gretel Adorno. Frankfurt am Main: Suhrkamp Verlag, 1955.

Über Haschisch: Novellistisches, Berichte, Materialien. Edited by Tillman Rexroth. Introduction by Hermann Schweppenhäuser. Frankfurt am Main: Suhrkamp Verlag, 1972.

Understanding Brecht. Introduction by Stanley Mitchell. Translated by Anna Bostock. London: NLB (New Left Books), 1973.

Ursprung des deutschen Trauerspiels. Edited by Rolf Tiedemann. Frankfurt am Main: Suhrkamp Taschenbuch Verlag, 1972.

Zur Kritik der Gewalt und andere Aufsätze. Afterword by Herbert Marcuse. Frankfurt am Main: edition Suhrkamp, 1965.

MAX HORKHEIMER

Anfänge der bürgerlichen Geschichtsphilosophie. Stuttgart: Kohlhammer, 1930.

Aus der Pubertät: Novellen und Tagebuchblätter. Munich: Kösel Verlag, 1974.

Critical Theory: Selected Essays. Translated by Matthew J. O'Connell and others. New York: Herder and Herder, 1972.

[Pseud. Heinrich Regius.] *Dämmerung: Notizen in Deutschland.* Zurich: Verlag Oprecht und Helbling, 1934.

Eclipse of Reason. [1947] New York: The Seabury Press, 1974.

Gesellschaft im Übergang: Aufsätze, Reden und Vorträge, 1942–1970. Edited by Werner Brede. Frankfurt am Main: Athenäum Fischer Taschenbuch Verlag, 1972.

"Hegel und das Problem der Metaphysik." In *Festschrift für Carl Grünberg: Zum 70. Geburtstag.* Leipzig: Verlag von C. L. Hirschfeld, 1932. Pp. 185–197.

Kritische Theorie: Eine Dokumentation. 2 vols. Edited by Alfred Schmidt. Frankfurt am Main: S. Fischer Verlag, 1968.

"Notes on Institute Activities." *Studies in Social Science* 9, 1 (1941): 123–125.

Sozialphilosophische Studien: Aufsätze, Reden und Vorträge, 1930–1972. Edited by Werner Brede. Frankfurt am Main: Athenäum Fischer Taschenbuch Verlag, 1972.

Traditionelle und Kritische Theorie: Vier Aufsätze. Frankfurt am Main: Fischer Bücherei, 1970.

Vernunft und Selbsterhaltung [1942]. Frankfurt am Main: S. Fischer Verlag, 1970.

MEMOIRS AND RECOLLECTIONS

Adorno, Theodor W., Ernst Bloch, Max Rycher, Gershom Scholem, Jean Selz, Hans Heinz Holz, and Ernst Fischer. *Über Walter Benjamin.* Frankfurt am Main: Suhrkamp Verlag, 1968.

Bunge, Hans. *Fragen Sie mehr über Brecht: Hanns Eisler im Gespräch.* Afterword by Stephen Hermlin. Munich: Rogner & Bernhard, 1970.

Gassen, Kurt, and Michael Landmann, eds. *Buch des Dankes an Georg Simmel.* Berlin: Duncker und Humblot, 1958.

Koestler, Arthur. *Arrow in the Blue: An Autobiography.* 2 vols. New York: The Macmillan Company, 1952.

Lacis, Asja. *Revolutionär im Beruf: Berichte über proletarisches Theater, über Meyerhold, Brecht, Benjamin und Piscator.* Edited by Hildegard Brenner. Munich: Rogner & Bernhard, 1971.

Mann, Thomas. *The Story of a Novel: The Genesis of Doctor Faustus.* Translated by Richard and Clara Winston. New York: Alfred A. Knopf, 1961.

Scholem, Gershom. *Walter Benjamin: Die Geschichte einer Freundschaft.* Frankfurt am Main: Suhrkamp Verlag, 1975.

Schweppenhäuser, Hermann, ed. *Theodor W. Adorno zum Gedächtnis: Eine Sammlung.* Frankfurt am Main: Suhrkamp Verlag, 1971.

Tillich, Hannah. *From Time to Time.* New York: Stein and Day, 1973.

Über Theodor W. Adorno: Mit Beiträgen von Kurt Oppens, Hans Kudszus, Jürgen Habermas, Bernard Willms, Hermann Schweppenhäuser und Ulrich Sonnemann. Frankfurt am Main: Suhrkamp Verlag, 1968.

Unseld, Siegfried, ed. *Ernst Bloch zu Ehren: Beiträge zu seinem Werk.* Frankfurt am Main: Suhrkamp Verlag, 1965.

OTHER PRIMARY WORKS

Bernfeld, Siegfried, Wilhelm Reich, W. Jurinetz, I. Sapir, and A. Stoljarov. *Psychoanalyse und Marxismus: Dokumentation einer Kontroverse.* Introduction by Hans Jörg Sandkühler. Frankfurt am Main: Suhrkamp Verlag, 1971.

Bloch, Ernst. *Geist der Utopie* [1918]. 2nd edition, revised. Berlin: Paul Cassirer, 1923.

Bloch, Ernst. *Spuren* [1930]. New edition, enlarged. Frankfurt am Main: Suhrkamp Verlag, 1969.

Bloch, Ernst. *Vom Hasard zur Katastrophe: Politische Aufsätze, 1934–1939.* Afterword by Oskar Negt. Frankfurt am Main: Suhrkamp Verlag, 1972.

Brecht, Bertolt. *Arbeitsjournal.* 2 vols. Edited by Werner Hecht. Frankfurt am Main: Suhrkamp Verlag, 1973.

Brecht, Bertolt. *Gesammelte Schriften.* Vol. 15: *Schriften zum Theater 1.* Frankfurt am Main: Suhrkamp Verlag, 1967.

Cornelius, Hans. *Grundlagen der Erkenntnistheorie: Transcendentale Systematik* [1916]. 2nd edition. Munich: Verlag von Ernst Reinhardt, 1926.

Dilthey, Wilhelm. *Das Erlebnis und die Dichtung* [1906]. 3rd edition, enlarged. Leipzig: B. G. Teubner, 1910.

Heidegger, Martin. *Being and Time* [1927]. Translated by John Macquarrie and Edward Robinson. London: SCM Press, 1962.

[Institut für Sozialforschung.] *Studien über Autorität und Familie.* Edited by Max Horkheimer. Paris: Felix Alcan, 1936.

[Institut für Sozialforschung.] *Zeitschrift für Sozialforschung* [1932-1941]. 2nd edition. 10 vols. Introduction by Alfred Schmidt. Munich: Kösel-Verlag, 1970.

Kracauer, Siegfried. *From Caligari to Hitler: A Psychological History of the German Film.* Princeton, N.J.: Princeton University Press, 1947.

Kracauer, Siegfried. *History: The Last Things before the Last.* New York: Oxford University Press, 1969.

Krenek, Ernst. Biographical essay on Mahler. In Bruno Walter. *Gustav Mahler.* New York: The Greystone Press, 1941. Pp. 155–220.

Krenek, Ernst. *Exploring Music.* Translated by Margaret Shenfield and Geoffrey Skelton. New York: October House, 1966.

Lenin, W. I. *Werke.* Vol. 14: *Materialismus und Empiriokritizismus* [1909; first German edition 1922]. Berlin: Dietz Verlag, 1968.

Lukács, Georg. *History and Class Consciousness* [1923]. Translated by Rodney Livingstone. Cambridge, Mass.: The M.I.T. Press, 1971.

Lukács, Georg. *Die Seelen und die Formen: Essays.* Berlin: Egon Fleischel & Co., 1911.

Lukács, Georg. *Die Theorie des Romans* [1916]. Neuwied: Luchterhand Verlag, 1971.

Lukács, Georg. *Die Zerstörung der Vernunft: Der Weg des Irrationalismus von Schelling zu Hitler.* Berlin: Aufbau Verlag, 1953.

Mannheim, Karl. *Ideologie und Utopie.* Bonn: F. Cohen, 1929.

Marcuse, Herbert. *Reason and Revolution: Hegel and the Rise of Social Theory.* 2nd edition, enlarged. New York: The Humanities Press, 1954.

Marcuse, Herbert. *Studies in Critical Philosophy.* Translated by Joris de Bres. Boston: Beacon Press, 1973.

Marx, Karl. *Capital: A Critique of Political Economy.* 3 vols. Edited by Frederick Engels. Translated from 3rd German edition by Samuel Moore and Edward Aveling. New York: International Publishers, 1967.

[Marx, Karl.] *Writings of the Young Marx on Philosophy and Society.* Translated and edited by Loyd D. Easton and Kurt H. Guddat. Garden City, N.Y.: Doubleday, Anchor Books, 1967.

Nietzsche, Friedrich. *The Will to Power.* Translated by Walter Kaufmann and R. J. Hollingdale. New York: Random House, 1967.

[Pfemfert, Franz.] *Ich schneide die Zeit aus: Expressionismus und Politik in Franz Pfemferts "Die Aktion," 1911–1918.* Edited by Paul Raabe. Munich: Deutscher Taschenbuch Verlag, 1964.

Reich, Wilhelm. *Massenpsychologie des Faschismus.* Copenhagen: Verlag für Sexualpolitik, 1933.

Rosenzweig, Franz. *The Star of Redemption* [1920]. Translated from 2nd German edition of 1930 by William W. Hallo. New York: Holt, Rinehart and Winston, 1970.

Sartre, Jean-Paul. *Nausea* [1938]. Translated by Lloyd Alexander. New York: New Directions Publishing, 1964.

Scholem, Gershom. *Major Trends in Jewish Mysticism.* New York: Schocken Books, 1967.

Scholem, Gershom. *The Messianic Idea in Judaism.* New York: Schocken Books, 1971.

Schönberg, Arnold. *Harmonielehre* [1911]. 3rd edition, revised and enlarged. Vienna: Universal-Edition, 1922.

Schönberg, Arnold. *Letters.* Edited by Erwin Stein. Translated by Eithne Wilkins and Ernst Kaiser. New York: St. Martin's Press, 1965.

Simmel, Georg. *Brücke und Tür.* Edited by Michael Landmann and Margarete Susman. Stuttgart: K. F. Koehler Verlag, 1957.

Sombart, Werner. "Technik und Kultur." *Archiv für Sozialwissenschaft und Sozialpolitik* 33 (1911): 305–347.

SECONDARY WORKS: BOOKS AND PERIODICALS

Bracher, Karl Dietrich. *Die Auflösung der Weimarer Republik.* 3rd edition, revised and enlarged. *Schriften des Instituts für politische Wissenschaft,* vol. 4. Villingen-Schwarzwald: Ring Verlag, 1960.

Breines, Paul. "Praxis and Its Theorists: The Impact of Lukács and Korsch in the 1920's." *Telos* 11 (Spring 1972): 67–103.

Bulthaup, Peter, ed. *Materialien zu Benjamins Thesen "Über den Begriff der Geschichte": Beiträge und Interpretationen.* Frankfurt am Main: Suhrkamp Verlag, 1975.

Butler, E. M. *The Tyranny of Greece over Germany.* Boston: Beacon Press, 1935.

Cerutti, Furio, D. Claussen, H.-J. Krahl, O. Negt, and A. Schmidt. *Geschichte und Klassenbewusstsein heute: Diskussion und Dokumentation.* Schwarze Reihe, no. 12. Amsterdam: Verlag de Munter, 1971.

Christie, Richard, and Marie Jahoda, eds. *Studies in the Scope and Method of "The Authoritarian Personality."* New York: Free Press, 1954.

Collaer, Paul. *A History of Modern Music.* Translated by Sally Abeles. New York: The World Publishing Company, 1961.

Eyck, Erich. *A History of the Weimar Republic.* 2 vols. Translated by Harlan P. Hanson and Robert G. L. Waite. New York: John Wiley & Sons, 1962.

Fetscher, Irving. "Bertolt Brecht and America." *Salmagundi* 10/11, *The Legacy of the German Refugee Intellectuals* (Fall 1969-Winter 1970): 265–280.

Frenzel, Ivo. "Utopia and Apocalypse in German Literature." *Social Research* 39 (Summer 1972): 306–321.

Friedrich, Otto. *Before the Deluge: A Portrait of Berlin in the 1920's.* New York: Harper & Row, 1972.

Gay, Peter. *Weimar Culture: The Outsider as Insider.* New York: Harper Torchbooks, 1968.

Grenz, Friedemann. *Adornos Philosophie in Grundbegriffen: Auflösungen einiger Deutungsprobleme.* Frankfurt am Main: Suhrkamp Verlag, 1974.

Gumnior, Helmut, and Rudolf Ringguth. *Max Horkheimer in Selbstzeugnissen und Bilddokumenten.* Rowohlts Monographien, edited by Kurt Kusenberg, no. 208. Hamburg: Rowohlt Taschenbuch Verlag, 1973.

Habermas, Jürgen. "Bewusstmachende oder rettende Kritik: Die Aktualität Walter Benjamins." *Kultur und Kritik: Verstreute Aufsätze.* Frankfurt am Main: Suhrkamp Taschenbuch Verlag, 1973. Pp. 302–344.

Honigsheim, Paul. "Der Max-Weber-Kreis in Heidelberg." *Kölner Vierteljahreshefte für Soziologie* 5 (1926): 270–287.

Jacoby, Russell. "Towards a Critique of Automatic Marxism: The Politics of Philosophy from Lukács to the Frankfurt School" *Telos* 10 (Winter 1971): 119-146.

Janik, Allan and Stephen Toulmin. *Wittgenstein's Vienna*. New York: Simon and Schuster, 1973.

Jay, Martin. *The Dialectical Imagination: A History of the Frankfurt School and the Institute of Social Research, 1923-1950*. Boston: Little, Brown, 1973.

Jay, Martin. "The Extraterritorial Life of Siegfried Kracauer." *Salmagundi* 31/32 (Fall 1975-Winter 1976): 49-106.

Jones, Gareth Stedman. "The Marxism of the Early Lukács: An Evaluation." *New Left Review* 70 (November-December 1971): 27-64.

Kaiser, Gerhard. *Benjamin. Adorno: Zwei Studien*. Frankfurt am Main: Fischer Athenäum Taschenbücher, 1974.

Kettler, David. *Marxismus und Kultur*. Neuwied: Luchterhand Verlag, 1967.

Laqueur, Walter. *Weimar: A Cultural History, 1918-1933*. New York: G. P. Putnam's Sons, 1974.

Leibowitz, René. *Schoenberg and His School: The Contemporary Stage of the Language of Music*. Translated by Dika Newlin. New York: Philosophical Library, 1949.

Lichtheim, George. *George Lukács*. Modern Masters Series, edited by Frank Kermode, no. 6. New York: The Viking Press, 1970.

Lorei, Madlen, and Richard Kirn. *Frankfurt und die goldenen zwanziger Jahren*. Frankfurt am Main: Verlag Frankfurter Bücher, 1966.

Mittenzwei, Werner. "Marxismus und Materialismus: Die Brecht-Lukács Debatte." *Das Argument 46* 10, 1/2 (March 1968): 12-43.

Mosse, George L. *Germans and Jews: The Right, the Left, and the Search for a "Third Force" in Pre-Nazi Germany*. New York: Howard Fertig, 1970.

Noth, Ernst Erich. "In der vermeintlichen Hochburg des Liberalismus: Wie man im Frankfurt der dreissiger Jahre studierte." *Frankfurter Rundschau*, no. 269, November 20, 1971, feuilleton, p. v.

Poggioli, Renato. *The Theory of the Avant-Garde*. Translated by Gerald Fitzgerald. Cambridge, Mass.: Belknap-Harvard University Press, 1968.

Ricoeur, Paul. *Freud and Philosophy: An Essay on Interpretation*. Translated by Denis Savage. New Haven, Conn.: Yale University Press, 1970.

Ringer, Fritz K. *The Decline of the German Mandarins: The German Academic Community, 1890-1933*. Cambridge, Mass.: Harvard University Press, 1969.

Schmidt, Alfred. *Der Begriff der Natur in der Lehre von Marx*. 2nd edition, revised and enlarged. Frankfurt am Main: Europäische Verlagsanstalt, 1971.

Schmidt, Alfred. "Die Zeitschrift für Sozialforschung: Geschichte und Gegenwärtige Bedeutung." Introduction to *Zeitschrift für Sozialforschung*, 2nd edition, vol. 1. Munich: Kösel-Verlag, 1970.

Schnitzler, Henry. "Gay Vienna: Myth and Reality." *Journal of the History of Ideas* 15, 1 (January 1954): 94-118.

Schorske, Carl E. "Politics and the Psyche in *Fin-de-siècle* Vienna: Schnitzler and Hofmannsthal." *American Historical Review* 66, 4 (July 1961): 930-946.

Shils, Edward. "Daydreams and Nightmares: Reflections on the Criticism of Mass Culture." *Sewanee Review* 65 (Autumn 1957): 587–608.

Steiner, George. "The Uncommon Reader." [A review of Walter Benjamin, *Gesammelte Schriften*, vol. I.] *Times Literary Supplement*, October 25, 1974, p. 1198.

Tiedemann, Rolf. "Editorisches Nachwort." In Walter Benjamin, *Charles Baudelaire: Ein Lyriker im Zeitalter des Hochkapitalismus.* Frankfurt am Main: Suhrkamp Verlag, 1969. Pp. 167–191.

Tiedemann, Rolf. *Studien zur Philosophie Walter Benjamins.* Introduction by Theodor W. Adorno. Institut für Sozialforschung, *Frankfurter Beiträge zur Soziologie,* edited by Theodor W. Adorno and Walter Dirks, vol. 16. Frankfurt am Main: Europäische Verlagsanstalt, 1965.

Tillich, Paul. "Theodor Wiesengrund-Adorno. Kierkegaard: Konstruktion des Aesthetischen." *Journal of Philosophy* 31 (November 8, 1934): 640.

Zohn, Harry. *Karl Kraus.* Twayne's World Author Series, edited by Sylvia E. Bowman, no. 116. New York: Twayne Publishers, 1971.

Index

Index

A

Adorno, Gretel: *see* Karplus, Gretel
Adorno, Theodor W.; *see also* Adorno-
    Benjamin debate; Method; Negative
    dialectics; Philosophy
  aesthetic theory, 15, 23, 37–42, 148–
    49, 234n
  and art, 3, 11, 122–24, 133–35, 148–49,
    170, 174
  The Authoritarian Personality, 68, 178–
    84, 187
  and Catholicism, 2, 192n
  childhood, 1–3
  as composer, 11–17, 123, 134, 137, 148,
    203–204n, 281n
  of philosophy, 101, 122, 131, 188–
    90
  as cultural critic, 101, 103–110, 187
  Current of Music, 176
  Dialektik der Aufklärung, 59–62, 68,
    87, 107, 132, 173, 178–79, 181, 230n
  "Der dialektische Komponist," 15,
    129–31, 143
  emigration, 136–39, 151–55, 165–67
  on history, 43–62, 168
  Husserl study (1934–1938), 138, 152
  inaugural lecture ("Die Aktualität der
    Philosophie," 1931), 23, 24, 27, 30,
    36, 46, 47, 52, 65, 69, 83, 86, 90,
    93, 95, 97, 102–103, 112–114, 129,
    140, 182, 238n
  transcending idealism, 10, 64–65, 69,
    76, 111–21, 130, 138, 188–90
  Kant-Freud study, 17–20, 22, 27, 179
  Kantgesellschaft speech ("Die Idee der

    Naturgeschichte," 1932), 52–62
  Kierkegaard study, 23, 27, 37, 65, 85,
    114–21, 122, 127, 136–37, 157
  Komposition für den Film, 167, 296n
  and language, 21, 23, 87–90, 93, 174–75
  Mannheim critique, 53, 226n, 234n
  Minima Moralia, 180–81
  move to Marx, 20–23, 25, 27, 45, 62, 65
  and music, 1, 11–17, 37–41, 129–31, 134,
    143, 187–89
  Negative Dialektik, 24, 53, 68–69, 85,
    133, 190
  "non-participation" (*nicht-mitmachen*),
    31, 37, 189, 219n
  and philosophy, 2–11, 24, 27–28, 42,
    66–69, 70–74, 111–21, 133
  on relativism, 50–53, 224–25n
  Reproduktionstheorie, 201n
  and science, 122–24
  as student, 2–20
  and Surrealism, 127–29, 142, 148
  and theology, 6–7, 8, 132, 140, 192n,
    282n
  "Über Jazz," 65, 100, 104–110, 149, 152
  Wagner critique, 98, 100, 122, 145
  "Zur gesellschaftlichen Lage der Musik,"
    37–41, 65, 78, 167, 218–19n
  "Zur Metakritik der Erkenntnistheorie,"
    10, 69
Adorno-Benjamin correspondence, 139,
    282n
Adorno-Benjamin debate, 89, 98, 102, 113–
    14
  alternative interpretations, 139, 141–
    46, 281–82n
  availability of source material, 139, 282n

325